CONVERSATIONAL COHERENCE

Sage's *Series in Interpersonal Communication* is designed to capture the breadth and depth of knowledge emanating from scientific examinations of face-to-face interaction. As such, the volumes in this series address the cognitive and overt behavior manifested by communicators as they pursue various conversational outcomes. The application of research findings to specific types of interpersonal relationships (e.g., marital, managerial) is also an important dimension of this series.

SAGE SERIES IN INTERPERSONAL COMMUNICATION

CONVERSATIONAL COHERENCE
FORM, STRUCTURE, AND STRATEGY

EDITED BY
ROBERT T. CRAIG
&
KAREN TRACY

Sage Series in Interpersonal Communication
Volume 2

SAGE PUBLICATIONS
Beverly Hills / London / New Delhi

For information address:

SAGE Publications, Inc.
275 South Beverly Drive
Beverly Hills, California 90212

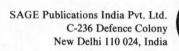   

SAGE Publications India Pvt. Ltd.
C-236 Defence Colony
New Delhi 110 024, India

SAGE Publications Ltd
28 Banner Street
London EC1Y 8QE, England

Printed in the United States of America

Library of Congress Cataloging in Publication Data

Main entry under title:

Conversational coherence.

    (Series in interpersonal communication ; v. 2)
    Bibliography; p.
    1. Conversation. 2. Discourse analysis. I. Craig, Robert T. II. Tracy, Karen. III. Series.
P95.45.C666   1983   001.54'2'019   83-13856
ISBN 0-8039-2121-7
ISBN 0-8039-2122-5 (pbk.)

FIRST PRINTING

CONTENTS

SERIES EDITOR'S FOREWORD

The studies of conversation reported in this volume represent more than their manifest content. Analyzing conversations is obviously vital for understanding the nature of interpersonal transactions. However, collectively, these studies also represent a scholarly movement that uses radically different methods, data bases, and conceptual frameworks for studying human interaction than those that dominated prior to the mid-1970s. Thus, even communication scholars whose work does not involve the study of conversations per se may profit from reading this book. It is a volume with many fresh perspectives on some persistent problems facing all of us who study human communication.

There are other books that focus on issues inherent in the study of conversations, but the distinctive feature of this volume is the explicit concern for communication issues by communication scholars. In their pursuit of understanding conversational coherence, form, and strategy, these authors confront (sometimes in quite different ways) central issues for anyone wishing to understand interpersonal transactions. These include

- *Mutual Influence.* How do the conversational behaviors of each interactant affect one another?

- *Process and Organization.* What sequential and/or recursive patterns characterize interaction components over time?

- *Multisignal Units.* To what extent do co-occurring paralinguistic units, facial expressions, gestures, and timing influence verbal responses in conversations?

- *Cognitive Processes.* To what extent are message units consciously produced? How do we know? To what extent do interactants pursue multiple goals in conversation? How do people interpret various message units and patterns found in conversations?

- *Multilevel Signals.* To what extent do message units simultaneously (or subsequently) send several different messages?

- *Perception of Signals.* Out of all the conversational stimuli available to us, what do we attend to? Why? To what extent are responses influenced by behaviors not overtly manifested in a conversation?

- *Contexts and Situations.* What is the role of the attending psychological, cultural, environmental, and behavioral features in determining conversational responses?

- *Researcher Influence.* How and to what extent is the researcher a part of his or her observations?

Another noteworthy feature of this volume is the B-K conversation. It not only provides a point of reference for viewing different perspectives and types of analysis, but it serves a useful function by putting an extended, transcribed conversation into the public domain. Actual conversations, unlike public speeches, are not readily available for researchers to examine. And many scholarly journals are not willing to devote the space needed to print extended conversations, which comprise the data base for conversation analysts. The publication of conversations such as this one, then, provides future researchers with common referents for discussion and further exploration.

Readers who expect a definitive analysis or even a definitive analytical procedure for examining the B-K conversation and readers who desire closure on the issues these authors are grappling with will probably be disappointed with this volume. Readers who are excited and challenged by the process of weighing the merits of diverse perspectives and who seek creative alternatives to persistent problems in the study of face-to-face interaction should enjoy the book. I did.

— Mark L. Knapp

ACKNOWLEDGMENTS

This volume grew out of the Third Annual Conference on Discourse Analysis, which was held at Temple University, March 1982. The editors wish to express their appreciation to Temple University and its Department of Speech for their continuing support of that series of conferences; to the many members of the department who contributed their efforts to the 1982 conference; and to our colleagues Herbert W. Simons and Arthur P. Bochner, who encouraged us to pursue this project.

INTRODUCTION
ROBERT T. CRAIG and KAREN TRACY

*"Conversation should touch everything but should
concentrate on nothing"*

— Oscar Wilde

EMERGENCE OF COMMUNICATION RESEARCH ON
CONVERSATION

The studies collected in this volume offer a current sample from
one of the most rapidly growing areas of communication research.
That such an obviously important aspect of interpersonal communication as conversation is only now emerging as a new area for communication research might be thought odd. In fact, the literature of
speech communication prior to the 1970s includes many articles on
the art of conversation (Matlon, 1980, p. 412), none of which, however, the reader will find mentioned in this book. As much as Oscar
Wilde would probably have been repulsed by a term like "conversational coherence," present-day communication scholars are often —
and often, rightly — rather embarrassed by the works of their
forebears.

It is indeed unfortunate that students of conversation pay so little
attention to a rich artistic tradition that ranges from classical treatises
on dialectic, through works like Richelieu's on the finer points of
conversation at the French royal court (Holmquest, 1981), to a long
line of literary wits and anecdotalists. The art of conversation, some
complain, has sadly lost its formerly high place in our culture (Sennett, 1978). If conversation is no longer a fine art, it is at least a
practical art, the cultural significance of which resides partly in a
history that current studies of conversation largely ignore.

Yet even though the academic discipline of communication has changed greatly since the day when essays on conversation bore titles like "The Fallacy of the First Name" (Konigsberg, 1957), and "Don't Be Afraid of Silence" (Dominick, 1958), the field has retained its characteristically practical orientation, which is evident in many of the studies collected here. The disciplinary culture tends to foster a pragmatic approach to the subject matter, and openness to the use of relevant knowledge from other fields. Communication research addresses questions such as: How is it done? What techniques or strategies are used? What is the association between strategies and effective outcomes? What are the elements of competence? Whereas in the past such questions might have been addressed by speculating about them or consulting traditional sources, today they are more likely to be a stimulus for original research.

However, we have not yet explained why conversation is just now emerging as a popular topic of communication research. In order to understand this, one must realize that the research process follows its own imperatives, which are not entirely those of everyday life. Systematic research depends upon the availability of concepts and methods for approaching problems. By the same token, the concepts and methods that are available at a given time tend to encourage researchers to address some problems rather than others.

In the 1950s and 1960s, communication research focused largely on the study of persuasion. The experimental method, which was considered to be the most scientifically rigorous way of doing research, required that questions be asked about the effects of independent variables (such as persuasive strategies) on dependent variables (such as attitudes). A focus on persuasion was also encouraged by the availability of concepts from such diverse sources as the traditions of rhetoric and public speaking, the latest theories of social psychology, and the studies of propaganda that flourished between the world wars. Conversation can certainly be studied experimentally (see Tracy & Moran, ch. 6), but in the intellectual climate of the time, a researcher's answer to the question, "Why don't you study conversation?" might well have been: "Conversation is certainly an important subject, but we don't know how to study it."

In the 1970s the study of *process* became an important concern of communication research. Berlo (1960) had insisted that communication was a continuous interaction, enormously complex, without fixed beginnings and ends or simple causes. Critics such as Smith (1972) complained that communication research, dominated by the persuasion experiment, had not yet accepted the implications of this process philosophy. Methods had to be found for studying communication as a continuous process of interpersonal interaction. The methods of interaction analysis and stochastic modeling seemed to answer this need. They were scientifically rigorous and consistent with the assumptions of the systems theories which were rapidly gaining in influence (Fisher & Hawes, 1971; Hewes, 1975; Rogers & Farace, 1975). Interaction analysis researchers, even though they studied the back and forth of communication, initially did not, however, think of themselves as studying conversation. The concepts that were available to guide research were derived from fields such as problem-solving group discussion and relational communication, in which the term "conversation" was not used. Only at the end of the 1970s did interaction researchers begin to use the word "conversation" to describe their subject (Capella, 1979; Cline, 1979; Stech, 1979). This change reflected the influence of new elements in the intellectual climate that were beginning to make possible entirely new styles of research.

Studies that related verbal to nonverbal communication were one source of influence. For example, Knapp and his associates had published papers on the behavior related to conversational turn-taking, greetings, and leave-takings (Knapp, Hart, Friedrich, & Shulman, 1973; Krivonos & Knapp, 1975; Wiemann & Knapp, 1975).

Another source of influence was the emergence of nonquantitative studies of conversation. Nofsinger (1975, 1976), Hawes (1976), and Frentz and Farrell (1976) published papers in which conversation was studied from a scientific point of view, but without the use of any statistical methods. This was considered at the time to be a radical idea. In 1977 a special issue of *Communication Quarterly* was devoted to arguments for various types of qualitative research ("Naturalistic Study of Communication: A Symposium," 1977). Quantitative research was indicted for its failure to provide the kinds of rich, descriptive information on which science of communication would have be be based (Nofsinger, 1977); talk, it was argued, should become a legitimate object of study in its own right, without the interference of overly rigid statistical models and assumptions (Litton-Hawes, 1977).

It is probably too early to say that these debates about methodology have been put behind us, but the studies collected in the present volume display a healthy variety of research styles and a general lack of rancor toward those who follow different styles. Several chapters combine qualitative and quantitative methods in clearly successful ways (for example, Tracy & Moran, Chapter 6; Crow, Chapter 7;

Ragan, Chapter 8). The loosening of methodological strictures, along with the introduction of a flood of new concepts from other disciplines (discussed below) has created an intellectual climate in which studies of conversation have proliferated and become one of the most vital fields of communication research. This book represents a sort of early maturity of communication research on conversation. Conversation is not, to be sure, a new phenomenon, but we have newly learned how to study it productively.

CONVERSATION AS A MULTIDISCIPLINARY FIELD OF STUDY

Another important influence on the growth of communication studies of conversation has been a virtual explosion of interest in conversation within several other academic disciplines. For reasons about which we will not attempt to speculate, the *zeitgeist* appears to have taken what Farrell (Chapter 13) refers to as a "conversational turn." In addition to the continental philosophers whom Farrell mentions (and whose ideas are especially important from the perspective of Hawes, Chapter 14), Rorty (1979) has argued that conversation should now become the basic metaphor of philosophy. The sociologist Sennett (1976) has made the fate of public conversation a centerpiece of his cultural criticism. Important studies and theoretical ideas about conversation have been contributed by philosophers (Austin, 1962; Grice, 1975; Searle, 1969); microsociologists (Duncan & Fiske, 1977; Goffman, 1961, 1969, 1971, 1976; Psathas, 1979; Schenkein, 1978; Sudnow, 1972); linguists (Bach & Harnish, 1979; Halliday & Hasan, 1976); sociolinguists (Goody, 1978; Hymes, 1974; Labov & Fanshel, 1977); developmental psycholinguists (Ochs & Schieffelin, 1979); cognitive psychologists (Just & Carpenter, 1977; Mandler & Johnson, 1977); and even artificial intelligence researchers interested in conversational computer systems (Reichman, 1978; Schank, 1977; Schank & Abelson, 1977) — and these are only examples from a literature already too vast even to mention here.

Ideas have traveled freely among the various disciplines, and many of those ideas have influenced communication studies of conversation such as those in this book. We noted earlier that communication research tends to have a unique disciplinary coloration reflective of its pragmatic and pedagogical interests, but communication has always been a discipline with a particular openness to other fields of knowledge. If the studies in this volume tend to share a certain disciplinary outlook, they also represent diverse schools of thought whose roots extend into other disciplines. As we describe each chapter in the course of an overview of the book, we attempt to explain the more important terms and concepts of other disciplines that have influenced, or are presupposed by, that chapter.

GENESIS AND RATIONALE OF A VOLUME ON CONVERSATIONAL COHERENCE

This book arose from a conference on conversational coherence that took place at Temple University in 1982. The conference theme seemed to locate a central thread connecting the various studies of conversation in the field. Each research program took a somewhat different approach to coherence, yet areas of agreement as well as certain issues in dispute became clearly apparent. It also seemed that work in the area had developed sufficiently to warrant publication in a form other than scattered journal articles. The organizers of the Temple conference proposed, then, to edit this book. Researchers doing relevant work, including several who had not attended the conference, were invited to submit proposals, the best of which were selected and, during the following year, developed into the chapters here assembled.

The title, *Conversational Coherence: Form, Structure, and Strategy,* suggests the basic orientation of the book. Coherence, form, and strategy are key terms that require some explanation.

"Coherence" refers to the fact that utterances produced by competent speakers in conversation usually seem to be connected to each other in orderly and meaningful ways. Coherence itself is a rather obvious phenomenon — a fact; but less obvious are the ways in which coherence can be described in detail and its production accounted for. How coherent is conversation? Are there different kinds, levels, or degrees of coherence? Does the coherence of conversation differ from that of other types of discourse, such as writing? Is coherence clearly marked in the discourse itself, or is it largely a product of the hearer, a kind of wishful thinking? How much and in what ways does the coherence of a conversation depend upon a social context of situation? What is it that competent speakers/hearers know that enables them to produce coherent conversations? These are some of the general questions that a study of conversational coherence might address.

Form and strategy are, from one point of view, contrasting approaches to coherence; from another point of view, they may be two aspects of it.

To understand coherence as form is to look for patterns or rules that conversationists follow in order to talk coherently. The patterns in question may range from the subtlest linguistic choices, to rules about turn-taking and the kinds of utterances that may follow each other, to structural formats for introducing and developing topics or telling stories, and even to the large-scale structure of whole conversations and the speech events in which they are embedded. A thoroughgoing formal account of coherence might attempt to show that coherent conversations can be generated from a set of rules (just as grammarians can generate sentences from rules), or that structures in conversations can be explained by matching them with certain standard patterns or forms. The role of the competent conversationist, from a formal point of view, is to follow the rules or script faithfully.

A "strategic" account of coherence, in contrast, would assume that conversationists behave strategically in pursuit of their individual goals, and that whatever structure conversation may have emerges from this process. Rules and standard patterns are not simply followed but are used as resources to accomplish goals. Rules may be broken, transformed, or used in nonobvious ways. Or if rules are followed strictly, as in a sport or game, they may be only a constitutive framework in which non-rule-governed strategic options are played out. The rules may permit a range of strategies from which conversationists select for their own, sometimes convoluted, purposes. Conversationists may confront paradoxes, dilemmas, and conflicts among goals, which they must act creatively to resolve.

Form and strategy are contrasting approaches to coherence, but they are not necessarily incompatible. It may be, for example, that to follow rules and standard patterns largely suits the needs of conversationists; thus the formal coherence of conversation might be explained strategically. Strategy, furthermore, depends upon form in the sense that rules and patterns must exist in order to be used strategically, and every strategy depends upon some fairly reliable expectation as to the response that a given choice of behavior will elicit. Strategies *are* indeed forms, and may become standard or rule-governed forms when used repeatedly — and thus subject to different kinds of strategic exploitation. A phrase such as "Speaking of X," might begin as a means of drawing a related topic out of an old one, then become a conventional way of doing so, then be used strategically to cheat by introducing rather digressive topics, then become a conventional way of licensing digression, and so on. The relation between form and strategy is, then, a considerable theoretical problem in its own right.

The chapters of this volume attribute various meanings to coherence and take various approaches to describing and explaining it. Form and strategy are pervasive themes. None of the chapters takes a purely formal or strategic view of coherence; all take up positions along a range in which relations between form and strategy are at issue. In the following section we give an overview of the structure of the book and of what we see as the central points and issues raised by each chapter.

OVERVIEW OF THE VOLUME

We have grouped the essays in this volume into four parts, each part emphasizing a particular issue. Each essay in Part I describes a perspective from which to view coherence and argues for its advantages over other perspectives.

Goldberg (Chapter 1) offers the most text-based approach. Pointing to the inherent vagaries of casual conversation, she argues for the importance of an adequate descriptive account of what is occurring in the discourse. The centerpiece of her descriptive model is the "move," a speech unit roughly analogous to a thought unit. Understanding of coherence is accomplished by categorizing moves into types based on semantic linkages with earlier moves, and then creating a conceptual map that charts the sequence of moves. The value of this approach, Goldberg argues, is its more accurate characterization of conversation as well as its ability to account for phenomena such as speech particles (e.g., you know), which other approaches have ignored and treated as meaningless.

Like Goldberg, Jacobs and Jackson (Chapter 2) indict attempts to explain coherence by appeals to sequencing rules models, for example, adjacency pair explanations. "Adjacency pair" refers to a discourse unit consisting of two "pair parts" (e.g., question-answer, request-grant, greeting-greeting). Adjacency pair models (Schegloff, 1972a) posit that whenever a first pair part occurs, the second pair part becomes "conditionally relevant" or expectable. Sequencing rules models in general attempt to account for the structure of conversation by rules that specify the order in which conversational acts must occur. Goldberg, and Jacobs and Jackson identify a number of problems with this type of explanation of coherence. However, in contrast to Goldberg, who deals with the problems by becoming more specific and descriptive, Jacobs and Jackson move in the opposite direction.

They offer a more abstract, general model, in their words, "a rational model," to account for communicators' understanding of certain sequences as coherent that cannot be explained by sequencing rules models. The rational model assumes that conversation is much like other rule-governed games. Players (conversants) have goals they are trying to achieve, and pursue those goals within the constraints imposed by the rules and the strategies most likely to succeed. The basic move in the game is the "speech act." Speech act approaches (see Searle, 1969) divide discourse into units based on the purpose or function ("illocutionary force") of a particular utterance, or in other words, the perceived intention of the speaker. Coherence requires that only certain speech acts may follow each other. However, the rational model rejects the possibility that these sequencing rules can be formulated at the level of discourse units. Instead, Jacobs and Jackson argue, the regularities are to be found at the level of interactants' goals and strategies. In their chapter Jacobs and Jackson attempt to describe the rational basis of conversational form and strategy.

Sanders (Chapter 3) offers a markedly different perspective on coherence. Rather than attempting to explain what utterance sequences would or would not count as coherent, as Jacobs and Jackson do, he assumes that conversations *are* coherent. One can imagine, he argues, a context in which almost any pair of utterances would be plausible and coherent. Therefore, the important task is to explain how items of discourse cohere and why conversants have chosen particular forms. In addition to sketching out how utterance sequences may cohere, he uses the B-K conversation (Appendix) to illustrate how coherence devices, particularly topic transitions, may have been used strategically to serve the needs of impression management for the conversants. The idea that conversational forms may be used for multiple purposes is touched on by many of the authors; Sanders, however, provides the richest exploration of this issue.

If we were to categorize approaches to coherence on a continuum ranging from text based to mind based, the chapters in Part I could be arrayed along that continuum with Chapter 1 located closest to the mind-based pole. Of all the essays, Hopper's (Chapter 4) is the closest to an exclusively mind-based approach to coherence. Hopper argues that coherence is produced by interpreters who have considerable freedom in the meanings othey choose to attribute to a piece of discourse. Not only may different interpreters come up with different meanings for a discourse, but these meanings, which have emerged over time, may be transformed over time. Coherence, one might say, is in the ear of the beholder. A central focus in his discussion of coherence is the notion of "2ness," the propensity for interpreters to understand and create meaning by pairing some item in the text with one other item in the text or context. Hopper illustrates the claim that interpretation produces coherence in a variety of texts including father-child teasing, a job interview, and the B-K conversation.

In Part II each of the four chapters focuses on strategies that conversationists use in various settings, for various reasons, to achieve degrees of conversational coherence. All of the studies point to specifics in the discourse that typically mean something. Thus, while their exact positions on the text-based/mind-based continuum may be unclear, all four studies can be seen as rejecting a radical mind-based approach.

Mura (Chapter 5) considers how communicators signal that they are adhering to Grice's (1975) supraordinate principle, "Be cooperative," while violating one or more of Grice's specific conversational maxims. She suggests that this is accomplished through the process of "licensing violations." That is, interactants, by explicitly cueing that they are violating a maxim, thereby inform their partner of their underlying cooperativeness. For each of Grice's four maxims, quantity, quality, relation, and manner, Mura describes the cues that conversationists use to license violations.

Tracy and Moran (Chapter 6) also begin with Grice (1975) and pose the question: What does it mean to be relevant? In contrast with the other chapters, Tracy and Moran draw upon an experimental methodology. People are presented messages under different goal conditions and are asked how they would respond. Response content is examined for particular semantic links with speaker messages. Underlying their work are the assumptions that relevance is a matter of degree and that it is pursued in conjunction with other goals in conversation. In addition to describing different types of topical links, Tracy and Moran suggest how the topic transition types link up with interactants' goals of being relevant, being an attentive listener, and introducing new topics of their own. In the second part of the chapter, the experimentally developed concepts are applied to the B-K conversation and the B-K conversation is used to suggest needed theoretical modifications.

Crow (Chapter 7) describes a typology of topic shifts inductively derived from a study of intimate couples' conversations. His typology partly parallels Goldberg's categorization of moves and Tracy and Moran's discussion of how new topics link with old ones. Of particular merit is the richness of his conversational examples, his integration of qualitative and quantitative methodologies, and his attempt to define coherence at a relational level that takes into account the success of a conversational move. In the conclusion Crow speculates on possible relationships between topic-shift patterns and marital satisfaction.

The fusion of qualitative and quantitative methodologies is also seen in Ragan's study (Chapter 8). Focusing on the job interview, she shows how both parties in the interview situation work to achieve coherence at the relational level. Coherence is created in the discourse through the use of different aligning devices that cue the nature of the situation and appropriate social roles. Drawing most heavily from the symbolic interactionist tradition (Scott & Lyman, 1968; Stokes & Hewitt, 1976), Ragan analyzes the job interviews and provides examples of aligning devices and comparisons between interviewers' and interviewees' use of them. In her last section, Ragan analyzes the B-K conversation in terms of the aligning devices used, and comes to some conclusions similar to those of Sanders regarding the social identities that B and K attempted strategically to present in their conversation.

Part III emphasizes the influence of context on the interpretation of discourse. In Chapter 9 Sigman identifies a number of social-situational factors that constrain what may be said or how an utterance will be interpreted at a particular place and time. Coherence, he argues, depends not only on relevance in the narrow sense — primarily a cognitive phenomenon — but also on the nature of the social relationship and the interactional setting. The social relationship affects the kinds of things that conversationists are expected to say — or not to say — and what can be taken for granted; the interactional setting implies an agenda for conversation that affects judgments of relevance. An utterance may be tied semantically to the immediately preceding utterance and yet, because of the relational or situational context, not be heard as relevant.

Whereas Sigman's work draws heavily upon an ethnographic tradition (Hymes, 1974), with its emphasis on speech situations determining acceptable communicative acts, Beach's essay (Chapter 10) is primarily influenced by the ethnomethodological perspective (see, for instance, Garfinkel, 1967). Ethnomethodology studies the methods everyday communicators use to make sense of their world; Beach focuses on the primary role of background understanding as a tool enabling people both to identify the social situation and to interpret the meaning of talk within it. Background understandings are the taken-for-granted, usually tacit knowledge that communicators use to make sense. Moreover, this sense making must be done reflexively, using the talk to help define the situation and using the situation to help assign meaning to the talk. Drawing upon three kinds of conversational sources — reconstructed conversations, videotaped group discussions, and the B-K conversation — Beach analyzes a large set of examples to show how interpretation works in situ. In the last section, he points to trade-offs among the three kinds of conversational data as resources for understanding communicators' sensemaking procedures.

In Chapter 11 Ellis examines the role of context in a manner quite different from Beach or Sigman. His concern is not only with discourse (i.e., connected text), but also language in the more traditional linguistic sense in which the sentence is the basic unit. Ellis considers how the communicative context influences all language levels including the phonemic (sound), morphemic (meaning unit), and syntactic (grammatical). He argues that language, similar to discourse, is fundamentally a communicative device; hence, the communicative purposes of individuals and the social requirements of situations constrain the possibilities of form at all levels. Moreover, Ellis rejects the possibility that the relationship between communicative purposes and language levels can be realized by a small set of rules. In the second part of the chapter, Ellis proposes three levels at which coherence can be analyzed, which he labels the depictive, the speech act, and the discourse levels. Finally, he discusses the possibility of individual style differences in the way coherence devices are used.

The essays in Part IV share a concern with the nature of the coherence requirements that distinguish conversation as a type or genre of discourse. In Chapter 12 Nofsinger provides an intriguing analysis of the coherence requirements of courtroom talk. He suggests that for courtroom discourse to be coherent, communicators need an understanding of lawyers' and witnesses' goals and need to be able to identify the particular questions and responses as tactics used to advance those goals. Nofsinger addresses a number of issues raised by earlier chapters in the volume. Like Ellis, he argues for the importance of conceptualizing coherence at various levels, but the coherence levels he proposes overlap only minimally with those Ellis describes. Similar to Jacobs and Jackson, he argues for the importance of understanding communicators' intentions as a basis of conversational coherence. In the last section of his essay Nofsinger suggests how coherence requirements in the courtroom differ from those which apply to everyday small talk such as the B-K conversation.

Nofsinger treats courtroom talk as one particular type of conversation, therein using a fairly broad definition of conversation that encompasses most interactive discourse. Farrell (Chapter 13), on the other hand, defines conversation more narrowly. His purpose is to distinguish conversation from rhetoric and consider how each is judged coherent. In Farrell's view, conversation is spontaneous, marked by its "sense of passage," and grounded in convention; it is, in other words, what we typically think of as small talk. Rhetoric, in contrast, is intentional or planned and makes use of particular kinds of discourse strategies. Farrell explores how conversation may become rhetorical and suggests that when it does, the same criteria that are used to judge rhetoric should be applied to conversation. This he illustrates by analysis of several examples, including segments of the B-K conversation. Rhetorical figures are identified in the conversation; the interactants' motives and choices are analyzed. In a very convincing way, Farrell points out the value of a tradition of thought (i.e., rhetoric) that conversational scholars have largely ignored.

Hawes's and Farrell's views of conversation differ markedly. Farrell suggests that it is never possible for a speaker to explicate exactly what he or she means, or to capture the full truth about any aspect of the external world or that internal to the speaker. Hawes, taking a philosophical perspective influenced by primarily European writers on semiotics (Barthes, 1967), deconstruction (Derrida, 1972), critical theory (Habermas, 1979), and phenomenology (though he cites none explicitly), posits an ideal notion of speech and emphasizes the importance of truthfulness as a condition for valid speech. Through a series of examples he points to the vapidity of much of what we consider conversation.

Hawes's essay (Chapter 14) is not in general an easy one to read. He challenges the interpretive resources — and perhaps the patience — of readers; but he challenges too our typical, unreflective assumptions about meaning, discourse, and the practical compromises of social life. A major point, similar to one of Hopper's, seems to be the ever-present possibility of multiple meanings and continual changes of meaning in conversation. Conversational coherence is thus a momentary and fleeting achievement. Yet "single-centered" meanings, he proposes, can emerge only from the process of dialectic or confrontation within the "double-centered universes" of conversation. He examines this process in several instances in which B and K correct each other or fail to do so.

Taken individually, each of the fourteen chapters raises and attempts to answer specific questions about conversational coherence. Taken as a whole, the volume develops at least five major ideas: (1) Form and strategy are interdependent. Wherever forms exist, the possibility of strategic use is there; strategies are themselves identifiable forms, having rationale, distribution, and consequences. (2) Coherence exists at multiple levels. What the important levels are is a matter of some dispute; the importance of distinguishing levels seems not to be in dispute. (3) Conversationists' goals must play a central role in any adequate explanation of discourse production and interpretation in conversations. The conversationist simultaneously pursues multiple, often conflicting, goals; hence the strategies used to reconcile various goals are an important subject for research. (4) Research must attend to the interpretation of conversational discourse as well as its production. (5) Obvious advantages are to be gained by using both qualitative and quantitative methodologies to study the same or related issues and phenomena.

Following the chapters is the Appendix, which contains a transcript of the B-K conversation that is analyzed throughout the volume. The chapter authors have most frequently used the B-K conversation to provide illustrative examples of concepts and claims. In four essays (Crow, Hawes, Hopper, and Sanders) however, the conversation is analyzed as a whole. Of particular interest are the differences among those authors in the number of topical units that they identify. The number of topics ranges from 7 to 36, attesting to the multiplicity of perspectives (and the inadequacy of our present notions of topic). In addition to the transcript, the Appendix includes background information about the conversation and an explanation of the notation symbols used.

Reference lists of all the chapters have been compiled in a general bibliography, which follows the Appendix. Author and subject indexes are also provided. Perusal of this scholarly apparatus will reveal that we have touched nearly everything; we hope, nonetheless, to have concentrated on something: the principles of coherence that underlie a practical art of communication essential to human society, the art of conversation.

<<<<<<<<<<<< >>>>>>>>>>>>

I

APPROACHES TO
COHERENCE

<<<<<<<<<<<< >>>>>>>>>>>>

1

A Move Toward Describing Conversational Coherence

< <JULIA A. GOLDBERG> >

< < < Coherence — that which differentiates the ado- > > > lescent's descriptions of events or recounting of stories from those of the preschooler, the young adult's conversational contributions from the senile geriatric's, the nonclinical individual's use of language from the schizophrenic's "salad bowl" speech — is said to be a necessary condition for the production of well-formed discourses. Yet coherence is no more than a pragmatic feature of discourse (see Grice, 1975) derived from judgments of propositional consistency and relevancy (Bellert, 1970; Manor, 1976; Nowakowska, 1976; Vuchinich, 1977). In fact, according to Grice's (1975) cooperative principle and conversational maxims virtually any locution/proposition can be made to cohere with another.

Since a well-formed discourse is a coherent one, a discourse grammar or model must be able to represent how coherence is produced. However, given that coherence is not a property of sentences (locutions), but of propositions, it cannot be formalized. This inability to formalize coherence has led many researchers to adopt the following two approaches to the modeling of well-formed discourse (Levinson, n.d.). Based on the assumption that propositional coherency is reflected in the serial arrangement and grammatical make-up of successive sentences, both approaches are centrally concerned with modeling the organization of discourse — accounting for within- and between-turn propositional coherence by means of sequencing constraints. It is these constraints that are generally held to be responsible for the creation of a well-formed discourse.

The two approaches differ, however, with respect to the theoretical nature of their inquiry. The first is interested in formally representing, through a set of concatenation rules, what is or is not a well-formed discourse. The models created are generative in that they produce or construct a coherent discourse sequence on the basis of a set of regulative and constitutive rules. Sequences that do not satisfy the conditions designated by these rules are treated as ill-formed and unacceptable (i.e., as incoherent). The second, accusing the first of engaging in premature formalizations, is engaged in descriptive analyses.

As can be seen from the transcript of the B-K conversation provided in the Appendix to this volume, control of the production processes are shared. Deciding what to say and interpreting what has been said are choices that each interactant must repeatedly make. Such choices affect and are affected by the organizational patterns and propositional content of the emerging discourse. As the discourse unfolds, coherency requirements and judgments will change. Generative models are unable to capture this mercurial characteristic of conversations.

Given the enormous complexity of multiparty interactions, therefore, it may well be wise to concentrate on the second (descriptive) approach before continuing to build predictive accounts of how the interaction should and will proceed. Until then, generative models will be severely limited to accounts of orderly, highly structured, and predictable discourse transactions.

The models described in the first section of this chapter are, by nature, generative. Although each focuses on different forms or levels of discourse coherence, each is centrally concerned with formally representing the sequencing rules that must be obligatorily followed if the discourse is to be well formed.

The move model presented in the second section provides a system for describing the coherence and sequential organization of discourse as it emerges. Like other descriptive approaches (see Brockway, 1979; Burton, 1978; Reichman, 1978; Sinclair, Forsyth, Coulthard, & Ashby, 1972) it examines, describes, and isolates one of the various techniques used for maintaining coherence. The move assigned to a locution is intended to reflect the extent to which that locution shares the same set of concerns with its immediate predecessor. It does not predict how the discourse shall progress.

Discourse coherence is promoted through the formation of thematic, act or illocutionary, and lexico-syntactic cohesive bonds holding between and across a series of locutions. Each type of cohesion is encoded within any discourse. Individually, each model enriches our understanding of the pragmatic and cognitive mechanisms underlying judgments of coherence. However, the relative prominence of each cohesive-based coherence model is dependent upon the discourse described. Thus, as Fillmore (1981, p. 165) noted, "samples of discourse that differ in significant pragmatic ways will be structured according to different sets of syntactic and semantic principles."

In the final section of this chapter, some advantages and applications of the move model for a richer descriptive analysis of discourse production and comprehension are suggested.

GENERATIVE MODELS

Generative models of discourse are constructed around each of the following three forms or levels of cohesive organization: thematic, illocutionary or activity-type, and lexico-syntactic or sentential. Each provides a set of concatenation rules for the production of locution sequences organized to ensure that the propositions they represent will be orderly and meaningfully arrayed. Two of the models examine locally operating cohesive techniques; the third models globally unifying structures.

Global Models

Global approaches to coherence, most notably associated with text/story grammars (Rumelhart, 1975; van Dijk, 1977a) and artificial intelligence/cognitive science (Schank & Abelson, 1975), suggest that well-formed discourses are constructed on the basis of general conversational or textual structures and organizational frameworks. (See Morgan & Sellner, 1980, for a critique of such models.)

A discourse may be coherent with respect to a particular theme: topic or event. Initially, it is the theme's generic macrostructure (i.e., the pattern of development intrinsic to a particular discourse type or genre) that is the salient cohesive device chaining one locution to the next. The actual structures found in the discourse are determined by lower-level, text-specific macrostructures. To illustrate this point consider the dime-store paperback romance novel. While all Harlequin Romances have the same theme or general organization, that is, generic macrostructure, each Harlequin Romance novel has its own unique set of text-specific macrostructures. In this way, no two Harlequin Romance tales will be in all ways identical.

The major drawback to these models is that they are unable to specify exactly how, within the locution set modeled, each locution is formally and specifically tied to the one preceding it. The emergent quality of the discourse tends to be glossed over and lost. The structure is already determined; all that is required of speakers is that they encode their locutions in the order specified by the discourse type. Determining what to say and how to say it are not at issue. Determining when to say whatever needs to be said is. For example, although the context- and content-specific features may vary for each joke told, the organizational pattern will be the same — governed by the generic joke script.

The data described are highly routinized and organized such as is found for jokes, sermons, restaurant interactions, or buying/selling routines. Even so, the global models work best as discourse comprehension models rather then encoding ones. As on-line production models, the representations provided would be both inelegant and complex. As van Dijk himself noted (1977a, pp. 158-159), the macrostructure assigned to an inital locution may have to be substituted for other macrostructures as the discourse unfolds. This is the case in Example 1[1] where B's particular response delimits and constrains the range of possible next responses as well as defines the schema or frame under which the discourse should proceed.

> **Example 1** A: Y'know, Rover won't come in here without you anymore.
> B: Why?
> He won't?
> Shit, but he's stupid!
> So, why not keep him in your room?
> Smart dog! He know who loves him.

This process is repeated at each step of the interaction. Furthermore, the models are based on the assumption of mutual orientation and shared participant frames in order to account for the coherence and comprehension of discourse like that found in Example 2.

> **Example 2** Well, I just thought I'd- re- better report to you what's happen' at Bullock's today. Well I-v-got outta my car at 5:30. I drove aroun' an' at first I had t'go by the front door

a' the store. An' there was two p'leece cars across the street andeh- colored lady wan 'tuh go in the main entrance there where the silver is an' all the gifts and things. And they, they wouldn't let 'er go in and he hadda gun in 'is hand a great big long gun. An'nen over on the other side, I mean to the right of there, where the employees come out there was a whole oh must a been ten uh eight 'r ten employees there [adapted from Sacks, 1968].

Nevertheless, it has been asserted that the global account is the model under which interactants operate while communicating with one another "since it [is] consistent with discourse-processing principles" (Tracy, 1981, p. viii; also see van Dijk, 1977a).

Local Models

Accounting for what can, at any given point in the locution set, follow what, is addressed by locally operating models of cohesion. These models describe the illocutionary or lexico-syntactic features that tie each locution to its immediate predecessor.

Lexico-syntactic. According to given-new (topic-comment or theme-rheme) models, successive locutions are chained together through the repeated use of various lexico-syntactic cohesive devices (Halliday & Hasan, 1976; also see Ellis, this volume). Each locution is structured to reveal the thematic relevance and informational salience of their respective propositions (Danes, 1974; Haviland & Clark, 1974). This is accomplished both lexically (e.g., through the use of definite/indefinite articles, synonyms, pro-forms, and reference) and syntactically (e.g., through the use of active/passive and other grammatical forms). When considered as a whole, it is found that the discourse (i.e., the ordered set of locutions) is organized around three basic patterns of thematic development (Danes, 1974): simple linear, constant theme, and derived theme. Each is schematized in Figure 1.1.

A simple linear thematic development occurs when the new information of a locution becomes the given, or known, background information of the next. A constant theme line of development occurs when the given information of successive locutions remains the same, all that changes is the new information predicated of the given information. Both patterns are exemplified in Example 3. The first two locutions of Example 3 follow the constant theme pattern (He is x; He

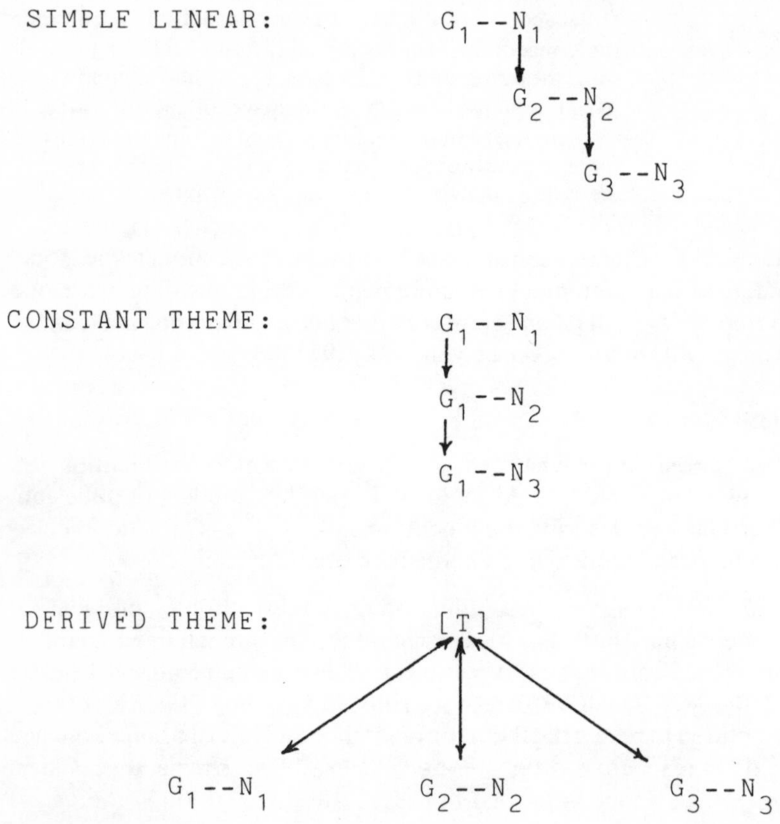

SIMPLE LINEAR:

$$G_1 - - N_1$$
$$\downarrow$$
$$G_2 - - N_2$$
$$\downarrow$$
$$G_3 - - N_3$$

CONSTANT THEME:

$$G_1 - - N_1$$
$$\downarrow$$
$$G_1 - - N_2$$
$$\downarrow$$
$$G_1 - - N_3$$

DERIVED THEME:

$$[T]$$

$$G_1 - - N_1 \qquad G_2 - - N_2 \qquad G_3 - - N_3$$

Note: G = Given; N = New; T = Topic.

Figure 1.1   Three Types of Thematic Development

is y), the latter two locutions follow the simple linear format ("argument" is the predicate of the first locution and subject of the second).

> **Example 3   062   B:**   He's a challenging person. ((laugh)) He um- he's a lawyer. So he only listens to as much as he needs to of what you're saying to make an argument against it. And if there is no argument going at the time he provokes one [B-K Conversation].

Finally, a discourse may be thematically coherent when each of the locutions address, albeit implicitly, an overriding, global theme. This is the pattern found in Example 4.

Example 4   New Jersey is flat along the coast and southern portion; the northwestern region is mountainous. The coastal climate is mild, but there is considerable cold in the mountain areas during the winter months. Summers are fairly hot. The leading industrial production includes chemicals, processed food, coal . . . [Danes, 1974, p. 120].

Illocutionary. Explanations of illocutionary coherence at the local level are derived from speech act (Searle, 1969) or adjacency-pair (Schegloff & Sacks, 1973) models of cohesion. The cohesive connections that link turns at talk (i.e., utterances) together are formalized such that the speech act or activity-type assigned to an utterance delimits the range of acceptable next acts encoded in immediately subsequent utterances (e.g., questions are followed by answers; complaints by apologies or justifications). The type of data analyzed by these models is best described as goal directed, interpersonal interactions where each utterance characteristically is made up of no more than one or two locutions (such as, for example, in interviews, directions, or problem-solving tasks). This is exemplified in Example 5.

Example 5   002 **K:**   So how are you doing?
((pause, rustling sounds))
003 **B:**   ((laugh)) As well as can be expected this time of the semester. How about you.
004 **K:**   ((animated)) Umm good.
005 **B:**   Are you sure that you don't want half? This is huge.
006 **K:**   No. Thanks. (I've finally) got my apple. [B-K Conversation].

Cohesion models of this sort are, mistakenly, based upon the theoretical assumption that illocutionary acts or activity types are consistently and uniquely related to one another. The sequencing rules and constraints proposed by each model are, thus, little more than formalized descriptions of inter-act compatibility. When activated, these rules are supposed to generate all the well-formed locution pairs and conventionalized interact units (e.g., repair sequences as described by Jefferson, 1972) found in conversational interactions.

In reality, the sequencing rules are only normative ones — reflecting the statistical probabilities that act *b* will follow act *a*. Thus, even though sequencing rules would not permit the generation of a sequence, it would be incorrect to assert that the sequence is, in all ways, ill-formed. Rather, all that can appropriately be claimed is that, according to the model, the chances of its occurrence are extremely low and not predicted.

Adjacency pair models do, to an extent, describe violations of the standard, speech act derived sequencing rules. For example, insertion sequences are regularized violations of the question-answer sequences (see Schegloff, 1972a).

Not all illocutionary acts, it should be noted, are amenable to sequencing rules. An assertion can, for example, be followed by almost anything. Consequently, neither speech act nor adjacency-pair models can adequately describe stretches of monologue-like talk. Adjacency-pair analysis is, however, a move toward surface structure textual coherence since the evaluated well formedness or appropriateness of a first or second pair part is assessed against situational relevance rather than speech act typologies. (See Levinson, 1980, for a detailed critique of illocutionary models of discourse.)

Each of the three major classes of models discussed above glosses over the emergent, interactive accomplishment of discourse. Each idealized the final product — the actual discourse the coherence of which they claim to be modeling — presenting an image of terse, direct, to-the-point interactions.

However, examination of most discourses, especially casual exchanges between familiar interactants, would reveal a unique blend of diverse discourse structures and organizational patterns. The development of the entire discourse rarely follows one pattern throughout. Rather, the discourse's developmental path may be diverted by forks, cul-de-sacs, and dead ends. Topics are raised only to be dropped before their completion or are cut off by side topics or tangential comments. Similarly, metacomments may crop up that are not part of the discourse topic itself. The move system described in the following section attempts to capture the developmental flavor of such interactions. As such, the model is purely descriptive.

A DESCRIPTIVE MODEL: MOVES

A descriptive model examines discourse for recurring patterns without later claiming that these patterns will always occur. In other words, the theoretical concern is not one of predictability but of negotiability. The emphasis is on representing what actually took place.

Descriptive models are designed to capture and demarcate the set of techniques that the interactants themselves employ in order to act upon and understand what has been said. These models stress that conversations are locally managed (cf. Sacks et al., 1974) with interactants signaling their intentions and analyses of the situation through the serial placement, as well as linguistic construction, of their remarks.

Conversational relatedness. Coherence is a matter of relatedness: consistency, relevancy, and order. Conversational interaction between familiars is, however, more often a matter of the reaffirmation of social relationships than the exchange of unknown information. In fact, silence or terseness are often heard as change of mood or relationship signals.

The need to keep the social/conversational channel open is complicated by the fact that the individual interactants might not have anything to say, might not have been listening to the other, and are simply egotistical. To minimize the relational consequences of these factors, interactants will often formulate their contributions to appear related to what the other had to say. It is this strategy that the move system addresses.

The Move System

Like the given-new model, the move system examines lexico-syntactic cohesive bonds. Unlike it, however, it does not specify which lexical item or syntactic structure creates the cohesive tie. Like the global models, it is concerned with general organizational cohesion, but unlike the global account it does not presuppose that the topic or event is agreed upon and, thus, addressed.[2] Furthermore, even given that the interactants are talking with respect to a particular topic or event, the talk itself rarely exhibits the preciseness and coherence that are said to exist by the rule-bound, generative models discussed above.

Assigning moves to locutions. Moves categorize each individual locution of an exchange in terms of its lexico-syntactic ties with preceding locutions both between and within turns of talk. The move assigned to the locution is intended to reflect the relationship of that locution to the immediately preceding body of information. Moves are assigned on the basis of the discourse referents (see Schank, 1977) contained in each locution with respect to those referents (i.e., the referential field) established in preceding contributions. In this way the system may be brought into line with the descriptions of topical transfer discussed by Crow (this volume) although the moves themselves are assigned independently of such topical descriptions.

Types of moves. The system is composed of four moves:[3]

(1) introducing;
(2) reintroducing;
(3) progressive-holding; and
(4) holding moves.

The operation of this system is schematically represented in Figure 1.2.

A locution is assigned to an *introducing move* if it introduces new referents and shares none with the immediately preceding locution. This is illustrated in Example 6 where the second locution is an introducing move.

Example 6   John bought a new car today.
➤Alligators have green feet.

A *reintroducing move* reintroduces referents found in locutions prior to, but not in, the immediately preceding locution (especially if the prior is a holding move).[4] Thus, assuming that in Example 6 alligators were being described prior to "John bought a new car today," then "Alligators have green feet" is a reintroducing move. For a *progressive-holding move* the locution shares some of the same referents as its prior locution while expanding or adding new referents not contained therein. When uttered by the same speaker (as in storytelling, for example) the move merely expands or elaborates upon the prior locution/proposition. However, the remark may be heard as supporting or challenging the comment that preceded it, especially when uttered by another. The second locution in Example 7 is an example of a *supportive* progressive-holding move, while in Example 8 it is illustrative of a *challenging* progressive-holding move.

Example 7   **A:**   John bought a new car today.
➤ **B:**   It is a red Mustang convertible.

Example 8   **A:**   John bought a new car today.
➤ **B:**   No, he would've told me if he did!

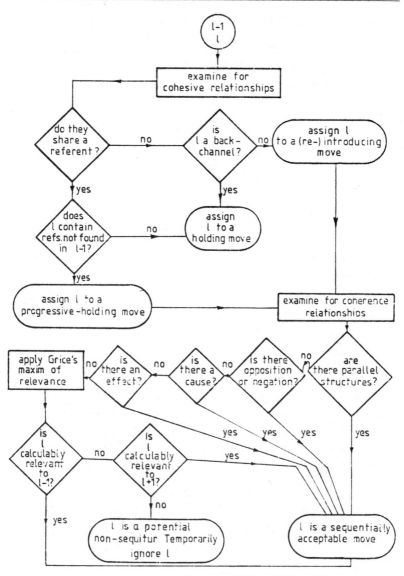

Note: L = current locution; L − 1 = immediately preceding L; and L + 1 = immediately following L.

Figure 1.2   Procedure for Assigning Moves to Locutions

A locution is assigned to a *holding move* if it is a backchannel or if its discourse referents are drawn only fro~. ~nose in the preceding locution (or locutions if the prior is itself a backchannel); that is, although referents may be subtracted or dropped no new referents may be added. Other holding moves include attention getters (e.g., Hey, listen to this; Got a minute?), metacomments (e.g., Shit!; Can I ask you a question?), and reiterations, minimal responses (e.g., Yes/No), or queries (e.g., Who?; Are you sure?; Why did you say that?). The "yeah" of Example 9 is a holding move.

Example 9   A: John bought a new car today.
    → **B:**   Yeah.

Advantages of the Move Model

Since conversation is linearly produced, the relationships between individual contributions are sequentially exhibited. A sequentially next locution relies on its immediately preceding locutions to produce the total coherent/cohesive effect. In this way assigning moves to locutions eventually may make it possible to describe and demarcate the various sections found in conversations where the break between one section (especially between one topic) and the next is often ill-defined.

The move system provides analysts with a necessary labeling device by which they may sharpen their intuitions on the structure of the talk found in casual, spontaneous discourse. The system itself, it should be stressed, does not claim to predict what is or will be a well-formed sequence or discourse. It only demonstrates how interactants are able to influence the course of the talk — how discourse develops, evolves, and revolves. Only after a move has been assigned to each and every locution does the analyst have a base from which to isolate the finer mechanisms by which interactants reveal how they intend to manipulate the course of the exchange or how their contributions should be heard as relating to that exchange.

Applications of the Move Model

Discourse particles. Discovering and describing the meaning and distribution of discourse particles was made possible by the move system (Goldberg, 1980; also, cf. Brockway, 1979, and Burton, 1978). The particles had previously been disregarded by researchers or cursorily treated as both randomly distributed and totally devoid of meaning except perhaps as fillers (which would therefore account for their random occurrence). However, when examined with respect to the move assigned to its host locution, the particles were found to be strongly correlated with particular move types. Thus, for example, a "y'know" tends to be associated with introducing or reintroducing moves. This relationship is illustrated in Example 10.

Example 10   P: Trying to get my remarks ready to (--) the building trades.
            D: So I understand.
            P: Yes, indeed, yeah.
        ➤   Y'know, I was thinking we ought to get the odds and ends uh, it was confirmed that- you remember we talked about resignations and so forth . . . [White House Transcripts: 16-4-73am:187].[2]

The typical move-particle association found for "well" is illustrated in Examples 11 and 12. The "well" of Example 11 and the first "well" of Example 12 are adjoined to progressive-holding moves.

Example 11   179   K: But I hafta kinda go along with what they want too. Like- I'd really like to do it over the week of New ((laughing)) Years but
            180   B: That's always a boring week.
        ➤   181   K: Well it'd be- in some ways it'd be good because I could be shown around - the office and the ins and outs and there wouldn't be a lot of interruptions. As far as, . . . [B-K Conversation].

Example 12   W: My name is Miss White. I am ringing on behalf of S.L.T. Electrical Engineering Company. And I would like to speak to Mr. Williams.
        ➤   S: Well, I am afraid he is going to be tied up most of the day, Miss White. Can you give me some idea of wha- the subject matter?
        ➤   W: Well, I really want to speak to him. I do not want to go into any details unless I can actually talk to him personally [Fast Food Bar:2-11:12.05].

The strength of the move-particle correlation was such as to suggest that a particle took on the meaning or function of the move it was associated with most often. The presence of the particle signaled or reinforced the move relationship holding between consecutive locutions: informing the other (the addressee) that the locution is acceptable and relevant to the talk at hand or, if not, that it is intended to break the established coherent/cohesive bonds unifying the discourse. The strategic use of particles occurred when the "meaning" of the particle and the move assigned to the locution failed to match. In such cases both move types operate together to describe the special relationship of the locution to the discourse. This is the case with M's second turn in Example 13 where the "y'know" that signifies an introducing move is attached to a progressive-holding locution. The result is a shift in topic. Similarly, since the second "well" in Example 12 is assigned to a reintroducing move and since the "well" represents progressive-holding moves, the locution can be heard as being tied back into the prior talk (reiterating a prior request) while at the same time moving the discourse forward onto tangential issues which indirectly answer S's question.

Example 13   S: How's your dog?
                 M: Stupid. (---) I think I found a place for him to stay?
                 S: Really? Where?
→ M: A friend of mine. (2.5) I like his girl friend, y'know. His girl friend is BEAUTIFUL. I've liked her for a LONG time, hh. (3.0) and, y'know what freaked me out? It was in 9th grade (.) I wanted to go out with her really ba::d (.) and I found out that she wanted to go out with me.
                 S: Oh, poor baby. Does she still want to? No?
                 M: 'Know how I found that out, too?
                 S: Uh uh.
                 M: This one girl that I met one night said she knew my name from someone. Then she remembered. She goes, "I know your name, cuz this girl I know, Sharon Jones, always used to like you." And I go, "(----)" [J/J: Getting Stoned:1].

Interaction quality and type. The type and quality of the interaction can be assessed through the move system.

Conversations are distinguished with respect to their developmental type: *symmetrical* versus *complementary* (see Leone & Martin, 1981). Symmetrical interactions are those where the theme (topic) or talk in general is jointly developed by both interactants. Both engage in topic initiations (i.e., introducing moves) and expansions (i.e., progressive-holding moves). This symmetrical pattern is found in Example 14. In this example both speakers can be described as controlling the conversation.

Example 14   A: But when ther on sale you can get them for a song.
                 B: Yeah. I know that. But I was // in a mood of madness.

A: Everybody's got to have their own mishegas.

B: Right. It was just a mishegas.

A: Well, it's nice when you can afford to have mishegases.

B: Well, look, y'know what I figure, I figure I'm going to kill myself on the highway. I might as well enjoy it.

A: Don't say that.

B: I might as well // enjoy it.

A: Oh, don't d-say that and oh well in other words you want what the second wife is going to get.

B: Right.

A: Okay. I'll talk about- I've covered a lot of stories today. R is going to a wedding today — one of the doctor friends whose wife committed suicide less than a year ago . . . [S/S:Sheets].

Complementary interactions, on the other hand, are those where one participant engages in the initiation and development of the discourse while the other passively supports this behavior through the use of backchannels and other holding moves. This type of interaction is found in Example 13: after the first turn M effectively controls the discourse. The same is true for Z in Example 15 for turns 7 through 13, and for B across turns 057 through 066 in the B-K conversation.

In addition to such general descriptions of conversational development, this research can be profitably expanded to include analyses of the type and quality of each interactant's individual behavior. After each locution is assigned to a move it would be possible to see if and, if so, how each interactant is supportive of the other; to see who switches topic or thematic/topical focus more often; to see in what manner the switch is achieved — baldly through the use of introducing moves or subtly through the use of progressive-holding moves which shift referents over one or more locutions (as in Example 13); and to see whether the interactants each address their own issues or each other's. The system could also indicate which interactant is the most competitive, repetitive, persistent, or manipulative.

Such an analysis would be quite instructive for conversations such as Example 15:

Example 15

Locution	Turn	Speaker	Utterance
1, 2	1	**Z:**	I haven't seen too many gay people lately, I guess, I just don't know what's happening.

3	2	**X:**	Yeah
4	3	**Y:**	There's all kinds, around here on this campus, in town
5	4	**X:**	Yeah
6, 7	5	**Z:**	Are there? I didn't know that ((clears throat))
8	6	**Y:**	(---) Central Illinois (---)
9, 10	7	**X:**	Well, what did you and E decide? You decided that =
11, 12	8	**Z:**	= Well, we were wondering just that, that if it's really possible to have it both ways . . . To be . . . to y'know . . . to uh . . . sort of use the sexploitation =
13	9	**X:**	umhmmm
12, 14 15	10	**Z:**	= for both sexes . . . That it really . . . that you get something else . . . That you can't . . . it's it's never going . . . that if you really do start using both sexes that it's never going to be really quite the same as before =
16	11	**X:**	= Okay
17, 18 19, 20	12	**Z:**	I don't know whether it's going to be better, worse, or neither . . . But it's . . . it's . . . The whole . . . . terms of the discourse get modified, I don't think you can do just a simple reversal of sex and treat men as sex objects in a commercial way . . . and just leave everything else constant.
21	13	**X:**	I don't think it works either.
22	14	**Y:**	But they use men as sex objects in women's magazines.
23	15	**X:**	Yeah
24, 25 26	16	**Z:**	Well, sure. I'm not saying that you can't do it. I'm saying it won't work the same way,
27	17	**Y:**	Well, I'm wondering if it doesn't work the same way.
28	18	**X:**	Yeah. =
29	19	**Y:**	= Like *Cosmopolitan* . . . (---) [Page:Office].

TABLE 1.1 A Sequential Description of Conversational Extract
Example 15

Turn	Locution	Speaker	Recipient*†	Move Type††
1	1	Z	X, Y	I (side topic)
	2			P (expand)
2	3	X	Z	H (backchannel)
3	4	Y	Z	R
4	5	X	Z	H (backchannel)
5	6	Z	Y	H (query)
	7		Y, X	P (expand)
6	8	Y	Z	P (expand)
7	9	X	Z	R (main topic)
	10		Z	P (expand/remind)
8	11	Z	X, Y	P (expand)
	12		X, Y	P (expand)
9	13	X	Z	H (backchannel)
10	12 con't	Z		
	14		X, Y	P (expand)
	15		X, Y	P (expand)
11	16	X	Z	H (backchannel)
12	17	Z	X, Y	P T10 (expand)
	18		X, Y	P (expand)
	19		X, Y	P (expand)
	20		X, Y	P (expand)
13	21	X	Z	P T12 (support)
14	22	Y	Z (X)	P (challenge)
15	23	X	Y	H (backchannel)
16	24	Z	Y	H T14 (min. resp.)
	25		Y	P (support)
	26		Y	P (challenge)
17	27	Y	Z	P (challenge)
18	28	X	Y	H (backchannel)
19	29	Y	Z (X)	P T17 (expand)

I = Introducing Move   R = Reintroducing Move   P = Progressive-Holding Move
H = Holding Move
*Y's remark (challenge) is primarily directed to Z. X is also addressed by virtue of
X having just supported Z.
†Recipient order designating which addressee is the primary recipient (e.g., X, Y
reads: mainly to X, only indirectly to Y.
††TN = Turn number to which move is addressed.

A description of this conversation in terms of the moves found therein
is provided by Tables 1.1 and 1.2

The move system highlights and confirms the analysts' interpretations of Example 15. Upon examination of Tables 1.1 and 1.2 it
becomes visibly apparent that not only is X supportive of both Z and

TABLE 1.2   The Distribution of Turns, Locutions, and Moves
by Speaker and Addressee

| | Speaker | | |
	X	Y	Z
Turns	8	5	6
Locutions	9	5	15
Moves			
(Re-)Introducing	1•Z	1•Z	*1•X(Y)
Progressive–Holding	2	4	12
expanding	1	*2	*10
supporting	1•Z	—	1•Y
challenging	—	2•Z	1•Y
Holding	6	—	2
backchannels	¥6 4•Z 2•Y	—	—
attention getters	—	—	—
metacomments	—	—	—
reiterations	—	—	—
minimal responses	—	—	1•Y
queries	—	—	1•Y

• = Addressee or recipient (e.g., Speaker Z, supporting move, 1 • Y (X) reads as "Z made one supporting move directed to Y and indirectly directed to X").
* = Addressed to Z's issues.
¥ = All supportive in tenor.

Y, but that the effect of this support is undermined. Z and Y do not see eye to eye, yet X indiscriminately concurs with both. Furthermore, all but one of X's nine locutions are supportive in nature and this (number 10) expands upon X's own locution (number 9, turn 7), which is itself used to bolster Z's face by reintroducing a topic raised earlier by Z.

Of the 29 locutions uttered across 19 turns, Y speaks the least: taking only 5 single-locution turns. Unlike X's contributions, Y utters only challenging, nonsupportive, substantive comments: 1 reintroducing and 4 progressive-holding moves. All are directed to Z. Similarly, 6 of X's are also directed to Z with only 2 directed to Y.

The initial impression that Z is the dominant interactant is somewhat mitigated by Y's locution/move profile. While it is true that of the 29 locutions, 15 are Z's, and that all 29 locutions are directed at Z's issues; at those two spots (turns 3 and 6, and turns 14, 17, and 19) where Y actively partakes in the discussion, the discourse changes from complementary to symmetrical and argumentative. The suggestion that Y may be equally dominant is borne out by both X and Z's readiness to support or accept Y's challenges or counterarguments. This is especially noticeable from turn 12 to 19.

Z's behavior in turn 16 is quite interesting. Is Z backing down from Y's challenge in recognition of Y's dominance or is Z manipulating these impressions? By the end of turn 16, Z's own position is repeated, albeit with less conviction or certainty: "it can't be done" in turns 10 and 12 is downgraded to "it can, but differently" in turn 16.

Describing the flow of talk. Through the assignment of moves to locutions it is possible to identify thematic and sequential boundaries as they occur in the discourse (Burton, 1978; Goldberg, 1980, 1982; Goodenough & Weiner, 1978; Sinclair et al., 1972). This is especially useful in cases of subtle topic shift (as found in Examples 13 and 14) for determining where one topic/sequence ended and the next began (Grimes, 1978; also see Crow, this volume; see Goldberg, 1980, for various procedures and strategies used in conjunction with moves for indicating and recognizing the point of topical transfer).

An example flow chart will suffice to illustrate how the move model indicates topical breaks, shifts, and boundaries. Applying the flow chart depicted in Figure 1.3 to Example 13, presented earlier, the reader can see where the topic shift occurred: "(2.5) I like his girl friend, y'know." And where it was secured: "His girl friend is BEAUTIFUL."

Eventually, the move model descriptions should encompass accounts of thematic or topical development. This could be done by the simple charting or tracking of each discourse referent from the time it is introduced up to the time it is dropped, and by simultaneously indicating the thematic or focal level (i.e., degree of relevance or salience at the time of mention) at which the referent is addressed (cf. Schank, 1977).

CONCLUSION

Under the move model it is evident that the chaining and tying of referents is the manner in which a fair amount of talk proceeds. Analysts without such a move system are unable to describe, let alone comprehend, how, when initiating a stretch of talk with, "Y'know, Rover won't come in here anymore without you," it can end, with each locution cohesively latched and tied to the last, with, "She goes,

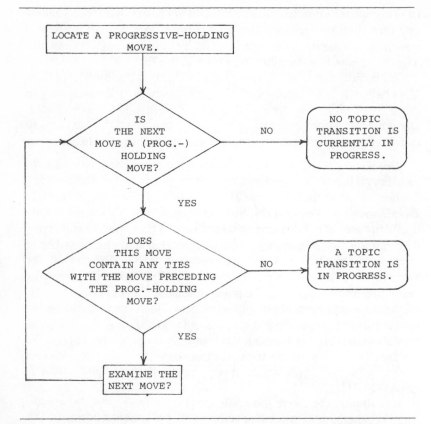

Figure 1.3 Procedure for Locating Topic Beginnings: Subtle (Unbounded) Topic Shifts

I know your name cuz this girl I know, Sharon Jones, always used to like you." In general, without the aid of the move model, analysts would be severely handicapped when it comes to describing casual conversation.

Throughout this chapter it has been stressed that much of conversation is composed of many interactively negotiated and achieved phenomena: Topic choice and structure are not predetermined. Each participant plays an ongoing and active role in the discourse's organization. They each interpret the other's utterances and formulate their own to fit their individual needs and/or understanding of the situation (see Sanders, this volume). These, in turn, affect the form and interpretation of subsequent contributions. And so the discourse evolves. In fact, as Schegloff noted (1981, pp. 26-27):

> There is a real, recurrent contingency concerning what whoever-gets-to-talk should talk *on;* the fact that the same speaker who talked before talks again and *talks more of the same thing* is an outcome achieved out of this contingency (they could have gone on to repair what preceded; they could have parenthesized into a comment about their talking; they could have "touched-off" into something entirely different, etc.) [Emphasis in original].

Schegloff adds (1981, p. 27) that "good analysis will retain a sense of the actual as an achievement from among possibles." This is the role of the move model. The advantages of the system do not end here. With the aid of the move model our understanding of the complex web of interpersonal, pragmatic, and cognitive mechanisms underlying and shaping a discourse has been vastly enriched. This is not possible with generative models of conversational coherence and development.

NOTES

1. In addition to symbols defined in the Appendix, the following special transcription symbols are used in this chapter:

(--) indicates inaudible segment (Examples 10, 13, 15);

(2.5) indicates pause timed in seconds (Example 13);

(.) indicates brief, untimed pause (Example 13);

... indicates pause, number of dots indicates approximate length (Example 15);

// indicates point at which following utterance interrupts current utterance (Example 14).

2. Like the global model the move system is interested in the larger organizational units of discourse. The system's labels are unitizing by nature. However, the unit described is open ended. That is, while there are introducing moves there are not terminating moves (as yet). The closure is accomplished by two or more passing moves or by introducing moves followed by holding or progressive-holding moves. In fact, much of topical closure is accomplished in just this way.

3. Similar models are devised by Keenan and Schieffelin (1976) and Sinclair et al. (1972). However, their moves apply to turns or larger constructional units.

4. This raises empirical issues regarding how far back into an exchange this assignment can reach and how far back in short-term memory a referent is retained (cf. Chafe, 1974).

2

Speech Act Structure in

Conversation
Rational Aspects of Pragmatic Coherence

< <SCOTT JACOBS and SALLY JACKSON > >

< < < This chapter presents an informal demonstra-> > >
tion of the potential power of a rational model for describing the
pragmatic aspects of conversational coherence. Specifically, the
chapter argues for an alternative to the conventionalist treatment of
coherence as the product of sequencing rules that operate directly on
speech act categories (cf. Jackson & Jacobs, 1980; Pomerantz, 1978;
Schegloff & Sacks, 1973). While any theory of conversational coherence must make reference to the pragmatic aspects of language, it is
not at all obvious that a sequencing rules theory is powerful enough to
do the job (for recent critiques, see Levinson, 1981; Mohan, 1974). We
argue that the theory of speech acts permits a deeper and more
parsimonious explanation than can be provided by a sequencing rules
theory, an explanation that appeals to rational principles of practical
action. Our argument for the superiority of a rational model has two
legs: first, the most notable conventional forms of conversational
sequencing identified by the sequencing rules approach (adjacency
pairs, embedded expansions, presequences) can be shown to be
derivable from a more fundamental system of rational principles for
producing cooperative speech activity; second, several anomalies for
the sequencing rules approach can be shown to derive from the *same*
underlying system of rational principles. In other words, a rational

model can subsume both the successes and the failures of the sequencing rules approach under a more abstract and inclusive model of conversational structure.

THE SEQUENCING RULES MODEL

The sequencing rules approach attempts to model the orderliness of dialogue on the assumptions that (1) the utterances of conversation may be analyzed as speech act categories and (2) the succession of utterances in conversation is regulated by rules that specify the range of speech act types that may appropriately follow any given speech act.[1] Such an approach promises to build a grammar of conversation by defining sequential coherence in terms of irreducible conventions that operate on the surface-level structure of turns at talk.

The centerpiece of the sequencing rules approach is the concept of the adjacency pair — conventional utterance pairings such as greeting/greeting, question/answer, request/grant (or refusal), and invitation/acceptance (or refusal). These sequential relations provide a conventional solution to the problem of how to make a relevant next turn in conversation. Adjacency pairs are defined by two sequential properties. First, the relation between pair parts is regulated by a rule that makes the appearance of the second pair part *conditionally relevant* on the occurrence of the first pair part (Schegloff, 1972a, p. 107). That is, the appearance of a first pair part creates a response demand: A member of the class of appropriate second pair parts is expectable and its absence is noticeable. Its appearance permits the closure of the sequence. Second, adjacency pairs are regulated by a *structural preference for agreement* between pair parts (Jackson & Jacobs, 1978; Pomerantz, 1978). The range of second pair parts that can appropriately combine with a given first pair part are structurally nonequivalent; that second pair part that agrees with the first pair part tends to occupy structurally preferred positions in conversation. So, for example, requests are designed to get grants, and yes/no questions are designed to get replies that are consistent with the presupposed answer. While refusals to grants and replies that negate the presupposed answer are *relevant* second pair parts, conversationists work to avoid, repair, or otherwise mitigate their appearance.

The sequencing rules approach can also claim as genuine achievements the discovery of presequences and embedded expansions (Jefferson, 1972; Schegloff, 1972a, 1980). These are patterns of sequential expansion generated by a rule permitting the repeated and recursive placement of subsidiary adjacency pairs before, within, and after a dominant adjacency pair. Presequences such as Example 1 are speech act sequences whose interpretation is relative to some adjacency pair *yet to come*. This prefatory character is part of their meaning.

Example 1   **A:**   Hey, did you hear about the game last night?
             B: No, what happened?
             A: We got blown away.
             B: That figures.

Embedded expansions are speech act sequences inserted between a first pair part and its second pair part. They too are interpreted with respect to the superordinate adjacency pair. Thus, certain kinds of questions and statements can be understood as objections or as contingent queries *by virtue of* their structural position between the first pair part and second pair part.

Example 2   **A:**   Wanna go to lunch?
             B: Where were you thinking of going?
             A: We thought we'd try out that new Japanese restaurant.
             B: Okay, that sounds good.

Sequencing rules models, then, offer an intuitively appealing direction for approaching problems of coherence in conversation. There is no getting around the intuitive strength of the adjacency-pair bonding, especially for highly goal-structured speech acts such as requesting and questioning. Likewise, the notion of sequential expansion appears to capture, in structural terms, some obvious patterns for constructing larger units of coherent development. These are sequential relations that any adequate model of coherence must recognize. This approach, however, leaves open a number of unanswered questions.

Most obviously, there are a variety of coherent replies to first pair parts that do not fit into the category of a second pair part. Consider, for example, some major classes of alternative responses to a request (3) or a question (4). Besides (i) direct replies, first pair parts can get (ii) passes that redirect the activity of the initiator, (iii) disagreeable responses that attempt to satisfy the demands of the first pair part, (iv) alternative proposals for action, (v) indirect refusals that address pragmatic preconditions for performance of the first pair part, and (vi) indirect replies that implicate the preferred second pair part (see also Levinson, 1981, p. 107; Sinclair & Coulthard, 1975, p. 133).

Example 3 R: Do you have a pen I could borrow?
      A: (i)   Sure.
           (ii) Ask John for one.
           (iii) I have a *pencil*.
           (iv) Let's just skip class today.
           (v) You never give them back.
           (vi) I just happened to bring an extra today.

Example 4 Q: What time is it?
      A: (i)   It's 11:00.
           (ii) There's a clock in the hall.
           (iii) It was 10:45 when we left for class.
           (iv) Quit worrying.
           (v) I don't have a watch.
           (vi) Class starts in three minutes.

An adjacency-pair analysis provides no obvious way of characteriz-ing the broad range of utterances that may constitute a coherent reply. The concept appears, rather, to capture a standardized pattern and not any general principle of coherence.

Just as adjacency-pair analysis has difficulty accounting for the full range of coherent responses to a first pair part, so also it has difficulty accounting for which speech acts can and cannot initiate an adjacency pair. A large number of speech acts establish no obvious conditional relevance. Statements, for example, do not place any obvious restrictions on how to make a reply — if they require a reply at all. A sequencing rules approach can accommodate this fact only as an ad hoc scope condition.

A third anomaly for the sequencing rules approach is the apparent diversity of sequential expansions. For example, one common varia-tion on the presequential pattern is the preempt where the issuing of, say, a prerequest leads at once to an offer (this and other variations are analyzed by Jacobs & Jackson, 1981). Likewise, replies to a contin-gent query after, say, an invitation, may obviate the need for a second pair part.

Example 5 A: Wanna come over Friday night?
      B: Did you get out of judging that speech contest?
      A: Oh, no. I forgot about that.

The simple fact of the diversity of patterns of sequential expansion suggests the need for deeper generative principles.

Finally, no account can be given within a sequencing rules model as to what makes some sequences structurally subordinate expansions and other sequences digressions or wholly unrelated intrusions into an exchange (cf. Dascal & Katriel, 1979). What, in other words, places some utterances within the structural environment of a dominant adjacency pair while excluding other temporally contiguous utterances?

A RATIONAL MODEL

It is important to recognize that while a sequencing rules approach uses speech acts as the *structural units* upon which coherent sequential relations are defined, the *functional properties* of speech acts do not enter into such definitions. The use of speech act categories as grammatical units is not dependent on the properties of practical action, nor does such use rely on notions of goals or functional preconditions for action. The rational model, which we will develop in the remainder of this chapter, argues that such notions are essential to an adequate understanding of pragmatic coherence and that the rules and structural patterns identified by a sequencing rules approach are the *consequences* of a more fundamental system of principles by which people rationally pursue goals in conversation.

A rational model of conversational coherence must show how coherent dialogue results from the application of practical reasoning to conventionally defined means of achieving goals (i.e., speech acts). Such a model must include systems of rules defining appropriate means of achieving particular kinds of goals, such as rules for performing requests, where the goal is to get an addressee to perform some future act (Labov & Fanshel, 1977; Searle, 1969), or rules for performing demand tickets, where the goal is to secure the attention of an addressee (Nofsinger, 1975). Since some rules will refer to general requirements for communication, such as Grice's (1975) cooperative principle, or Habermas's (1979) universal validity claims, while others will refer only to narrowly defined goals, different levels of abstractness will be apparent among these rule systems. In addition to these rules, a rational model must include a theory of practical reasoning, such as the principles outlined by Mohan (1974). Coherent discourse must be shown to be the orderly output of practical reasoning about goals, constrained by institutionally defined means of *achieving* those goals.

Conversation as a Language Game

At an intuitive level the nature of a rational model of conversational coherence can best be understood by seeing conversation as a language game or collection of language games (Wittgenstein, 1958). Games are social activities defined by rules; their players are held accountable to the rules. Players have knowledge of the rules and varying degrees of skill in using the rules to make moves that realize their goals. Games are characterized by varying degrees of mutual constraint: Each player's actions will constrain, in some degree, the actions of the other. As an individual game unfolds, however, the contributions of each player produce emergent, transpersonal patterns resulting in end states that may or may not represent the end state envisioned by either player. In planning their own line of moves, then, players must take into account the plans of other players. They are continually faced with the task of inducing the willing or unwitting collaboration of their fellow players.

From this viewpoint the question of how people construct and recognize coherent discourse is equivalent to asking how the game is played. As with any game, a perfectly satisfying type of explanation comes from a description of the primary rules and elements that define the game and a demonstration of how those rules are applied to the players' goals to produce moves appropriate to the point of the game. That is the sort of explanation that can be found in any chess handbook, and we think that an adequate theory of conversational coherence will be a formalized equivalent of such accounts. An adequate account has two levels of description.

First, there is a level representing the primary knowledge that is needed to play the game. Chess handbooks lay out the point of the game, the elements or basic components, and the primary rules operating on those components — the procedures for making allowable moves. Notice that there are no sequencing rules in chess; handbooks on the game rely on informal illustrations of practical reasoning to explain sequencing.

Second, there is a level of knowledge representing not rules but rational play within rules. Corresponding to this level of description, a chess handbook might lay out general strategies and standardized patterns with their variations. Standard ("book") openings belong to this secondary level of knowledge, as do standard lines of end-game play and general strategic principles (such as "Control the center of the board," or "Place rooks on open files"). Such patterns and strategies are not themselves normatively enforced, as rules are. They may be conventional in the sense that there can be strong mutual expectations concerning their use (especially among sophisticated players), but there are no rules prescribing their use. They are used because they are rational solutions to the problems presented by the structure of the game. Such strategies and patterns are ultimately derivable from the way that the primary rules serve to constrain the range of possible and effective moves as the game unfolds. Strategies can be seen as rational ways to pursue goals and standard lines of play as the principled interlocking of two individual strategic plans. One major difference between the sequencing rules approach and a rational model is that the sequencing rules approach treats this secondary level of knowledge as comprising the system of primary rules, rather than as derivations from primary rules.

A rational model of conversation assumes that the point of the game is to achieve one (or more) of a restricted set of goals through the use of rule-defined moves. The analogy between conversation and chess is a good one. It clarifies our analytic task (How is this game played?) and it points to important distinctions between levels of knowledge possessed by players (systemic versus strategic). The analogy also clarifies the sense in which conversation is a *cooperative* activity: as in chess, conversationists pursue their goals with respect to a *social* structure, even when individual goals compete. As in any game, each conversationist must adhere to a set of cooperative restrictions and must act on the assumption that others are doing likewise.

The sense in which rationality depends upon some form of cooperative principle can be intuitively demonstrated by examining two manifest properties of coherent dialogue: *goal orientation* and *alignment*. A model of conversation as an idealized game assumes that players try to approximate the properties of rational agents: they establish goals, plan means for achieving goals, and make moves contributing to the achievement of those goals. Of course, players are never perfectly rational, but they try to be — which is why they subject themselves and others to criticism.

Coherent conversation requires that each player's contributions bear a rational relation to some goal. That is part of what it means for an utterance to be coherent: it ought to have a point. The goal can be very limited (as with Nofsinger's, 1974, demand ticket) or be very broad (as when a single-target goal requires the achievement of several subgoals); it can be very focused (as with a specific request for action or information) or be very diffuse (as when the only point is to simply generate a topic for talk); goals can be intrinsic to the conversation (as with self-disclosure) or be extrinsic to the conversation (as where the goal of getting something done is mediated by the act of giving instruction). But in any case, the sense of an utterance — its coherence — is to be found in its relations to *some* goal.

The sense of coherence in conversation also derives from its transpersonal structuring. Players pursue goals in a system of mutual awareness and mutual dependency, using communication to establish a reciprocity of perspectives and a consensual agreement of purpose. Coherent conversation requires a cooperative pursuit of goals as opposed to simple individual pursuit of goals. The actions and beliefs of any individual must be *aligned* with the actions and beliefs of other individuals and with the requirements of an institutionally defined system (Stokes & Hewitt, 1976). This dual process of alignment leads to an emergent social orientation that Mead (1934) tried to capture with his notion of the generalized other: Individuals align with one another with respect to the way each aligns with the social system.

Because each player is a necessary instrumental agent for the achievement or obstruction of the other's goals, he or she must be adjusted to in any plan. Rational players do not initiate goals they think will be obstructed by others. They search for goals and means compatible with the possibilities offered by others. Most important, they acknowledge their own involvement in the goals and plans of others. The simultaneous orientation of players to an institutional system results in more than the coordinated pursuit of individual lines of action: it involves the joint pursuit of socially defined goals. The goals initiated by either player create a prima facie demand on the other by virtue of their mutual participation in a transpersonal system. The appropriateness of any act and the legitimacy of any goal will be negotiated with reference to institutionally defined standards.

The notion of alignment is not limited to cases of achieved agreement: it involves entry into an effort to reach agreement. Disagreements and arguments may be cooperative activity involving good faith efforts by individuals to align actions and beliefs. Alignment suggests that rational players engage in an ongoing effort to achieve what Goffman termed a "working consensus" (1959, p. 10). Alignment does not mean consensus of belief; it involves fitting lines of action into a set of transpersonal structures (such as rules for performing valid requests).

The task of a rational model of conversation is to explicate the nature of the institutional constraints and the nature of the practical reasoning within such constraints that account for the appearance of cooperative (i.e., coherent) activity in conversation. It is important to see that all of the obvious deviations from the ideal of cooperative action — deception, confusion, pretense, and so on — are organized with respect to the way in which they preserve the appearance of cooperative dialogue (Jacobs, 1977). If one can make it look like he or she is trying to cooperate, the institutional demands are satisfied. For this reason, we take a model of rational action — an ideal conception of cooperativity — to be a fundamental step in understanding how any utterance makes a coherent contribution to a conversation.

Conversational Moves

Let us begin by specifying that moves in conversation are illocutionary acts. As has been noted repeatedly, the performance of any illocutionary act presupposes some set of beliefs and wants for the hearer and commits the speaker to some (partly overlapping) set of beliefs and wants. Illocutionary acts may be seen as attempts by one player to change the beliefs and/or wants of another. That is, conversational moves have force as transformations of a starting state (a belief/want context) into a new state (a different belief/want context) (cf. Mohan, 1974). As in chess, the current position of each player affects the moves that can be appropriately and effectively performed.

Every illocutionary act has associated with it some set of preconditions defining appropriate performance of that act type (e.g., felicity conditions, but also see Levinson, 1979). Searle (1969) has provided an abstract description of these conditions: Every act type will have associated with it some restricted set of permissible propositional contents, a (set of) sincerity condition(s), a (set of) preparatory condition(s), and a (set of) essential condition(s). For example, the propositional content of a request must convey a future act by the hearer, while a compliment's propositional content must refer to an attribute or act of the hearer. Sincerity conditions describe the internal states to which speakers commit themselves in performing an act. For requests, the speaker must actually want the requested act to be performed; for compliments, the sincerity condition requires the speaker actually to approve the attribute or act referred to. Preparatory conditions represent beliefs that are logical prerequisites for the success of the illocutionary act. For requests, they include the speaker's belief that the hearer is able and willing to do the act requested and that the act would not have been done without its being requested; for compliments, the preparatory conditions include the speaker's belief that the hearer is responsible for the attribute or act and that the hearer approves the attribute or act. The essential condition corresponds to what Searle (1975b) has termed the "illocutionary point" of an act: the intent a speaker communicates in performing the act. For requesting, the utterance must count as an effort to get the hearer to do the desired action by virtue of placing him or her under obligation to do so; for compliments, the essential condition is that the utterance count as the speaker's expressed intention to give the hearer positive face by expressing approval for the hearer's attribute or act (Brown & Levinson, 1978).

Every distinct type of illocutionary act has its own particular set of rules within this common set of abstract categories. The propositional content, sincerity, and preparatory conditions define the values that must obtain in a belief/want context for the appropriate performance of an act; the essential condition defines the transformation in the belief/want context that occurs by virtue of the act being communicated. This communicative structure of illocutionary acts provides the basis for the pursuit of three types of goals in conversation — goals that themselves involve a further transformation to a new belief/want context.

First, every illocutionary act is associated with some conventional perlocutionary effect — an institutionally defined goal that consists of the response by the hearer called for by the appropriate performance of the illocutionary act. Conventional perlocutionary effects may involve some action on the part of the hearer (e.g., performing a requested action or accepting a compliment) or they may involve only a change in the hearer's belief state (e.g., believing the stated proposition). Second, illocutionary acts may *implicate* a wide range of intended consequences by virtue of the hearer recognizing that the speaker is purposefully *using* the illocutionary act to express those intentions (Grice, 1975; Searle, 1975b). The pursuit of both types of goals involve the communication of the intent to achieve those goals. So, for example, in asking what time it is, a speaker may express the intention to get the hearer to provide such information (the illocutionary point) and thereby get the hearer to provide such information (the conventional perlocutionary effect). But in using such an act, the speaker may also intend to implicate a chain of reasoning that leads the hearer to see that it is time for a meeting to end and to thereby call an end to it (the chain of reasoning being triggered by the hearer wondering why the speaker would ask such a question and seeing that the speaker intends for him/her to wonder why).

Third, through the achievement of these communicative goals, illocutionary acts can establish subgoals in the pursuit of broader goals. So, for example, in obtaining a negative answer to whether or not the hearer has heard about an event, as in Example 1, the speaker establishes a precondition for the appropriate performance of a reporting of that event.

Primary Rules

From the point of view of a rational model of conversational coherence, people initiate acts in order to change current belief/want contexts in ways that are congruent with the achievement of some goal state, that is, some desired belief/want context. Likewise, people respond not to acts per se, but to the goals communicated by those acts and to the belief/want contexts created by those acts. The overall structure of a series of utterances, then, has a sense of coherence not dependent so much on surface-structure issues of utterance-by-utterance sequencing as on deep-structure issues of how any utterance contributes to or obstructs the unfolding of a goal-based plan by signifying changes in belief/want contexts. Correspondingly, the rules for the production of coherent conversation will be found not to operate on acts as units, but on state changes in belief/want contexts. In addition to some very abstract principles for cooperative action (such as Grice's, 1975, conversational maxims or Habermas's, 1979, universal validity claims), we suggest the following rules as necessary elements in an explanation of coherence.

Validity rule. Any illocutionary act is validly performed if and only if the speaker believes that the preconditions for the act are satisfied and the speaker sincerely intends to achieve the communicated goals. Speakers should not do any illocutionary act they do not believe is valid. In performing an illocutionary act, the speaker is committed to believing the preconditions hold and to sincerely intending what is expressed. In other words, conversationalists are under obligation to align their utterances with the demands of the social system. Obviously, since every act has its own set of preconditions and can be associated with an indefinite variety of implicatures, the validity rule will have variable implications for different kinds of talk.

Reason rule. Conversationalists are also under obligation to align their utterances with the beliefs and wants of others. One party's expressed beliefs and wants are a prima facie reason for another party to come to have those beliefs and wants and, thereby, for those beliefs and wants to structure the range of appropriate utterances that party can contribute to the conversation. If a speaker expresses belief X, and the hearer neither believes nor disbelieves X, then the speaker's expressed belief in X is reason for the hearer to believe X and to make his or her contributions conform to that belief. Likewise, if the speaker expresses want Y, and the hearer neither wants nor opposes Y, then the speaker's expressed wanting of Y is reason for the hearer to come to want Y and to make his or her contributions pursue that want. The reason rule requires conversationalists not only to try to satisfy one another's goals, but also to try to agree with subordinate beliefs and wants conveyed by the performance of an illocutionary act. For example, the reason rule not only obliges the hearer to accept an invitation in the absence of good reason not to; it also obliges the hearer to believe that the preconditions for that invitation hold unless he or she has reason to disbelieve that such preconditions hold.

Of course, cooperative agents may have good reason to disbelieve that such preconditions hold or have good reason not to want the goal expressed in an illocutionary act. In such cases the reason rule will still operate to constrain the range of utterances a cooperative hearer may contribute: here a cooperative agent will indicate the failure of an illocutionary act to produce its intended effects and will identify the point of obstruction.

Practical Reasoning

The validity and reason rules establish a basic logic for the pursuit of social consequences through illocutionary action: by appropriately performing an illocutionary act, the speaker creates a belief/want context that places a demand on the hearer to act in a way that aligns his or her own belief/want context with that expressed by the speaker. Such a process, however, is fallible. Specifically, cooperative agents may differ in their assessments of whether or not a given illocutionary act satisfies the demands of the validity rule. In such cases the expressed goals of an illocutionary act will be obstructed, conflict between belief/want contexts will appear, and conversationalists will be forced to reassess or readjust their goals or their belief/want contexts in order to continue the pursuit of social goals.

In order to cooperatively pursue conversational goals in the ways provided by the validity and reason rules, rational agents must be able to reason about which (combination) of the available means in conversation will achieve their goals. In other words, they must be able to reason according to the following basic principle of practical reasoning:

> **Principle 1:**   Whenever anyone wants to achieve an objective and this objective can be achieved by performing a certain action, then one thing for him or her to do is perform this action.

Rational agents can also be expected to develop more elaborate plans and strategies that anticipate and overcome potential barriers to alignment, that locate and repair sources of misalignment, and that confirm the achievement of alignment when that state is in doubt. In his discussion of the logic behind patterns of presequencing, Mohan (1974) has proposed two principles of practical reasoning that apply to a wide group of patterns of coherent development in conversation. Specifically, he has proposed the following:

Principle 2: "Whenever anyone wants to achieve an objective and cannot achieve this objective unless he performs a certain action, then one thing for him to do is to perform this action" (p. 80).

Principle 3: "Whenever anyone wants to achieve an objective and cannot achieve this objective unless a certain state of affairs obtains, then one thing for him to do is to determine whether this state of affairs obtains" (p. 80).

Every speech act, whether structured around some limited and specific goal or around some broad and ill-defined goal, presupposes some belief/want context that must obtain as a precondition for its appropriate performance; and any conversational goal (a projected belief/want context) will be associated with some (set of) illocutionary act(s) that conventionally achieve that objective. These principles of practical reasoning, together with the primary rules for making coherent contributions to a conversation, provide the basis for building and carrying out plans that pursue social goals and for monitoring the progress of such plans over the course of a conversation. Pragmatic coherence consists of this sort of activity. In the next section we defend this claim in a preliminary way by showing how a rational model can absorb and extend the achievements of a sequencing rules approach.

OUTPUT FROM A RATIONAL MODEL

In this section our strategy will be to show that our model can account for the brute facts of sequential coherence in terms of operations on belief/want contexts. Additionally, we will address the major anomalies that have been charged up against sequencing rules accounts of coherence as a demonstration of the greater explanatory power of a rational model.

The Successes and Failures of the Adjacency Pair

The first thing to notice in reconceptualizing the nature of adjacency pairs is that these exchanges look very much like the kind of speech acts Hancher (1979) calls "cooperative" speech acts. These are compound speech acts such as betting or giving where the act requires the performance of two separate illocutionary acts in order to be performed (in these two cases, types of offers and acceptances). The illocutionary point of any first pair part projects just this sort of social completion as its goal. The first pair part of any adjacency pair *counts as* an attempt to establish a jointly held belief/want context which occurs through a speech act performed by the hearer (the preferred second pair part).

Thus greetings have as their conventional perlocutionary effect the creation of a mutual focus, a state established by another greeting. Questions have as their conventional perlocutionary effect the obtaining of information, a state established by an answer. Requests and offers have as intermediate conventional perlocutionary effects the establishment of a social contract to perform some action, a state established by a grant and an acceptance. So, adjacency pairs can be seen as a simple solution to the problem of an initiator communicating goals that a hearer must satisfy through performance of another illocutionary act, and then the hearer responding in a way that satisfies or, in the case of a dispreferred second pair part, obstructs those goals.

From the perspective of our model the adjacency pair can be seen as a limited special case of a general rational structure. Specifically, the bond between first pair part and second pair part can be derived from the illocutionary structure of the two acts performed in the pair parts and from the application of principle 1 of practical reasoning to the demands of the reason rule. Elsewhere (Jacobs & Jackson, 1981), we have argued that requests and promises of compliance (i.e., grants) have mirror-image felicity conditions and identical propositional content conditions. The same symmetry exists in the belief/want contexts associated with the pair parts of any adjacency pair. This means that when performance of the first pair part is valid, the validity of the preferred second pair part is also guaranteed. And the performance of the preferred second pair part is a reasonable means of achieving the objectives of the first pair part. Where the first pair part is not validly performed, however, the preferred second pair part cannot be validly performed either. In this circumstance, performance of the dispreferred second pair part is a reasonable means of satisfying the demand of the reason rule to indicate a misfiring of the projected consequences.

So, both the conditional relevance of second pair parts given the occurrence of first pair parts and the preference for agreement between pair parts find a rationale in the application of practical reasoning principles to the demands of the cooperative pursuit of social goals. The adjacency pair is not simply the output of surface-level rules for sequencing; it is generated from the rational relationship between the preconditions and goals of the constituent act types.

Our analysis does more, however, than explain why adjacency pairs should have such a standardized appearance; it also explains a variety of phenomena outside the scope of the adjacency-pair concept. First, our analysis provides an account for the variety of coherent replies to first pair parts that do not fit into the category of a second pair part. Passes, such as those illustrated in Examples 3(ii) and 4(ii), and "agreeable disagreeables," such as those illustrated in Examples 3(iii) and 4(iii), are ways that a cooperative agent can attempt to meet — or at least approximate — the goals communicated by an illocutionary act when the preferred second pair part cannot be validly performed. Indirect replies, such as those illustrated in Examples 3(vi) and 4(vi), are another way of using principle 1 to satisfy the goals of the illucotionary act, though they do so by implicating rather than by directly expressing what is called for. Finally, counterproposals, such as those illustrated in Example 3(iv) and 4(iv), and indirect refusals, such as those illustrated in Examples 3(v) and 4(v), are relevant replies by virtue of the way they identify the point of obstruction in satisfying the goals of the first pair part. The latter type of reply, in fact, can be seen as less than a full-blown refusal since it opens the possibility of repairing the defective precondition it identifies. It is in this sense a cooperative solution to the problem of simultaneously satisfying the demands of the validity and reason rules (Jackson & Jacobs, 1981). Once it is realized that replies to first pair parts are the result of practical reasoning principles applied to the cooperative demands placed on illocutionary action rather than the result of sequencing rules operating simply on speech act units, a far more flexible system of coherent replies can be accommodated.[2]

Second, a rational model of pragmatic coherence is able to explain which speech acts can and cannot initiate an adjacency pairing. Our analysis explains the weakness of the bond any illocutionary act creates in terms of the same principles that explain the strength of the demand characteristics created by other illocutionary acts. The conventional perlocutionary effect and implicated goals associated with any illocutionary act create different constraints on how the hearer might satisfy the reason rule. The conventional perlocutionary effect of a statement, for example, may only go so far as to require that the hearer recognize the speaker's expressed belief in some proposition. In such circumstances the hearer can align his or her contributions in any way consistent with that recognition. The conventional perlocutionary effect of a question, on the other hand, goes beyond a change in the hearer's beliefs to the causing of the hearer to perform a narrow set of goal-relevant responses.

This sort of analysis does not imply that large classes of illocutionary acts establish *no* pragmatic constraints on the range of contributions that a hearer may make; rather, those contraints will be of a very general nature and may be satisfied by a wide variety of illocutionary acts. Consider, for example, the appearance of acknowledgments in conversation. Because the principle outcome of an illocutionary act is a private mental process not directly accessible to the speaker, hearers must cooperate in the joint pursuit of even very diffuse goals by indicating that alignment exists when that state is in doubt. And even for ordinary conversational events such as telling stories or expressing opinions, alignment must exist with respect to assumptions about the knowledge and interest of each party. Recipients of such acts may still feel the need to express their appreciation for the significance of, and their interest in, what is being said. Of course, that pragmatic function can be implicated in the performance of any number of illocutionary acts that extend the topic, but it can also be directly performed through a variety of stereotypical feedback cues. Consider K's contributions in Example 6:

Example 6 057 **K:** Are you going to be gone long?

058 **B:** It seems like long. It's going to be two weeks.

059 **K:** Hmm::!

    [

060 **B:**   My father and I haven't spent two

weeks together in quite some time. ((snicker))

061 **K:** A real challenge? ((pause)) Or will it be fun.

    [

062 **B:**   He's a

challenging person. ((laugh)) He um - he's a

lawyer so he only listens to as much as he needs

to of what you're saying to make an argument

against it. And if there is no argument going at

the time he provokes one.

063 **K:** Ah:::!

064 **B:** Every once in a while you have to just sit down

and tell him to back off. ((snicker)) .hhh That's

done if you're willing t'either burst into tears or

duck. ((laugh))

065 **K:** Oh::heheh [B-K Conversation,].

From the point of view of a rational model the primary difference between tightly structured exchanges, such as those in an adjacency pair, and loosely coupled exchanges, such as those in casual conversation, is not to be found in different kinds of sequencing rules, but in the different kinds of pragmatic goals that speech acts are used to pursue. The same system of rational constraints produces quite different output depending on the goals that must be satisfied in a conversation.

The Regularities and Irregularities of Expansion

Our model explains presequences and embedded sequences, not as the output of structural expansion rules, but again as rational output from a set of means for transforming belief/want contexts. Consider presequences first, specifically prerequests. The target illocutionary act — a request — can be appropriately performed only in a specific, well-defined belief/want context. The preconditions for appropriate requesting obviously do not always hold, and even when they do hold, this is not always apparent to the prospective requestor. A rational procedure for the speaker in such circumstances is to try to determine whether or not the conditions hold (Principle 3), or if a condition seems *not* to hold, to try to establish the condition (Principle 2). The validity rule, operating through principles of practical reasoning, generates presequences as a rational strategy.

The way we hear presequences such as prerequests as prefatory is also explained by the model. The interpretive and sequential connections between the prerequest and the request result from the way prerequests contribute to (feed) a request-relevant belief/want context (Mohan, 1974). Specifically, the recognizability of a prerequest appears to be a function of the directness of its association with a felcity condition for requesting (Jacobs & Jackson, 1981).

Embedded sequences, likewise, derive their coherence from links to the belief/want context associated with the superordinate act. Embedded sequences vary greatly in the degree to which they disrupt the normal flow of discourse — the degree to which they are coherent. These variations, we maintain, reflect degrees of association with the preconditions for superordinate speech acts. Not just any question/ answer pair can be inserted between a request and its response; the range of coherent embedded sequences is constrained by the belief/ want context of requesting. We have argued elsewhere that argument and persuasion around requests must be organized by the felicity conditions for requesting; such organization is what makes an utterance understandable as a reason for or against a request (Jackson & Jacobs, 1980; Jacobs & Jackson, 1981). Such hearings are based on conversationists' unerstanding of the rational application of Principles 2 and 3 of practical reasoning. Where a respondent to a request is not sure that the preconditions hold, he or she can inquire about such circumstances; where the respondent sees the basis for a potential obstruction, he or she can raise an objection in order to invite a response that overcomes that objection — as in Example 7:

> **Example 7   A:**   Let's eat at Denny's.
> **B:**   That's pretty far away.
> **A:**   We can drive.
> **B:**   All right. Let me get my coat.

So, embedded expansions, like presequences, owe whatever coherence they have to their contributions to the belief/want context defined by the superordinate illocutionary acts.

Preemptions, which create special difficulties for a sequencing rules approach, are also generated as coherent contributions by a rational model. A preempt occurs in response to a presequential move when (1) the utterance is recognizable as prefatory or incomplete; (2) the nature of the broader goal can be inferred from background knowledge; and (3) the preconditions for the target act are known to be satisfied. Because a presequential act is primarily an effort to establish the preconditions for pursuing some further goal, a reply aligning with that goal will satisfy the demands of the reason rule even if it does not literally answer the presequential act. So, for example, the offer in Example 8 is a coherent reply even though it does not directly supply the information requested. Likewise, the rejection in Example 9 is coherent because it shows the question to be pointless.

> **Example 8   A:**   Did you drive into school today?
> **B:**   Would you like a ride home?

> **Example 9   A:**   Do you own a copy of Cox and Willard?
> **B:**   I lent it out to Paul.

Regular forms of expansion — presequences and embedded expansions — can be partially explained in terms of sequencing rules. Specifically, it is possible to give a structural description of episode-level units of discourse in terms of more basic components such as adjacency pairs. But the *coherence* of such events is not derivable from sequential structure; it is derived, we maintain, from the functional relationships among the belief/want conditions for the various individual utterances. Irregular forms of expansion — such as preempts — are not explainable by sequencing rules. Nevertheless, they are coherent, and the way in which they are coherent is an argument for the necessity of a rational model. Like adjacency pairs, both orderly and disorderly forms of expansion can be explained as the output of practical reasoning principles operating on a system of rules for transforming belief/want contexts.

CONVERSATIONAL COHERENCE

It has been apparent for some time that a sequencing rules approach is not powerful enough to account for the facts of pragmatic coherence. Although adjacency pairs unquestionably represent a conventional solution to the problem of replying coherently to certain classes of illocutionary acts, they cannot account for the diversity of coherent sequences found in ordinary conversation. Understanding conversation as a goal-directed activity requiring alignment of participant's beliefs and wants suggests that any contribution to a conversation be seen as an effort to transform an initial belief/want state in a way that moves toward a goal. An utterance is coherent if it proceeds *rationally* toward the achievement of some goal or toward modification or obstruction of the goal. Thus, presequences probing a hearer's initial belief/want state can be seen to cohere with subsequent illocutionary acts by way of the operation of practical reasoning principles on the performative structure of illocutionary acts. Likewise, illocutionary acts can take all sorts of coherent replies, including direct action on their underlying goals, inspection of their preconditions, clarification of their propositional content or implicatures, challenges to their validity, and many other classes of response. Finally, incoherent utterances are those which have no apparent goal, or which ignore apparent goals behind other utterances, or which pursue goals in an irrational manner.

A rational model can account for all aspects of coherence explained by a sequencing rules approach. Additionally, however, a rational model can account for aspects of coherence standing as counterexamles to a sequencing rules approach. No fully adequate rational model yet exists. This chapter provides just a skeletal and provisional outline of what such a model should include. But even in skeletal and provisional form, the superiority of a rational model over a sequencing rules model is evident.

NOTES

1. For purposes of this discussion we will ignore the problem of how utterances are assigned to speech act categories, although we are aware of the intimate relation

between the way one approaches problems of sequencing and problems of interpretation (cf. Jacobs & Jackson, 1981). We suspect that a system of rational principles very similar to the ones we shall suggest for conversational sequencing operate for conversational expression and interpretation (cf. Grice, 1975).

2. By tracing the adjacency relation back to the illocutionary structure of each act, a rational model is also able to differentiate between normal forms like request/ grant and incidental variations like complaint/complaint-about-complaint (cf. Matoesian, 1981).

3

Tools for Cohering Discourse and
Their Strategic Utilization
Markers of Structural Connections and
Meaning Relations

< < ROBERT E. SANDERS > >

< < < It seems not just self-evident, but a truism, to > > >
say that communicators are obligated to make their discourse coherent. But coherence, especially in conversation, is a feature of discourse that gets more puzzling the more closely it is examined. If we
say that being coherent is obligatory, then the obvious research question is how communicators go about the job of fulfilling that obligation. A reasonable first answer is enveloped in the work on topic
management in conversations (e.g., Sacks, Schegloff, & Jefferson,
1974; Nofsinger & Boyd, 1979), which treats messages as combining
with each other coherently if there is a semantic overlap among them
— if, that is, they are about the same thing (are topically relevant to
each other). From there the problem boils down to operationalizing
the condition of two items of discourse being about the same thing,
with such an operationalization being adequate the extent to which it
identifies surface markers that communicators can use to establish
the meaning relations required for coherence.

But there are prior considerations. First, it appears that an item of
discourse does not have to be about the same thing as (topically
relevant to) every other item for the discourse to cohere. Jefferson

(1972) began to get at this when she pointed to the existence of "side sequences"; an item can provoke a digression (as when a question provokes a request for clarification), and items topically relevant to that first one will as a result be several steps removed (as when the question is answered once it is clarified). This sort of thing was treated in a more sweeping and richer way by Reichman (1978), who observed that conversations often consist of a jumble of separate topics (context spaces), with talk jumping back and forth among them even within a single turn. The job of being coherent thus demands that communicators mark their contributions in terms of whether they are continuing or shifting topics — and if so, to which other topic — and Reichman identifies a number of such devices. They range from fairly explicit transition markers (e.g., "well, anyway . . . ") to much subtler ones having to do with patterns of naming and pronominalization.

Second, Schank (1977) makes a strong, if ad hoc, case that being topically relevant is a necessary condition, *but not a sufficient one,* for being coherent. His central point is that items of discourse that are functionally superfluous, even though topically relevant, are anomalous (incoherent?). Thus, in precisely the same way that it would be anomalous to ask a question after its answer had already been stated, it would also be anomalous to overtly say something which had already been either semantically or pragmatically presupposed. The following pairs each involve such anomalies:

Example 1   A: I'm going home.
             *B: Where are you going?

Example 2   A: I've just traded in my old car for a 1983 model.
             *B: The new models have been designed and
                  manufactured.

Example 3   A: My plane left Chicago a half hour late this morning.
             *B: An airplane is a means of transportation.

Reichman's (1978) and Schank's (1977) analyses indicate that it is not easy to fulfill the obligation of being coherent. Reichman's analysis raises the question of how the number of topics, and the rapidity of switching back and forth among topics, is constrained. Such constraints would mean that topical relevance, with items marked according to which topic they are linked to, is not enough to ensure being coherent. (Of course, there might not be any such constraints, which would mean that a sequence of utterances, each topically unrelated to the others, would cohere as long as they were marked as being topically distinct from each other. This is an empirical question.) That topical relevance is not enough to establish coherence is precisely Schank's point, of course, but the constraints against functionally superfluous items of discourse are relative, if not altogether fluid. Whether an item actually is superfluous depends (at least with respect to pragmatic presuppositions) on what can safely be treated as a presupposition under the circumstances. In addition, Heritage and Watson (1979) exhibit numerous instances in which reiterating the substance of prior talk is clearly functional, for example, to check on the accuracy of one's understanding or to redirect subsequent talk toward an antecedently peripheral issue.

But the job of being coherent goes from complicated to confounded when Grice's (1967, 1975) analysis is factored in. Grice's treatment of conversational implicature rests on the idea that we always presume each other to be speaking relevantly (among other things), so that we always try to supply a basis for relevance when one is missing on the surface. If instances of failing to be topically relevant (coherent) are explained away so as to establish relevance in any case, on the presumption under the cooperative principle that all items in a discourse were included as they were deliberately and for good reason, then topical relevance is entirely in the eye of the beholder, and it is impossible to be incoherent (constraints as above to the side for the present). That is, whether an item is relevant depends entirely on the interpreter's ability (or willingness) to infer or invent a situationally plausible, topically relevant motive for the communicator's having included the item: no principled basis for saying categorically that an item is relevant or not seems to exist. This is the moral of the tale preached in the novel/movie *Being There* (Kosinski, 1970): significance, even profundity, and thus inclusion in the flow of talk, can be accorded the utterances of fools and children as long as they are presumed to be competent. From this perspective even Schank's (1977) idea that items can be functionally superfluous is dubious, considering that if such items are put forward, they would likely be presumed to be functional and interpreted to make them so.

On the basis of the foregoing, the question of what has to be done to achieve coherence (or what failings result in incoherence) is clearly muddled. It would thus seem that the analysis got off to the wrong start, and that the thing to do would be to garner samples of coherent and incoherent discourse, and compare them in hopes of better identifying their distinguishing features. But going that route would assume that incoherent discourse even exists, and that it can be reliably and validly identified, whereas that is precisely what is in doubt.

The only other way to proceed in the face of this muddle is to abandon the idea that coherence is a feature of discourse at all — and to abandon the postulate that coherence is something that communicators are obligated to work at producing. Grice's analysis, coupled with Reichman's, indicates that it is never problematic *whether* the items of discourse will cohere, at least in the eye of the beholder; it is only problematic *how* the items of discourse will cohere, how communicators and interpreters will end up integrating the parts into a whole (with the caveat that interpreters can choose not to work at establishing coherence if they believe the communicator is incompetent on the grounds of some physical or mental flaw, or if the cost of the effort involved seems to outweigh any benefits that success could bring). In confronting this problem communicators have the *option* of utilizing the arsenal of devices at their disposal for exercising some control over the way in which constituent items of discourse will be integrated. If such devices are not used for this purpose, or are utilized by habit or accident, the result will not be incoherence; it will be an integration of the parts into a whole by interpreters that may be surprising, and at times even detrimental, to the communicator.

COHERING ITEMS OF DISCOURSE INTO A WHOLE

Items of discourse, like the parts of a sentence, can be integrated into a whole in terms of their structural connections or the meaning relations among them. Accordingly, some of the devices that communicators can use to exercise some control over the way that their contributions are integrated into the whole mark structural boundaries and connections. Other such devices can be employed to indicate how specific items should be interpreted, and in that way these devices serve to influence the meaning relations among the items of a discourse. It is of course basic to cohering the items of a discourse that structural relations and boundaries can be identified, and on the presumption that they exist, interpreters will identify such relations and boundaries even if the communicator fails actively to guide them. But identifying structural relations and boundaries is not typically an end in itself: The goal is to identify meaning relations (among structurally distinct items) and to cohere the discourse in terms of them. A concern with meaning relations will thus be dominant below, which is to say, a concern with the means of exercising some control over the interpretation of specific items, or of deciding on their interpretation whether or not the communicator seeks to exert such influence.

Identifying Structural Relations and Boundaries

Although diverse ideas exist about how (or whether) discourse is structured (see, for example, Becker's, 1965, and Christensen's, 1967, pp. 52-81, efforts to identify the structural parts of a paragraph), there are few structural distinctions that are made and overtly marked. In writing, such markers comprise punctuation up to the structural level of the sentence, and the visual device of indentation beyond that. In ordinary communication, particularly in conversation, it appears that only (some functional approximation of) sentences, turns at talk, and topics are structurally distinguished. The primary markers of grammatical segments in speech up to the level of the sentence appear to be intonational, particularly vocal stress and tonal duration (Morton & Jassem, 1965; Lieberman, 1967). It should be noted that there is evidence that despite individual differences among communicators in the use of these devices, there is a high degree of consistency among interpreters in the way they grammatically segment utterances (Scholes, 1971). Thus, even at this level, despite what communicators do (or neglect to do) to establish coherence, interpreters independently go about the business of cohering discourse (as long as the communicator is presumed to be competent).

The markers of turns at talk are also predominantly nonverbal, again utilizing intonation (stress and tonal duration, plus loudness and pitch changes) as well as muscle relaxation (Duncan, Brunner, & Fiske, 1979). There has also been considerable attention to the role of gaze in marking turns at talk (e.g., Beattie, 1978; Rutter, Stephenson, Ayling, & White, 1978; Kendon, 1978), though Duncan and associates (1979) argue that it is likely a superfluous marker as well as one that does not differentiate smooth transitions between turns from confused ones.

In contrast, there are predominantly verbal devices for marking topic boundaries, and — if several topics have been introduced — marking utterances as to which topic they are about. Reichman (1978) provides an excellent treatment of these. Even so, there are intonational markers of topic changes as well (Brown, Currie, & Kenworthy, 1980, pp. 34-36).

Obviously, if the structural boundaries and connections within sentences could not be reliably identified, their interpretation according to the rules of language, constitutive rules of speech acts, or the like, would be impossible. Likewise, if paragraphs, turns at talk, and topic shifts could not be reliably identified, then the organization of items of discourse into, for instance, main and subsidiary points, issues and events, claim and supporting evidence, the parts of ritual exchanges, prologues and epilogues, and the like would be impossible. Thus discourse could not cohere unless such structural distinctions are made (or at least can be made by interpreters), but making them does not in and of itself cohere the discourse: it is meaning relations that link structural components to each other.

Identifying Meaning Relations

Given that the requisite structural boundaries and connections are marked, the items of discourse involved cohere according to the meaning relations among them. Because the meaning relations within a discourse are directly contingent on the way in which specific items are interpreted, the matter at hand boils down to a concern with the ways in which communicators can (purposely or accidentally) influence the interpretation of specific items.

Work on the interpretation of uttered expressions has tended to sidestep the key problem faced by interpreters. Much has been done on the principles for assigning one or another of the distinct types of interpretation utterances can have, but not for choosing among them. At minimum, a given utterance can be understood semantically, or in terms of its presuppositions or implicatures, or as an illocutionary act. For example, the sentence, "You have spinach between your teeth" can be said to mean (1) what it semantically claims, that the hearer has spinach on his or her teeth; (2) what it could in certain settings implicate, that the speaker finds the hearer unattractive because of the spinach; or (3) that the speaker has the intention of embarrassing the hearer, and thus performed the illocutionary act of insulting or ridiculing. The problem for interpreters, given the rules of language and conventions of use establishing what an uttered expression *could* mean, is to choose between alternative interpretations and decide what its *communicative value* under the circumstances is — what meaning among those alternatives the speaker intended to communicate. While deciding on the communicative value of an uttered expression may at times be a function of special knowledge (based on knowing the speaker's private codes, telepathy, or the like), I have proposed elsewhere that it is generally a function of the way in which the uttered expression is relevant to the antecedent sequence of messages, behaviors, and events (Sanders, 1980, 1981, 1982).

On the surface, there is a circularity here. The central concern is to establish how items of discourse cohere according to the meaning relations among them — but I have postulated elsewhere that what particular utterances mean, their communicative value, depends on the way they fit into the antecedent sequence. In other words, a discourse presumably coheres in terms of what its constituents mean; but the communicative value of its constituents depends on how they fit (cohere) in the antecedent sequence. This circularity is not accidental, or indicative of a flawed analysis. It presumes that as the discourse unfolds, decisions about how to cohere its constituent parts are checked and balanced against decisions about how to interpret specific utterances. Problems with interpreting an utterance so that it meshes with the antecedent sequence coherently may foster a reappraisal of how to cohere the parts of that sequence into a whole; and conversely, a problem cohering the parts of a sequence may foster reconsiderations of the communicative value (interpretation) of some of its constituent utterances.

The first of the specific ways in which an uttered expression can fit into the antecedent sequence involves overlaps in the features of the state of affairs specified by the uttered expression and features of the state of affairs specified in the interpreted antecedent sequence. This is commonly marked by shared lexical material (even if deleted on the surface), as illustrated by W's utterances in Examples 4 through 6:

Example 4 **A :** *Lasagna* is too fattening for me to eat very often.
  W: I make *it* with tofu — cuts the calories in half.

Example 5 **C :** The Bergers asked me to water their plants while *they're gone*.
  W: It's a little early to be *vacationing,* isn't it?

Example 6 **K :** I'll probably *get the gardening finished* this weekend.
  W: If it doesn't rain [you'll *get the gardening finished*].

Of course, it is not this simple. Such overlaps also occur in the anomalous cases cited by Schank (1977), in which the utterance is a gratuitous response. They also occur in cases that Tracy (1982) considers defective, when the utterance follows up on an antecedently mentioned event but not the covering issue. And there are overlaps in lexical material at the same time utterances are relevant to their antecedents in other ways as well and interpreted accordingly. However, these problems can be avoided if the warrant for deciding that the communicative value of an utterance is not only that features of the states of affairs it specifies overlap features of states of affairs specified antecedently, *but in addition the utterance has to add to the coherence of the whole sequence on that interpretation.*

An uttered expansion can also be relevant to its antecedent(s) in terms of the universe of discourse (i.e., scripts) attached to the state of affairs specified by the utterance and/or its antecedent(s). When it is relevant to the antecedent sequence on this basis, the utterance has the communicative value of an implicature. Consider for example W's responses in Examples 7 and 8:

Example 7   D: I'm amazed at how expensive books have gotten — this paperback is nearly $20.
W: That's a really useful reference to have on your shelves.

Example 8   T : I tried to call you last night.
W: That's funny — I was home all evening.

Although W's responses do have a minimal connection to their antecedents on semantic grounds (through a proform "that"), there is also a substantial overlap within the universe of discourse (script) attached to D's and T's utterances: in Example 7 D's utterance involves the universe of discourse of "investments and returns," and it is in those terms that W responds — the communicative value of the utterance is the implication of a belief that the cost of the book is justified. Similarly, T's utterance in Example 8 involves the universe of discourse (script) of using the telephone: assuming that T did not successfully telephone W the previous night, then W's response is relevant to the conditions in that script for failing to transact a phone call, and has the communicative value of an implicature that the failure was not due to the scripted condition of the call's recipient being absent. However, in addition to relevance in terms of associated universes of discourse, W's responses are, as noted, also (marginally) relevant on semantic grounds. Therefore, the fact that there is relevance in terms of associated universes of discourse does not in itself warrant a decision that the communicative values of W's responses are implicatures. In addition, the utterances have to add to the coherence of the whole on that interpretation (and of course, without more background information regarding Examples 7 and 8, it is unclear whether W's responses do that).

Third, an uttered expression can be relevant to specific antecedents in terms of the felicity conditions specified for the performance of illocutionary acts. An uttered expression can specify a state of affairs that includes features of the felicity conditions of an act which the antecedent could count as (e.g., when the response to a putative threat is to assert that the person who made the threat does not have the requisite power to follow through on it). Conversely, the utterance in question could potentially be an illocutionary act, the felicity conditions for which were antecedently specified (e.g., when someone expresses a desire for something, and the response is a stated intention to provide that thing, the response could potentially count as a promise, and the felicity conditions of a promise are relevant to the antecedently stated desire). In such cases the uttered expression has the communicative value of an illocutionary act (assuming, again, that in addition the utterance on that interpretation adds to the coherence of the whole). Hence, all else being equal, W's responses in Examples 9 and 10 are illocutionary acts (of a rebuff or repudiation, and a warning, respectively):

Example 9 **B :** How about taking out the garbage?
          W: I don't have to do things just because you say to.

Example 10 **K :** I've finally been invited to the Smiths; I'm going for afternoon tea.
           W: Their dog bit the mailman yesterday.

The general proposition here — that the interpretation of what people say and do is not a simple function of specific features of the utterance and the situation, but rather a somewhat fluid result of efforts to cohere the overall sequence as it unfolds — has consequences for an analysis of message strategy. First, consider that if there are specific ways in which utterances can be linked to their antecedents, and their interpretations depend on how they are made relevant, then there are constraints at any juncture in a sequence on what can meaningfully be said or done next. On this basis, communicators with the intention of having the sequence unfold in the direction of a particular goal (or away from an undesired one) must aim to manipulate the constraints of the sequence on what others can meaningfully say or do. In the same vein, an intention that one's own utterances be interpreted in a specific way requires that they be formulated so as to be relevant to the antecedent sequence on the appropriate basis. Obviously, if a communicator does not exercise control over the way in which his or her utterances mesh with the antecedent sequence, and the way in which the antecedent sequence has constrained what can meaningfully come next, that will not result in incoherence: it will result in interpretations, and perhaps outcomes, which the communicator may not have anticipated.

The Strategic Use of Cohering Devices:
A Case Study

Given that it is optional rather than obligatory to actively utilize cohering devices, the point of actively using them is to exercise some control over the interpretation of specific items, and thus the meaning relations among them. Communicators are most likely to actively utilize cohering devices, of course, when different ways of cohering the items of a discourse could lead to different outcomes, and the communicator has a stake in facilitating or averting one of them. *When cohering devices are utilized to advance the communicator's interests, then they have the status of strategic rather than enabling tools of communication.* A case in point is the elicited conversation (see the Appendix) between B and K.

On the surface, and perhaps in actuality, the conversation between B and K is superficial, mundane, even boring. It seems as inconsequential as one would expect a conversation to be if carried on by two casual acquaintances going through the motions for the sake of helping out in a research project. From the analysis of the way in which communicative values are decided, the impression of dull and mundane talk results from having to take what each woman says at face value (in terms of the semantics of the uttered expressions) because of the basis of relevance each utterance has to its antecedents. The conversation is extremely orderly, talk about most of the topics covered is remarkably prolonged, and most important, the constituent utterances are semantically chained within and across topics.

However, there are certain patterns in the way that the conversation unfolds that do not square with this surface appearance of mundane talk and routine conversation. There is an argument for cohering the overall sequence around a contest waged by B against K to assert her (B's) superiority, and on that basis for saying that it would be a mistake to take many of their constituent utterances at face value — even though the basis of relevance in every case warrants doing just that. In that case, *there is reason to speculate that the semantic chaining that so dominates the conversation is a strategem* – not something that is obligatory for the sake of being coherent. The semantic chaining provides warrants for treating the conversation as routine and mundane, and keeps the underlying contest sufficiently below the surface to prevent an overt confrontation. All the observer (and perhaps one or both participants) can do is speculate that some of the utterances were meant as putdowns and ridicule, self-aggrandizement or self-defense, that they have the communicative value of implicatures and illocutionary acts rather than references and assertions.

There is some basis in biographical facts about B and K that are provided in the covering paragraph in the Appendix, and in the conversation itself, for saying that a contest of sorts was being waged between them. B is several years older than K (27 years compared with K's 21), the child of professional parents, a broken home, brought up in an environment of Eastern old money (Philadelphia), and in general worldly-wise; K is the ordinary child of ordinary parents, brought up in smaller cities of the Midwest, limited in experience or interests to what would have come her way while at home in high school, on visits home while in college, and in Madison during her four years there. These differences are striking enough that it would not have been surprising for there to have been a less tranquil exchange between the two. The differences could easily have provoked displays of contempt or patronizing curiosity, and thereafter conflict from whichever of the two felt more secure about herself and her background. B, of course, could easily have been contemptuous of K's provincialism, but just as easily envious of her stable and ordinary family and personal life; and K could easily have been envious of B's experience and worldliness, or contemptuous of her broken family and the elitist East Coast tradition she is allied with.

The contest between them that is suggested by patterns of topic development and response was initiated by B. K was on the defensive, and the objective that B apparently had was to establish herself as a superior rather than a peer (as opposed to being vindictive in some way). The criterion for superiority in this case involves the notion of "original and exotic" contrasted with qualities of "conventional and mundane." In reading the conversation as a contest along these dimensions, I have punctuated it around seven major topics as follows:

	Initial *Utterance*	*Topic*	*Duration* *(min:sec)*
(1)	017	Xmas Gifts for Family	1:20
(2)	034	Home at Xmas/Family	4:45
(3)	105	Self on Skis	4:15
(4)	166	K's Internship/Home	5:30
(5)	228	B in Philadelphia	6:50
(6)	301	Winter Recreation	4:15
(7)	342	California Weather	tape ends

(1) *Xmas Gifts for Family* develops talk that indicates common attitudes and experiences between the two women. Talk on this topic is shorter than on any other following by a considerable margin, and it is B who initiates the change.

(2) *Home at Xmas/Family* opens with an initial exchange of travel plans, and descriptions of family, that reveals sharp differences along the "exotic-ordinary" dimension. B follows with talk about step-siblings and their schooling in Switzerland, accentuating the differences between them. K tries to compete by referring to a friend who will be flying to Switzerland over the Christmas break to go skiing. B trumps that move by citing her step-brother's world-class prowess on the slopes. At that point, the topic is changed — by K (in defeat?).

(3) *Self on Skis* opens with B being self-deprecating (confident in victory?), K reciprocates, and B carries it forward with talk about fear of heights. At that point K successfully reverses field on B, claiming no fear of heights, and instead an active interest in the exotic and original activity of ballooning. B responds by establishing that she has also been interested in the activity, and shows that she is better informed about it. K is then forced to admit that some of her fantasies about the subject came from *McCalls,* and finally concedes that she would not try it even if she had the chance ("too impractical"). B changes the topic to one that permits K to talk in positive ways about herself (magnanimous in victory?).

(4) *K's Internship/Home* begins with K talking diffidently and vaguely about her upcoming internship, and then proceeds to talk about her hometown and her life there. As K shifts to talk about home, B returns to the offensive (utterances 202, 204, and 206, and more subtly, 223 and 225. Perhaps in defense against slurs on her hometown, and where those could lead, K changes topic (utterance 228).

(5) *B in Philadelphia* is an extended self-aggrandizing review of B's background that stands in sharp contrast to the feeble treatment of home that K had been able to present. The quibble about the meaning of "ferrier" (utterances 267-284) is a last gasp by K to stay even, and it is rapidly disposed of. B finally changes the topic, from here to the end in control and apparently determined to finish the job properly.

(6) *Winter Recreation* opens with B maximally distancing herself by asking " Do you do anything besides ski? . . . What do people in Wisconsin do for exercise in the winter?" The distance that has been created is confirmed by K's subsequent evasion of B's offer to let K ski on B's land, and B's evasion of K's effort to elicit B's interest in trying K's sport. The topic is again changed by B.

(7) *California Weather* begins with a transition from the preceding topic based on K's reference to weather patterns. B says, "I had forgotten that you knew all about that weather stuff," the tone and

language of an aristocrat condescending to a technician, and then asks K for information about weather that might help her decide about where to go on to graduate school. This is the greatest distancing and depersonalization evident in the conversation, and at that point, the tape ends.

ACHIEVING AN ADEQUATE THEORY OF ORDINARY COMMUNICATION

There is a clear difference in the consequences of viewing coherence as something that communicators are obligated to ensure, compared with the view that there are tools for cohering discourse which communicators have the option of actively using and which can be used strategically. That difference is indicated by the foregoing analysis of B's and K's conversation. If coherence is treated as obligatory, and topical relevance the principal means of securing it, then the chains of semantically overlapping utterances created by the two women represent the competent fulfillment of their obligations as communicators. But that view prevents one from seeing what took place as a tacit battle for status, coated over with the trappings of casual small talk, or to account for any suspicions along those lines formed by observers or by the women themselves.

If all this boiled down to the question of whether a framework that makes possible the voicing of unprovable suspicions about communicators' intentions and actions is preferable to one that does not, then admittedly I have concocted a tempest in a teapot. But a more general and more important issue is involved. The difference between the view that coherence is something communicators are obligated to bring about, and the view that there are cohering devices communicators have the option of actively using, is this: the latter distinguishes the properties of the tools of ordinary communication from the conventional, normative, and strategic uses those tools are given; the former does not. Failing to distinguish characteristics of the tools from their typical, and not so typical uses, guarantees inadequate descriptions and overly weak predictions. The analogy would be an anthropologist witnessing the use of a primitive tool for cultivating soil, and explaining its design in terms of the uses he or she had witnessed (agricultural). Suppose, however, that that same tool anomalously showed up in ritual dances celebrating past battles and the prowess of the group's warriors. It could have been the case that this predominantly agricultural group had historically been preyed upon by neighboring warlike peoples, and that it had fashioned agricultural tools that could double as weapons in the event of surprise attacks on workers in the fields. Descriptions and generalizations of the tool on the basis of its observed uses thus turned out to be deficient. The analysis would have been more likely correct had the design of the tool itself been examined, independent of its observed uses, and served as the basis for projecting the uses it *might* have gotten.

It could, of course, turn out in many instances that distinguishing the characteristics of tools from their uses fosters precisely the same conclusions that were arrived at by observers who failed to do so. However, there will almost certainly be instances in which the distinction fosters better descriptions and predictions, and never an instance in which failing to make the distinction provides better results. Just on the grounds of observational caution, if not going with the better odds of success, making a distinction between tools and their uses wherever possible is an important research concern.

This is particularly so in studies of ordinary communication. The most noteworthy feature of ordinary communication is the opportunities it affords for creativity about what goals to pursue and how to pursue them. People are constantly innovating things that can be achieved through ordinary communication (from self-realization to earning a college degree to having friends to obtaining food and shelter in the wasteland of modern cities) and even more rapidly innovating ways in which they can communicate to bring about desired results. An adequate theory of ordinary communication must therefore have built into it the basis for explaining such creativity. Failing to distinguish properties of the tools of communication from their typical uses means shutting the theoretical door to positing sources of atypicality (creativity), and that is precisely the wrong direction to take. Treating coherence as something that communicators are obligated to bring about is a prototypical case: it treats the tools for cohering discourse as markers that communicators are obligated to actively use, and to use solely for the purpose of ensuring coherence. Their strategic utility is thus lost to observers and unexplained in theory.

4

Interpretation as Coherence Production

<< ROBERT HOPPER >>

< < < Most writing about conversational coherence > > > seems to suggest that speakers achieve coherence primarily by making orderly noises. This view overlooks the production of coherence through interpretation. The present essay displays conversational coherence as interpretively produced and offers speculations describing this process.

Production of conversational coherence through interpersonal communication involves ancient, yet poorly understood, human technology. Coherence is produced through cooperative action, just as are art works, automobiles, and hybrid corn. Interpretation seems the most basic and necessary aspect of coherence production. Yet interpretation is difficult to describe since none of the five senses can measure it precisely. Interpretation works through common sense more than through material senses of sight, hearing, touch, and the like.

Interpretation is sense making, or coherence building. Speech is the manufacture of noises; interpretation is the manufacture of coherence. Interpreters rarely question whether coherence exists. Rather, interpreters appear to operate under a *will to cohere,* an assumption

Author's Note: The assistance of Christopher Zahn, Janet Alberts, Anntarie L. Sims, and Susan Koch is gratefully acknowledged.

that coherence inheres in discourse and emerges as a matter of interactive course.

The present essay describes some episodes in coherence manufacture, discusses some problems that recur as interpreters try to build coherence, and meanders on a pilgrimage toward explication of this riddle: How do interactors preserve facades of coherence in the face of what (to this analyst) appear as a continuous coherence breaches in everyday communicative performance?

Example 1	161	K:	NO:,
	162	B:	One balloon lesson?
			[ ]
	163	K:	that's not - too practical
	164	B:	No::/
			((pause))
	165	K:	Nah, it's not worth it. I'm in to ((laughing)) practical - a lot of times/
	166	B:	Umm. (pause) Have you heard anything about your internship, speaking of practical?=
	167	K:	=Um::: No I forgot to call about that. [B-K Conversation].

Analysis of Example 1

The editors of this volume asked chapter authors to comment on coherence in the B-K Conversation. Mostly I found myself noticing segments such as in Example 1, in which coherence appears limited to question-answer pairing and repetition of a few words. Five of seven utterances in Example 1 use negation in the first few words, three utterances make prominent use of the word "practical," there are symmetrical vocalized pauses beginning the last two utterances, and there are question-answer pairings. Does the occurrence of such features classify this talk as coherent? Are we then willing to certify any talk as incoherent? Do the above-noted features provide much clue about what the actors are *doing* in the segment? In order to satisfy such inquiries and present an interpretation-based approach to coherence, it seems necessary to begin by discussing the importance of two concepts: technology and interpretation.

INTERPERSONAL COMMUNICATION AS TECHNOLOGY

If we speculate about the evolution of communication, it is evident that a very important stage in this evolution occurs when the organism gradually ceases to respond quite "automatically" to the mood-signs of another and becomes able to recognize the sign as a signal . . . which can be trusted, distrusted, falsified, denied, amplified, corrected and so forth. Clearly, this realization that signals are signals is by no means complete even among the human species [Bateson, 1972, p. 178].

Why is speech communication so important to establishment of coherence and cooperation? Why do our attempts to use speech communication frequently leave us frustrated? Some answers to these questions emerge if one considers talk as technology — humanmade instrumentality that partially restructures the world. Speech communication transforms life worlds just as do innovations that are more commonly regarded as technologies, such as industrialization, agriculture, and mass communication.

Technology emerges when a series of purposeful actions becomes associated with obtaining certain goals. Plant a seed to grow wheat; divide tasks in a factory to cut costs; follow instructions in order to coordinate activity. Technologies seem simple at first — do X and achieve Y. However, technologies also have damage records. Technology frequently does ecological violence. If you build factories, you may achieve environmental pollution and exploitation of wage earners as well as economic efficiency. Plant a seed and as you care for the growing plant, you invent categories such as "weed" or "pest-insect." Become aware of interpretation, and you open Pandora boxes such as deception, propaganda, self-disclosure, and reticence.

We have been speaking and interpreting for millennia, but we still have very little ecological understanding of talk technologies. To say that utterances consist of "speech acts" (Searle, 1969, 1980), or that language exists only for communication (Clark & Clark, 1977, p. 3) is to obscure technological multifacetedness, and to lead us to believe that we control messages more completely than we actually do. When we listen and speak, we have a tiger by the tail, whirlwinds to reap, a mad scientist on the loose. With speech technology as with all technology, undesired impact is subtly systemic. We cannot expect to do only one thing when we interpret a text any more than when we erect a factory or plant corn. When we listen to each other, we invoke deep magic. We know how to do it, but we control it only incompletely.

An example: It is sometimes claimed that men and women speak different dialects of English (Lakoff, 1975; Kramerae, 1981). Men speak "powerfully," in assertions, strong expletives, interruptions, and directives. Women are described as asking questions, using qualifiers, and showing high degrees of adherence to grammatical correctness. Closer examination shows, however, that actual male-female speech differences are ephemeral to nonexistent; rather, *listeners interpretively create male and female dialects* by responding to their stereotypes, rather than actual male/female speech differences. Men and women are not different classes of speakers, rather their speech is interpreted as different (Haas, 1979; Kramerae, 1981).

Street and Hopper (1982) pose a similar argument in their review of research in language attitudes and accommodation: Numerous studies indicate that speaker-listeners respond to the dialect features they *perceive* the other is speaking more than to the others' actual speech features. Thus, if a caucasian person believes that black persons speak a unique ethnic dialect of English, he or she may hear such speech features with selective emphasis when they occur. Such differences may even be perceived or recalled in their absence. Interpretive strategies, in sum, may rely upon difficult-to-change, counterproductive stereotypes and habits. Such habits, much as industrial pollutants, may persist even after one begins to notice some of their ecological side effects. Suppose, for example, that a listener who understands that men and women, blacks, and caucasians actually speak similarly. Even such a listener may continue to emphasize speech differences between social groups.

Coherence production is a complex matter, and probably more coherence is produced interpretively than we have noted in either our theories or our instructional practices. We can no longer rely upon a model of communication that emphasizes the role of the speaker over that of the listener, or one that emphasizes message transportation over message interpretation. This essay's purpose is to redress such imbalance by describing the sense in which interpretation produces coherence, and by offering some speculation about the nature and workings of coherence-producing interpretive processes.

Example 2	509	5:	Put me down (whispered)
	510	F:	I'm gonna okay I'll pack my clothes and le:ave
	511	5:	Put me down
	512	F:	You old mama's girl
	513	5:	BA:M BA:M BA:M ((with sounds and gestures))
	514	F:	Gimme some sugar
	515	5:	BAM BAM
	516	F:	After I get some sugar you can get down

517 **5:** B A::M B A::M B A::M B A::M B A::M B A::M
B A::M
518 **F:** After I get some sugar you can get down I said
after I get some sugar (0.5) (ugh ugh) see you
gonna knock the hem out your dress 5!! 3 3 5 told
me I could pack my clothes and leave
519 **5:** N:o I did:n't N:O I

[Source: Collected and transcribed by Anntarie L. Sims, Detroit,
Michigan, January 1, 1982 Scene: Holiday family gathering. Daughter,
age 5, is on Father's (F's) lap.]

Analysis of Example 2

There is coherence here at the word, phrase, and pair-part levels
as in Example 1. But in addition there is a story: The child is trying to
escape, and the father (who continues to hold her) peppers her with a
variety of quasi-courtship hazings. Here are a pair of intimates,
people who know one another and are used to coordinating their
interpersonal communication. The dance has few missed steps, the
coherence production lines roll at breakneck speeds. Consider the
following things the father suggests about courtship: physical restraint by the male, withdrawal of affection if sexual favors are not
forthcoming, an offer to trade freedom from restraint for physical
affection (some sugar), a mock accusation that the child is a "mama's
girl" because she resists, a warning not to knock the hem out of her
dress (unladylike), and a taunt bringing the five-year-old's sister (3)
into the fray. The whole thing is a tease sequence besides. More on
that later. . . .

INTERPRETATION:
THE SILENT PARTNER

What is interpretation, this key process in coherence production?
A primitive but useful hint is to note that interpretation seems more
closely related to listening than to talking. Given a distinction between speech and listening, one must admit that most of theory and
teaching in communication have aimed to improve the making of
speech noises. Perhaps we have focused upon talking at the expense
of deeper understandings of listening and interpretation. To note
these facts is neither to defend the speaker/listener distinction nor to
argue that speech is irrelevant to interpretation. Rather it is asserted

that, given a common-sense speaker/listener dichotomy, listening is the closer of these terms to interpretation.

As one way of illustrating the affinity between the terms "listening" and "interpretation," consider Schramm's (1954) information-theory model of communication. Schramm pictures communication as the travel of a message in an oval orbit between two parties. Each party is pictured as a circle with three parts: decoder, interpreter, encoder. A message is decoded, then interpreted. Encoding occurs only after interpretation is complete, which illustrates an affinity between listening and interpretation. Listening might be roughly defined as hearing plus interpretation (Hopper, 1976, ch. 1).

To illustrate the importance of interpretation to any understanding of interpersonal communication, let us consider briefly whether one might better define communication as encoding-speech or as listening-interpretation. The latter works much better. No amount of speaking, or even message planning/invention, assures that communication will occur. There must be interpretation, the making sense of messages, for the description "communication" to apply. Even if there is no (intended) message, one cannot not be communicating because interpretation by itself seems sufficient to constitute action as communicative.

It may be sloppy to offer "listening" too strongly as a synonym for "interpretation," but interpretation is surely more identified with the listener role than with the speaker role. Interpretation is the silent partner in communication, the essential component that makes no noise. It is not nonverbal either, but rather distinguishable from encoding. The bringing-togetherness of interpretive coherence is invisible and silent, like the invisible grace celebrated by sacramental signs. Interpretation is nonmaterial "light industry."

Interpretation, then, is the manufacture of coherence. Its workings are silent and invisible: non-sense at the sources of sense making. We observe only the results of coherence manufacture. Talk seems coherent largely due to the activities of the silent partner. Interpretation performs the dance of coherence; speech hums the tune.

Additionally, consider the role of interpretation in the probable origins of human speech communication. It seems implausible to suppose that humans first gained control of speak-able intentions that they somehow displayed so that others could understand (interpret) them. Rather, communicators probably came first to realize that others' actions could be taken interpretively. Later, the rhetorical realization presumably dawned: Since others could be expected to interpret one's actions, one could self-control those actions to steer others' interpretations in desired directions. Speech has been a much exploited resource in this regard, though we may presently be developing nonverbal intentionality in similar ways.

To summarize: Interpretation, the silent partner, seems the foundation and beginning for interpersonal communication — both conceptually and chronologically. Therefore, it appears justifiable to approach conversational coherence based upon the premise that coherence is produced interpretively. What is the nature of such interpretive processing? This question may be informed by studies in hermeneutics that involve textual interpretation. Hermeneutical studies have been based upon literary and historical texts, but the following points may be applied to interpersonal communication.

First, interpretation crucially involves selective binary pairings. Interpretation involves selection by the interpreter of details to be paired. This view not only increases the influence attributed to interpretation, it also emphasizes the essential incompleteness and ambiguity involved in interpretation. No interpretation is ever final.

Second, and closely related, interpretation is emergent in time. Interpretation of any utterance draws upon past interpretation as well as plausible future expectation. Present interpretations may alter past ones or transform one sort of textual coherence into another that is quite different.

Each of these characteristics of interpretive coherence-production will be discussed subsequently.

Example 3	**Interviewer:**	Uhu-um—huhum. What kinds of things did you have in college — at the university that particularly equipped you to — uh — to take on this kind of an assignment — uh courses you had, experiences you had:
	Applicant:	Well, I had no management; I had very little business — but a lot of government and I really feel strongly that it's important to understand how policy is made and how — how it works right now, because we are facing a — a time right now in health care where we just don't know how much of a role government's going to continue to play. And I think I've had just kinda — kind of a natural knack for organization and so those are really — I couldn't tell you that I've had twelve hours of management and because I really don't think those things necessarily prepare you to do something like this

[Source: Collected and transcribed by Sandra L. Ragan. Situation: A simulated employment interview, in which the part of interviewer is played by a teacher and that of interviewee is played by a student].

Analysis of Example 3

The interviewer in this segment asks a question about educational experience. It appears to be a straightforward, even innocently general request. The applicant's answer, however, offers only brief description of educational experience. Most of the response is devoted to justifying the failure to have chosen a different major altogether. One must explain this response in terms of the applicant's interpretive choices in regard to the interviewer's question. Actually, such unasked-for accountings are relatively commonplace in job interviews examined by Ragan (see Chapter 8, this volume), and they appear to emerge out of the applicant's definition of the interview situation. Example 3 is presented as an illustration of interpretively produced coherence.

2ness

One characteristic of interpretation seems to be the crucial importance of *2ness,* the bringing together and pairing of selected elements of text/context. 2ness is aural double vision, a stereo fusion at the heart of coherence production. The Oxford Dictionary of English Etymology traces the word "coherence" to roots meaning the joining together of binary pairs. To *co-here* is to fasten together two disparate items.

Perhaps this concept of interpretation relates to speculations by many scholars that there is an inherent "double structure" to speech action (Habermas, 1979, pp. 41-44). Habermas labels the two components of double structure "illocution" and "proposition," and notes that this double structuring is closely connected with the "inherent reflexivity" of talk (p. 42). The task of the silent-partner interpretation is to cohere swirls of 2ness.

In interpretive processes there seems some special significance to the number 2. Consider this sampling of double-lamination metaphors descriptive of language: Langue and parole, expression and content, competence and performance, deep and surface structure, diachronic and synchronic, task and relationship. Additionally, many concepts are descriptive of double-structuring phenomena: ambiguity, teasing, play, deception, dialectic, distinctive features, role distance, bit, and double bind. Though it operates differently in different concepts, the theme of 2ness or double structuring runs throughout, suggesting that interpretation crucially involves selection of two elements at a time and bringing them to foreground to be paired/compared.

The term "2ness" is an invention of Russell Hoban's (1980) fictional hero, Riddley Walker. Walker lives 2000 years after the Big Nuke. He is trying to revive civilization through some innovative uses of listening and storytelling. The following passage describes Walker's view of interpretive process. This passage is also kind of a metalog, an example of itself, due to Hoban's invention of a new dialect of English, in which the entire book is written:

> Lykin for the 1 you wil aul ways fyn thay 2. . . . I cud feal it in the guts and barrils of me. You try to make your self 1 with some thing or some body but try as you wil the 2ness of every thing is working agaenst you all the way. You try to take hold of the 1ness and it comes in 2 in your hans [p. 140].

Speech appears to achieve partial systemic ordering into a number of layers or language games that are only loosely connected with one another (Pearce & Cronen, 1980; Frentz & Farrell, 1976; Wittgenstein, 1953; Hofstadter, 1979). This multitextured nature of discourse is fertile ground for textual interpretation. Every listener, to a degree, must construct an interpretation, perhaps by centering mainly upon one level of analysis (taking for granted, perhaps, certain others). Interpretation may draw on connections between levels of analysis, or, as Bateson (1979) suggests, take connections between levels as a level of analysis. To some degree each paired connection produces coherence. And each bit of coherence is open to testing, refinement, or discarding. How bits of coherence may be combined is a matter beyond the scope of this chapter. Perhaps there exists some connection here with constructivist approaches that view intelligence as ability to make large numbers of distinctions and to integrate them.

In constructing interpretive pairings the interpreter may use well-known, even trite interpretive templates, reach for novel ones, or stumble across serendipitous connections. Interpretive pairings may provide a surprise at any moment: a pun, a sudden revelation of a long-standing deception, a spoonerism, an apt metaphor, a Freudian slip, or a turn to self-reference. There are moments in talk that bubble over with serendipity and creative play; perhaps these moments are best captured by Bales's term "dramatizes" (1970, p. 477). These moments have been considered fertile ground for analysis, at least since Freud's work.

The controversial assertion here is that, in some sense, the fundamental unit of interpretation is the pair. Pairs of items are selectively brought to foreground and compared, fused, or juxtaposed. Probably the process often recurs several times in an instant, and the results of certain pairings become grist for others. Perhaps the bases for the process are in perception of contrast; probably the concept of negation is crucially involved as well.

The preceding paragraphs have assembled evidence that a theme of 2ness seems important in the interpretive process. Another way to discuss 2ness is by inductive example. The notion first came to my attention in analyses of teasing in intimate relationships.

In a study of couples' "personal idioms" (Hopper, Knapp, & Scott, 1981) one of the most important and commonly used kinds of idioms used by lovers with only each other was called the *teasing* ✓ *insult*. The double term seems necessary to describe the combination of hostility with playfulness. Here are just a few of the teasing insults supplied by our informants: futtbutt, fluffybutt, bigbutt, fatboy, jerk, wimp, asshole, bouncy-bouncy, animal, turkey-face, chops, scarface, tarpot, honsky, mopsy, and spaghetti-head. Most of the utterers of these terms felt that they were expressing good-natured endearments, though many of the targets of the endearments felt belittled or denigrated. These teasing insults are examples of playing rough in intimacy. The words are hostile, though at least much of the illocution is playful. Notably, informants in the personal idiom study reported an association between use of such idioms and satisfied/happy feelings about their relationship. The couple that plays/teases together seems to be the well-adjusted, satisfied couple (Betcher, 1981). How do teases simultaneously maim and build? What does such 2ness tell about interpretive coherence?

We conducted a conversational analysis of 15 teasing episodes (Alberts & Hopper, 1983). The conversations in which the teasing episodes occurred were heavily laden with 2ness: combinations of verbal hostility with playful intent, use of ambiguity, display of indirection, simultaneous use of truth and falsity, dramatic episodic shifts, and use of metacommunicative signals. Examples 2, 4, and 5 are taken from this teasing research, and display play braided with seeming-hostility.

Example 4 607 **3:** Daddy where's 5; Daddy where's 5; Daddy where's 5

608 **F:** Gone

609 **3:** Gone where?

610 **F:** Home over to Dawn and Ivy's

611 **3:** Where she is?

612 **F:** She gone. Call her and see if she's gone

613 **3:** 5! 5! Where's 5; Daddy where's 5

614 **F:** Gone. She said she don't want to be your sister no more

615 **3:** (ugh)

616 **F:** ain't but the two of us now

617 **3:** Mama

618 **F:** You can have all 5's toys her new baby doll its yours

619 **3:** (unintelligible) I can have em

620 **F:** Yea you take 5's skates and send them to Stacey

621 **3:** Yea cause she she too big

622 **F:** Yea now what else you want to give away of 5's and what you want to keep of 5's

623 **3:** I take 5's

624 **F:** You take 5's doll

625 **3:** Yea

626 **F:** You can have 5's watch

627 **3:** Yea

628 **F:** What else can you have of 5's

[Source: Collected and transcribed by Anntarie L. Sims. Situation: Family holiday gathering, about a minute after the conversation that appears in Example 2].

Analysis of Example 4

This is the same father as in Example 2, and the same teasing style. This time the target is a three-year-old daughter, and the tease concerns the location of the older sister. The game is a variant of peek-a-boo, or hide-and-seek, since the missing sister is under F's chair. The game appears to have a teaching function. Bruner (1975) describes the operation of these kinds of teaching routines in parent-child interaction. Once F's deportment is put into an instructional frame, many aspects of his role march to different coherences. The lessons concern concrete operations (612), possession (618-628), family separation (614-617), and English as a first language (622ff). Of course, there is also instruction in the 2ness of talk; the sequence is a laboratory tutorial on teasing techniques. The family-instruction aspect of this transcript emerges as a dominant factor when this conversation is reexamined in terms of the courtship-family themes in Example 2 (and a lesson on names of uncles and cousins that occurred in the minute between Examples 2 and 4). Perhaps teasing is daddy's classroom, a cooperative game that fathers play with children as part of interpretation instruction.

TEMPORAL EMERGENCE

In considering Examples 2 and 4, with material in-between concerning kinship, the theme "instruction about family" comes up so frequently that it becomes, in some sense, the topic of the conversation. There is no single moment at which this is, in particular, evident. Rather, the theme appears in fragments across time. It is best observed by noting its recurrence throughout the sequence. The nature of the sequence is emergent in time. As Jack Burden remarks in *All the King's Men:*

> reality is not a function of the event as event, but of the relationship of that event to past and future events. We seem to have here a paradox: that the reality of an event, which is not real in itself, arises from other events which, likewise, in themselves are not real. But this only affirms what we must affirm: that direction is all [Warren, 1949, p. 407].

The ordering of events in sequential time frequently seems an important tie to the interpretive process. Interpretation is always operative in the present, but interpreters arrive at formulations by achieving some sense of the past and future (Cicourel, 1972). In some sense, interpretation "travels in time" (Beach & Japp, 1983). These are figurative metaphors for a set of interpretive abilities we use to compare various uses of a term at various times, or to recognize familiar phrases and story-patterns.

Situation definitions frequently emerge in time (McHugh, 1968). Communicators seem able to draw on wide varieties of cues about situation construction, use these cues to define the situation, then reflexively pretend that the situation definitions had been in place all along. In normal speaking and listening, such interpretive processes leave few obvious traces. Deeper analyses from drama and life, however, show many effects of situation definition and its reflexive emergence (Habermas, 1979; Garfinkel, 1967). In drama, rapid plot shifts frequently occur as new information is revealed or new acts change the meanings of former ones (Goffman, 1974). Conversational analysis displays similar rapid shifts of situation direction in everyday talk. (See essays by Goodwin and Jefferson in Psathas, 1979). Example 5 presents an example of a teasing episode that is transformed and retransformed within a few seconds, while an observer scores the changes in the game from the safe distance of laughter.

Example 5	90	**L:**	. . . don't? — do I have a good j-voice? J____? (.6) Do I have a, re:ally good voice? Do you really
	91	**K:**	((undistinguishable sounds))
	92	**J:**	Dad you you *have* a good voice but you don't sing good.
	93	**K:**	(nnha ha H A HA HA HA .hhh Ha Ha un .hhh) Fi:::ne distinction there (he he he)=
	94	**L:**	((snort)) (heh HEH HEH)
	95	**L:**	=That's pretty funny there J____=
	96	**K:**	=I don't think he was intendin to be funny=
	97	**L:**	=You having dinner tonight?=
	98	**K:**	=((softly)) (ha ha)=
	99	**J:**	=Ye::ah=
	100	**L:**	=(uhha), no:::you're not (ha ha)=
	101	**J:**	=(ha ha) go::od I ( )
	102	**K:**	GOOD! (HA HA HA) He got you on that one (.hhh ha ha)

[Source: Collected and transcribed by Janet K. Alberts; transcript appears in Alberts and Hopper, 1983. Situation: L is cooking dinner for his seven-year-old son, J. K is L's fiancee].

Analysis of Example 5

This is another father-child tease, actually a temporally emergent series of teases. The son casts the first tease (92), which is certified as amusing by the observer (93), and finally accepted by the butt of the tease (94 and 95). The father retaliates with a set-up (97) and counter-tease (100), but the son retransforms the episode immediately by making the threatened punishment (losing supper) into a reward (101), adding teasing's implicit criticism of the father's cooking to the earlier critique of his singing voice.

Note the rapid transformations of the episode's nature at each tease (92, 100, 101). These utterances are interpreted by the observer as events deserving of verbal applause (93, 102). Any useful theory of conversational coherence must account for such rapid emergence flip-flops. Erving Goffman provides some terms toward this task in *Frame Analysis* (1974). It is in Goffman's sense that the term "transformation" is used (see Hopper, 1981).

ALIGNMENT AND ALIGNMENT TALK

Alignment is a metaphor for a set of coherence-building, sense-making ethnomethods. This term has been suggested by symbolic interactionists as descriptive of numerous verbal devices used in impression management; for example, disclaimers, accounts, motive talk, and remedial rituals are labeled "aligning actions" (Stokes & Hewitt, 1976). Alignment is at least double layered, constituting some coherence building at the level of interpersonal relationship (alignment between communicators) and some alignment of interactants with social norms (prescriptions).

Morris and Hopper (1982) extend the alignment metaphor by suggesting it as a term to subsume a decade of research on communication and rules. Alignment is viewed as a continuous process, reflected in many aspects of talk. They use the term "alignment talk" to refer to speech features that do relatively explicitly comment on action. *Accounts* (see Example 3) are one kind of alignment talk. B uses an account in turn 263 of the Appendix. ("It saved you a lot of money in vet bills.") K uses an account in turn 276 ("I was wondering what they were, so I finally checked it out.") Another alignment talk feature is the *formulation*. Formulations include utterances in which a communicator states the gist of a situation definition or summarizes a longer strip of dialogue. Sandra Ragan (this volume) describes how accounts and formulations function in one kind of communication situation, the job interview.

The alignment process is holistic, ongoing, and multifaceted. Alignment talk is one part of alignment. Alignment talk appears when problems emerge that need to be set right. Otherwise, one assumes alignment is taking place just out of focus yet still in the conversation. It occurs reflexively, emergently, through interpretation of little-noticed peripheral features, the parapraxes that fascinated Freud, the 2nesses, the quirks of emergence, the odd points of simultaneity, the puns, the teases.

Alignment is offered as one metaphor for applied coherence building. Interpreters seem able to use many acts as alignment signals. For instance, we utilize many rhythmic variables for alignment purposes — stress patterns, speech rate, pause length, smoothness of turn-taking, and synchrony of eye contact (Street, 1982). Also, word choices, language choices, choice of dialect, and many other variables can be taken as coherence builders. Speakers unleash fantastic numbers of stimuli upon the world. Interpreters sample these stimuli; the selecting and pairing are presumably important sources of situation definition.

Interpreters read alignment on the fly of temporal emergence. Situation definitions then become clues that guide subsequent interpretive formulation. Actors accommodate their speech to that of others (Giles & Powesland, 1975), which, when done artfully, helps communicators believe they are building a piece of coherence together. That you do coherence is, of course, taken for granted.

TOPICAL COHERENCE IN B AND K's CONVERSATION

In light of the above speculations about 2ness, temporal emergence, and alignment as facets of interpretive coherence production, let us return to the B-K conversation (Appendix). This is a casual pastime sort of conversation with few external demands for coherence. Small coherences such as those involving pair-parts or mini-episodes might seem to be needles of coherence in haystacks of hapless meandering. However, if one looks for repetition of themes across time, one finds some larger patterns. B and K reach early alignment that B is in the role "teller of outrageous stories" about how much she suffers, which also contain brags about family prominence, and a dose of self-deprecation (turns 62-66, 80-84, 96-102, 106-116). K responds with stories emphasizing suburbs, little brothers and a self-typification of practicality (turns 71-73, 77, 195-201, 207-209, 213 — see also Example 1). Where does such alignment come from? If we taught communicators to align better would we do it by telling them to pay attention to the interpretation of the out-of-focus indicators? Such an injunction seems to be a double bind, since attention to out-of-focus indicators removes them from being out of focus. This is no mere wrinkle of paradox, but a major problem for communication instruction.

Some even larger topical patterns emerge if one examines the entire B-K conversation. The following topics (numbered by turns) dominate:

(1) home and family topics: 18-104; 189-215; 226-237; 337.
(2) skiing: 89-122; 217; 301; 308-322; 329-337.
(3) other recreation: 124-165 (ballooning); 241-301 (horses); and 301-347 (misc.)

In brief, it rapidly becomes apparent that this conversation concerns mostly two topics: family and recreation. In "Unexample" 6 below, the conversation is schematized chronologically as an alternation between these two topics: family, recreation, family, recreation. Other topics seem to appear mainly as transitions between major topics.

Unexample 6: Topical Sequences in B and K's conversation (Appendix)

Turn	FAMILY TOPICS	Transitional Topics	RECREATION TOPICS
1-19		lunch, turkey, holi- days	
19-104	family themes —B's dad —K's brother —B's brother		
82-122		Switzerland	skiing
123-160			*Balloon Fantasia*
161-167		(Example 1)	
166-184		K's internship Rock County	
184-228	K's home town		
228-241	B's home town		
241-300			*Horse Opera* —B rode a lot —ferrier fight
301-347			Winter recreation in Madison, K's advice

Analysis of Example 6: The Big Picture of B-K Coherence

Seen from the Olympian retrospective posture of Unexample 6, B and K's conversation turns on two primary topic domains, family and recreation. No other topic draws sustained mention. Much of what happens in the conversation might be explained in terms of navigating a course to and from these topics. The two italicized segments that are titled *Balloon Fantasia* and *Horse Opera* strike me as the most interesting episodes on the transcript. The balloon fantasia (123-160) is marked by fantasy chains involving colors, scenery, romance, and, best of all, by relational symmetry between K and B. For this brief stretch the two are aligned in fantasy, contributing enthusiastically to a common excitement. The horse opera segment (241-300) is examined by Hawes (this volume). It contains the only emotional fireworks in the conversation.

Taking Unexample 6 as a topical coherence map of the B and K conversation, some other patterns begin to emerge. Examples include symmetrical question pairs (66 and 79; 105 and 118) and the repetitive chaining out on certain terms, most notably the word "ski." The most instructive coherence lesson that emerges from this view, however, concerns the words that appear as Example 1. Example 1 occurs just at the end of the balloon fantasia, which practical K has begun to bring to earth" with alignment talk in utterance 153 ("Oh:. This is just a dream . . . "). B's attempt to rescue the fantasy gets "No" (161) and "not practical" (twice, in 163 and 165). K is shutting the fantasy down, using practicality as a bludgeon. B pauses, then abruptly changes to a topic not previously discussed in this conversation, but apparently known to both parties (K's internship) and nails the new topic firmly in place using K's own word (166: "Have you heard anything about your internship. Speaking of practical.") Within a few turns, K converts the discussion of the internship to another family discussion. B counters with some stories of her own; note that family topics always appear in symmetrical speaker alternation. To add redundant coherence: the conversation of 161 through 167, which at first glance is coherent only in fragmentary ways, turns out to be the plaster over the biggest procedural crack in the B-K conversation. Coherence shows many faces.

CONCLUSION: SOME PERSONAL REFLECTIONS ON CONVERSATIONAL ANALYSIS

I constructed this essay as a three-party "conversation" alternating the voices of exposition, data, and analysis. The central idea is: Let us emphasize the role of interpretation in conversational coherence. Technology-based metaphors are used to illustrate four claims about interpretive processes in coherence production: (1) Interpretation involves primarily the listener role; (2) Interpretive coherence is produced as *2ness*, or the bringing to foreground of paired elements selected from text/context; (3) Interpretive coherence production is emergent in time, frequently involving abrupt transformations of situation definition; and (4) aligning actions are important to coherence production.

The proposed change in emphasis from a speaker's perspective to an interpreter's perspective is justified by the importance of interpretive work to situation definition. Interpretation constitutes communication; the interpreter's insistence that situations be constructed as coherent maintains social order.

This is a primitive view of interpretive process, but these concepts shed some light on conversations. For instance, I originally focused on six utterances in the B-K conversation because they showed little overall pattern or direction (Example 1). Early drafts of the present chapter used this transcript to question the notion of coherence and raise the issue of possible incoherence. However, my analysis (over a year-long period) displayed the very temporal emergence represented by the two treatments of this B-K passage (in Example 1 and Unexample 6). My view of this passage changed shape dramatically, and I now conclude that the passage performs a primary piece of topic-transition work. I presume that the passage does other things as well. Further analysis might retransform what is presented here.

Such emergence recurs in my attempts to describe conversation. As another example: I initially was drawn to the recordings from which Examples 2 and 4 are taken by their strong dramatic flavor. I judged the father's speech style somewhat negatively at first. He seemed a "hard" teaser, one who gave few clues that he was teasing, and continued to tease for long periods of time. I was also put off by his apparent sexism. However, across multiple listenings to a two-hour recording, and especially the five-minute segment surrounding the transcripts presented, a new view emerged: the father as teacher. Eventually this view eclipsed the harsher first impression because it seemed intuitively more basic and more typical of the entire conversation. I came to admire the father's teaching style as directive, tenacious, and compelling. In sum, conversational analysis should allow itself emergence, just as do the interpreters we study.

This chapter should soon appear naive, but let's not solidify our concepts too quickly. We are just learning a few ways to gather specimens. Still, there seem to be instructional implications of this work. Based upon the above, I argue for increased emphasis on teaching of interpretation: listening skills, processes of inference, practical understanding of emergence, and *using* ambiguity instead of trying to eradicate it. Recent developments mandate increased communication teaching, especially at primary levels. Curriculum innovation may revitalize our discipline in the coming years.

<<<<<<<<<<<< >>>>>>>>>>>>

II

STUDIES OF
STRATEGIES

<<<<<<<<<<<< >>>>>>>>>>>>

5

Licensing Violations
Legitimate Violations of Grice's Conversational Principle

< <SUSAN SWAN MURA> >

< < < Despite the claim by linguist Noam Chomsky > > >
that "communication is only one function of language, and by no
means an essential one," (1975, p. 69) many theorists typically consider language to be almost synonymous with the study of communication. One may go about studying the phenomenon of language in
many ways, focusing on its sound system, its grammatical system, or
its conventional meaning system, but the most important aspect of
language in regard to communication is not in these areas. It is rather
in pragmatics, the use of language to communicate. The domain of
pragmatics thus falls not into a field that delineates the linguistic
competence of the ideal speaker (i.e., traditional linguistics), but
rather into one which is properly and naturally concerned with the
practical use of language to think and to interact with others (i.e.,
communication). Save for a few rhetorical theorists, however, the
study of language vis-à-vis communication has been left to linguistics,
psychology, anthropology, sociology, and philosophy; it has not taken
its rightful place in the mainstream of communication theory.

With Cushman and Whiting's (1972) outline of a rules approach to
communication, this situation did begin to change. Publications
began to appear in our field looking not only at the rules-theory base
for pragmatics (Pearce, 1973; Cushman & Pearce, 1977; Donohue,
Cushman, & Nofsinger, 1980; Cushman, 1982), but presenting re-

search looking at some specific rules of doing conversation (Nof-singer, 1975, 1976; Stech, 1975; Bowers, Elliott, & Desmond, 1977). A general trend was followed to depend upon the groundwork laid out by philosophers John Austin, John Searle, and H. Paul Grice. It will be the purpose of this chapter to examine the contribution of one of these philosophers, Grice, to understand better the implications of his theory for a communication theory of conversation and to suggest an extension of his theory.

THE BASIC THEORY

In 1957, Paul Grice began a series of articles (1961, 1968, 1969, 1975, 1978) concerned with meaning in natural language in which he attempted first to distinguish between natural and nonnatural mean-ing (essentially Burke's (1978) motion/action dichotomy) and later to distinguish between the conventional and nonconventional aspects of nonnatural or symbolic meaning. His concern was to make

> a distinction between what the speaker has said . . . and what he has 'implicated' (e.g., implied, indicated, suggested, etc.) taking into account the fact that what he has implicated may be either *conventionally* implicated (implicated by virtue of the meaning of some word or phrase which he has used) or *non-conventionally* implicated (in which case the specification of the implicature falls outside the specification of the conventional meaning of the words used) [Grice, 1968, p. 55].

In following up on the nonconventional implicatures, Grice began to look at a special case called conversational implicatures, formulating in 1967 a general principle of conversation called the cooperative principle (CP; Grice, 1975). This principle, which participants are expected to observe, is stated prescriptively: "Make your conversa-tional contribution such as is required, at the stage at which it occurs, by the accepted purpose or direction of the talk exchange in which you are engaged" (Grice, 1975, p. 46). As support for this general principle, Grice also posited four maxims of conversation — quality, quantity, relation, and manner. These maxims may be summarized, respectively, as: be truthful; be succinct, yet complete; be relevant; and be clear and orderly.

Typically, Grice (1975) assumes that these four maxims and the supraordinate CP will be overtly observed in order to preserve coher-ent and cooperative communication and it was hypothesized that interactants would, in general and "in absence of indicators to the contrary" (p. 47-48), proceed to interpret conversation in the manner prescribed by these maxims. Intuitively, this principle is evidenced both by a lack of randomly generated contributions to conversation and by the indignation typically felt when someone in a conversation is clearly uncooperative. Conversational implicature comes into play when the CP and its maxims are not overtly observed. In such cases one may fail to fulfill a maxim when actually keeping, in spirit, the CP. As a result, a double message is given: a literal or direct message the meaning of which is determined conventionally and which fails to fulfill at least one of the maxims, and a nonliteral or indirect message which maintains the CP. The working out of this nonliteral or indirect message is the process of discovering the conversational meaning or implicature. In the absence of cues to the contrary, then, a listener will do his or her utmost to interpret an utterance in accordance with the CP; the cues to the contrary, however, provide a potential explanation for how one makes sense out of irony, figures of speech, hints, circumlocutions, ambiguities, and other nonliteral, indirect, or apparently uncooperative ways of saying things. A key question therefore is what are these cues or indicators to the contrary? What is their effect upon interaction? How do they function in conversation? What forms do they take? It is to these questions that the remainder of this chapter is directed.

VIOLATIONS OF CONVERSATIONAL MAXIMS

In general, the expectation that conversation will proceed smoothly and nonproblematically is realized as interactants "orient their conduct toward one another and toward a common set of objects. In this mutual orientation of conduct, an effort is made by the participants to align their individual acts, one to another, in the creation of joint or social acts" (Stokes & Hewitt, 1976, p. 843). Failures to live up to expectations do however occur and mismatches between intended acts and expectations may result; often these mismatches and the consequential misunderstandings are due to a failure to fulfill the CP and its maxims. Grice (1975) recognized this potential for nonfulfillment and suggested four classes of maxim violation. One could (1) violate a maxim "quietly and unostentatiously" (p. 49) with an intent to *mislead;* (2) *opt out* of a situation by withdrawing from the interaction when one is unwilling or unable to be cooperative; (3) be faced with a *clash* of maxims such that the choice of one maxim violates another; or (4) *flout* a maxim by blatantly violating it with an intent for strategic or artful cooperation.

In order to prevent misunderstanding, therefore, cues or indicators to the latter three classes of violations are needed. Indeed, in each of the classes, including that designed to mislead, a knowledge of conversational implicature is required such that the listener may make educated guesses concerning the speaker's intentions based on certain cues given. Of course, in the case of deception where only an appearance of cooperation is desired, the speaker hopes that any cues go undetected. Without such cues, the process of conversation would be inhibited and the potential for misunderstanding increased. In other words, an interactant may, in certain circumstances, choose to violate a maxim with an ultimate intent to fulfill the CP; as an indication of the ultimate intent, the interactant thus marks or cues the violation so as to qualify and clarify the interpretation. These cues sidestep the interpretation suggested by common expectation and redirect it in the direction desired by the speaker, thus reducing the potential for misunderstanding. The violation is overtly addressed (with the exception of those intended to mislead), brought to the attention of the listener, and recast in a cooperative light. These cues or indicators, in essence, grant a license for a violation of a maxim by pinpointing a supraordinate effort to meet the CP; as such, these cues are referred to as licenses for violations.

The behavior suggested by the licensing of violations of maxims is not exclusive to Grice. A close parallel may be found in Stokes and Hewitt's (1976) notion of aligning actions. For them, aligning actions are "forms of conduct, mainly verbal, in which individuals . . . sustain the flow of joint actions by bringing individual acts into line with one another in problematic circumstances" (p. 844). Licenses for violations thus allow a communicator to "'account' for seemingly deviant acts by showing they are congruent 'in spirit' with prevailing norms" (Stokes & Hewitt, 1976, p. 847). Inclusive in the alignment approach is alignment with social requirements *outside* the structure of conversation (e.g., morality); licensing of violations however is strictly in regard to the cooperative norms *within* the structure of conversation (e.g., dominating the floor).

One of the more important stylistic elements for achieving licensing and thus achieving an aligning action is the qualifier (i.e., an element that softens, mitigates, excuses, or explains statements and often requests forbearance and understanding). Two major types of qualifiers exist, according to Eakins and Eakins (1978): *hedges,* short phrases that reduce the impact of a statement (e.g., well, perhaps, I think) and *disclaimers,* introductory expressions that place contingencies upon the qualifications of the speaker or the validity and propriety of the message (e.g., I'm not an expert, but . . .). Disclaimers particularly are important in "disclaiming the apparent negative implications of a word or deed . . . [so that] the person 'gets away' with his intended act and joint action proceeds on its course" (Stokes & Hewitt, 1976, p. 846). If licensing does indeed exist as a means to qualify potential or perceived failures to meet the CP and its maxims, an examination of conversation should reveal it.

ANALYSIS

In order to provide a logical progression through each of the four conversational maxims, this section will present separate discussions of each. The transcripts used for this study come from two primary sources. The first represents a series of transcripts from an earlier study (Mura, 1980) and includes the first minute of each of 24 dyadic interactions centering around the topic of "talking a professor out of an exam." These are designated with the initials C and S (for confederate and subject). The second is the B-K conversation included in the Appendix. These transcripts were analyzed by pinpointing instances of qualifiers, eliminating those not addressing the conversational interaction, and then categorizing them in terms of Grice's maxims. The examples represent a sample of these instances. In a few instances, the transcripts did not contain examples of a particular type of license; for these few cases, anecdotal evidence is used. Such use was not thought to be problematic as (1) this study is exploratory and not definitive in nature and (2) the samples given seem to represent common, not idiosyncratic, experience.

Licensing Violations of the Maxim of Quality

As stated by Grice (1975, p. 46), "it is obvious that the observance of some of these maxims is a matter of less urgency than is the observance of others." He further suggests that the maxim of quality is the maxim of primary import. One would expect therefore to find a proliferation of qualifiers in statements that compromise the integrity of this maxim. Such appears to be the case in the present corpus. There are so many qualifiers for this maxim, in fact, that it is appropriate to break them up into two categories, namely "be truthful" and "have evidence for what you say." These submaxims closely approximate Pomerantz's three-category system (1980b) to explain assumptions operative when formulating and interpreting evidence: objective truth, direct access, and limitation of knowledge. "Be truthful" subsumes the first of these; "Have evidence" subsumes the latter two. Licensing of violations of the maxim of quality should be representative of exceptions to these submaxims.

"Be truthful." It is typically assumed that what one says represents objective truth. Violations of this assumption call for a license to qualify any presentation of something not wholly true. Absence of these licenses may lead to a misinterpretation of the truth value of a given statement. Take, for example,

228 **K:**   . . . Did you grow up in Philadelphia?
229 **B:**   In the Philadelphia area. Not really *in* Philadelphia. (pause) Uhm, (pause) this is embarrassing to admit, I was a Main Line kid. (pause) In the uh - n'there's a stream - of - of cities or towns - that go around Philadelphia.
230 **K:**   Um hmm/
231 **B:**   That are called the Main Line and (pause) they range from suburban to rural.
232 **K:**   Um::!
233 **B:**   As rural as you get - in Philadelphia an'the - Pennsylvania farms don't look anything like Wisconsin farms. You don't see a lot of - of fields with - wheat and corn. You see a few - but - there are a lot of horse farms. . . .
234 **K:**   ((high pitch)) Hmm!
235 **B:**   . . . And the vegetation is different and looks somewhat lusher. I=
236 **K:**   Um. Yeah.
237 **B:**   =mean, it's not - doesn't hold a candle to Virginia, for example, but- also it's a much - moister climate than here. (pause) Well, you can't get much moister than Madison summers I guess, but- ((laugh)) [B-K Conversation].

First, if both interactants assume objective truth, B's response to K in 229 may be problematic as it was implied earlier (045-046) that B's father lived *in* Philadelphia. If K remembers this, a misalignment could result; B sees that clarification is necessary and provides in 229 both a qualifier to expand the reference to the Philadelphia *area* and a disclaimer to license her apparent disregard for objective truth. Second, as if to make up for this disregard, B then provides a series of qualifiers for "rural," "a lot of farms," "lusher," and "moister," using self-corrections ("I mean," "well," and "but") and hedges ("somewhat" and "I guess") to lessen the perceived degree of objective truth being presented.

Situations may occur too when a license is used, but is not picked up by the listener, thus calling for an additional reinforcing license. For example:

202 **B:** N'yeah, East Molene is the one that stands out in my mind that's really a thrill.
((pause))
203 **K:** Why.
[
204 **B:** One of the uglier places ((laughing)) on - on earth I think. I- I went through there once after it flooded [B-K Conversation].

Turns 202 and 204 provide apparent contradictions of one another. Turn 202 was probably accompanied with the paralinguistic cues appropriate to sarcasm, but apparently B did not think this sufficient ✓ for she laughs to reinforce the nontruthfulness of her statement *and* follows it with a clarification in 204 of what she intended to mean. There is no indication that K needed this clarification, but, if she had, the reinforcing licenses would have provided the proper realignment with objective truth.

In the above samples, the "be truthful" submaxim was compromised, but without any intent to deceive. In most of these, the license used could be and was understood immediately and no misunderstanding occurred; in others, reinforcing licensing was required to either prevent or repair confusion.

"Have evidence." More commonly occurring are those qualifications of direct access to, and limitations of, knowledge; the licensing of these qualify the use of information for which the speaker has inadequate evidence. For licensing of direct access violations, crediting or the presenting of sources seems to be a common strategy if one must present knowledge that is other than firsthand. Such strategies imply that the second- or third-hand knowledge is based upon someone else's credible and direct access to the information. Samples of how this is accomplished vary, but one variation follows:

1C: . . . I had this professor who used to tell a story about the people coming in and when they started talking about getting out of finals he says "here's a list of all the ones I've heard" you know "if you've got a new one just add your name to it"
2S: Yeah?
3C: Yeah-it was like "I'm up to here with all the same old thing"

In this exchange C is crediting a professor he had had *who used to tell this story.* The use of indirect evidence is further licensed by the continuation of the story in a narrative form, reinforcing it as someone else's story while at the same time making it a part of the direct experience of the dyad. A sample, which includes both crediting and clarification of objective truth, is found below:

> **1S:** But umm No- I've heard of like I can remember when I had physics I heard of this one girl who the quarter before um in fact I talked to her- she told me that . . .

In this example, the crediting is given in line 2 to the girl she had heard of and a realignment with objective truth occurs that has the additional effect of bringing access to the information from third-hand to at least direct access to the first-hand evidence. Common phrases for licensing the use of nondirect evidence include, "I understand that . . . " or "I've heard that . . . ;" these allow the use of information for which the speaker does not have direct access, but which he or she feels is relevant to the topic under discussion.

Related to the licensing of the use of indirect access is the licensing of information based on limited experience or knowledge. The most common type of this licensing may be found in hedging, using items such as, "I guess," "somewhat," "kind of," and "it seems." Of greater interest, however, is the use of disclaimers directly exposing one's limited knowledge to prevent any chance of misalignment. This may include a speaker indicating that he or she is not willing to be held strictly accountable for what is said (e.g., "I could have been mistaken, but . . . ") or an attempt to sidestep disbelief or suspicion of a statement for which the speaker has little evidence (e.g., "well, I'm not the expert, but . . . "). Samples of such licensing is found in the transcripts, including,

> 342 **B:** Hmm. (pause) I had forgotten that you knew all about all that weather stuff.
> 343 **K:** ((laugh)) I really don't. I just pretend I do.
>   ((pause))
> 344 **B:** Tell me what you know about weather - on: the Pacific coast . . .
> 347 **K:** (I really haven't ever) studied anything that specific. There are some areas, (I think more like the Los Angeles area where because of the mount-) [B-K Conversation].

In this instance disclaimers (343 K; 347 K, line 1) combine qualifiers with hedges (like "I think") to give license to the speaker for possible future maxim violation. In this case K qualifies the objective truth of

B's assumption that she knows *all* about the weather; B pauses (perhaps to consider this qualification), but does not seem to accept it, proceeding in 344 to question K specifically about Pacific weather. Clearly, K believes that she does not have sufficient knowledge — or at least she feels some social pressure against admitting she does (as Brown & Levinson, 1978, would suggest), but once she has established this, she can answer B's question, safe conversationally because she has licensed any violation due to lack of knowledge by qualifying the evidence upon which her response is based.

The above approach is quite different from one in which the same disclaimers are given but with the intent of opting out of presenting evidence due to knowledge limitation. In such a case the speaker obtains a license for appearing uncooperative in the conversation for the sake of preserving the maxim of quality. For example:

> 1C: Umm I don't know, I've never gotten out of a final. Have you ever gotten out of one?
>
> 2S: No::unless they told us before- I- we never talked somebody out of it — probably depends on the teacher
>
> 3C: Yeah . . . well, you've got a little more experience than I do (pause) Oh, I don't know . . . I've only had like two communication courses. How would you get out?

In this sample C consistently states her position of inexperience and shifts the turn back to S. S qualifies her experience, but still hazards some guess as to how to handle the situation. Both thus qualify their limited knowledge, but use the license for quite different violations of the cooperative maxim: C licenses a limitation to explain her lack of quantity in contribution, while S licenses a limitation to qualify her lack of evidence for the ideas she presents.

Qualification can also occur in the form of crediting, where limitation of knowledge is attributed to someone else's failure to cooperate, thus absolving the interactant from blame for potential violation.

> 1C: But that's still a test — it doesn't count, does it?
>
> 2S: Yeah, I don't know — I'm not sure what she's trying to get at but, I think that would probably be considered a final.

In this manner S is able to make an assessment of the situation and make a judgement, but one which is sufficiently qualified to show that *S* is cooperating and any misalignment is the fault of the researcher.

Qualifications of, or licensing of, violations of the maxim of quality thus appear to be quite common, reinforcing Grice's suggestion that this maxim may be of primary import in maintaining a spirit of cooperation. With such licensing, necessary evidence that violates the letter of the CP may be presented as part of the interaction, but the spirit of the principle is maintained by showing the necessity for such deviance. Cooperative interaction may continue then with lower levels of misunderstanding than would otherwise be possible.

Licensing Violations of the Maxim of Quantity

Licensing does occur for the three other conversational maxims — quantity, relation, and manner — although not to the extent as has been seen with quality. The licensing of the violations of the maxim of quantity provide opportunities for cooperative instances of insufficient or excessive contribution to a conversation. A few examples of licensing insufficient quantity may be found in crediting the limitation to some outside force (e.g., "Well, I'm not at liberty to say," or "that is classified information"). These strategies shift any blame for uncooperativeness from the immediate interactant. Licensing may also occur when the interactant feels that he or she is taking too much time or is saying more than is necessary. In such instances, the speaker may head off or repair any misalignment by licensing and legitimizing the apparent failure to say only what is necessary (as with, "I know this is long and involved, but it really is important," or "Oh, I am so sorry. I really have been rambling on. What do you think about . . . ?").

In some instances, these strategies also provide a license for violations of the maxim of manner, which, in terms of brevity, is similar to the maxim of quantity. These devices show that the communicator is aware of the violation, yet the violation is allowed as the communicator makes it clear that either a legitimate reason exists for the breach or it was unintentional and should not be regarded as seriously uncooperative. One other strategy that may be used by a communicator anticipating a violation is to shift the responsibility of the violation onto the other interactant. Take for example:

1C: How did you and your husband meet?
2S :   We::ll, that's a lo:::ng story!
3C: OK, I'm not going anywhere, let's hear it.

In this exchange S is aware that to plunge into the long account of the meeting would be a violation of the quantity maxim. To prevent this she makes C aware that the answer is long, but in so doing obtains C's permission to violate the maxim. As a result S gets to tell the story and both feel that the spirit of cooperation has been negotiated between themselves and has been fulfilled to their satisfaction.

Licensing Violations of the Maxim of Relation

Various sorts of violations of relation exist, also. One sort of licensing occurs when it is necessary to exact a topic shift, but a smooth transition is not easily had. Take for example a dyad that has continued for about one minute with no reference to the assigned topic:

    1S: I just got back from my gym class right now-it's like blah!
    2C: Yeah, Gee::
    3S: I don't know
    4C: Oh, well — let's think of getting out of an exam.

In this sample an abrupt shift of topic is accomplished by a direct reference to the task at hand, licensing the surface irrelevance by a reference to a higher level of relevant topics.

Licenses for relation violation must also be given when interactants are conversing with divergent notions of the topic. For instance in the following sample, K directs the conversation toward "lessons" and it is not until several exchanges later that B realizes there is a problem. She then is obligated to show that her lack of relation is unintentional (286); K then feels obligated to clarify what she intended the topic to be.

  278 **K:** Oo. ((laugh)) (pause) I suppose when you take lessons that's also when you - just sort of learn to - to y'just take it in stride . . .
  279 B-283 **B:** When you ah - when you put a shoe on a horse. . . . I don't ((laughing)) think it's the sort of thing you ever get used to or learn how to deal with
  284 **K:** ((laugh)) That's- that's not what I was talking about. But I — mean just as a kid taking ho- lessons . . .
          [   ]
  285 **B:**   ((cough))
  286 **B:** Oh, that kind of ((laughing)) lessons.
       [
  287 **K:** Y'know, learning - learning to groom horses an- and things like that . . . [B-K Conversation].

Other licenses for apparent relation violation appear when one speaker uses a bridge to move the conversation in a different direction without appearing to introduce an irrelevant topic or being inattentive to the present topic. One may refer, for example, to a past mutual experience for the bridge, as with, "I meant to ask you the other day" (052 K), or by repeating the topic in a "speaking of . . . " approach. Another type of relevance licensing occurs when an interactant wants to make a point about or return to a topic already passed. For instance, the following sample occurs after an extended discussion of horseback riding:

301   **B:**   Yes, well - you just ((laughing)) don't go on the field without a baseball bat or a two by four. (pause) Do you do anything besides ski- besides cross country skiing in the winter here? What do people in Wisconsin do for exercise in the winter [B-K Conversation].

B appears to be jumping to a totally different topic, but on second glance, the "besides skiing" phrase acts as a cue and as a license to violate the relevance at one level by appealing to a higher level; she is returning the topic to that immediately preceding the digression on horses, namely that of skiing at Christmas. Other licenses such as "getting back to what we were talking about earlier," and, either humourously or viciously, depending on the intonation, "well, before we were so rudely interrupted, we were talking about . . . " are used similarly. In sum, each of these licenses either suspends judgment of relevancy long enough for the relevance to become evident or metacommunicates about the situation in order to license a violation that maintains the spirit of cooperation by showing how the contribution does fit into the structure of the conversation.

Licensing Violations of the Maxim of Manner

The final maxim to be considered is that of manner. Grice (1975) includes a supermaxim for this: "Be perspicuous," or, in other words, present what has to be said so that it is plainly understood, especially in regard to clarity and precision of presentation. As mentioned earlier, the maxim of quantity overlaps with that of manner in that both place a premium on brevity. It is seen also as overlapping with the maxim of quality in that obscurity of expression often involves convoluted modes of saying something simple, perhaps in order to prevent being pinned down to the objective truth. Some devices may be found, however, that directly license the use of obscurity or at least place it in a context so that it does not result in misalignment. Often these strategies are in the form of crediting (e.g., "And I quote . . . " or "Remember these are their words not mine . . . ") or in reference to some attempt at humour (e.g., "eschew obfuscation").

An additional aspect of manner that merits attention is that of orderliness, both in terms of presentation of an utterance and in terms of the regulation of turns. In the former case it is not uncommon to hear individuals stop in the middle of an explanation to say, "Wait, let me simplify that." These devices call attention to the violation, licensing it, and then proceed to rectify the problem with no loss of cooperative spirit. The latter case involves, in part, the responsibility of each interactant to make his or her contribution to the interaction at the proper place and time. Some instances occur too when the speaker needs to buy time to think before speaking rather than violate one of the other maxims. Vocalized pauses such as "well" and "um" are routinely used for this, but other strategies blatantly call attention to the need for delay. For example:

1S: You probably know more than (pause) I would, umm (pause 7 sec) I don't know — 've you ever heard of anyone that's gotten out of a final?

2C: I don't think so.

3S: (pause 4 sec) I'm trying to think (pause 3 sec) my older brother goes here and . . .

In this exchange C is not taking up her part of the conversation and rather than let it appear that S is at fault, S uses the stalling device, "I'm trying to think" to delay the need for a response. S also uses vocalized pauses as delay tactics. Other devices such as "just a minute" and "wait a sec" can also function as place-holder licenses for an interactant when immediate response is not possible. With the use of these licenses, the interactant may legitimately hold the attention of the other interactant longer than conventionally allowable and a relatively problem-free cooperative interaction is maintained.

Finally, a special case of violations of manner may be found when one goes beyond the literal level of conversation to a figurative level; the purpose in such a case is to enrich the conversation, not to mislead the listener and thus requires a slight extension of Grice's theory beyond the purely informational (Snyder, 1982). So if, for instance, one says, as B does in turns 202-204, "that's really a thrill" and means "that's one of the ugliest places," it is not with an intent to deceive or mislead, but to add richness and variety to the conversation — to take it beyond mere informational exchange to the level of creative exchange. Obvious exaggerations, as when B proclaims in 301 that the lesson she learned about being kicked by a horse is, "don't go on the field without a baseball bat or a two by four," her laugh should be sufficient to prevent her statement being taken literally. The same is true in K and B's discussion of the problems of buying presents for their fathers.

> 023 **K:** = *Yes.* I have that same problem. I finally resorted to saying ((louder, mock exasperation)) "Dad, what do you *want*" ((high pitch, comical)) "I don't need anything."
> 024 **B:** That's exact- I think we've got the same father ((laugh)) [B-K Conversation].

Note that B's reply is obviously not true, thus violating the maxim to be truthful and to be clear and unambiguous — her laughter, however, along with the blatant obviousness of the statement's falsity circumvent a literal interpretation, the violation is licensed, and the conversation enriched.

CONCLUSIONS

This study has looked at the licensing of violations of Grice's maxims of conversation; the licensing or qualifying of violations for each of the four maxims is similar in function, namely, to provide for problem-free interaction in circumstances that otherwise would result in misalignment and possible incoherent interaction. While Grice suggested that the use of these maxims would result in cooperative interaction, this analysis has shown that indications contrary to following the maxims may also function in a cooperative manner. In response to the questions asked at the beginning of this chapter, one may now see that the indicators or licenses exist as markers of deviance away from the letter of cooperation, while acting to preserve a greater cooperation. They exist most frequently for the maxim of quality, suggesting the salience of truth as a cooperative variable. The weighting in the direction of quality lends credence to the notion that interactants are sensitive to potential violations of the truth and evidence assumptions and indicates that they anticipate violations by softening their impact. Licensing exists also for potential violations of quality, relation, and manner, particularly in the forms of hedges and disclaimers. The effect of the licensing is to bring to the attention of the interactants the potential or actual violation, to provide legitimation for it, and to place it in an overall context of cooperation. In addition to providing examples of how such licensing of violations look and function, this study also provides preliminary evidence that the cooperative principle represents a psychologically real construct, modeling the behavioral (in a non-Skinnerian sense of the term) basis for conversational formulation and interpretation. If the CP were not a valid construct, there would be no need to provide licensing for violations of it; this chapter provides evidence that there is such a need and thus is suggestive of the validity of the theory.

Other aspects of this phenomenon of licensing violations remain to be investigated. For example, it is possible and indeed desirable to empirically verify the claim that licensing of quality violations occur more frequently than other types of licensing. Also, the correspondence between the types of violations and the contexts in which they occur needs to be explored to determine the salience of specific types of violations in various contexts. Additionally, it would be desirable to look at the conventional use of such violation licensing in regard to such things as storytelling and comedy or as it is affected by social variables such as status or gender. I hope that this study has provided a descriptive base upon which other such investigations may be built.

<<<<<<<<<<<< >>>>>>>>>>>>

6

Conversational Relevance in Multiple-Goal Settings

<< KAREN TRACY and JOHN P. MORAN III >>

<<< Grice (1975) argued that conversations seem >>> coherent because communicators cooperate with each other and follow rules. One of these rules, which he labeled the "relevancy maxim," specifies that conversants are to make their comments relate to the prior discourse. Grice, however, did not specify the nature of relevancy. The question, "What counts as relevancy in conversation?" is the focus of this chapter. In examining the question we make two assumptions. First, we assume that relevancy, while an important goal, is but one of many goals that communicators possess in everyday interchanges. Hence, to understand relevancy adequately, we must understand its relationship to the other goals that communicators typically pursue. Second, we conceive of relevancy as a continuum where particular remarks can be assessed, although perhaps imperfectly, in terms of their degree of connectedness to the prior discourse. In other words, relevancy is a matter of degree rather than a dichotomous choice.

In this chapter we will first present an overview of the research pertinent to our question and present a number of conceptual distinctions about topicality and relevance. Then we illustrate these distinctions in a discourse situation where the goals communicators possessed were partially controlled and the messages to which they responded followed a particular structure. In the final section we examine the B-K conversation from two perspectives. We show how the theoretical concepts illuminate our understanding of this specific everyday conversation, and we show how close scrutiny of the conversation enriches, adds depth to, and suggests modifications of our theoretical constructs.

RESEARCH OVERVIEW

Recently a series of studies (Tracy, 1982, in press-a, in press-b; Tracy & Moran, 1982) have attempted to explicate the concept of conversational relevance and relate it to judgments of competence and effectiveness in communication. All of the studies have used an experimental methodology: people are brought into situations that are varied systematically on certain dimensions, are presented messages, and are asked either to evaluate a set of possible responses or to indicate what they would say as a response. If one examines the studies chronologically, each subsequent study approximates more closely the complexity of conditions in natural discourse situations. Let us consider each study to see what we can learn about conversational relevance.

Study I

At first glance the question, "What is conversational relevance?" seems an easy one. Everyday conversants, while perhaps not able to define it, appear to know what it means. As evidence, consider the not infrequent accusation one communicator makes of another that he or she "changed the subject." If this accusation is meaningful, there must be at least a partially shared conception of what relevance is, and of where a topic begins and ends. Closer examination of the question reveals, however, that understanding of conversational relevance is not so obvious. Two quite different definitions are found in prior research.

The *local* definition sees relevance as a matter of sentence-to-sentence links. If a communicator links his or her comment to the immediately preceding sentence, a relevant remark has been made. For example, imagine that a speaker (Person A) says: "The weather has been so crummy lately," and the conversational partner (Person B) responds "Yeah, I know, my car got stuck in the snow coming to work." In this case most of us would see Person B's response as relevant. The reason, according to Schank (1977) and Halliday and Hasan (1976) is that Person B's response linked to key concepts in A's sentence (i.e., linking snow to crummy weather is a lexical connective). While in many cases this definition of relevance is satisfactory, it is inadequate in others. Consider the same sentence of A's in a different context.

> I feel as if everything has been going wrong for me. I broke my thumb three weeks ago. My husband and I have been fighting. The weather has been so crummy lately.

If we consider Person B's response to this larger discourse situation, it is less likely to seem highly relevant. While connected to the past discourse, it does not respond to the main point.

The second definition of relevance, the *global* definition, takes this into account (van Dijk, 1977a, 1977b). A relevant remark is one that responds to the central point of the speaker's utterance. When a speaker's message is more than one sentence in length, the main point often will not be captured in the last sentence. It can frequently be captured, however, by application of an issue-event structure (Reichman, 1978) where an issue is an abstract statement or a generalization about a belief or feeling, and an event is a specific example or instance. Applying this conversational structure to A's remarks, the issue would be the speaker's feeling that everything is going wrong; the events are the specific instances of thumb breaking, fighting, and crummy weather.

In the first study (Tracy, 1982), two predictions were made. First, it was predicted that communicators would make topicality judgments on a global basis, considering the entire utterance rather than solely the last sentence. In other words, if given a choice between an issue and an event when a conversation included both, people would select the issue as the topic. This prediction was supported. The second prediction concerned people's evaluations of conversational extensions. It was expected that communicators would judge extensions of the conversational issue as more competent (a better thing to say) than extensions of the event. This prediction was supported but only weakly. In one of four conversations the results were the opposite of prediction; in another there was no clear preference.

Study II

The first study demonstrated a preference for issue extensions rather than event ones in some situations but not in others. The purpose of the second study (Tracy, in press-a) was to delineate more carefully the conditions when issue extensions are preferred over event ones and to do so in a more natural (ecologically valid) situation. Thus, rather than having subjects read written conversational messages and evaluate extensions as had been done in the first study, Study II presented tape recorded messages.

Two conditions were predicted to influence when issue extensions *would not* be the preferred conversational response. One condition was the perceived understandability of the speaker's message. If the listener found it difficult to infer the speaker's main point — in this case, the issue — then extensions of more peripheral parts of the discourse (parts of the event) were expected to be evaluated as equally competent to issue extensions. By either providing or omitting background information about the speaker's message, the understandability of the message was varied. The effect was as predicted. When the background information was present, issue extensions were strongly preferred; when it was absent, the preference was significantly smaller.

The second condition was the perceived importance of the message to the speaker. If the listener perceived that the speaker was not strongly invested in his or her message, then extensions of the more peripheral event were expected to be acceptable. On the other hand, if the speaker appeared strongly invested in his or her message, as communicated by delivery cues and linguistic choices, then extensions of the peripheral parts of the discourse would be sanctioned strongly. Interestingly, this prediction was not supported. Instead, regardless of whether the message was high or low in importance for the speaker, issue extensions were seen as the more desirable and relevant type of conversational response.

In summary, Study II provided strong evidence that communicators evaluate extensions of issues as more competent and relevant than event extensions, particularly when the speaker's issue is easy to understand.

Study III

The first two studies provide evidence that third-party observers evaluate issue extensions of the conversation as more relevant and competent than event ones. We do not, however, know if this preference is reflected in the conversational behavior of communicators. People do not always do what they say is preferred behavior (Clark, 1979; Sherman, 1980). The third study (Tracy, press-b) asked communicators to generate their own messages. Subjects were asked to imagine that they were conversing with someone whom they did not know well; they heard tape-recorded messages, and after each wrote down what they would say in response.

Communicators were expected to adhere to Grice's (1975) relevancy maxim and interpret it to mean "extend the conversational issue." With the qualification noted in Study II (the speaker's message could not be difficult to comprehend), the preference for issue extensions was found. Whenever the speaker was perceived easily understandable, respondents extended the issue.

A second attempt was made to test message importance. Clearly, conversationalists possess goals other than being attentive and extending the speaker's issue. One obvious goal is the desire to move the conversation to a topic of interest to self. Thus when a speaker appears not to be highly invested in the message, conversants could be expected to respond in a greater variety of ways; that is they would more frequently produce remarks that were tied less closely to the speaker's issue. Similar to Study II, no support was found for this prediction. Subjects were more likely to extend the issue than the event, regardless of how important the message was to the speaker.

Study IV

Results of Studies II and III did not show any evidence that the importance of the message to the speaker influences the preference for issue extensions. Across conditions of high and low message importance, issues were extended equally often and events were evaluated equally negatively. This result seems puzzling. It suggests that the only goal conversants had was to be attentive and extend the partner's topic. Yet everyday experience patently contradicts this: Conversants often attempt to move the topic to an area of greater interest to themselves.

If we look at the structure of Study III, an explanation is possible: Subjects had no motivation to introduce new topics. Given no instructions to the contrary, it is not surprising they did not try to change the topic in response to their tape-recorded partner's message.

Study IV (Tracy & Moran, 1982) examined what communicators say in response to another's messages when they clearly have something they wish to talk about. Conversational extensions were examined with two factors varied: the first, the previously established condition of speaker understandability; the second, the ranking of two communication goals. All respondents were asked to try to achieve two goals: to be attentive to their partner and to introduce a new topic (a movie they had recently seen). In one condition the most important goal was to introduce the new topic, while the goal of being attentive was secondary. In the other condition the goal priorities were reversed; being attentive was the primary goal, introducing the new topic was secondary. As in Study III, subjects listened to tape-recorded messages and wrote down what they would say in response. It was expected that respondents would be more successful at introducing the new topic when it was a primary rather than a secondary goal. This prediction was strongly supported. Because of the greater difficulty inherent in accomplishing two goals within a single utterance, it was also expected that conversational extensions would be less well connected to the issue when the respondent's primary goal was introduction of a new topic; this prediction was also supported.

Summary

Earlier research (Planalp & Tracy, 1980) demonstrated that a remark will be judged more relevant and competent if it links to the immediately prior conversation rather than to something that was said many comments earlier in the discussion or to a situational occurrence. This set of four studies further defines relevance: A relevant remark is one that responds to the main point of a speaker's immediately preceding message. When a message follows the issue-event structure, that is, a story that makes a point, the issue is the main point and a relevant and competent response is one that extends the issue.

In the next section the conversational data from Tracy and Moran (1982) are examined with the purpose of illustrating the issue-event distinction in terms of what people say as they respond to the conversational issue. We describe several types of strategies that respondents used in their efforts to introduce a new topic while responding relevantly to the speaker's issue.

CONVERSATIONAL EXTENSIONS IN A COMPETING GOAL SITUATION

When faced with the task of being an attentive partner and introducing a new topic, respondents produced three generally different kinds of messages: messages that continued the old topic, messages that closed the old topic and introduced the new, and messages that linked the new topic with the old. Let us consider examples of these three message types, the relationship of each type to the two goals, and the likely degree of conversational relevance. In all cases conversants were attempting to introduce a specific movie they had recently seen. Table 6.1 displays the taped messages to which the conversants responded.

TABLE 6.1   Speaker Messages Used in Experiments II, III, and IV

Conversation 1:

McDonald's*

People badmouth eating at McDonald's but it seems to me it's somewhat uncalled for. It serves a number of different needs—it has a function. Sara and I went to Burdeen's the other day. The service was not very good. It took two hours and I was late for my meeting.

Conversation 2:

Watching TV

I'm not against watching TV. I mean, some people can be so snooty about it but it's relaxing and doesn't have bad effects. The other night I laughed almost continuously for three hours. I thought my sides were going to split. The next day I was in a good mood all day.

Conversation 3:

Monopoly

It seems that playing Monopoly can be so irritating. It uses up your time, saps your energy and you get very little satisfaction. It's a hard-to-win activity. Last night I was with Jim, Ted, and Mary Ann. I lost most of my property and a good deal of my money to them.

Conversation 4:

Parking Tickets

I suppose cops shouldn't spend so much of their time giving parking tickets. Everywhere I go I see them giving some. There are some more important things to do. The other day when we had that big snow that brought down a lot of branches and stuff, I saw cars colliding or slipping off the road and there were no cops to help.

Conversation 5:

Time Magazine

Reading *Time* is just like the advertisements say. One finds it not uninteresting—it's not a bad way to pass time and you learn something. Last week I learned about those sets of separated twins who have grown up not knowing each other and yet are still very similar.

Conversation 6:

Weight Reducing

Weight reducing salons are not only questionable but not of any great worth and probably dishonest. I suppose it should be closed down. Jill paid $300—She doesn't have much much money. Anyway for that money she got five pounds—that's $40 a pound.

(continued)

TABLE 6.1   Continued

Conversation 7:

Monkeys

I guess monkeys are kind of like us—in many ways. Indeed the similarities are sort of amazing. Yesterday on my way home from work I stopped to see them. There they were sitting, giving each other backrubs.

---

*For purposes of brevity and clarity, the comprehensibility cue has been incorporated into the message. In the experiments, messages began with a vague pronominal reference (e.g., "they" for "monkeys"), which, in the high comprehensibility condition, was prefaced by a short cue.

Continue Old Topic

One type of conversational extension, found most frequently when the respondent's primary goal was to be attentive, was an extension of the conversational issue with no attempt to introduce the desired new topic. For example, in Conversation 7 (Table 6.1), where the speaker's issue was the similarity of monkeys and people, the following kinds of comments were made:

Example 1   We can really learn a lot about ourselves watching monkeys relate to each other. Their very primitive societies are the roots of our own.

Example 2   Yeah, I believe they are pretty much like us.

Example 3   I know what you mean. When my wife and I go to the zoo the monkeys are always the first animals we go see. They are so fascinating the way they resemble humans.

This type of response stands in marked contrast to ones where the respondent introduced the new topic as well as responding to the issue:

Example 4   Monkeys are the most similar animal to man. They need touching like humans. In the movie *Ordinary People,* the mother never showed any emotions or touching toward the son and he was suffering psychologically from the lack of his mother expressing care and emotion for him by touching.

Example 5   Talking about monkeys, in the film *Superman* young Clark Kent was treated like a monkey because he wasn't allowed to play sports because of his super powers, just delivered water.

Close Old Topic and Introduce New

Another method respondents used to deal with the goals of responding to the other and introducing a new topic was to make a comment that unequivocally closed off the previous speaker's topic, after which they proceeded to introduce a new one. Consider the following comments:

Example 6   I never really dwelt on it too much. That reminds me did you see *American Gigilo?*

Example 7   Let's talk about something on the brighter side. Have you seen *Raiders of the Lost Ark?*

Example 8   Well enough of that, let's talk about the movie I saw last week. It was so funny. Did you ever see *Young Frankenstein* with Gene Wilder and Peter Boyle?

Example 9   I don't know about that but going on to something else, have you seen *Raiders?*

Each of these remarks acknowledges the speaker's topic, although minimally, cues that the old topic is finished, and introduces the new one. This type of remark establishes relevance by explicitly cueing that the respondent is not interested in the speaker's issue and is not continuing it. While lacking in social attentiveness, this strategy type is understandable, does not provoke confusion, and indicates clearly what is occurring in the conversation.

Linkage of New Topic with Old

Responses that only continue the old topic or introduce the new without attempting to link it with the old, are similar in one respect: Both abandon one goal in the interaction. The former abandons the goal of introducing the new topic; the latter the goal of being attentive. While achieving two goals within a single utterance may be difficult, it is often possible. Conversationists can and do accomplish both goals in a single utterance. Four types of strategies for linking the old with the new were present in our data.

Script linkages. One way to link a new topic to an old one is to relate both topics to the same "script." A script, according to Schank and Abelson (1977), is a common set of expectations about how some aspect of life is structured. They argue, for instance, that we are able to understand a story about a man entering a restaurant, looking at a menu, eating food, and paying a bill because we have a "restaurant script." The script allows us to make connections among diverse ideas because the events are connected in our everyday experience of going to a restaurant.

One script that was pertinent to our data was what we labeled the "night out script." This script consists of expectations about what is involved in going out for an evening of entertainment. Specifically, a night out involves doing an activity and getting some refreshment. Consider responses to Conversation 1 where the speaker makes comments about how eating at McDonald's is not a bad thing to do:

Example 10   I think they're useful. I had a date the other night. We had to catch something to eat before we went to the movie. We saved time and also put something in our stomachs. We were on time for the movie. We saw *Private Lessons*.

Example 11   Yeah, I like to go to fast food places sometimes too. We went to Roy Rogers the other day before we went to see *Time Bandits*. If we'd gone to any other kind of restaurant, we would have missed half the movie.

Example 12   I ate at an excellent restaurant in Center City last night. We stopped in for a snack after seeing the *French Lieutenant's Women*. It topped the evening off after seeing such a wonderful film.

Common idea linkages. A second way to link a comment to the prior message is by using an idea that was present in the partner's message. This idea could either be the issue, the event, or some subpart of either. Common idea linkages explicitly refer to an idea the speaker mentions. Consider how this is done in Conversation 5. The speaker maintains that reading *Time* magazine is just like the advertisements say: You learn a lot. The speaker goes on to illustrate this with a story about twins who were separated.

Example 13   Ads can be misleading just like anything else. But the ad for *Modern Problems* was pretty accurate.

Example 14   You always read about that long-lost twins story. Speaking of advertisements, you know those ads on the radio for the new flick, *Madman,* well the scenes that go over the radio aren't even in the flick. I was real disappointed.

Example 15   I think it is a good idea to keep on trying to learn throughout one's life. You know watching movies is a good way to learn.

Example 16   I spent time working in a movie theater as an usher and learned a great deal about my sensitivity to people while watching *The Elephant Man*.

In each of these examples the conversationist explicitly links to an idea or word mentioned by the speaker ("ads" and "learning"). To a certain degree both goals (i.e., attentiveness and new topic introduction) are accomplished in each of these messages. However, although each of these accomplishes both goals, previous research (Tracy, 1982, in press-a) suggests that 15 and 16 would be judged more relevant and competent than 13 and 14: The idea of learning from activities is a more central part of the issue than comments about advertisements.

Meta-issue linkages. A third way to link one topic with another is to show that the previous topic is really an instance of some more abstract topic or issue. For example, in Conversation 3 the speaker talks about how playing Monopoly is irritating. This can be seen as an instance of the larger issue that participating in activities leads to feelings.

Example 17   You know the way you're saying you felt about this is just how I feel about a movie I saw last night. It wasted my energy for sure — I was drained — emotionally and physically because it really made me sick.

Example 18   What the hell did you play for if you feel like that? It's just a game. You should have come to the movie with me and Marie, dummy. I told you it was supposed to be good. That's what you get.

In Conversation 2, where the speaker's topic was how watching TV is a good thing to do, a number of conversants treated this as an example of the larger issue of how to spend time.

Example 19   TV is OK but I like going to the movies looking at a large screen. The other night I went to see *True Confessions,* it was very relaxing.

Example 20   TV is alright but I feel you have to break its monotony by going to see a movie in a theater. I saw *Private Lessons* the other night.

Where common idea linkages refer explicitly to an idea mentioned by the speaker, meta-issue linkages create a new idea. The conversationist takes an idea in the speaker's message (e.g., watching TV), relates it to·a more abstract issue (e.g., ways to spend time), and then links the new topic (e.g., a particular movie) to the more abstract issue. Common idea and meta-issue linkages may be distinguished conceptually with relative ease. Actual discourse, however, does not always fall neatly into one category or another. In fact, these strategy types are best conceived as fuzzy sets (Rosch, 1977). While many utterances will fall clearly in one or the other category; others will have characteristics of both.

Procedural linkage. In the final type of linkage the conversant maintains that his or her comment is indeed linked to what the speaker said, but the nature of the link is vague and unclear. Few explicit cues are provided about the nature of the link. In contrast with the other kinds of linkage strategies, the inferential task required by the use of the procedural linkage is quite difficult. For instance, in Conversation 4, where the speaker talked about cops giving parking tickets and illustrated with a story about an snowstorm and an accident, one respondent said:

> **Example 21**   I know what you mean. The other night I had the same problem on the way to see the movie *Ragtime*. Have you seen that movie?

What does the conversationist in 21 mean? What is the "same problem?" Is it getting a parking ticket? Not having police around to help for an accident? Getting stuck in the snow? The procedural link makes it difficult to discern this. Another example of a procedural linkage is seen in response to Conversation 6 about weight-reducing salons:

> **Example 22**   That reminds me of a movie I just saw. An overweight boy just keeps right on eating and his friends more or less made fun of him. I guess he wasn't very interested in losing weight.

Again we might ask what the conversant is referring to with the statement, "That reminds me." What exactly is *that?* If we insert the speaker's issue (weight-reducing salons are fradulent and should be closed down), the comment makes little sense. We can make sense of 22 only if we interpret "that" to mean concerns about weight. To come up with this interpretation, however, the partner is required to do a lot of mental work. A procedural link, then, is one in which a conversant suggests that his or her comment is linked to the speaker's but provides few cues to guide the other's mental search to understand the link.

Of the four types of linkage strategies, procedural linkages are likely to be the least relevant; a large amount of cognitive work is left to the partner. However, procedural links are very successful at accomplishing the goal of new topic introduction and show some degree of attentiveness — at least more so than closing off the speaker's topic.

Each of the three major strategy types (continue old topic, close old and introduce new topic, and introduce new) gives different weights to the goals of being relevant, attentive, and introducing a new topic. To a certain degree, these goals compete with each other. Yet, as we have seen, it is possible to accomplish all three simultaneously.

Summary

The research reported here looked at conversational extensions in a controlled experimental situation. This type of approach has both advantages and disadvantages. The experimental approach is advantageous because it permits us to make attributions and to draw conclusions that we would otherwise be unable to do. For example, in Study IV we knew what the goals of the interactants were because we provided them and checked to make sure communicators actually pursued them. Hence the experimental research allows us to draw conclusions about how people combine goals and how these goal combinations are realized in discourse. In everyday interaction we rarely have access to this type of information. We do not know what goals communicators possess, nor how important any particular goal is. While it is possible to make reasoned guesses about communicators' goals, the complexity of everyday situations necessitates that these guesses be quite tentative.

On the other hand, it is everyday conversational interaction that we are interested in understanding. Experiments are valuable insofar as their results apply to real-life phenomena and enrich our understanding of those phenomena. In the next section we consider how well our experimentally gleaned understanding of relevance applies to an ordinary conversation, the B-K conversation (see Appendix).

ANALYSIS OF THE B-K CONVERSATION

In our analysis of the B-K conversation we take up three questions: (1) How applicable is the issue-event distinction to describing ordinary discourse? (2) Is there evidence for the significant role of comprehensibility in influencing the selection of conversational extensions? (3) Do the linkage strategies identified experimentally occur in an ordinary conversation?

Applicability of the Issue-Event Distinction

In looking for instances of the issue-event structure we are looking for discourse examples where a communicator tells a story (the event) to illustrate a specifically made point (the issue). Examination of the B-K conversation reveals many instances of this type of structure. It also reveals a good deal of variation in the way this form is manifest.

In turns 259-263 we see a segment of conversation conforming to an issue-event structure. B claims that she did not own a horse but leased one (the issue) and proceeds to tell a story about the summer she leased a horse (the event). Although B's issue is not very abstract in an absolute sense, it certainly is more abstract than the event and is the main point of her story. This is consistent with Tracy's claim (1982) that issue and event are not absolute categories but rather are relative to each other.

In turns 106-116 we see a slightly different variation of the issue-event form. In response to a question from K, B mentions her issue (she doesn't ski), tells an elaborate story about the traumas of her few attempts to ski (the event), and then finally reiterates and clarifes the issue. ("I hated it, I got . . . very cold and unhappy ((laughing)) and quit.")

In an ongoing conversation all of the comments except the initiating one have the prior discourse as background. This means that each speaker may respond to the other's issue, event, or both, and/or may introduce his or her own issue and event. Thus conversation is likely to reveal a complex interweaving of one conversationist's issues and events with the other's. This is illustrated in turns 202-209 in the B-K transcript. B has just made a comment that East Moline is not very pretty, and illustrates her issue by telling a short story about going through it during a flood. K responds to this issue and event in a complex way. First she tells a story about her experiences with a flood there (a response to B's event), then she extends B's issue by disagreeing with it ("There's just so- but there's so much to *do* in those towns"), and then supports her issue with an event detailing all the things to do there (e.g., "theaters, little theaters that are affordable for college students.")

A third variation of the structure is seen where a conversational issue is developed over several turns with input from both conversants.

Example 23 017 **B :** K (pause) what are you giving ((laughing)) people for Christmas this year? ((both laughing)) I've started thinking about it'n - my -

ability to be inventive - without spending much ((laughing)) money is - very very small.

[   ]

018	**K:**	(oh)

019 **K:** Like family? Friends?

020 **B:** Family mostly.

021 **K:** Family hhoh:: (pause) What do you buy men in your family for Christmas?

022 **B:** My father is the main problem.=

023 **K:** *Yes.* I have that same problem. I finally resorted to saying ((louder, mock exasperation)) " Dad? What do you *want?*" ((high pitch, comical)) "I don't need anything."

024 **B:** That's exact- I think we've got the same father. ((laugh))

In Example 23 K and B jointly construct the issue — fathers are hard to buy gifts for — and then in subsequent turns each provides an event illustrating it.

In summary, the issue-event structure frequently occurs in everyday discourse: People do a lot of storytelling in which they explicitly state the main point. This finding, that the issue-event structure occurs with some frequency in informal initial interaction is consistent with the research of scholars of natural discourse in other settings, including therapeutic discourse (Labov & Fanshel, 1977) and conversation between friends (Reichman, 1978; Ryave, 1978).

Role of Comprehension in Influencing Extensions

One important claim of our research has been that extensions of the conversational issue occur more frequently and will be judged more relevant and competent than event extensions when the issue is easily understood. In other words, when a speaker's main point (the issue) is unclear, there is likely to be greater variety in the parts of the message that are extended than when the issue is clearly stated. This is not to suggest that every clear statement of an issue would automatically result in its extension but, in contrast to conversations where the issue is complicated and difficult to follow, the likelihood of issue extensions is much greater when the issue is clear.

Let us consider the kinds of conversational continuations that occurred in the B-K conversation where the issue was either difficult to infer or very easily inferable. In turns 229-237 we have an instance where B's issue is difficult to remember and understand because of the sheer length of the accompanying event. B goes on for an extended time, punctuated only by "uhms" and "yeahs" from K, to describe the suburban area she is from. Her issue seems to be something to the effect of, "I'm from the Main Line, a surburban area of Philadelphia." Her event is an extended description of the area. B concludes her description by comparing the climate in her home town to Madison. K responds (turn 238) to the most recently mentioned comment about Madison's climate, clearly an event extension rather than a response to B's issue.

At a somewhat earlier point in the conversation, we see another example of a difficult-to-comprehend issue. This time the comprehension difficulty can be traced to a series of false starts and nonfluencies.

> **Example 24** 145 **K:** Oh well *tha:t* would be nice/ hhh .hhh I al'ys thought- California's supposed to have- when I- first started getting interested in it - they had - they were one of the few places that had - pla- where you could go, and, someone would either take you up or learn- teach you how to do it and you could go. So that's what I want to do on my honeymoon. Go to California and- and balloon. ((laugh))
>
> [
>
> 146 **B:** ((laugh)) (pause) Hmm::.

The issue in Example 24 is something concerning K's attitudes toward ballooning, California, and honeymoons. But the exact point K is making is far from clear. B's pause and then minimal response of "hmm" suggest that she too may have been at a loss for how to respond. Similar kinds of minimal responses (e.g. "yeah sure," "I see your point") were seen in the low understandability condition in earlier research (Tracy, in press-b).

In contrast to these difficult-to-understand segments, there are two examples in the B-K transcript where the issue is stated with extreme clarity and the subsequent responses unequivocally continue the issue. In turns 96-102 B tells a story about her stepbrother who was asked to be on two Olympic teams but broke his knee in training. B concludes stating the issue that the kneebreaking was "the only thing that saved poor little D from growing up to be a ski bum." In the next utterance K's response clearly extends this issue, "Which I'm sure his family was glad of/" (turn 103).

Another instance of an easily inferable issue is seen in B's tale about how she hates to ski (turns 106-116). Again, we see B finishing up her story by specifically stating the issue: "and I hated it, I got very cold and unhappy ((laughing)) and quit." K's response again continues the main point rather than picking out some subpart of her rather lengthy story: "Tha:t would be about my reaction too."

The experimentally documented link between message comprehensibility and conversational extension type appears to operate in the B-K conversation. When the issue is clearly stated and easily inferable, the partner is likely to respond to the issue. When the issue is difficult to infer, less central parts of the conversation are continued.

Linkage strategies

Finally, let us examine the B-K transcript to see what evidence there is for the strategies noted in Study IV (Tracy & Moran, 1982). In a single conversation we would not expect to see all types of strategies but we should find evidence of several. In the B-K conversation the most frequently used strategy was to link the new topic with the old; instances of common idea, metatopic, and script linkages are easily found.

A common idea linkage is used at turn 85. B is talking about her stepsiblings and mentions that they went to school in Switzerland. K continues the conversation by linking to the idea of Switzerland. K then proceeds to tell a story about her friend ("Speaking of Switzerland a good friend of mine is going there for Christmas. He's an AFS student . . . "; turn 85).

Another and somewhat more subtle example of a common idea linkage is seen in turns 122-128. B has been talking about skiing and not liking heights; K refers to the idea of heights and then links to ballooning.

> **Example 25** 122   **B:** I don't mind the speed on- on the flat but
> I'm-terrified of heights. Which makes me a
> ((laughing)) bad candidate for skiing.
>
> 123-128 **K:** (I love) I love the heights. [B: Umm] Tha's
> [B: um] .hh- hhh I'm gonna learn how to
> balloon or something like that so I can - see
> the world.

A metatopic link is illustrated at turns 306-307. K and B had been talking about winter activities and specifically mentioned swimming. B comments on baths and skating. Then K says, "I get into taking showers that's about it. ((laugh))." B's response ("I take long baths.

I'm looking for somebody who - wouldn't be embarrassed to start skating. I'd like to skate with another beginner.") is understandable because baths, a joke on swimming, are related to skating via the metatopic of winter activities.

The use of script linkages is not common in the B-K conversation, but we do see one instance. K and B have been discussing difficulties in buying gifts for their fathers; B then introduces the idea of going home for Christmas.

> **Example 26** 031-033 **K:** I don't think my dad would be hurt. Cuz he really doesn't he- enjoys - Christmas and birthdays - just - as a family activity. [B: Um hmm] And he's ra- uh rather give (pause) But (pause) it's just not the same. ((pause))
>
> 034 **B:** Are you going home for Christmas?

These two utterances are linked because of culturally shared knowledge about the holidays. The Christmas script involves buying gifts for relatives and going to visit them. However, this is not the only linkage operating. The two utterances are linked by repetition of a common idea (Christmas) and, if one looks even further back in the conversation, by the use of a metatopic linking Thanksgiving as a holiday to Christmas.

This points to one of the central complexities of ordinary conversation. With a single remark links can be forged with multiple parts of the conversation. This is even better illustrated in lines 85-103 of the transcript. K has been talking about her friend who will be going to Switzerland to ski over Christmas and comments how hard he has been working to earn money to go. B responds by telling a story about her stepbrother's opportunities to ski in Switzerland. If we view B's remark solely in light of K's immediately prior utterance, we would say that the remark establishes relevancy by extending a minor part of K's event (skiing in Switzerland) rather than K's issue (her interesting friend) However, if we go back further in the discourse, B's remark appears more competent. It can, in fact, be seen as returning to her immediately earlier issue (her family), which K changed by linking to B's event (experiences in Switzerland).

K and B appeared to use the strategy of continuing the old topic with no attempt to introduce the new one. However, since we lack knowledge of K and B's topic goals it is difficult to assign any particular response to this category; just about all utterances involve a certain degree of topic shift. Whether the intent of the speaker is to respond in an interesting and attentive way to the speaker's old topic or to shift the conversational focus to his or her own "new" preferred topic is difficult to ascertain without knowledge of the interactants' goals. Perhaps of more interest is the almost complete absence of utterances that unequivocally close off the old topic to introduce the new. The closest example of this strategy is seen in the middle of turn 308. K, in response to B's statement about skating, responds briefly about skating and then says, "I don't really know! When I have free time I ski. I don't even think of anything else." While K's, "I don't really know" does act to close off B's topic of skating, the rest of the response acts to soften this move by linking the newly introduced topic (skiing) with skating.

The concepts developed and refined in the experimental situation have helped us understand the B-K conversation. By no means, however, is the influence process one-way. Study of the B-K conversation suggests directions for theoretical development and empirical research.

Implications for Theoretical Development
Suggested by the B-K Conversation

Study of the B-K transcript suggests three issues that need consideration. First, this ordinary conversation makes salient the importance of the larger discourse context. The experimental research treated each message as the initiating one in interaction; the role of all prior discourse except the immediately preceding utterance was ignored. While the immediately preceding utterance may be the most important in determining the next utterance's relevance, it is likely that the relationship of that utterance with other parts of the discourse also has an impact. Thus it may be possible for an utterance with a moderate degree of relevance to the immediately preceding comment but many connections with earlier sections of the discourse, to be a much more relevant comment than one with a slightly higher degree of relevance to the immediately preceding comment.

Second, the main thrust of the experimental research has been study of one conversational form — the issue-event structure. While it is true that the B-K conversation shows numerous examples of this form, it is also true that a good portion of the discourse does not use this form. Hence conclusions about relevancy must be limited to this one form which characterizes only part of the conversation. A theoretical move that would deal with this problem is to treat the issue-event structure as one specific way to identify the main point in discourse. Other structures would signal the speaker's main point in different discourse types. A job of future research, then would be specifying these structures, or to put it another way, specifying the mechanisms speakers use to cue and listeners use to interpret the main point.

A third point suggested by study of the B-K conversation is the complex relationship among communicator goals, conversational behavior, and assessments of individuals' conversational skill. If, in the course of a conversation, communicators are trying to make their remarks relevant, be attentive to the partner, and talk about topics of particular interest to themselves, it seems probable that the importance of relevance as a goal will vary. Thus it may be the case that at least in certain situations, as long as a person's comment meets some minimal standard of relevance, the assessment of his or her communicative effectiveness will hinge on successful attainment of the other goals salient in the situation.

CONCLUSION

At the outset we posed the question, "What counts as relevancy in conversation?" Four experiments were reviewed that addressed this question in conversations that had an issue-event structure. Results indicated that extensions of the conversational issue were generally more relevant than extensions of the event, that the comprehensibility of a speaker influences the strength of this preference, and communicators whose primary goal is introduction of a new topic will be less successful in linking to the issue than those whose primary goal is attention to the speaker. Three strategy types were identified that communicators use to deal with competing goals.

The second part of the chapter applied the theoretical concepts developed in the experimental setting to the B-K conversation, suggested possible modifications of the theoretical framework, and showed how the B-K conversation illuminated directions for future research and possible modifications of the theoretical framework. Too frequently researchers identify either with a naturalistic-qualitative perspective or an experimental-quantitative one and dismiss the value of the other. This chapter illustrates how the two perspectives can be used in a complementary manner to enrich our understanding of conversational behavior.

<<<<<<<<<<<<< >>>>>>>>>>>>

7

Topic Shifts in
Couples' Conversations

<< BRYAN K. CROW >>

<<< Every conversation can be analyzed pragmati- >>>
cally as a text situated within a context. Conversational *texts* are
typically analyzed at one of three levels: act, sequence, or episode.
The *conversational act,* verbal or nonverbal-vocal, is the minimal
pragmatic unit, ranging in length from one word ("Hi!") to a long and
complex sentence.[1] Participants in a conversation choose not only
the informational content of their acts but also pragmatic strategies
for communicating the content in ways most appropriate to the communicative context and most likely to achieve intended responses.
Conversational pragmatics encompasses choices made by the participants in placing a conversational act in an ongoing string of talk (its
pragmatic *form*), in maintaining or shifting the *topic* that is on the
floor, and in performing certain pragmatic *functions* through the construction of conversational acts. When two or more consecutive
conversational acts (either by the same person or by different
speakers) exhibit contingencies in form, topic, or function, they constitute a *conversational sequence. Conversational episodes* are constructed as participants coordinate a common topic through two or
more consecutive sequences of conversational acts. The conversational *context* includes a *social frame* within which a text is constructed (while eating in a restaurant, talking on the telephone, being
interviewed, etc.) and a *relational frame* that participants bring to a

conversation if they have expectations based on prior interaction with each other.

When a conversation lasts longer than one sequence, it generally consists of coherent topical talk (Donaldson, 1979). If talk is non-coherent and nontopical, we might hesitate to call it conversation if we define conversation as collaborative work toward the construction of a coherent communicative text (Speier, 1973). Coherence and topicality, even if not always achieved, must be desired before conversation can even take place. As a conversational text is being constructed, participants must attend to the formulation, mainte-nance, and shifting of topics in order to avoid random conversational behavior. Participants' normally routine accomplishment of topical coherence by attending to these pragmatic problems is a matter of central interest in a theory of conversational pragmatics.

Researchers in diverse fields have studied topical coherence in one way or another, but, as Hurtig (1977) reports, there is no fully articulated theory of topics. Reichman (1978) offers perhaps the most advanced theoretical treatment to date of conversational coherency. She uses the term "context space" to describe the topical relationship between a group of utterances. An *active* context space is used to interpret the topic under discussion at a given point in a conversation; an *open* context space is one concerning an unfinished topic that may become active again; and a *closed* context space circumscribes a topic that has been fully discussed. Topic shifts, then, involve the transition from one context space to another. Reichman summarizes the theory as follows:

> As a conversation proceeds, each conversant builds a discourse model that includes the conversation's context space structure, a notion of the present discourse topic, and a list of items being focused upon. Conversational coherency depends upon a lack of conflict between the respective models of the participants [1978, p. 283].

Defining "topic" with any greater specificity than "what a conver-sation is *about* at any given moment" usually entails focusing on topic boundaries and shifts. Hurtig (1977, p. 95), for example, develops a formal logic of topics based on the premise that a topic can be reduced to one or more related propositions. Once one propositional set or idea is established in the construction of a conversation, subsequent topics may be defined in relation to it. The original propositional set may be expanded to include new propositions, in which case it may be difficult to say whether the topic has changed or has simply diffused. When a new propositional set is constructed that has no logical links with an antecedent set, the shift in topics is easier to isolate. Nothing is inherent to the definition of a topic, however, that states how widely or narrowly a topic may range. Thus the need for a typology of topic shifts arises.

Various types of topical moves have been documented in studies of conversation, and several studies have formulated fairly complete typologies (Keenan & Schieffelin, 1976; Planalp & Tracy, 1980; Reichman, 1978; Vuchinich, 1977). The purpose of this chapter is to synthesize and revise these typologies in order to describe the accomplishment of topical coherence in a particular relational frame: ✓ that of the intimate couple, conversing spontaneously in the social frame of their home.

PROCEDURE

The decision to focus on pragmatic resources of intimate couples was based on several considerations. For one, dyadic interactions present fewer transcription problems than interactions between three or more people, in terms of assigning utterances to the right speaker and sorting out what was said in cases of overlapped utterances. The conversations of intimate couples, speaking spontaneously and at length in their own homes, are a largely untapped (and untaped) resource for conversation analysis, despite their inherent claim to typicality. Most analyses to date have drawn upon data obtained in a laboratory or therapeutic setting (Gottman, 1979; Mishler & Waxler, 1968; Rogers-Millar & Millar, 1979). Conversational topics were supplied or prompted by the researchers and recording was done in the lab or in the home with a researcher present. Relatively little systematic attention has been directed to perhaps the most common and critical interpersonal occurrence — everyday talk between intimate couples. The couple can be viewed, in fact, as the institution in which conversation as a system reaches its fruition: Couples are formed in part to assure oneself a conversational partner with whom to develop a wealth of episodes, and conversation serves as a primary means of developing and enriching a relationship. If a couple's conversational episodes become banal or unproductive, or even fail to achieve episodic stature, the relationship will no doubt suffer.

Recent studies of communication in intimate relationships (Fitzpatrick & Indvik, 1982; Gottman, 1979) stress the importance of a pretheoretical *descriptive* phase of investigation. Gottman (1979) in particular defines theory as "explaining patterns in well-described phenomena" (p. 292). Descriptive categories should be grounded in naturally occurring discourse, which makes it important that we work from a large and diverse data base in building and testing models of conversation.

In order to obtain a sample of conversations as representative as possible of those that couples normally have on their own, the following method was developed. Couples (anyone who defined themselves as such) were solicited through an ad in a weekly shopper newspaper in a Midwestern university town. After initial telephone interviews with over 25 volunteers, five couples were selected for the study. Criteria for inclusion were (1) that the couple had been living together for at least six months, and (2) that they reported frequently engaging in topically focused conversations of 30 minutes or longer. The five couples selected were all in a low-income bracket (average combined annual income = $10,700), young (average age for males = 30, females = 28), and well educated (average = four years of college). Each couple agreed to keep a tape recorder in their home for two weeks and to turn it on whenever they felt that they were likely to carry on a conversation for at least 30 minutes. Each couple was given six tapes lasting 45 minutes each, and they were encouraged to fill up as much of each tape as possible with a different conversation on different days.

Participants were given control over the conversational recording for methodological and ethical reasons. Methodologically, this procedure was expected to be superior to lab recordings, interviews, and conversation prompting in eliciting conversations typical of those the couples normally engage in when they are not being recorded. All five couples reported that once they got involved in a conversation, they tended to forget about the tape recorder's presence and were not conscious of any constraints it imposed upon their talk. Ethically, the advantage is that no invasion of privacy can be claimed. If participants find that a conversation reveals more about their private lives than they had intended, they simply erase the tape and record another one.

For purposes of analysis, only the last three conversations recorded by each couple were transcribed, on the assumption that the tape recorder's presence would become less noticeable or obtrusive with repeated use.[2] Fifteen conversations, ranging from 24 to 45 minutes and totalling about 10 hours, were transcribed following the notational system developed by Sacks and his associates (see Schenkein, 1978). Initially the transcripts were unitized according to two criteria: speaker change and pauses at the end of syntactic clauses within one speaker's turn. Typologies for coding form, topic, and function of conversational acts were then developed, drawing from previous research those categories that were applicable to the data and generating new categories that were not adequately accounted for by previous research. The categorization schemes were then used to further isolate pragmatic units *within* a speaker's turn, resulting in a total of 20,116 conversational acts. Applying these procedures to the B-K conversation (Appendix, this volume), for example, turn 228 would be unitized into two acts. The first, "there's little brooks, and bridges, and - all sorts of fun things" is nonoverlapping and incomplete in form (it concludes the sentence initiated in K's previous turn), it maintains the prior topic, and it functions as elaboration on the previous information. The second act, "Did you grow up in Philadelphia," is nonoverlapping and complete in form, shifts the topic from K's home to B's background, and functions to elicit information from B.

The topical analyses are presented below in two sections. First, the typology for coding topic shifts will be discussed and illustrated with examples from the data as well as from the B-K conversation. Then, frequencies of each type of shift will be reported so that patterns within and across couples may be observed, and formal and functional aspects of topic-shifting acts noted.

TYPOLOGY

In the typology offered here, the emphasis is on topic *shifting* as the pragmatic resource of primary interest. Once topical talk is under way, no distinction is made in the coding as to different ways in which the topic is maintained. Every conversational act can be said to belong to one topic or another, even if the act is nothing more than a buffer or a pause. But only some acts perform topic shifts, and those are the acts that the typology attempts to isolate and differentiate from one another. Once a topic is on the floor — once both partners begin to talk about the same general body of content — the topic determines the coherence of subsequent acts. After a brief discussion of topic maintaining devices, four types of shifts will be presented: coherent shift, renewal, noncoherent shift, and insert.

Maintaining

Acts that maintain or terminate an established topic are categorized together since they involve no topic shift. Once a topic has the floor, all acts that fall within the range of the conversation occupied by that topic may be coded as contributing to the maintenance of the topic. Topic maintenance is the norm for most acts of a conversation. One utterance about a topic is usually followed by a coherent and relevant utterance about the same topic, either by the same person or by the partner, in what Keenan and Schieffelin (1976) call "topic-collaborating sequences." Consecutive utterances may be linked semantically by maintaining a common referent (A: "I think I might take a bath this morning." B: "I took one last night."); they may be linked lexically or syntactically by such devices as ellipsis (A: "Why don't you write a letter to Brendan?" B: "Why don't *you*?"), conjunction (A: "We have two like that don't we?" B: "Mm hm." A: "And one's smaller a bit."), repetition (A: "It's inevitable it's gonna happen to you sometime though." B: "What's gonna happen to you sometime?"), and pronominalization ("Reagan is probably making himself unpopular with a lot of the people who voted for him now because of his decontrolling of the oil industry. He *said* he was gonna *do* it, . . . "); and they may be linked pragmatically by sequential implicature (A: "She wants a key to the house?" B: "Mm hm." A: "Really?"). Vuchinich (1977), Reichman (1978), and Halliday and Hasan (1976) discuss topic maintenance in greater detail than the scope of the present chapter allows.

Coherent Shift

The structurally preferred mechanism for topic change within a conversation is the coherent shift. Coherent shifts include acts of initiation and shading, and they are often marked explicitly by topic-bounding devices (Schegloff & Sacks, 1973) or transition markers. *Topic initiation* is an attempt to introduce a new topic either at the beginning of a conversation, after a prior topic has been apparently terminated, or after a period of nontopical talk ("drift") or silence. Topic initiation has elsewhere been referred to as "introducing discourse topics" (Keenan & Schieffelin, 1976) and, when the initiation is prompted by information available from the participants' social or physical environment, "environmental topic change" (Planalp & Tracy, 1980). We find an example of a conventional conversation-opening topic initiation in turn 2 of the B-K conversation: "So how are you doing?"

The transition to a new topic may be signalled by using one of a relatively small number of *pre-acts* that function as topic-bounding devices, in which case the pre-act should be considered the act that performs the topic shift since it is no longer part of the prior topic. Conventional bounding devices include "Oh say," "I tell you what,"

"One more thing," "Listen, there's something I've gotta tell you," "You know what?" "Before I forget," "By the way," "Incidentally." Such acts have also been referred to as "disjunct markers" (Jefferson, 1978), "clue word shifts" (Reichman, 1978), and "explicit topic changes" (Planalp & Tracy, 1980). Address terms are also used as pre-acts for topic initiation, as in turn 17 of the B-K conversation: "*K, what are you giving people for Christmas this year?*"

The more common form of the coherent topical shift is *topic shading,* which introduces a new topic by first establishing its relevance to or connection with the topic that has been on the floor. The new topic may be quite closely related to the prior one, particularly if it maintains the same characters, situations, feelings, ideas, or other salient features. In such cases even though the conversation has simply shifted to a different aspect or subtopic of the same topic, the introduction of the new aspect is still coded as a coherent shift. For example, one person may be telling a story about how a co-worker, Mary, was mistreated at the office. When the partner asks, "Have I ever met Mary?" and the conversation turns from the story to a description of Mary, a minimal sort of shift has occurred in the focus of the conversation, and it takes the form of a topical shading. Topic shading accomplishes what Schegloff and Sacks (1973) call "fitting" of a new topic to prior talk, allowing a prior topic to serve as a sufficient source for raising a new topic that will be perceived as relevant to the first. One topic blends into another. Topic shading has also been referred to as "topic-incorporating sequence" (Keenan & Schieffelin, 1976) and "immediate topic change" (Planalp & Tracy, 1980).

Goodenough and Weiner (1978) call topic shading an "inefficient" practice because the first speaker may not have finished with the prior topic. They state, "To be efficient and responsive to a partner's wishes we assume that a speaker will not shift topics unless she understands that her partner has completed her turns on the topic" (p. 396). As a maxim for an ideal speech situation, this assumption may be appropriate, but it does not adequately reflect the unproblematic routineness with which participants actually move from one aspect of a topic to another. Goodenough and Weiner (1978) argue that clearly marked topic boundaries are preferable to shading, and that the use of such markers may facilitate the processing of conversational information. In fact, topic shading often does employ topic-bounding devices, the most common of which are, "Speaking of X," and "That reminds me, . . . " Jefferson (1978) refers to these markers as "embedded repetitions" that locate a prior item as the trigger for a next item, and she reports that the person who uses the embedded repetition will usually wait until the prior utterance is completed to avoid overlap. In the B-K conversation, topic shading is overtly marked twice: once in the standard pre-act form in turn 85 ("Speaking of Switzerland,") and once as a post-act in turn 166 ("Have you heard anything about your internship. Speaking of practical."). Whether the coherent topic shift takes the form of initiation or shading, it will not occasion a request for topical coherence clarification — that is, will not be challenged by such statements as, "I'm not sure what that has to do with anything."

The four following examples from the couples' conversations show topic shifts in roughly decreasing order of coherence.[3]

Example 1
  ⟶**M:** I tell you what love, if we eat any more of those potato chips, I won't be able to eat my dinner
    F: Yeah, no more

Example 1 illustrates the most straightforward type of topic initiation. M's utterance comes after a three-second silence that had followed the closing of the previous topic. He initiates a new topic by using a pre-act ("I tell you what") and an address term ("love"). F's response indicates that M has succeeded in establishing a new topic.

Example 2
    M: And there was something so incredibly strange about that place, y'know
    F: Uh huh
        [[
    M: Here's some guy singing ((sings)) "Tiny bubbles, in the wa-" y'know it was just so incredibly - strange sitting out there in the middle of the water
⟶**F :** Speaking of that I heard a strange song today that I haven't heard since I was a little kid and used to listen to Arthur Godfrey on the radio with my mother
        [
    M: Oh yeah

In Example 2, F uses the standard bounding device to indicate topic shading, but her shift is only semicoherent. The referent in "speaking of that" is ambiguous. Normally, "that" would apply to the prior topic as a whole — in this case, a singer in an Italian restaurant where the couple once ate. The actual link between the two topics, though, is the idea of a song and, more specifically, the notion that the song or the singing was strange. Otherwise, the song that she goes on to talk about has nothing in common with "Tiny Bubbles" (unless perhaps Arthur Godfrey sang both of them).

Example 3   M: I gotta go to community auction, - check it out
             F: And may- maybe I'll go with you
             M: Mm hm, then we'd just walk down
                 Don't take our purse or wallets along
             F: heh
        →   *That* Henry, I-
                 I don't know, I think he - maybe did take my purse, y'know
             M: Mm *hm*

The female in Example 3 performs a subtle topic shade, from plans about the auction to characterization of one of the auction workers. M's suggestion that they not take a purse or wallet along is clearly intended as a reference to what happened to F's purse the last time they went to the auction, and F goes on to indicate her uptake of M's implicit reference. The syntax of her final utterance is evidence that this is a topic that is being renewed from an earlier conversation.

Example 4   F: Well, -
                 (4.0)
        →   I just hope Pat handled it alright
             M: Oh, the card reminds you of Pat
             F: Mm hm, - yeah
        → M: That is *such* a beautiful card
             F: I love it it's my favorite one

Example 4 follows a 7.8-second lull in the conversation. F uses a buffer ("Well"), which may be seen as signaling a topic initiation, although buffers themselves are not coded as performing topic shifts. Her next utterance initiates a new topic, which must be a renewal of a topic from an earlier conversation; but the initiation apparently was momentarily puzzling for M, who signals his resolution of the puzzle by clarifying the trigger of F's initiation — an environmental cue. After receiving confirmation of his hypothesis, M shades into the topic of the card itself instead of maintaining F's intended topic of Pat. F lets her topic drop and both partners continue talking about the card, perhaps to relieve the tension due to uncertainty about Pat.

Renewal

A shift back to an earlier topic after one or more other topics or topic-shifting attempts have intervened is defined as a renewal of the earlier topic. The renewal has properties of both coherent and non-coherent topic shifts. Without the nonimmediately prior context, a renewal might appear to be a noncoherent shift away from the immediately prior topic. But if the renewal secures the topical floor for the renewed topic, we can assume that it has been understood by the partner as a coherent return to a previous topic. Schank (1977) refers to the intraconversational looping back to a previous topic as a "topic pop," which he says is often triggered by a lull in the conversation or by the dullness of the immediately prior topic, and which is often marked syntactically. Renewals have also been called "re-introducing discourse topic" (Keenan & Schieffelin, 1976) and "earlier topic change" (Planalp & Tracy, 1980). Renewal may be marked by a pre-act that gets the conversation back on topic, usually in the form of "Anyway," "Like I told you," or "Getting back to the subject, . . . " In Reichman's (1978) terms, such markers signal a return to an interrupted context space. If there is a break in the conversation, a topic may be renewed by the use of "reorientation markers," such as, "As I was saying," and, "Now, where were we?" (Speier, 1973). Renewal may also be marked by a pre-act that signals the return to a prior topic ("Oh, one more thing about tomorrow").

If a turn is not topically coherent, the partner may choose to terminate the prior topic or to maintain it. If the previous topic "rides" over the noncoherent turn (Vuchinich, 1977), in effect ignoring it, the initial act of continuation is considered a renewal. The same holds for what Vuchinich (1977) calls a "contribute," when the noncoherent turn is incorporated into the previous topic reference and becomes understood as a contribution to it, even if it was not intended as such. A renewal may be unsuccessful in holding the floor for more than one turn if it is immediately followed by a topic shift by the partner. But as long as the attempted shift by the first person can be linked with some prior topic, it is still coded as a renewal. Two examples are offered from the data.

Example 5	F :	Want some tea?
	M:	Ahhhh I think I've got enough for now
		Maybe in a little bit
→F :		No, I don't have any plans
	M:	Oh, (I forgot that was)

In this excerpt, F's second utterance appears incongruous unless it is perceived as a renewal. The original initiation of the topic had occurred before the tape began. M's response indicates that he has solved the temporary puzzle created by F's answer to an apparently unasked question.

Example 6   M: I said I'd never *do* that, I'm *say*ing though, I'm
saying I've had all kinds o' opportunities 'n I've
never *done* it, that's what I was *say*ing
Y'know

→ **F:**   What were we talking about before this?

M: What
Before what

F :   Before this
I can't remember
Oh, oh, oh, nothing
Mm
I had the same boyfriend from first grade to sixth
grade

[   ]

M: Oh

Example 6 starts with the conclusion of a conflict episode having to do
with the possibility of M cheating on F. After a brief latency, F renews
a slot for the preconflict topic, even though she has forgotten the
content of the topic. After a metacommunicative side sequence, she
finally signals recall and then completes the renewal of the prior topic
— childhood relationships — a safer version of the conflictful topic of
potential relationships.

Renewal undoubtedly occurs across conversations as well, requiring more explicit marking than it would within a conversation. For
example, in the B-K conversation, K uses a pre-act in turn 53 to renew
the topic of an earlier conversation: "*I meant to ask you the other day,*
are you flying down?" Had she omitted the pre-act, no shift would
have been involved. The pre-act is useful, though, in signalling K's
recall of the earlier discussion of B's flying to Florida. B's response in
turn 54 ("Um hmm, and I hate planes") demonstrates less competent
recall of the earlier conversation, reiterating information that K already knew, as K is quick to point out in turn 55 ("I:: know you said
that"). In long-term relationships, we might expect even more inter-
conversational topic renewals, and we might find that there is less
need to mark the renewals with pre-acts.

Noncoherent Shift

An abrupt shift that succeeds in gaining the topical floor is coded
as a noncoherent shift. The abruptness of the shift is usually due to its
not being marked for initiation, shading, or renewal, or to its noncoherent use of a topic-bounding device. Such shifts may occur at any
point — in the middle of topical talk by the partner, immediately after

a coherent topic-maintaining act by oneself, and so on. The coherence of the shift may be challenged by the partner, but in any case the partner drops the prior topic and takes up the new one. Even if coherence is not challenged, a shift is still considered noncoherent from the analyst's viewpoint if, looking at the sequential development of the conversation, the new topic bears no identifiable propositional relationship to any prior topic (and is not a postsilence or postdrift topic initiation). Vuchinich (1977) refers to such shifts, in which the noncoherent turn is allowed to be the new topic and the old topic is dropped, as a "focus." Planalp and Tracy (1980) refer to both marked and unmarked noncoherent shifts as "unspecified topic changes." As an example of a marked noncoherent shift, Planalp and Tracy (1980) offer the conventional pre-act, "Not to change the subject, but . . . ," which licenses the speaker to go ahead and change the subject anyway. An equivalent but more honest marker is "This is off the subject, but. . . . " Keenan and Schieffelin's (1976) category "introducing discourse topic" applies to noncoherent as well as coherent shifts since the authors make no distinction between the two. As in the other topical categories, only the first act of a noncoherent topic shift is coded as a shift, since subsequent acts then maintain the new topic or eventually shift again to other topics.

In the first example below, the noncoherent shift is followed six acts later by a renewal of the previous topic.

Example 7 **F :** And they were telling about a show - - uh, a new
movie with - about a guy who - was in Howard
Hughes's will or something (2.0)
Just an ordinary . . . -
[
→ **M:** Did *you* wanta cut your hair?
And make it look short
F : I wasn't planning to but I feel like it
M: Oh::!, I think you (   ), not letting it - letting it
down in the wash
[
F : I *might* after a while
(2.6)
→ Are you interested in this?
M: Oh in what they said? *oh* yeah
F : They s- the- both of them thought it was a great movie

Example 7 illustrates a phenomenon often associated with renewal: *persistence* in trying to gain the topical floor. This couple exhibits a very regular pattern in which the male cuts short the female's attempts to get him onto her topic, and then she persists until her topic is eventually acknowledged. His resistance appears to be not so much a function of domineeringness but simply of not being able to keep his attention focused for very long in a casual conversation. Her persistence in trying to gain the floor seems to take this into account because her frustration never turns into anger toward him for cutting her off. His noncoherent shift in this case was probably prompted by the feeling that her recounting of the film review did not seem to be going anywhere. Once she renews the recounting, he renews his apparent interest.

The next excerpt occurred five minutes after M had talked about an auction that he and Dave had attended. Several other topics were raised in the meantime, culminating in a discussion about getting distilled water from a food co-op.

> **Example 8** **F :** I wish you'd find one of those um - dis- *water*
> dispensers thrown away sometime boy *that*'d be
> pretty handy
> → **M:** heheh Dave bought this mo- - speaking of uh water
> dispensers Dave bought this Model T uh luggage
> rack?
> He was -
> [[
> **F :** That's what he told me

M's utterance steers the conversation back to the general topic of the auction, although the specific topic of Dave's luggage rack is not a renewal of any previous discussion of the rack. M marks the shift, after an incomplete unmarked version of the same act, with a topic-bounding device to indicate coherent shading. But the new topic has nothing to do with the prior topic of water dispensers, and so it is coded as a noncoherent shift. The only possible connection between the two is that both objects belong to the class of things that can be salvaged after they have been thrown away, but M's "speaking of water dispensers" in no way clarifies the relationship. This may be a case in which he is simply using the marker out of habit, as a way of getting the floor that usually will not evoke a request for coherence clarification.

Insert

An abrupt shift that does not succeed in gaining the topical floor is defined as an insert. Inserts literally appear to be inserted into the transcript of an ongoing topical conversation, with no pre-act to mark their disjunctiveness. For example, husband says, "Well it's time to go to bed." Wife does not respond. Husband then says, "This is a pretty thick book," and both partners talk about the book for several turns. The husband's first utterance is considered an insert because it failed to gain any response from the wife. His second utterance is a within-turn topic intiation. Even if he had followed his first act with one or more acts on the inserted topic ("I'm sleepy. I had a long day."), his topic-shifting attempt would still be considered an insert because his partner's next act ignores the attempted topic shift. Nothing distinguishes an insert from a noncoherent shift when the acts are viewed in isolation. The coding decision must be determined by the topical allegiance of subsequent acts.

Inserts are routinely placed within one person's turn at talk without disrupting the ongoing topical talk, as in the following examples.

Example 9	**M:**	So seven years ago he left - the priesthood -
→		*I'll* have one of those
→		and came back
Example 10	**F:**	It's up to *you,* whatever you feel comfortable with
	M:	Well I don't feel comfortable with=
→		=*Oh* no more milk ((opening refrigerator))
→**F:**		Then what're you gonna *do* it for?

In both cases, the second shift is an immediate renewal of the prior topic. The conversational system seems to be able to sustain such minor interruptions without the need for reorientation markers after the insert, particularly when the insert accompanies some action that is going on concurrently with the conversation.

The topic of the insert may be related in some way to the topic that was on the floor and that rides over the insert. In such cases the attempted shift could arguably be called unsuccessful topic shading. The following rule of thumb is offered to clarify the distinction between the two: If the attempted topic is successfully renewed two or more acts later, the attempt is coded as a coherent shift (shading). If the attempted topic is not subsequently renewed, it is coded as an insert. The following excerpt shows an example of the latter case. The excerpt contains three shifts: a noncoherent shift, an insert, and an immediate renewal of the pre-insert topic.

Example 11	**M:**	Well, I don't think if he made that much money he'd
		work that *hard*

➤ F: How does my hair look?
        Looks better, doesn't it?

M: Uh huh

F: I got it trimmed out
        Took her a *hour*
        An *hour*
        [[

M: Gee
        What'd she do, each hair individually?

F: First she took - me back and washed my hair,
        y'know?

M: Mm hm

F: Which *feels* great, 'cause they have a wonderful kind
        of massage that they do, y'know when
        they - wash your hair
        [   ]

M: Uh *huh*

F: It's *just* so nice to get your hair washed by somebody
        I don't know how they - - y'know, just kinda

➤ M: *I* went to a professional barber in 1969 when I went
        to work for my father
                  [   ]   [   ]

F: (   )
        And *then* they rinse it and put - they wash
        she washed it twice and then she put - a rinse on it,
        creme rinse on it

M's first utterance here is the final maintaining act of the prior topic, which had to do with the auction that he had attended the night before and one of the auctioneers in particular. This topic had occupied much of the first fifteen minutes of the conversation. Since F did not attend the auction, it is to be expected that she would eventually tire of hearing all about it, and what she does here is shift noncoherently to her *own* story about an experience that *he* had not participated in, thereby claiming equal floor time for herself. He attempts to grab a piece of the topic for himself by talking about *his* trip to the barber, but she overrides and overlaps his insert, and he never renews the story of his experience. Her continuation is coded as a renewal. If she had commented on his statement or asked questions about his experience, his act would be coded as a coherent shift (shade) instead of an insert.

RESULTS

Coding reliability was measured for two separate processes: unitizing and categorizing of topic shifts. Three coders trained in the typology listened to a tape of one conversation and unitized a transcript of the tape according to topic shifts. Unitizing reliability was calculated as the number of agreements between researcher and coder divided by the number of agreements plus omission errors plus commission errors. Errors of omission are instances in which a coder did not count as a topic shift an act that the researcher had originally counted as one, while errors of commission are acts that were considered shifts by a coder but not by the researcher. The average intercoder unitizing reliability was .50, ranging from .44 to .58 as each coder's units were compared with those of the researcher. Once they had unitized the transcripts, the coders were told which acts in the same conversation were considered topic shifts by the researcher, and they categorized these preunitized acts using the typology. Categorizing reliability was calculated as the number of agreements between coder and researcher divided by the number of agreements plus disagreements. Average intercoder categorizing reliability was .78, ranging from .73 to .85.

The lower reliability for unitizing is an indication of the difficulty of establishing satisfactory rules for identification of topic shifts. It is clear that no two people will hear a conversation in the same way, and what sounds like a topic shade to one coder might be considered topic maintenance by another. These coders tended to punctuate the transcript more finely than the researcher had done — their errors of commission more than doubled their errors of omission. However, the higher figures for categorizing reliability indicate that, given more clearcut unitizing rules, the typology can be used reliably.

Table 7.1 reports the frequencies of topic shifts for each conversation, the overall frequencies of each type of shift, the mean number of topic shifts per couple, and the mean number of conversational acts per minute (topic-shifting as well as topic-maintaining) for each conversation. Nearly 60 percent of the observed shifts were coded as coherent shifts, 23 percent were renewals, 12 percent noncoherent shifts, and only 5 percent inserts. A distribution of this sort is to be expected for conversations which, on the surface, appear to be largely coherent to the observer and would probably be reported as coherent by the participants.

The couples differed to some extent in their tendency to use certain shifts. The most obvious case is couple 3's use of inserts, which accounts for over 40 percent of all observed inserts. A breakdown by gender reveals that the male in couple 3 contributed 11 of the 13 inserts. Similarly, in couple 5, the male contributed 9 of the 10 inserts. In each case the number of inserts is probably not so much a sign of the male's lack of competence at gaining the topical floor (in fact, the males in couples 3 and 5 contributed more coherent shifts

TABLE 7.1 Frequencies of Topic Shifts

Couple and Conversation Number	Maintaining	Coherent Shift	Renewal	Noncoherent Shift	Insert	Shifts per Conv.	$\bar{X}$ Shifts per Couple	$\bar{X}$ Acts per Minute
Couple 1								
Conv. 2	2003	27	5	2	0	34	26.0	45.3
Conv. 4	1658	6	8	5	2	21		37.3
Conv. 6	903	19	3	1	0	23		38.5
Couple 2								
Conv. 4	1237	33	3	16	2	54	49.7	31.5
Conv. 5	1562	46	9	3	0	58		36.0
Conv. 6	918	28	7	2	0	37		35.4
Couple 3								
Conv. 6	1718	42	17	10	7	76	72.3	39.9
Conv. 7	1219	46	11	8	2	67		36.7
Conv. 8	1612	40	19	11	4	74		37.5
Couple 4								
Conv. 4	1145	18	13	6	5	42	37.3	26.4
Conv. 5	836	17	10	2	0	29		19.2
Conv. 6	1105	25	11	4	1	41		25.7
Couple 5								
Conv. 4	1078	27	10	5	1	43	53.7	38.7
Conv. 5	1087	31	29	7	2	69		38.5
Conv. 6	1318	24	15	3	7	49		40.2
Total	19399	429	170	85	33	717		
Percentage of total	96.4	2.1	0.8	0.4	0.2			

than did their partners) as it is a sign of the female's intolerance of an attempted topic change in the middle of an ongoing topic. Couple 3 had a much higher mean for topic shifts in general than any other couple. Since the conversations varied in length, and since the number of acts per conversation ranged from 926 to 2037, it is reasonable to expect that the number of topic shifts in a conversation is a function of the mean number of acts per minute. Within each couple's set of conversations this generally holds true. But comparing across couples, the conversations with the highest means for acts per minute are not at all those with the greatest number of topic shifts (r = .24). The lack of a clear relationship may be due to the nature of the particular conversation — its tendency toward topic stability versus topic drift — as well as the nature of the couple and their communication style. In general, the longer the couple has been together, the more topic shifts they perform in their conversations (Spearman r_s = .87). This may be an indication that more recently formed couples are working harder to maintain each other's topics, while couples with a longer shared past have worked through more topics together and require less careful monitoring in renewing them.

Since each act was coded for form and function as well as topic, it is possible to describe acts that performed topic shifts in more detail. Most topic shifts (79 percent) occurred in the form of nonoverlapping complete acts. Very few shifts were performed in the process of overlapping the prior speaker. When an overlap *was* a successful topic shift, it was almost always syntactically complete and held the floor after the point at which the prior speaker stopped talking. The functions or "illocutionary forces" of topic-shifting acts were most often assertions (23 percent), information elicitations (15 percent), pre-acts (13 percent), recountings of past events (11 percent), and predictions of future events (10 percent). Most topic-shifting *assertions* performed coherent shifts, most likely as topic shades since initiation often requires the more overt marking made possible through pre-acts. For example, after a discussion of problems with their freezer, M says, "I can't believe ice cream has not gone on sale," an assertion that shades into a new but related topic. The majority of topic-shifting *pre-acts* were used coherently to initiate, shade, or renew a topic (see Examples 1 and 2). Only in six cases were pre-acts used noncoherently, at least from the point of view of an observer who is limited to the contextual information available from within the conversation (see Example 8). *Eliciting information* is also a standard way to perform a coherent shift, since a question or an invitation to speak about a new or related topic is relevant at any point at which it may occur to a participant in a conversation, as in, "Well, did you have a good day today?" (In the B-K conversation, 15 of the 36 topic shifts functioned to elicit information, which is not surprising given the context.) New topics may also be initiated by *recounting* a past event ("I went to the Psych library today, and . . . ") or *predicting* a future state ("We could have a giant family and everything, you know?"). In both cases, the shift in the temporal frame of the conversation from here and now to then and there almost inevitably performs a topic shift.

CONCLUSION

Six main points may be drawn from this study. First, for these five couples, topic shifts were fairly frequent (one every 48 seconds, on the average), and were largely coherent. All five couples reported that they were moderately to extremely happy with their relationship and perceived it to be extremely strong, communicative, and involved in comparison with other couples they knew. It is tempting to conclude that topical coherence is symptomatic of a healthy relationship, but such a conclusion is unwarranted. Conversational samples from distressed couples might exhibit even greater topical coherence, particularly if the whole conversation is focused on one arguable issue. Lack of topical coherence may be more a sign of relational neutrality than relational distress. Still, the study of conversational features, particularly in longitudinal samples, has much to tell us about relationship initiation, maintenance, and dissolution.

Second, a number of methodological issues in conversation analysis have been highlighted by this study. The procedure for acquiring tapes of naturally occurring conversations was found to be quite useful, and from follow-up interviews with the couples it seemed to be unobtrusive. The use of more than one conversation from each set of participants allows for greater understanding of idiosyncratic patterns within each relational frame. The study's recognition of topic shifts *within* turns as well as between turns points up the advantages of treating the conversational act as the unit of analysis, instead of using the entire turn at talk as the unit.

Third, in defining topic shifts relationally instead of at the individual level, this study emphasizes the dimension of *success* as a topical pragmatic consideration. Success in changing topics can only be gauged by looking at the topic of subsequent acts by the partner.

Fourth, like others before it, this study has not produced a precise definition of "topic." The preference has been to define by unitization of transcripts into series of topics, such that a shift or a shade defines a new topic. The recognition of shading as a type of coherent shift means that many more shifts will be isolated than if only explicit changes in the course of the conversation are counted as topic shifts. The topic at time *n* may no longer be the same as the topic at time 1, even though no explicit and intentional shift occurred in the meantime but only a gradual shading from one subtopic to another. A typology of topic shifts must include shading as perhaps the most important, though most elusive, mechanism for extending a conversation. The lack of precise rules for recognizing topic shades is probably the main cause of unreliability in unitizing these conversations, and such rules must be developed before further topic-shift coding is done.

Fifth, as outside observers, our judgments as to the *competence* exhibited in the participants' performance of various shifts are limited. Competence is a function of context, not just of text. While Planalp and Tracy (1980) offer evidence that some types of shifts are perceived as more competent than others, the relative competence of a shift may vary greatly depending on the conversational context in which it is used. A pair of individuals high in conversational competence, for instance, might occasionally prefer the unconstrained, stream-of-consciousness type of rambling that produces noncoherent topical moves over the more sequentially organized conversation that results from working to achieve topical coherence, but we cannot say that they exhibit less *competence* in the former — only less coherence. Our measures of communicative competence currently lack the precision necessary for linking competence with specific pragmatic choices.

Finally, this study has focused on coherence in contrast to cohesion. Discourse cohesion, as richly outlined by Halliday and Hasan (1976), is revealed by tracing utterance-to-utterance connections, but without taking into account pragmatic connections among utterances. Conversational coherence is a pragmatic rather than a grammatical accomplishment, the description of which requires freedom of movement from microlevels to macrolevels of conversational organization, from acts to sequences to episodes to intertextual ties. Changes in the topical flow of a conversation can usually be attributed to specific acts, but the resultant implications for coherence can only be seen from the vantage point of the higher order conversational structures.

NOTES

1. In the model of conversational pragmatics offered here, one person's utterance or turn at talk can consist of more than one conversational act. This model favors within-turn unitization, unlike previous analyses that have treated the turn or utterance as the unit of analysis. A single turn frequently performs more than one act, as in the case of B answering A's question and then immediately asking A a question. If we were coding B's turn as one unit, we would have to code it as either an answer or a question, or else as a double-duty utterance.

2. For couple 1, the fifth conversation occurred during task-oriented work and hence was subsidiary to the nondiscursive action. Conversation 2 was chosen as a replacement instead of conversation 3 because conversation 2 was longer and more varied topically.

3. Each excerpt from the transcripts contains at least one topic shift (indicated by an arrow to the left of the utterance). Prior and subsequent acts are included to show how the shift fits into the ongoing conversation.

<< <<<<<<<<<< >>>>>>>>>>>>>

8

Alignment and Conversational Coherence

<< SANDRA L. RAGAN >>

A: What was your major in college?
B: Business administration.
A: And did that prepare you for a managerial position?
B: Yes. I think my management courses were excellent.

Conversational coherence makes the presupposition that communicators talk in ordered, patterned, nonrandom ways enabling them to define and to make sense of their conversational situation. One sense-making issue in the construction of coherent, meaningful dialogue involves actors' perceptions of their social identities in conversation. Social or role identities shape conversation; they delineate what kind of conversation the speakers are in. For example, in the above excerpt we can easily observe that the conversational situation is that of an interview — one party questions, the other responds. Since we know, by convention, that the interviewer generally asks the questions while the interviewee generally responds, we can conjecture, and in all likelihood be correct, that A is assuming the role of interviewer in this conversation while B is playing the interviewee role. Thus, at least in this sort of highly patterned dialogue, we receive conversational cues that help define speaker role.

Participants in any conversation define their relation to each other and their social roles through their talk. In fact, communication theorists tell us that every spoken message inherently contains a metacommunicative component, one that displays relational cues enabling us to know what kind of relationship we have with the other communicator. Again, noting the example above, we might assume that the relationship between A and B is an asymmetrical one: A asks and B answers; furthermore, B responds to A's queries directly and concisely, apparently as a matter of course, as if this were prescribed behavior in this setting. A and B are conforming to conventionalized role behavior, most probably tacitly agreed upon prior to their conversation yet also enacted during their conversation. Their talk confirms for them the kind of conversational situation they are in — an interview — as well as displaying their role relationship, that of interviewer and interviewee.

This chapter focuses on how communicators coherently construct their role identities through their conversation. Alignment talk, metacommunicative talk that displays speaker role, is discussed as one type of conversational device that defines communicator identities and role relationships. The chapter also provides an empirical example of the use of alignment devices as they appear in one interpersonal communication context, the job selection interview (Ragan, 1981). It concludes with a look at how alignment talk works to manifest speaker role in another interpersonal context, the B-K conversation (Appendix).

ALIGNMENT TALK

One kind of conversational cue that functions to display or to promote speaker role is alignment talk. What constitutes alignment talk? The term "alignment" is one coined by symbolic interactionists Stokes and Hewitt (1976). They refer to aligning actions as verbal strategies that communicators can use to repair misunderstandings or disruptions in conversation, as in the example, "What do you mean by that?" Through use of alignment talk, actors are presumed to reach definitions of their social situation and to manage their roles in that situation (Stokes & Hewitt, 1976; Hewitt & Stokes, 1975; Scott & Lyman, 1968).

Several aligning strategies are claimed to be useful in attaining these sense-making goals: *motive talk* (Mills, 1940), which legitimizes potentially inappropriate acts; *accounts* (Scott & Lyman, 1968), which are justifications and excuses exonerating a breach of social or conversational norms; and *disclaimers* (Hewitt & Stokes, 1975), which prospectively interpret and rectify possible problematic events and speaker identities. Goffman's *remedial process* (1971), a ritualized four-stage sequence of messages designed to correct problematic conversation, also functions as an aligning strategy.

The notion of alignment can be expanded and clarified by recognizing aligning messages as a subset of metacommunication and by looking at ethnomethodological research on actual talk. Metacommunication has been discussed as a framing property of a message, as message segments that are used to interpret or characterize other messages (Bateson, 1955, 1972; Goffman, 1974). Alignment talk functions metacommunicatively in that it places an interpretive frame around other talk that instructs communicators how a message should be taken, how it should "count" (Hopper, 1981). For example, "metatalk" does alignment work by questioning problematic utterances and initiating their repair; for example, "could you repeat that, please?" (Schiffrin, 1980).

Communicator alignment is further clarified if its metacommunicative properties are seen in the context of natural conversation. Ethnomethodology, a research approach that describes the microdetails of everyday talk, examines features of talk as they are embedded within their conversational contexts. Conversational analysts in the ethnomethodological tradition have described several features of conversation that function to do alignment work, such as *side sequences* (Jefferson, 1972), *formulations* (Heritage & Watson, 1979) and *"my side" tellings* (Pomerantz, 1980a). These message sequences align communicators and meaning by placing an interpretive bracket around some portion of talk. This bracket provides commentary on the conversational situation the communicators are in, and in doing so, clarifies meanings, repairs disruption, and manages communicators' roles.

Looking at these features of talk that do alignment work and recognizing their metacommunicative function expands the notion of alignment. Rather than being limited to remedial processes in talk, alignment can be seen to function in a larger sense to inform communicators how a message should be interpreted and how their relationship within that conversation should be seen. Thus, an amplified notion of alignment talk is metacommunicative talk used to frame messages for purposes of clarifying, interpreting, and managing conversational meaning and communicator roles. This view of alignment allows us to see its potential coherence-managing function in conversation.

METHOD

Given this expanded concept of conversational alignment, the task was then to locate alignment features in actual talk. The employment interview was chosen as a site for describing and analyzing alignment talk since it is a context in which aligning features could be expected to occur, both to promote positive impressions and to manifest conventional communicator roles.

The descriptive method of this project drew both from ethnomethodology and from grounded theory (Glaser & Strauss, 1967). Ethnomethodology provided the model for using transcripts to examine conversational microdetails. Grounded theory recommended procedures through which categories emerge from data during the process of descriptive analysis. These perspectives guided the analysis; hence, the categories of alignment actions presented below grew from the data as much as from the literature. In this way the concept of conversational alignment emerged as it was established by the job interview conversations themselves.

The conventional roles of interviewer and interviewee have been discussed in two recent studies of the job interview. In an examination of simulated job interviews, Shaw (1983) found that applicants conformed to notions of what they perceived as interviewers' norms for appropriate responses, thereby constraining their communicative choices. Apparently, job applicants reciprocated the applicant role that they assumed to be defined by the interviewer. Kress and Fowler (1979) analyzed dialogue in job interviews to find that participants defined their identities, statuses, and rights through their language; applicants unwittingly yet cooperatively defined themselves as inferior to the interviewer.

The purpose of the present study was to explore how alignment functioned in one significant interpersonal context, the job interview. From this descriptive analysis the emergent findings focused on differences in use of aligning features by the interviewer and the interviewee. The study thus became one of communicator role management through conversational alignment.

Categories of Aligning Actions

Twelve job interviews were videotaped and transcribed for the study. Six of these interviews were role-play situations conducted as practice interviews for graduate students applying for internships in health care administration. The remaining six were natural job interviews of undergraduate students applying for positions in data processing and personnel. For all twelve interviews, both applicant and interviewer were aware of the videotaping and consented to releasing the transcriptions from the videotapes to the researcher.

Six male and six female applicants' interviews were transcribed. Interviewers for the twelve interviews consisted of three males (one interviewer for the simulated set of six interviews and two interviewers for the six actual job interviews). Each was well trained in interviewing procedures. Since the differences in use of alignment strategies in the simulated and the actual interviews were not substantive, the entire set of twelve interviews was treated as one corpus of data for the purposes of this study. The interviews and the circumstances under which they were conducted indicate nothing that would mark them as atypical job selection interviews.

An analysis of alignment talk in the twelve interview transcripts uncovered these seven aligning strategies: accounts, formulations, metatalk, side sequences, metacommunicative digressions, qualifiers, and "you knows." Although frequency counts were tallied for each of these aligning strategies, a qualitative analysis of the function of each aligning action in its conversational context comprised the major portion of the study and yielded its most important conclusions.

A brief description of occurrence of use of each of the seven coded aligning actions follows, along with an example of each aligning action from the job interview conversations.

Accounts. Accounts (Scott and Lyman, 1968) were coded as statements offered to explain unanticipated or questionable behavior. An account consisted of a justification or an excuse for conduct deemed untoward, either within the interview, or, more commonly, outside its context. For example:

I :   Um hm, What kinds of things did you have in college — at the university — that particularly equipped you to uh to take on this kind of an assignment — uh courses you had, experiences you had?

A: Well, I had no management; I had very little business — but a lot of government and I really feel strongly that it's important to understand how policy is made and how how it works right now, because we are just facing a a time right now in health care where we just don't know how much of a role government's going to continue to play. And I think I've had just kinda kind of a natural knack for organization and so those are really — I couldn't tell you that I've had twelve hours of management and because I really don't think those things necessarily prepare you to do something like this.

Formulations. Formulations (Heritage & Watson, 1979) were coded as utterances that summarized previous utterances or which offered interpretations — gists — of the conversation in progress. Formulations conformed to the constraints for adjacency pair parts: A formulation was followed either by a confirming statement or by a disconfirming one, but speakers displayed a decided preference for confirmation. For example:

I : When are you available for employment?
A: I'm available for employment uh in town I could start sooner because I wouldn't have to move.
I : Yeah.
A: Out of town I could start as soon as June.
I : Okay.
A: But it would be fine with me if I could start in the middle of July or the beginning of August.
I : Want to take some time off, is that
A: That's right. I've been going to school for about five or six years and I'd like to take a little vacation before starting full time.

Metatalk. This consisted of items or utterances referring explicitly to the verbal properties of another message. Metatalk could focus on the speaker's talk (e.g., "like I say"), on the receiver's talk (e.g., "you mean"), or on the interview process itself (e.g., "Could I ask a few questions?").

Since metatalk was the most frequently occurring aligning action of the seven aligning features isolated for the study, it was further coded according to its function within the interview context. Six categories of metatalk emerged; these were derived by determining the primary illocutionary force of the 251 examples of metatalk in the twelve interview transcripts:

(1) *Clarifying* — attempts to refine the meaning of a previously expressed message or to express the need for making that meaning clearer; rephrasing for the sake of greater clarity. For example: I mean, I assume you're talking about; You're talking about.

(2) *Remediating* — attempts to express misunderstanding or mishearing or to provide apology, correction, or disclaimer for behavior that otherwise might be seen as untoward. For example: I misunderstood you on that; It's gonna sound funny; Excuse me.

(3) *Directing* — messages that masquerade as asking permission to perform certain speech behaviors while functioning, in fact, to actually perform these behaviors (similar to Schegloff's, 1980, preliminaries to preliminaries; e.g., "Can I ask a question?"). For

example: Well, allow me to make one point if I can; Let me interrupt you for just a moment.

(4) *Requesting* — messages that make actual requests of the receiver or of his or her talk. For example: What else can I respond to?; Maybe you can describe that for me.

(5) *Agendizing* — messages that may also function as requests but as requests that specifically announce an agenda for the interview stage or process. For example: If you have anything you'd like to ask me or wrap up with; Let me more formally introduce myself.

(6) *Side particles* — messages referring to or qualifying prior or subsequent messages; often idiosyncratic speech habit. For example: I said; You mentioned; Quite frankly.

Side sequences. These (Jefferson, 1972) were coded as conversational sequences constituting a metacommunicative break in the conversation, after which the ongoing conversation resumed. Side sequences were frequently ritualized sequences, such as repeats or interrogatives, that functioned to ensure consensus on a point. For example:

A: Allright.
I : All together?
A: All together.
I : Okay?
A: Okay.

Metacommunicative digressions. These were conversational sequences or single turns at talk that were similar to side sequences in that they constituted a metacommunicative break in conversation, but more elaborated and less ritualized than side sequences. Generally, metacommunicative digressions consisted of extended sequences of metatalk during which applicant and interviewer talked about some aspect of the interview process or shared somewhat personal, job-peripheral information. For example:

I : Is that what we have?
A: Yeah, you have (unintelligible) framing.
I : Hm. See, this is very embarrassing, but I see no reason to deny (or admit defeat).
A: I know.
I : That I don't you, I don't do business applications programming. You know what I do for a living? I'm a personnel man.
A: Okay.
I : That has a Ph.D. in this field, so don't ask me how I got there, I don't know, but but I'm making excuses but I must.

Qualifiers. Qualifiers were coded as words and phrases that explicitly manifested tentativeness, uncertainty, and nonassertiveness such that they evaded issues or diluted expressions of opinion. For example:

> I've had just *kinda – kind of* a natural knack for organization. So I feel that that qualifies me *somewhat* . . . *I don't know,* I'm *I'm sort of* the belief that

"You knows" were counted each time a speaker used the phrase as a metacommunicative aside to the recipient, allegedly for purposes of emphasis or topic tracking (Goldberg, 1981). For example:

> *You know,* I can tell you. It depends on who you're managing . . . . . . an administrative capacity 'n helps them with a lot of paper work *you know*

Definitional criteria for each of the seven coded aligning actions described above, along with examples of each aligning action from the interview transcripts, comprised a manual of coding procedures. This manual was used to train a second coder who provided reliability estimates for the study. Agreement was reached on 92 percent of the coding decisions for these aligning actions: accounts, formulations, side sequences, metacommunicative digressions, qualifiers, and "you knows." For the category of metatalk, which was further divided into six subcategories according to its function in talk, the two coders agreed on 90 percent of their judgements. Any disagreements on coding decisions were resolved through discussion.

RESULTS

Frequency of use of each of the seven aligning actions for interviewers and applicants shows marked disparity: interviewers used more formulations, metatalk, side sequences, and metacommunicative digressions; applicants used far more accounts, qualifiers, and "you knows."

While these numerical differences are dramatic, qualitative differences reflect even greater inequity in the alignment talk of interviewers and applicants. In short, interviewers used alignment strategies that controlled conversational pace and progress; applicants, on the other hand, utilized those alignment forms that explained or justified their behavior. The function of each aligning action in the interview transcripts reveals two differential patterns.

TABLE 8.1   Frequency of Use of Aligning Actions for 12 Interviews

	Interviewers	*Applicants*	*Totals*
Accounts	3	20	23
Formulations	32	17	49
Metatalk	157	94	251
Side Sequences	36	0	36
Metacommunicative Digressions	19	3	22
Qualifiers	30	43	73
"You knows"	11	50	61

Accounts. These functioned in the interview to defend and to justify behavior that otherwise might be judged as inappropriate. In the twelve interview conversations, job applicants used most of the accounts invoked (20:3). Moreover, applicants sometimes anticipated that their qualifications might be evaluated negatively, and thus offered accounts even when unnecessary. Account giving appeared to place the speaker in a defensive posture; that applicants dominated use of accounts in the interview conversations may attest to their greater defensiveness and their inferior status vis-à-vis the interviewer.

Formulations. On the other hand, formulations are verbal strategies that exerted control over the interview conversations by interpreting, summarizing, and pacing the progress of talk. Interviewers not only used more formulations than applicants (32:17); they were also more likely to disconfirm an applicant's formulation. In the rare instances in which an applicant disagreed with an interviewer's interpretation or summary of the conversation, the disconfirmation was so equivocal as to appear confirming. The applicant, in fact, appeared loath to disagree with a framing comment offered by an interviewer. For example, in the following formulation sequence, conversational alignment is adroitly managed by the applicant's polite and equivocal disconfirmation:

I : Rather than internally operating the facility, you want to see what's done uh in relation to the society out there, the political uh lobbying for example, is this am I paraphrasing accurately?

A: Well, you probably are from your impression, but I feel like the strongest thing about the residency is that I do need a grasp of the internal which I don't have now and I don't have by going to school, so I am very interested in just seeing the way that it runs internally.

TABLE 8.2   Frequency of Use of Kinds of Metatalk for 12 Interviews

	Interviewers	*Applicants*	*Totals*
Clarifying	33	17	50
Remediating	24	18	42
Directing	20	4	24
Requesting	28	8	36
Agendizing	19	0	19
Side Particles	33	47	80
Totals	157	94	251

Metatalk. Metatalk is the third category of alignment reflecting disparity in interviewer and applicant use. One-half of applicant use of metatalk was coded as functionless or trivial speech particles (i.e., side particles) rather than as purposeful alignment attempts. Interviewer use of metatalk, on the other hand, accomplished the more meaningful alignment functions of clarifying and remediating. Interviewer metatalk also helped manage applicants' views of interviewer influence manuevers in the job interview conversations. For example, interviewers almost exclusively used those forms of metatalk that exerted control over the interview by framing talk as directing, requesting, and agendizing.

The initiation of *side sequences* and *metacommunicative digressions,* both of which are monopolized by interviewers (36:0 and 19:3, respectively; see Table 8.1), also reflects disparate use of alignment by the two parties to the interview. Each of these devices worked to achieve consensus, clarity, and rapport. Applicants appeared unwilling to interrupt the flow of talk to begin these metacommunicative asides. They rarely subjected talk to close scrutiny but rather observed the "let it pass" rule, which states that conversational difficulties will be remedied in time as the conversation proceeds (Garfinkel, 1967).

Qualifiers and "you knows" were considered less significant to the process of conversational alignment in the interview transcripts. That is, neither of these aligning devices appeared to function in as meaningful ways as the other coded aligning actions in terms of managing meaning or intention. Qualifiers and "you knows" have also been investigated as verbal fillers indicating powerless speech (Erickson, Lind, Johnson, & O'Barr, 1978). These two aligning features were most frequently used by applicants (43:30 and 50:11, respectively; see Table 8.1).

Thus, the aligning items and sequences that appeared to exercise the most influence over the interview conversations by coordinating meaning, managing communicator intention, and influencing the progress of talk — that is, formulations, metatalk (except side particles), side sequences, and metacommunicative digressions — were used more often by interviewers than by applicants in these twelve job interview conversations. Those aligning features that promoted speaker typification as defensive, tentative, and deferential — that is, accounts, side particles, qualifiers, and "you knows" — constituted the majority of applicants' use of aligning actions.

DISCUSSION

Communicator alignment is achieved in the interview conversations primarily through aligning features that clarify, correct, and interpret messages. The subsuming or end product of alignment talk, however, is the management of speaker typification or role. In other words, the study of alignment talk in these conversations is also the study of how communicator roles are enacted. Aligning actions create, maintain, and enforce the differential power and status of interviewer and applicant. An important finding of the study, therefore, is that alignment talk reflexively creates dissimilar roles of interviewer and applicant, while also apparently establishing norms for interview talk.

If we consider aligning actions as conversational influence moves, we see that they function rhetorically to direct topic, pace and movement of job interview conversations. They also typify the speaker as being engaged in these influence processes. Two fairly distinctive patterns emerge with regard to speaker influence in the interviews.

(1) Interviewers use primarily those aligning actions that exert control over talk and thus that typify them as the more powerful communicator.

(2) Applicants use those aligning actions that signify tentativeness and powerlessness — markers of low-status communicators.

Thus, alignment talk displays asymmetrical roles, and, in all probability, also aids in the enactment, maintenance, and enforcement of these differential roles of interviewer and applicant. If the power positions of interviewer and applicant were not clearly differentiated prior to the interview, alignment talk in the interview conversation itself could create this differential. Interview talk both substantiates and reinforces the status disparity of interviewer and applicant.

Alignment Talk in the B-K Conversation

Unlike that of the job interview context, the conversational situation for B and K is not inherently inequitable vis-à-vis status. Both women are students; they are engaging in everyday conversation rather than in structured talk with a specific purpose. No conventionalized role relationships exist a priori as with the interviewer and the interviewee in the job interview; neither do such dramatic role disparities emerge in their talk. Nonetheless, both conversants utilize alignment strategies that serve to construct and to clarify their communicative identities in the conversation.

An analysis of the types and functions of alignment talk in this transcript reveals, first of all, that the communicators do not use grossly dissimilar patterns of alignment as in the job interviews. Use of accounts, qualifiers, side sequences, and formulations shows little or no disparity. Neither party offers any accounts; both use qualifiers only twice (179 K; 278 K; 257 B; 320 B); each initiates several metacommunicative side sequences or digressions; for example:

Example 1	002	**K:**	So how are you doing?
	003	**B:**	((laugh)) As well as can be expected this time of the semester. How about you.
	004	**K:**	((animated)) Umm, good.
	005	**B:**	Are you sure that you don't want half? This is huge.
Example 2	009	**B:**	Umm (pause) a bonus. ((extended laugh))
			[ ]
	010	**K:**	Wha:t?
	011	**B:**	A *bonus*. [B-K Conversation].

Both the number and the function of these digressions are similar for K and B; each is willing to interrupt conversation to offer digressing or remediating asides. And, although K uses more formulations than B, this disparity is again only a slight one (045 K; 061 K; 254 K; 154 B; 220 B).

Despite this similarity in their use of qualifiers, side sequences/ digressions, and formulations, subtle differences emerge when one looks at the phrase "you know" and, more importantly, at metatalk in the transcript. K uses "you know" twice as much as B does (8:4, respectively). Whether as an idiosyncratic speech filler or as an indicator of insecurity, use of "you know" has nevertheless been perceived as a mark of powerlessness (Erickson et al., 1978).

K also uses 14 instances of metatalk while B uses only 6. In addition, a qualitative difference in the function of their metatalk appears. K, in seven utterances, offers metatalk that apparently functions to clarify or to emphasize a previous utterance; for example, she uses the phrase "I mean" six times. She also comments directly on her talk with such phrases as: "I meant to ask you" (053 K); "in other words if I had asked you" (254 K); "I was going to say" (258 K); and "that's not what I was talking about" (248 K). In one instance, she metacommunicates, "That's a good question" (302 K).

B, by contrast, offers "I mean" only twice to clarify her remarks (235/237 B; 311 B). She does, however, use metatalk in two instances that function as remediating metatalk, almost as a disclaimer for behavior that might otherwise be seen by K as untoward.

229 B: This is embarrassing to admit . . .
279 B: This is going to show up great on tape . . .

This disparity in frequency and function of metatalk might suggest a subtle disparity in communicator roles. While the power dimension does not seem as much an issue here as with the job interviews, K is the communicator who manifests relatively more need to be understood in this conversation. Whether that manifestation springs from communicative anxiety, communicative competence, or some other communication-related propensity cannot be decided on the basis of a transcript. Neither can it be claimed with any degree of certainty that K's more frequent use of "you know" and her metatalk mark her as a powerless speaker vis-à-vis B.

It is revealing to note, however, that each instance of K's use of "I mean" occurs immediately following a potentially awkward conversational incident. For example:

Example 3   152   B: Have you picked out the long suffering man who is going to put up with that kind of a honeymoon yehht?
             153   K: Oh:. This is just a dream *I mean* (someone can plan this type things)
Example 4   268   K: = Yes.
             269   B: uh::,
                        [
             270   K: Oh! - Ferriers are horse doctors.

271 **B:** Um::. Well, out there they're- they're mostly - concerned with the feet. The vet takes care of the horse from the ankles up.

   . . . .

277 **B:** They're the people who get paid outrageous amounts of money to get kicked.

278 **K:** Oo. ((laugh)) (pause) I suppose when you take lessons that's also when you - just sort of learn to - to y'just take it in stride, getting kicked and bit an' - *I mean* you don't like it, but - (you know it's)

Example 5 284 **K:** ((laugh)) That's - that's not what I was talking about. But *I mean* just as a kid taking ho lessons.

Example 6 331 **K:** You might like it. It's - more of an endera-end*u*rance type - thing than anything. There's not a lot of - talent to it at all. Believe *me*. .hhhhh

                                                [

332 **B:**   Why, thank you. =

333 **K:** = ((laugh)) =

334 **K:** = ((laugh)) =

335 **K:** = .hhh No. But *I mean* it's not something that'a- you could - pick it up in a morning. It's not something you have to spend - weeks and months learning how to do properly.

Example 7 336 **B:** Perfecting you technique.

337 **K:** Yes. *I mean,* - I taught my little brother - up three years ago - how to ski . . .

"I mean" thus serves a remediating function in K's talk; she uses the phrase to clarify, to ameliorate misunderstanding. As a result, K's metatalk helps to construct her role in this conversation as that of a smoothing communicator, relative to B; she displays in a seemingly nonrandom, coherent pattern a form of metatalk that remedies, clarifies, and interprets. Conversation can then proceed without undue awkward breaks, obsessive scrutiny, or uncorrected misunderstandings. K's use of alignment talk thus not only serves to remedy problematic incidents in the conversation; it also helps display and promote a coherent communicator role.

CONCLUSION

The present study suggests that alignment talk, both in twelve job interview conversations and in the B-K transcript, is apparently nonrandom and coherently constructed. In the job interviews two distinctive patterns of alignment talk work to enact and to maintain the inequitable status of interviewer and interviewee. In the B-K conversation, K's use of metatalk displays relatively more concern for conversational clarity than B's — perhaps an indicator of status/power differences between the two. In both sets of transcripts, talk appears both to construct and to reflect coherent speaker identities.

Additional research in conversational coherence might explore other patterned features of a communicator's talk, alignment talk being only a minor subset of linguistic style. Particularly if "linguistic style simultaneously expresses and constructs an ideology" (Fowler, 1981, p. 29), consistent use of a feature of talk can be examined as a manifestation of and a clue to speakers' roles and conversational relationships. And if consistently different patterns of use emerge in two speakers' talk, we can speculate that the differences are meaningful indicators of role disparity, at least within the confines of their conversation.

Gumperz (1982) claims that language differences signal information as well as "creating and maintaining the subtle boundaries of power, status, role, and occupational specialization that make up the fabric of our social life" (p. 6-7). Fowler (1981) writes of the inherent asymmetry in all relationships — "much communication is concerned with establishing and maintaining unequal power relationships between individuals" (p. 29). Alignment talk is but one feature of talk that appears to get used in patterned, coherent fashion by speakers. Differences in these patterns suggest that indeed talk does construct for communicators subtle social identity boundaries and power relationships. Such construction enables communicators to define coherently for each other who they are in the conversational situation they are in.

<<<<<<<<<<<<< >>>>>>>>>>>>

III

THE INFLUENCE OF CONTEXT

<<<<<<<<<<<<< >>>>>>>>>>>>

9

Some Multiple Constraints
Placed on Conversational Topics

<< STUART J. SIGMAN >>

<<< One of the discourse elements suggested to be >>> productive of coherence in conversation is topicality, that is, speakers' adherence to rules for constructing topics. Topic negotiation researchers (e.g., Adato, n.d.; Keenan & Schieffelin, 1976; Litton-Hawes, 1977) examine the processes of topic introduction, maintenance, dissolution, recycling, and so forth. Furthermore, these researchers suggest that conversational participants produce connected speech through adherence to certain discourse metarules, specifically Haviland and Clark's (1974) notion of the "given-new contract" and Grice's (1975) concept of "relevance."

The present chapter examines some of the assumptions underlying the theory and methodology of the topic negotiation literature, and provides a critique of certain of these presuppositions. In light of the critique, certain additional constraints seen as shaping topic behavior are explored. In general, this chapter is informed by, and argues for, an analytic perspective on discourse that recognizes three critical tenets of social communication theory (see Bateson, 1972; Birdwhistell, 1970; Scheflen, 1974; Sigman, 1980; Zabor, 1978): (1) communication behavior is multifunctional; (2) rule governedness is context bound, that is, it is shaped by an interactional context and the definition of a situation; and (3) interpersonal behavior is both a resource for, and a product of, participants' construction of their social relationships. With regard to the specific purposes of the present volume, the research perspective outlined here suggests that communication scholars doing discourse analysis should extend their investigatory focus beyond the discourse text itself and toward the relationship between discourse and the encompassing social context.

TOPIC NEGOTIATION LITERATURE

The investigation of topic as one interaction component worthy of study in its own right is a relatively recent research direction, especially when this is compared with an area such as turn-taking, which received considerably earlier attention (Duncan, 1972, 1973; Sacks, Schegloff, & Jefferson, 1974). As late as 1976 Keenan and Schieffelin remark that "there has been no systematic study in linguistics of the way in which topics are initiated, sustained, and/or dropped in naturally occurring discourse" (p. 337). Litton-Hawes (1977) also observes that "scholars interested in systematically studying such everyday discourse . . . find neither an integrated literature nor an organized conceptual framework" (p. 2).

The three studies discussed in the present section represent a linguistic, an ethnomethodological, and a speech communication perspective on topic negotiation. A common concern of these works is with the examination of *discourse structure,* that is to say, with the behaviors and rules individuals appear to employ in contributing the interdependent utterances constituting a connected stream of discourse. Topic negotiation researchers hypothesize that, as conversations progress temporally, shifts in topical focus take place, and that individuals manage topic continuations, substitutions, recursions, and so on. However, conversationists are constrained by how their statements may fit into the ongoing and connected discourse stream, that is, into the flow of shared information already produced. Researchers state that topics may be seen to reflect speakers' adherence to the conversational maxims of "relevance" (Grice, 1975) and/or the "given-new contract" (Haviland & Clark, 1974). It is assumed that speakers build on previous relationship knowledge or events transpiring within the interaction when contributing to the topic at hand. Speakers take into account presumably old information or information already shared by the participants, mark this linguistically, and then build on this with new or as yet unshared information. When relevance is not retrievable from immediately preceding speech (Keenan & Schieffelin, 1976), or from other contemporaneous events (Adato, n.d.), then linguistic devices must be employed by speakers to signal this (at least in English).

Keenan and Schieffelin (1976) note that discourse may develop temporally in one of two ways, and that each utterance produced by the speakers may serve the developmental progression differently. In order to create *continuous discourse,* individuals either collaborate on the topic underlying the immediately preceding utterance, or they incorporate some of its propositional content, thus talking on a new but related topic. *Discontinuous* discourse is produced whenever two adjacent utterances are not focused on the same topic. This may be accomplished through the introduction of a topic that does not incorporate any of the content of the previous utterance, or through the reintroduction of a discourse topic other than the immediately preceding one.

Three additional characteristics of topical sequencing are noted by discourse researchers. First, Litton-Hawes (1977) considers that "any utterance of a [conversation] member can be heard as containing or implying relevant and, therefore, appropriate topics on which the other member may comment" (p. 9). Litton-Hawes suggests that speakers cannot always control the implications of their own statements or the way in which others reply. Adato (n.d.) similarly notes that an utterance does not constrain the selection of a theme for subsequent utterances. Second, according to Litton-Hawes (1977), the relevance of a previous statement and the function it serves in interaction are not delegated until *after* the next statement (which presumably builds upon it) is produced. This suggests that the topic of an utterance is dependent upon the response it yields from the subsequent speaker. As Schank (1977) writes, "Sentences . . . do not have topics in isolation. Only conversations can be said to have topics" (p. 425). The final consideration is that speakers have a wide latitude in elaborating on previous statements, and in either maintaining or shifting the topic sequences (Litton-Hawes, 1977). Congruent with the perspective outline by Sacks and associates (1974), conversation can be characterized by a lack of prespecification of turn length and turn content. For example, comments on previous statements may take the form of questions about omitted information, reflections on the speaker's attitude toward what has just been said, or expansions through reference to additional information.

Gaps in the Topic Negotiation Literature

With these considerations as background, we may now discuss several critical issues related to the topic negotiation literature. First, the above research does not indicate the likelihood of different conversations being composed of different percentages or blends of, for

example, connected and unconnected topics. In a sense this research
✳⌐ provides an idealized grammar or taxonomy of discourse techniques,
but it does not specify contextual regulations on the appearances of
the various conversational devices. The writers seem to assume a
cross-situational consistency in that it is left up to *individual choice* as
to how to go about contributing to ongoing discourse. Litton-Hawes
(1977) does not indicate *when* any of the techniques for elaborating on
or shifting a topic is most likely to be employed by speakers, *with
whom,* and *with which topics;* she only oulines the theoretical
possibilities. Similarly, the principal constraint that Keenan and
Schieffelin (1976) propose for topical sequencing is adherence to the
⌊ relevance rule.

In contrast to this, situational differences may be hypothesized
with regard to the relative appearance and evaluation of the two
characterizations of discourse noted by Keenan and Schieffelin.
Whereas a rambling or discontinuous approach may be appropriate
and highly valued on some occasions, for example, for its informality,
there are many circumstances, such as the classroom, in which it
would be considered a conversational shortcoming (cf. Aldrich, 1972;
Mc Dermont & Hall, 1977). In short, topic negotiation researchers
apparently do not consider discourse patterning in the introduction
and reintroduction of topics (or, at least, do not see this as a feature to
be noted by a discourse analysis of topics).

/ Second, a monofunctional perspective on topics is assumed by
these reseachers (see Levinson's, 1981, remarks on discourse analysis
in general). Keenan and Schieffelin's (1976) and Litton-Hawes' (1977)
research are predicated on the belief that topics serve primarily an
/ information-bearing function, and that the construction of such topics
\ requires speaker adherence to rules of relevance only. Thus when a
topic change occurs individuals must account for its relevance. One
might hypothesize instead that some topic transitions may not be
bound by rules of relevance as narrowly viewed by the above research, and that there may be other constraints upon the continuity
and discontinuity of discourse. As the following discussion indicates,
conversations and the constituent topics may serve both the new
√ information and a phatic (group creation and maintenance) function
(Birdwhistell, 1970; Malinowski, 1923).

Often the aim of some topics is not the provision of information to
coparticipants, but the provision of a ritual transition from one topic
to another. Under these circumstances adherence to rules of relevance may not be warranted. This may be seen in terms of a dis-
placement function of topics (Aragon, 1978). A specific next topic

may be employed by a speaker, not for the (new) information trans-
mitted, but because it supplies a framework that eases social interaction and social tensions. This is to say that a social level integrational
function, along with an informational function, may be served by
topics and topic changes. Aragon's example of a child's introduction
of talk about family vacation experiences at the time when another
topic may be precipitating a confrontation within the family system,
indicates that easing tension-filled interactions may be accomplished
through topic changes, but that relevance need not always be marked
or accounted for.

Aldrich (1972) provides a related example from a Mensa meeting,
in which the introduction of a topic inappropriate to the tacitly
prescribed communicational code results in the substitution of
another topic:

> After the brief exchange between Craig and Paul, and the group's
> humorous response to Paul's tongue-in-cheek complaint, the con-
> versation returned to a focus on religious education. Mary, Al, and
> then Paul mentioned instances of the suppression of books that
> challenged conventional religious wisdom. Craig's and Paul's per-
> sonal references were simply dropped [p. 174].

In this example certain levels of topic-related information were inap-
propriately included in the group's conversation by Craig and Paul,
and these were subsequently "dropped" by the other participants
who returned to the usual topic boundaries of Mensa meetings. Interestingly, the latter speakers apparently did not have to account for
the relevance of the newly introduced statements in moving away
from or not developing Craig's or Paul's propositions. *The very
occasion of the meeting seems to have warranted their remarks and
not the others'*. Thus, in addition to behavioral mechanisms for
producing continuous and discontinuous conversation, there are
probably rules not considered by topic negotiation researchers which
account for *when* interactants converse continuously and discontinu-
ously. In addition, the discourse literature apparently fails to consider
that both the informational requirements of particular groups, and
their integrational or phatic needs, may be met by a communicational
coding of conversational topics.

Third, methodological issues may be raised about the topic negotiation literature surveyed here. It is important to note that, while the
research examined here is concerned with the underlying coherence
of topics in discourse, it nevertheless posits this in strictly linear
fashion. Specifically, the connecting or typing (Litton-Hawes, 1977)

of utterances and their concomitant relevance to discourse are only analyzed in terms of immediately preceding utterances. The speakers in these studies are assumed to orient themselves to the immediately preceding other's statement when providing for the relevance of their own statements (see Tracy's, 1982, discussion of local coherence). Discourse structure seems to exist here in the conjoining of any two temporally adjacent utterances. Thus, no provision is made for a series of conversational "embeddings" (cf. Goffman, 1971), or for speakers' awareness of and orientation to future (as well as previous) moves for accomplishing certain ends in conversation.

Scheflen (1973) has remarked that the linear analysis of conversational turns fails to consider that speakers respond, not only to immediately preceding utterances, but "within broader systems of events — to what has been said hours or even months before, to something unsaid, to what might be said, and to matters unrelated to the immediate transaction" (p. 6). Consider in this respect the example of talk on hiring chorus soloists provided by Clancy (1972, p. 82):

> The primary explanation for the changing among these subjects lies in the different roles of the speakers. These roles give certain responsibilities to fulfill, so that each speaker takes the opportunity when it arises to contribute to the discussion his specialized knowledge. Thus, goals of the speakers cause the subject of discussion to shift in a repetitive, rather cyclical manner.

In this discussion speakers were oriented to (1) the main topic of the hiring; (2) the special (subtopic) contribution each could make to this; (3) providing this information repetitively throughout the conversation and (4) reintroducing this information when it was warranted by a particular juncture (subtopic) in the conversation itself. In general, *speakers appear to direct their verbal contributions to the interaction as a totality,* its goals, and their role requirements, and not only to the immediately preceding utterance(s).

Researchers also face definitional problems, specifically in the isolation and unitization of topic-related behavior. For example, Keenan and Schieffelin (1976) define a topic as "the proposition (or set of propositions) about which the speaker is either providing or requesting *new* information" (p. 4; emphasis added). In addition, their scheme warrants labeling a topic change whenever the propositional content of two adjacent statements is not identical, even though some propositional content may be shared. In this manner Keenan and Schieffelin (1976) appear to lack a distinction between topic and comment, preferring to view any changes in the propositional content of specific comments as changes in the topic itself. Furthermore, theirs is an a priori (non-emic) categorization of topics. Based on the new versus old information discriminations that are assumed to go into a speaker's statements, it is the researchers themselves who judge shifts in topic rather than native informants. Two considerations must be examined in this regard.

First, Keenan and Schieffelin (1976) suppose that the set of propositions, or the topic, rests on an unstated "question of immediate concern." This is to say that a topic is seen as addressing or answering such a tacit question. When this question of immediate concern is altered, so too is the topic regarding it. Consider the apocryphal example of two women who ride in the same car pool each morning to work, whose conversation is one day recorded:

Woman 1: We saw that new movie Saturday night. It was good.
Woman 2: Jack and I also went . . . uh, bowling . . . on Sunday.

According to my understanding of Keenan and Schieffelin's work, these two sentences would presuppose two very different questions of immediate concern. In specific, the second speaker does not appear to have either collaborated on or incorporated any of the propositional content of the first speaker's utterance ("new movie," "Saturday night"); a *new* topic has apparently been introduced, and, moreover, this topic must be judged as irrelevant with regard to the first. However, this analysis falls short of considering that both speakers may be conversing on the same higher order topic, but that the particular subtopics employed for talking on that main topic may be different. In other words, *a relationship between the two topics may indeed exist, although not in terms of what is immediately being spoken about.* While it may be true that, individually, the first statement is directed at the topic, "Did you see that new movie?" and the second one at, "What did you do on Sunday?" both may be collectively addressing the question, "What did you do this weekend?" Even though the immediate (i.e., surface) propositional content of the two utterances is different, both may be relevantly adhering to the same regularly patterned, but largely unstated, topic (and interaction framework) for Monday-on-the-way-to-work talk, namely, weekend events.[1]

An important (and limiting) feature of much discourse analysis, then, is that the researchers do not employ native informants to decide either relevance or topic transition, but instead rely on their own categories to make such judgments (cf. Planalp and Tracy, 1980).

A second definitional question that arises is how topic negotiation analysts, as well as cospeakers in an interaction, may come to understand a question of immediate concern, especially when it is not directly stated. Here one would hope for Keenan and Schieffelin to consider social variables serving as constraints on such questions, or relationship parameters defining repetitive topic appearances. While they do admit that awareness of shared background knowledge may be of use in ascertaining the question of immediate concern, they nevertheless focus only on contemporaneous events in the actual analyses. Keenan and Schieffelin (1976, p. 345) write:

> Given that question of immediate concern may be drawn from both verbal and non-verbal dimensions of the immediate situation, it is to the advantage of the observer to have available the most complete record (i.e., both video and audio) of the situation.

Adato (n.d.) also suggests that it is the immediate circumstances surrounding an interaction that engender topics. He contends that topic introductions are warranted by (1) events occurring simultaneously with the interaction itself; and (2) dialogic focus on making those event known in common by all participants. In contrast to this, the implication of the mock dialogue between the two women is that topic determinations do not require reference to only immediate propositional content. Rather, the analyst must be able to make reference to conversations engaged in over an extended period of time, that is, to discourse embedded in a continuous social relationship.

This does not deny that interactants may orient to a shared question of immediate concern in formulating statements. It seems to me that this is the same thing as saying that individuals talk on a topic. Rather, the issue I am raising here is whether the question (and, by implication, the topic) is retrievable from *immediate* contexts alone. The answer that is drawn by the topic negotiation researchers seems to be an unqualified yes.

The topic negotiation research is thus subject to the criticism that it takes into account only "the immediately sensible punctiform present" (Birdwhistell, 1956, p. 149), rather than temporally and spatially more encompassing social contexts that monitor and constrain individual interactions. To the extent that discrete (bound) interpersonal exchanges reflect a social-level code for communication behavior, then focus on only the immediately observable spatial and temporal dimensions of an interaction, limits boundaries of research too severely. The spatial and temporal dimensions of a communication event are generally viewed by discourse researchers in terms of the initiation and subsequent termination of visual and auditory contact by individual actors. The meaning of a particular *bit* of conversational behavior is related to time as measured by an observer's stopwatch, or to territory as determined by the limits of one's vision. Nevertheless, *some conversational relationships are enduring social enterprises,* and the significance of any one interactional engagement is regulated by the larger ongoing social process. As Scheflen (1973) indicates, social context may be viewed as a hierarchical structuring of levels, and an isolable behavior may be related to more and more hierarchically superordinate, levels of the total social communicational stream.

In summary, the sequential organization of topics is viewed by topic negotiation researchers as only a participant controlled phenomenon within the "ongoing physical context" (Keenan & Schieffelin, 1976) of discourse. These researchers consider the moment-by-moment behaviors that go into producing a topic or changes in topic, rather than the larger relational or situational context for providing topic choices. As noted above, these studies do not consider *what* one may speak about in employing these techniques, only *how* one may speak on *any* topic. The various studies examine the mechanism for maintaining or altering discourse topics, but they fail to consider that part of the work that may go into the creation, sustaining, or dissolution of a topic is the degree to which the topic (or the topic change) is an expected, unexpected, rule-abiding, or rule-breaking act within a larger social interactional framework. Topic negotiation researchers adhere to a notion of an idealized speaker/ hearer who requires only knowledge of particular linguistic devices for creating discourse. Relevance as it is employed in this research is a cognitive phenomenon, taking into account information that is shared and not shared; it is not a matter of social acceptability, that is, social relevance (cf. Hymes, 1972).

INFORMATION AND SOCIAL RELATIONSHIPS

The previous section discussed the various ways discourse utterances are said to construct meaningful and coherent topics. However, it was argued that the topic negotiation literature has tended to emphasize only the *internal units* productive of coherent or integrated discourse, and has not considered the multiple functions of discourse utterances and the larger situation or context that influences topic behavior. The present section and the next one suggest that constraints other than internal relevance can be postulated: in specific, the information status of social relationships and agenda patterns. The attempt, in the remainder of this chapter, can be seen as a looking out from discourse to the broader communication context of interaction.

Unpublished reports by Aragon (1978), Sigman (1979), and Winkin (1979) indicate the existence of context-sensitive rules constraining topic selections. The data from these studies are consistent with the view on language behavior articulated by Firth (1964, p. 67):

> Speech is not . . . "boundless chaos". . . . For most of us the (social) roles and the (verbal) lines are there, and that being so, the lines can be classified and correlated with the part and also with the episodes, scenes and acts. Conversation is much more of a roughly prescribed ritual than most people think.

This section employs this perspective on discourse in order to point to some of the social constraints on the introduction, stability, and/or alteration of topics.

Discourse rules, especially those serving to pattern topic selection and development, may be seen as abstract principles guiding the information states of particular social relationships (and interaction contexts). More specifically, they may be taken as summaries of the verbal information that must, may, and/or may not pass among interactants at a particular phase of relationship development (and in particular interaction settings). As will be suggested, these information states provide for the relevance and situatedness of discourse behavior, and serve as constraints in their own right on topic selection.

Definitions of social relationships can be seen to serve as regulators of discourse units, that is, they provide for a range of acceptable or preferred behaviors (cf. Haley, 1963; Hymes, 1974). Reciprocally, the behavioral units of face-to-face interaction may be used by social actors as resources in the generation of social messages. That is to say, they provide a repertoire of behaviors for the construction, maintenance, and redefinition of social relationships. Relationships establish limitations on what may form as the object of conversational attention (either in passing or during extended discourse episodes) by the comembers, and specific social relationships are organized around particular discourse rules (see Goffman, 1959, and McCall & Simmons, 1978, for useful treatments of information control). These rules, seen by the analyst either as socially given constraints or as ongoing (negotiated) emergents (see Shimanoff, 1980; Sigman, 1980) in turn delimit the appropriateness of each participant's behavior.

Three aspects of the information states of social relationships will be briefly considered here: (1) the information that may be taken for granted by relationship comembers; (2) the information that is expected and must be exchanged by relationship comembers; and (3) the information that must be excluded from a relationship.

Taken-for-Granted Information

As suggested in the critique of the topic negotiation literature, discourse units are relevant, not only to what has just been said in conversation, but also to what has not been said, or, perhaps more often, to what need not be said. In other words, discourse relevance must be seen in terms of the information states presupposed by particular social relationships. During the course of individuals' continuous negotiation of who they are vis-à-vis each other, certain information is extended about each individual that becomes part of a general storehouse of knowledge. Included in this store of information are shared-in-common experiences, some of which may be directly related to previous discourse. Excellent treatments of how such background understandings and taken-for-granted information are patterned in discourse are provided by Beach (this volume), Haslett (1982), and Hopper (1981). Hopper, for example, discusses the relationship between relevance conditions as discussed above and "TFG" (taken-for-granted information) in the following manner:

> The relevance maxim gives no guide to listener or analyst for answering the question: relevant to what? One must look for relationships between the utterance in question and other discourse or events [1981, p. 204].

Discourse relevance and coherence can be seen to have an historical continuity across particular interaction events; that is, they are dependent upon accumulated information. Relevance of particular discourse units is in part defined by that information which is tacitly assumed or explicitly noted to exist within the extant information repository of the relationship.

There are several discourse implications of taken-for-granted information. One research direction is concerned with the process by which TFG information enters or becomes part of everyday conversation. With respect to interpersonal relationship development, at what point in a social relationship do the comembers agree to make use of TFG information, and how do they signal their intentions to do so? In investigating this question, one should not assume a directly linear relation between the (usually gradual) accumulation of information that *can* be taken for granted by discourse participants, and the actual implementation or utilization of this information in ongoing discourse. A speaker's decision to employ TFG information should not be considered by researchers to be a simple product or consequence of the existence of the information itself. Under certain conditions, information may be shared or held implicitly by relationship comembers, and subsequent messages may appear as redundant with this information. That is, at certain times information held by the relationship comembers may *not* be taken as given or assumed. To refer to tacit knowledge may imply an intimacy (or other relationship defintion) that one or both comembers may be unwilling to admit at that time.

Conversely, TFG information may be seen to be implemented by a speaker some time before the reference information is, in fact, securely held in common by all participants. This may signal a redefinition of the relationship, and, perhaps, permit the building of a storehouse of relationship knowledge. That is, reference to TFG information that is not actually held may signal a recalibration of the relationship parameters, increased intimate feelings, and the need to exchange at some point the information which will give rise to the actual information. The TFG information under these circumstances is presupposed by the existence of a signal indicating permission or desire to hold certain information in common (and participate in a particular social relationship), rather than the TFG information presupposing or preceding the signal for its retrieval.

Congruent with this perspective, one can observe that, as part of the negotiation of their overall relationship, individuals continuously signal (1) their awareness of the progression of the relationship itself; and (2) their familiarity with and ability to retrieve previous relationship knowledge. In the B-K dialogue, for example, there are at least two instances in which one of the participants cues the other into the repetitiveness of current information when it is cross-referenced against the existing information store:

053 **K:** Hmm::! I meant to ask you the other day, are you flying down?
054 **B:** Um hmm, and I hate planes.

```
055  K:   I:: know you said that.
          ((pause))
056  B:   Yup/

294  B:        It was a horse I'd never seen before.
295  K:   .hhh I remember when you said that! He attacked you.
          ((laugh))=

                                              [    ]
297  B:                                        (Hm::)!
297  B:   = He did! He just came running up out of ((laughing))
          nowhere [B-K Conversation] .
```

From a purely discourse-analytic perspective, these subtle reminders may be seen as attempts to sanction the speaker for including repetitive information and for veering away from a conversational obligation to present new information. However, within a perspective that views discourse as a resource or device for communicating about social relationships, one can postulate other functions served by this behavior.

K's remarks appear to do more than mark repetitions. In the dialogue, K is able to communicate to B her information state vis-à-vis the latter individual and the total relationship. She makes a reference to the existing history of interaction and to the amount and type of information that the relationship currently contains. In a sense, she may be said to be "stock taking." K is stating what information *can* be taken for granted. She is informing her partner about the status of a particular item of information by referring to previous talk on the subject. One important observation that should be made here is that B (in excerpt 294-297) does not stop talking about the repetitive information, and K collaborates on that topic with her. Therefore, it is reasonable to assume that B does not take K's comment as a "rebuke," that is, as a sanction for a breach of discourse rules.

In the following excerpt, retrieval of previous information serves as a "prerequest" (see Sacks, 1972) for asking for *additional information* on the named topic:

```
342  B:   Hmm. (pause) I had forgotten that you knew all about all that
          weather stuff.
343  K:   ((laugh)) I really don't. I just pretend I do.
          ((pause))
344  B:   Tell me what you know about the weather - on: the Pacific. . . .
          [B-K Conversation].
```

Reportable Information

An additional means to analyze the information states of social relationships is to consider what I will call "reportability." Reportable

information is the information that must be exchanged between relationship comembers. In this case the definition of a particular relationship provides an expectation for the sharing of certain verbalizable information. Unreportable information is that information which
must be excluded from a relationship. In terms of discourse, reportability regulations may be seen to provide a warrant for the
inclusion of certain topics in conversation.[2]

There are a number of general rule statements that can be used to
capture the underlying structure of discourse reportability, including,
"I am obliged to tell X what I hear Y say (about X or someone/thing
else)." "I observe something which X will need or want to know."
"Congruent with my relationship with X, I must report all I know
about Y (a person, event or thing) to X." Various examples of such
reportable (and reported) information can be found in a corpus of
conversational materials I collected in People's Home, a nursing
home located in Philadelphia.[3] For example, residents constantly
monitored (observed and evaluated) each other's behavior — especially that of newcomers to the facility and of presumed "seniles" —
and reported the results of the monitoring to their peers. One of the
concerns that the residents expressed was to be made aware of the
mental and health status of the other residents in the facility. Such
reportability was a constraining feature of the institution's social
relationships, and residents were chastised when they did not report
to their peers.

Lillian: Mrs. O'Keefe [staff nurse] said so.
Gladys: I know. I know. I was there when the ambulance pulled up.
Lillian: You should have
Thelma: Why didn't you tell us? What time was it?
Gladys: Before lunch. I forget. You know, a sponge. *(She points to her head.)*
Lillian: You should have told come told us. We knew she was failing, but this

An interesting combination of reportability requirements and the
existence of previously exchanged topics appears in the B-K transcript:

165 **K:** Nah, it's not worth it. I'm in to ((laughing)) practical - a lot of times/
166 **B:** Umm. (pause) Have you heard anything about your internship.
            Speaking of practical. =
167 **K:** = Um:::. No I forgot to call about that.

168 **B:**   Um hmm/ ((tone of mock reprimand)) And that was very bad
             you'll have to call about that today. [B-K Conversation].

There are several possible functions of B's remark at turn 166 to be
noted. First, B seems to be reminded of a previous conversation with
K in which an internship application is discussed. B thus signals
remembrance of the conversation and the conversational topic. Further, B indicates the status of the topic as relationship information that
may enter into subsequent interactions, and she suggests to K that she
talk about it at this particular point. B thus conveys to K some degree
of expectation that she be notified about the outcome of the internship
process. In brief, B appears to establish an item of reportability (or, at
least, an assumption that such reportability already exists) with K at
turn 166.

Excluded Information

As suggested, reportability limitations can also be seen in terms of
the nonexchange of information. For example, nurses at People's
Home were not allowed to share certain types of information with
patients labeled by the administration as suffering from the "Doctor
Johnson syndrome." Dr. Johnson was a patient who had been told by
his family that entry into People's Home was only for a brief re-
cuperative stay; in actuality, however, the family intended this as a
permanent placement. Staff members' conversations with Dr.
Johnson and similar residents were constrained by an administrative
decision not to inform the residents of their family members' intentions. The rule for such unreportable information can be phrased as,
"I possess information about Y (a person, an event, a thing) which I
am not allowed to tell X."

The reportability dimensions of social relationships (the information excluded as well as included) can be seen to account for the
continuity and repetition of topics. In specific, they pattern the kinds
of information speakers are likely to share with each other over time.
As Aragon (1978) observes, "If only certain topics are routinely
discussed with certain persons, then the nature of the knowledge
which these persons share through talk becomes boundary-defined"
(p. 14). Moreover, reportability constraints appear to establish the
relevance and connectedness of topics. Note the following People's
Home conversation:

Edith: I smell fish today.
Louise: No, I think it's grilled cheese. Some sort of cheese thing.

Edith:	Oh, well, that's fine. It's better than that (?) they serve.
Louise:	Oh, yes. I don't like *that* at all.
Edith:	And they put so much seasoning on it. That's the most fattening thing they can serve.
Louise:	I know.
Pearl:	I don't like it with all those spices.
Edith:	Let's just say that we have nothing else to complain about, so we complain about the food.
Louise:	We're not complaining. We're just passing remarks.
Edith:	That's true. Yes.
Pearl:	Yes.

Edith's utterance, "we have nothing else to complain about," appears to me as a (locally) coherent utterance when compared with the rest of the dialogue. It seems to employ one possible mechanism for collaborating on a previous utterance's propositional content. Nevertheless, it is not positively interpreted by the others involved in the scene. In part, this may be because a "no complaints" rule defined what in this group of residents in the nursing home was heard as relevant at the relational level. Certain topics, such as negative feelings about nursing home life, were unreportable to one's wardmates (cf. Bennett, 1964). Utterances employing these topic frames — no matter their connectedness to previous discourse — were judged as unacceptable. In this regard an important distinction should be drawn between *relevance*, which is a relation between sentences, and *appropriateness*, which is a relation between discourse and a social context (cf. Hymes, 1972).

Interpersonal communication researchers note that the information exchanged between relationship comembers changes as the relationship definition changes (Bochner, 1978; Miller, 1978). Nevertheless, an important aspect of reportable information per se is that it is not necessarily new or previously untransmitted information. Rather, as suggested above, reportable information may be recurrent information, and its repetitiveness may be demanded by the situation and by the relationship. Reminding us of the various functions that discourse utterances may serve, Aragon (1978, p. 19-20) writes in this regard:

> When two adolescent girls talk for hours every night on the telephone, they may be providing each other with no more information more important than the fact that they continue to be each other's best friend.

Finally, it should also be noted that breaches of reportability constraints may be message-ful for individuals in their dual roles as relationship members and discourse participants:

> Since lazy nurses can increase the aide's work, the latter may retaliate by cutting down on her own "charting" or by abstaining altogether. With nurses who are "unco-operative," she withholds information. The aide's chief weapon . . . is merely the withholding of information that she would ordinarily feed back through channels [Strauss, Schatzman, Bucher, Erlich, & Sabshin, 1964, p. 258].

In brief, discourse participants seem to adhere to constraints on their behavior that are defined by the nature of conversational interaction (e.g., rules of relevance) and by the organization of their interpersonal relationships. Discourse analyses must be responsive to both sets of constraints.

INTERACTION AGENDAS

One claim advanced throughout this chapter is that an utterance may be tied to the immediately preceding one, yet it will not, in all cases, be heard as relevant and as contributing to the coherence of the total discourse. Interaction events can be seen to establish and to be guided by a general rules framework. This abstract framework is informed by the "definition of the situation" held by the participants, and this, in part, directs and defines the relevance, appropriateness, and coherence of talk behavior. Social interaction situations comprise boundaries for external information flow, as well as for internal information flow (see Birdwhistell, 1970; Goffman, 1969; Parks, 1982). By external flow I mean constraints on the information which participants in a given social encounter convey to outsiders, and by internal flow I refer to limits on the messages shared among the participants themselves. Interaction *agendas* and *programs* establish frameworks which permit action, define what is relevant and acceptable (or irrelevant and unacceptable), provide for the meaning and functioning of behavior, and link several encounters together (cf. McCall & Simmons, 1978; Scheflen, 1968). These frameworks also establish entailments or expectations for behavioral sequences, and contingency plans for when the traditional program cannot be completed. I will provide here one extended example of how an agenda may be implemented in conversation and how this constrains discourse contributions.

The conversations I will consider are taken from meetings held by the admissions board of Sisters of Faith Home (SFH).[4] The conversation I am initially concerned with begins with a question by Catherine Anderson, the administrative assistant. Her remarks focus on the first discussion topic of the meeting:

> **Catherine:** Why don't we begin with going over the empty beds?
> **Wilson:** Cathy, excuse me (I'm sorry). Do you have down there 102-B is available, Mr. Kelly died last night.

Mrs. Wilson is the director of nursing. The others present at this discussion are Sister Marie, the head administrator, Ted Smith, the business manager, John Stevens, the chief social worker, and Sister Rose, the staff assistant in charge of proceising applications. These six individuals comprise the admissions board, which meets every four weeks and which is charged with the task of voting on applications to the home that have been sent to Sister Rose during the previous month. Although it is called the *admissions* board, in actuality the board does not admit individuals to SFH (or, at least, this was not its original function). Rather, the members usually decide either to accept or reject applicants, or to delay a decision, and they place names on the entry wait list.

Certain interesting features of the above and subsequent talk may be noted at this point. First, Catherine's question is not directly answered. Rather, it immediately initiates a particular activity, a discussion of available beds at SFH. Mrs. Wilson, the second speaker, does not say whether she agrees that this is the way the meeting should begin. Instead, she follows through with Catherine's suggestion by providing one piece of the requested information.

Second, all previous and subsequent admissions board interactions that I was able to record or observe began with a statement by Catherine or Sister Marie noting how the particular meeting was to be structured. Thus, Catherine's specific statement above is one of a class of *possible opening utterances*. From a transcript of one occasion:

> **Sister Marie:** (As she enters the room) Sorry I'm late. Rose, how many applications do we have to do today?
> **Sister Rose:** There's only two, we lost one in the hospital this morning.
> **Sister Marie:** Oh, (pause) well, why don't you read the first one. What's the name?

And from field notes based on another meeting:

> The meeting began with Sr. Marie reminding everyone about the special convocation for Fr. Montgomery's twenty-fifth anniversary. Sr. Marie then asked if the applications were divided between private pay and Medicaid patients, and when Sr. Rose said yes, Sr. Marie asked her to start with the former applications.

As can be seen, the discussions of the admissions board begin with some comment about how the interaction should proceed.[5]

The apparent significance of Catherine's comment is that it not only directs the initial activity of the group, but that it does so through a selection of one element from various other possibilities. Board meetings begin in a number of ways, but Catherine's statement specifically delimits how the particular meeting she heads will begin. Moreover, further analysis indicates that Catherine's utterance establishes an agenda which provides for the relevance of *all* subsequent remarks. In specific, Catherine's statement appears to set the tone and direction for the remainder of the interaction:

Sister Marie:	Let me see if we have consensus. We're saying to approve the application and admit her this week. Let the
All:	Yes
Sister Marie:	Let the doctor decide later.
Catherine:	If we bring everyone on the waiting list, this week, is that what we said?
Sister Rose:	There are three names, female beds on the wait list.
Catherine:	Then all applications today are priority.
Sister Rose:	Going on the wait list.
Catherine:	They'll be priority on the wait list, on top.

In contrast, in those discussions which immediately began with deliberations on the applicant pool, there was rarely any mention made of the number of people already on the wait list or the current number of available beds. In fact, when this did occur, the board members present at the meeting commented on the inappropriate placement of the remarks. For example:

Ted Smith:	We can't, there's no way we can bring in all those M.A. (public assistance patients).
Catherine:	Let's wait until after the applications, okay?
Sister Marie:	We don't have to do that here.

In the meeting under analysis here, that is, the one which was initiated by Catherine, the conversationists were repeatedly oriented to the fact that the people voted on would be immediately offered beds or moved further up the list as others already on were admitted. Catherine's initial statement thus serves to delimit future action by the others, and to provide a *framework in which their topical con- tributions are interpreted as significant, relevant, permissible, and so on.*

Selections from behavioral alternatives can thus be seen to give rise to entailments, i.e., behaviors that must (or may) cooccur with or folow the alternative chosen. Catherine's selection has implications not only for the initial phase of interaction, that is, the first discussion topic, but for the content of subsequent phases as well. Catherine's selection can be interpreted as calling into play an agenda that directs the interaction and that contrasts with the agendas established on other occasions. A statement by Catherine that initiates discussion of bed vacancies and a statement that requests consideration of the first application — while equivalent in the sense that they both may fill the beginning structuring slot — are not equivalent in that they set very different directions (agendas) for the remainder of the group's interac- tion. As Scheflen (1968) notes, behavior units such as these implicate different interactional progressions.

Interaction agendas may have an historical continuity in that there may exist a limited yet enduring repertoire of programs for specific interaction events. At the same time, agendas are negotiated moment by moment; specific ones may be invoked, chosen, or implemented at different times and for different purposes. It should be noted that in the next meeting of the admissions board, a month after the one discussed at length here, Catherine again attempted to direct the group's initial task to the wait list. This time, however, Catherine's effort was thwarted by John, who indicated to me that he had con- sulted his job description and that he intended to remain solely re- sponsible for resident placements (see Sigman, 1982). He also confer- red privately with the administrator about this. During this next meeting, John informed Catherine that the direction she wanted to follow (the agenda she intended to implement) was now unacceptable to him:

Catherine: Did anyone get the list of empty beds from nursing? I think
John: Catherine, I'll follow through after the meeting (pause) with the wait list.
Catherine: Oh, okay.

John does not allow Catherine to complete her statement, which presumably would have again directed the group to consider the availability of beds and the bringing in of new patients. Moreover, he apparently ignores the surface content of her message (the receipt of the list), and instead focuses on what he perceives as the intent of that message. John does not state whether he has or has not received the weekly census, yet his utterance is a notification that this information will be used after the meeting to begin admissions of new patients. In this manner he does not allow Catherine an opportunity to follow through on her agenda selection.

In the present context use of the term "agenda" is not intended to suggest an explicit or formalized statement of interaction task, topic, or direction. Rather, I conceive of an agenda as any abstract framework which defines meaningful and relevant communicational activity. An agenda may be implemented by an explicit utterance such as a directive, but this need not always be the case. Some agendas may be pre-set from the concluding moments of a previous discussion, while others may be momentarily implemented through a selection from some repertoire. In this manner there may be coherence and continuity, not only between discourse units (utterances), but also between discourse episodes. In all cases, however, agendas establish entailments, and discourse, in order for it to be heard as coherent, must fit the agenda (see Tracy, 1982, in press-a; Tracy & Moran, this volume, for a related discussion of relevance to conversational issues).

SUMMARY

Much of the research on coherence focuses on what might be called "internal relevancy constraints," that is, on how one unit of verbal behavior can be heard as following from another. The present chapter has argued that discourse coherence, and, more generally, conversational units of all sorts, are patterned as appropriate, inappropriate, linked, relevant, irrelevant, and so on with regard to more than the content or organization of particular turns at talk. I have described some of these additional constraints as follows:

(1) Definitions of social relationships can be seen to serve as constraints on discourse units. At the same time, the behavioral units of face-to-face interaction may be used by social actors to negotiate particular social relationships. The relevance of particular discourse units is, in part, defined by three aspects of social relationships:

    (a.)   the information that may be taken for granted by relationship comembers;

    (b.)   the information that is expected and must be exchanged by relationship comembers; and

(c.)   the information that must be excluded from a relationship.
(2)   Particular interaction settings prescribe and proscribe particular orders of conversational behavior. A theory of discourse must be grounded in an analysis of the demands placed on interactants by the larger frame. Interaction agendas and programs establish frameworks which permit action, define what is relevant and acceptable, and provide for the meaning and coherence (continuity) of behavior.

The recent naturalistic emphasis in communication is an important attempt by interpersonal researchers to examine the structural properties of face-to-face behavior. Nevertheless, communication scholars must not lose sight of disciplinary history. Questions about social situations and interpersonal relationships should not be subverted by or substituted with exclusive focus on the doing of conversation. Rather, the study of the former can and should serve to illuminate and contextualize data provided by the latter. In brief, conversational behavior must be examined with regard to its interpersonal features and its multilevel constraints.

NOTES

1. By taking in a larger observational framework for the analysis of the talk produced by the two women, I am, admittedly, still affirming the sharedness of topics. But I am also contending that relevance claims need not be linked to immediately preceding utterances, or even to any utterance which appears in that particular discourse episode. The analyst who considers that topics can have a multievent continuity through time will need to postulate rules and behaviors for retrieving shared background information, reapplying high generality topics on each new occasion, and employing previous interaction frameworks or agendas (cf. Hopper, 1981).

2. Reportability constraints may be used to explain why particular initial utterances are heard as relevant and worthy of talk, and others are not. That which must be taken for granted when a conversation is begun is not simply background knowledge of a topic, but rather the degree to which the topic itself (or, discussion on the topic) may be taken for granted and assumed to be acceptable.

3. See Sigman (1982) for details about the research questions, methodology, and data of the People's Home study. All names herein are pseudonyms.

4. The data in this section are derived from audio recordings of scheduled meetings of the admissions board of a nursing home located in a township adjacent to Philadelphia. See Sigman (1982) for an ethnographic study of SFH's administrative organization and patterns of communication behavior.

5. This analysis is limited by the data as collected. One means of ascertaining the full normative force of a regularity is to consider examples of violations to the proposed rule and resulting reactions. Thus, I am only suggesting here that admissions board meetings can be seen to begin with certain types of remarks, not that they *must* do so.

10

Background Understandings and the Situated Accomplishment of Conversational Telling-Expansions

<< WAYNE A. BEACH >>

<<< How are individual background under->>> standings and shared knowledge among speakers and hearers essential to the achievement of conversational coherence? Throughout this chapter attention is given to how everyday interactants use their social knowledge to organize understandings in social contexts. The specific focus rests with the interface of language and meaning as speakers and hearers attempt to disambiguate particular utterances, make coherent sense of connections among utterances, and coordinate turn-taking sequences within which utterances and their connections are embedded.

To accomplish this communicative work, it is suggested that speakers and hearers must work *reflexively* with discourse *presuppositions*. The term "reflexivity" is intended to draw attention to two interrelated features of social interaction. First, there is a mutual elaboration between reality and setting. As Leiter's (1980, p. 139) oft-quoted statement illustrates, "The setting gives meaning to talk and behavior within it, while at the same time, it exists in and through that very talk and behavior." Second, speakers and hearers are constantly involved in making sense of how others are making sense, such that conversation can be used as a resource for creating understandings and as a topic of investigation when understandings become problematic. The term "presuppositions" refers to those properties of language use that remain unspoken, tacit, or unexplicated. Thus, speakers and hearers must often draw inferences beyond spoken discourse in order to achieve conversational coherence. As Tyler (1978, p. 459) notes, the "said" and the "unsaid" are reflexively constituted:

> Every act of saying is a momentary intersection of the "said" and the "unsaid." Because it is surrounded by an aureola of the unsaid, an utterance speaks of more than it says, mediates between past and future, transcends the speaker's conscious thought, passes beyond his manipulative control, and creates in the mind of the hearer worlds unanticipated. From within the infinity of the "unsaid," the speaker and hearer, by a joint act of will, bring into being what was "said."

These pragmatic concerns with natural language are most clearly evident in recent work (van Dijk, 1977a; Coulter, 1979, 1980; Kreckel, 1981; and Clark & Carlson, 1982), whose empirical goals rest with the discovery of relationships among interactants' knowledge and the knowledgeable use of context-bound discourse structures (e.g., the strategic and situated use of speech acts). The realization of such empirical goals, however, need not be grounded upon psychological, experiential, subjective, or other inherently mentalistic concepts. Rather, it is assumed that ordinary discourse *is itself* an organized reflection of how interactants interpret, reason, make sense, monitor, and otherwise use their knowledge to structure everyday interactions. Coulter (1980, pp. 6, 34) observes,

> Real intentions, real motives, real thoughts, and real understandings are social phenomena through and through . . . the real problems of description and explanation of human action and interaction are not psychological or mentalistic in nature, but arise due to the occasionality, defeasibility, and normative negotiability of substantive descriptions of actions *and* substantive explanations of those actions. . . . [Mental categories] can themselves be treated in terms of the mechanisms of social-reality production and sense-assembly in everyday, practical, commonsense affairs.

The study of *conversational* coherence is thus equivalent to the investigation of how social understandings are *scenic accomplishments* (Coulter, 1980), that is, occurring within the observable, seeable, describable social world. These accomplishments presuppose, in their structural organization, how speakers and hearers commonsensically orient themselves to the occasion at hand. Such is the case when utterance connections appear vague and essentially incomplete to an uninformed observer, while being understood with relative ease by interactants sharing background knowledge:

> **Example 1** 1 **W:** Heard you're falling in love
> 2 **D :** (laughing) I wish I had recordings of those meetings!

Example 1 illustrates Goffman's (1976, p. 258) views on *normatively residual ambiguities,* whereby "What is 'said' is obscure; what is 'meant' is obvious and clear." It also evidences the kind of analytic mentality promoted herein, namely, to begin unpacking what Mohan (1974, p. 88) has described as "the link between rational order and temporal sequence" in everyday conversation. In most simple terms a rational explanation of this short sequence requires an understanding of the shared background understanding possessed by W and D. First, D had been absent from meetings held by W and others in which D had become a topic of conversation. Second, before this particular interchange, D had already discovered that his "falling in love" (turn 1) had been discussed by conversing with someone (other than W) who had also attended the meeting. Consequently, D recognized the source of W's comment without needing to expand the sequence and seek clarification. Finally, W interpreted D's response in light of the fact that (1) D could not have made such a reply without (2) prior knowledge of his being mentioned in an earlier meeting.

In this chapter three different data sources are employed to examine how conversational coherence is achieved in and through the background understandings and shared knowledge possessed by various speakers and hearers. Attention is first given to the interface of *social knowledge* and *social context* by analyzing how interactants work reflexively with discourse presuppositions. Numerous conversational instances, naturalistically observed and *reconstructed* by the author and those involved in each instance, constitute the data for this portion of the analysis. Consideration is then given to the sequential organization of longer segments of interaction, transcribed from video recordings of small groups. The specific focus is upon how group members use background understandings and expand sequences when producing *tellings,* by integrating past experiences into present interactional circumstances. Data for the third and final level of empirical analysis were drawn from the B-K conversation (reproduced in the Appendix of this volume) in which cultural knowledge, reconstructions, and tellings are deemed functionally significant.

WORKING REFLEXIVELY WITH DISCOURSE PRESUPPOSITIONS

Because we look not to the things that are seen but to the things that are unseen; for the things that are seen are transient, but the things that are unseen are eternal [II Corinthian 4:18].

Background understandings are communicatively relevant as tacit resources informing the orderly production of natural language. Conversational organization presupposes background understandings, just as ordinary social interaction would not be possible among interactants devoid of *cultural* (e.g., biographical, geographical), *relational* (rule-specific, code-dependent), and *linguistic* (syntactic, semantic) knowledge.[1] Interactants methodically rely on residual experiences when attempting simply to figure out what's going on face to face.

It is in this sense that speakers and hearers are themselves practical methodologists and theoreticians, reflexively engaged in language-based, puzzle-solving tasks (Garfinkel, 1967; Silverman, 1973). Everyday interactants are constantly designing and structuring, predicting and controlling, describing and explaining the often subtle nuances and intricate connections between language and meaning. This routine work involves levels of interpretive ambiguity, requiring speakers to disambiguate speakers' inferences and, conversely, hearers to disambigutate hearers' intentions as conversation is organized within situated occasions. How this communicative work is accomplished influences, and is influenced by, speakers' and hearers' methods for rendering social actions meaningful and coherent (e.g., see Grimshaw, 1980). A closer examination of these methods reveals complex interrelationships among *social knowledge, social context,* and the use of natural language as a vehicle for achieving interactional understandings (and variants thereof).

Social Knowledge

Following Garfinkel's (1967) early work on background understandings and practical reasoning in everyday life, it becomes clear that speakers' and hearers' expectations function as sets of pre-suppositions defining the ground rules. To the extent that interactants share expectations in the process of constructing a "perceivedly normal environment," there is a greater correspondence between *signs* and *referents* (e.g., utterance/meaning, behavior/action) and thus an increased likelihood that interaction will reflect a "mutually recognized texture of events" (Garfinkel, 1967, p. 46).[2]

To study conversational organization, however, it is necessary to display how notions such as "intersubjectivity" are grounded within those *culturally available* (scenic) *resources* (Coulter, 1980) actually used to structure interaction. For example, the following reconstruction illustrates how a discussion and earlier events in the day influenced the correct interpretation and presupposed meaning underlying an utterance:

> **Example 2**   (Setting: W and A are getting ready to eat dinner. W is in the dining room, unable to directly observe A in the kitchen.)
>
> 1   **W:**   What are you making in there?
> 2   **A :**   Brown rice. It looks like it got worse.
> 3   **W:**   What, your leg?
> 4   **A :**   Ya.

The potential ambiguity in this series of turns stems from W's clarification of A's utterance "Brown rice. It looks like it got worse" (turn 2). The question is: How did W know that A was indirectly referring to the worsening condition of her leg, rather than the brown rice being cooked for dinner? The answer resides within the shared knowledge between W and A, namely, (1) an infected mosquito bite had been the topic of discussion earlier that day in the back yard, which (2) led into a rather extended conversation of mosquitoes in general. This discussion had a residual influence, as evidenced by W's correct "guess" (turn 3).

Now, suppose that immediately after A's last utterance "Ya" (turn 4), A wanted to know how W had guessed the "leg" rather than the "rice." And W responds _____. What might you respond if you were W? Given your knowledge from reading about Example 2, how might you respond to A? It is not difficult to provide a coherent utterance informing A of (1) your remembering of the earlier discussion of mosquitoes that day; (2) how we were getting bitten in the back yard; and (3) how your bitten leg led us into talking about mosquitoes in the first place. For example, W might say, "From our discussion about mosquitoes in the back yard today"; or simply, "Remember the yard?" And while this last query might appear somewhat vague and ambiguous, it is normal that a person like A would, in Cicourel's (1973) terms, enact the "et cetera" principle by "filling in" the unexplicated information; In Garfinkel's (1967) terms, engage in "adhocing" procedures, similar to coders having to improvise their way through inherently ambiguous coding procedures; in Wieder's (1974) terms, "connect the behavior with the code," whereby "code" is synonymous with unexplicated but known features of the setting, as in his study of "telling the convict code" in a halfway house; or, in specific terms, behave according to Garfinkel's discussion of Mannheim's "documentary method of interpretation." Garfinkel (1967, p. 78) writes,

> The method consists of treating an actual appearance as "the document of," as "pointing to," as "standing on behalf of," a presupposed underlying pattern. Not only is the underlying pattern derived from its individual documentary evidences, but the individual documentary evidences, in their turn, are interpreted on the basis of "what is known" about the underlying pattern. Each is used to elaborate the other. . . . The method is recognizable for the everyday necessities of recognizing what a person is "talking about" given that he does not exactly say what he means.

In practice, Example 2 visibly displays what a theory of documentary method of interpretation attempts to describe. Such a method lies at the core of thinking ethnomethodologically. One must think reflexively to identify and understand a presupposed underlying pattern. The merging of interpretive practices and conversational structures is most meaningful in this regard. By examining how interactants connect *utterances* (as social structure) with *codes* (as the commonsensical sense of social structure), it becomes clear that commonsense reasoning is evident *within* conversational structures and functions to assemble and organize social reality in discourse (see Beach & Dunning, 1982).

Example 2 also gives rise to a series of questions that have been systematically addressed within Kreckel's (1981) work on shared knowledge in family discourse. Several of these issues are particularly relevant to the present analysis, especially her elaborations of the interactional relevance of *private, shared,* and *common* knowledge. Private knowledge consists of individuals' personal histories and experiences of past events. While private knowledge may be meaningful or lasting, it is not directly communicated during interaction. In contrast, the "knowledge acquired in mutual interaction between communicants provides the basis for shared knowledge, whereas knowledge acquired separately can at best be common knowledge" (Kreckel, 1981, p. 28). Because interactional involvement tends to promote the development of shared knowledge, conversational coherence becomes possible through speakers' and hearers' abilities to *reflexively monitor* both presupposed *and* explicit information resources (verbal, nonverbal, and environmental messages). Clearly, "not everything that is available is taken up and not everything that is said is shared between the interactors" (Kreckel, 1981, p. 22). Yet relationships are structured through the workings of private, shared, and common knowledge as they influence the uptake of certain kinds of information (see Brown & Levinson, 1978; Grimshaw, 1980) while swaying interactants to overlook, ignore, or simply fail to consider alternative interpretations of behaviors and/or events. Cicourel (1980, p. 104) reinforces the importance of this communicative work:

> Continuous feedback to speaker and hearer presumes monitoring or reflexive thought that can result in the building and interaction of more complex predicates about what is happening in the conversation, its present and future course or direction, and plans or strategies for elaborating, blocking, and terminating the conversation.

In contrast to Example 2, however, interactants' shared knowledge — as background understandings formed through mutual interaction — does not always ensure correct guesses regarding presuppositions. Reflexive monitoring can also result in the use of such moves as *clarifications* and *elaborations* in order to reduce ambiguity about previous experiences, as in Examples 3 and 4:

Example 3 1 A : This place reminds me of that restaurant,
remember, Our House?
                  2 W: What? This reminds you of our house?
                  3 A : No! The restaurant Our House.
                  4 W: Our house?
                  5 A : No, that restaurant where we ate pie, over by
Baskin Robbins, with a lot of older people.
                  6 W: Oh.

Example 4 1 A : Did you remember that broccoli is the second
most nutritious vegetable?
                  2 W: To *what?*
                  3 A : What?
                  4 W: To *what?*
                   5 A : I don't understand.

6 **W:** Well, if broccoli is the *second* most nutritious
         vegetable, what's the *first?*
7 **A :** Oh, tha:::t's what you mean! I didn't understand
         what you were getting at. Collard greens are more
         nutritious than broccoli.

In both instances the sequence was expanded because of the lack of conversational coherence. In Example 3 W did not commonsensically connect the Our House reference with a restaurant in which W and A had dined. Eventually (turn 5), A had to provide more details about Our House for W to grasp her intended meaning. And in Example 4, A did not recognize the intended references for W's "To *what?*" clarification (turn 2), even though W appears to be cognizant of their background understandings and is simply seeking additional information about the most nutritious vegetable. In this case, W had to offer more details in such a way as to provide A with a more specific (less ambiguous) sense of meaning (turn 6).

Both Examples 3 and 4 illustrate how background understandings are reflexively constituted: they can simultaneously be a resource for sharing social meaning *and* a topic for examination when ambiguity arises. In the process of disambiguating utterances to create understanding, interactants have little choice but to commonsensically examine those presuppositions glossed by the utterance themselves.

Social Context

All conversation involves the knowledgeable use of language in context (Bates, 1976). How interactants work reflexively with discourse presuppositions cannot be separated from the indexical (context-specific) features surrounding conversation. In most simple terms, social meanings and actions are reflexively tied; each functions to elaborate the other (Heap, 1975; Mishler, 1979; Leiter, 1980). Interantants are *influenced by* ethnographic particulars (e.g., physical settings and the persons comprising them, activities cooccurring with talk) *and influence* the relative impact each of these particulars might have on the sequencing and achievement of conversational coherence. We have characterized this work as *indexing* (Beach & Dunning, 1982), since a good portion of the interpretive work required to organize conversation coherently depends on how interactants go about sequentially inserting or placing utterances in light of the goals and priorities of any given occasion (e.g., being strategically indirect, playful, and/or protective of self-identity).

Reflexively, Ochs (1979, p. 9) explicates how language functions *in* context and *as* context: "Speakers and hearers must not only rely upon a context in order to comprehend discourse, but they are in fact embedded within the same context they create." Moreover, the organization of conversation is facilitated by *extrasituational knowledge* transcending the boundaries of any given context. To create a "situated condition for adequate, practical comprehension" (Coulter, 1979, p. 173), that is, to work coherently with what Searle (1975b) has termed "context bound presuppositions," interactants must collaborate on integrating those variables — internal and external to a given context — directly or indirectly influencing the interpretation and use of utterances.[3]

An illustration of these contextual issues appears in Example 5, a reconstructed pre-dinner sequence that was tied to an earlier discussion between W and A:

Example 5 1 **A :** We need to get a wok.
            2 **W:** A walk? Right now?
            3 **A :** No, later.
            4 **W:** After dinner?
            5 **A :** Maybe next week.
            6 **W:** What are you talking about?
            7 **A :** A wok, ya know, Chinese cooking? (Pointing at the kitchen.)
            8 **W:** Oh:::hh, a *wok!*

Of course, spoken discourse is heard differently than reconstructed discourse appears in text. The terms "wok" and "walk" sound essentially the same when uttered, so the context of interaction plays a major role in deciphering the meanings of any given term or phrase. In this example, A (turn 1) initially assumed that W would utilize his background understanding to make sense of an earlier shared agreement: the need to purchase *a wok utensil* for cooking. Her comment was also influenced by the obvious fact that friends were using a wok utensil for that evening's dinner. Yet, in response, W (turn 2) supplied a context of meaning quite different from A's focus of intention: walking. The following sequence became expanded to accommodate for the ambiguity in their conversation, leading up to W's direct question (turn 6) and A's direct answer (turn 7). Together, A and W solved the puzzle and reduced the ambiguity by contextualizing their discussion in light of the setting of which they were an integral part.

It can be assumed, therefore, that individuals can attend to different features of a given setting by relying upon shared background understandings in contrasting ways, and/or by possessing dissimilar knowledge about the present context. The latter is the case in Example 6:

Example 6   (Setting: Persons H and B are watching a lively jazz trio on TV. Person B had read a *TV Guide* description of this trio as being comprised of a father and two sons. H was unaware of the family relationships among the musicians.)

Utterances	*Interpretations*
B: Wo::ww, *playin* with your pa	(Gee, wouldn't it be great to be able to play music like that with your father? I'll bet his sons really appreciate having a father who's such a great pianist. It's nice that they can generate such music as a family unit.)
H: Ya . . . playing with your *el*bow, too!	(I can't believe that young drummer uses his whole arm like that. He's quick, isn't he?)
B: Hmm::::mm??? . . . Oh:::hh, yaa . . .	(What's he talking about??? Elbow? . . . Oh, I see, when I referred to "pa" and meant "father," he thought "pa" (paw) referred to "hands" . . .)

(B and H continue watching TV)

It is clear that B relied upon his reading of the *TV Guide* to initiate his first utterance. It also appears that (1) H interpreted "pa" to mean "paw," and (2) H did not possess adequate background knowledge to interpret B's utterance as a comment on a family jazz trio. Consequently, since B came to an understanding of H's commonsense reasoning,[4] a coherent sense of social structure was maintained for B while H remained unaware of the momentary *lack* of coherence (i.e., B's confusion). In this particular case B did not seek clarification of H's utterance because of his realization that H had linked "pa" with drummer's performance. Thus, B understood that words can possess multiple meanings, that it is normal for individuals to make different sense of the same context, and also that H was likely unaware that B had problems understanding the coherence of his agreement with B's original statement. If B had explicitly informed H that the intention of H's utterance ("Oh:::hh, ya . . . ") was understood, or if H had doubted B's acknowledgement, then H would have been more likely to make some reference to the incoherence of the sequence.

Competing claims of social reality are constantly emerging during conversation, resulting in what Pollner (1975) has called *reality disjunctures*. As has been illustrated, interactants can make sense of the same context in dissimilar fashions, due largely to differences in the kinds of knowledge relied upon when attempting to solve language-based puzzles. Consider the following example of a man talking after church with a recently married couple:

Example 7	1	**W:**	Hey Bud, how are you?
	2	**B :**	Fine, thanks, and you?
	3	**W:**	OK. Last time I saw you you were looking for a girl//
	4	**C :**	(joking, yet concerned) He was, huh? He never *tells* me about *these* things. Just like I told you Bud//
	5	**W:**	No, not *that!* Bud was working on a suicide case.
	6	**B :**	(Bud elaborates and justifies his "looking for a girl" to C.)

The sequencing of Example 7 is understood by W and B, yet C (Bud's wife) has difficulty figuring out the presuppositional nature of Bud's "looking" (turns 3 and 4). (Might she be jealous and protective of her new husband?) W senses her discomfort (turn 5), however, as evidenced by what his, "No, not that!" glosses and leaves unspoken. Bud then (turn 6) describes his background understanding with A: Being a University policeman, he knocked on W's (a professor) door one evening and asked him if he had seen a woman on the floor of that particular building. Apparently, there was a woman threatening suicide, and Bud had been assigned to locate and stop her from harming herself. This mutual interaction had produced shared knowledge between the professor and Bud. But until C was informed of their shared experience, she had little choice but to supply her own context for interpreting the unspoken meanings underlying W's "Last time I saw you you were looking for a girl." Jumping to conclusions can, of course, lead to ungrounded assumptions, false accusations, and/or arguments concerning the implications of any given action or utterance.

Reality disjunctures also emerge when different interpretations of previous discussions lead to interactional trouble, as with the *disagreement* in Example 8:

Example 8	1	**P:**	She said she could wait until next week to give her a call.

2 **D:** No, she didn't. We'd better call her right away or we might not get the reservations we need.

3 **P:** Will you just be *patient!* If you'd have listened carefully enough you'd know that she doesn't even *need* to know until next Monday or so.

4 **D:** Forget it. I'm gonna call her after lunch to make sure.

5 **P:** Why can't you believe what I'm telling you?

6 **D:** You've been wrong before.

7 **P:** Right, and *you* haven't huh?

and with the *confusion* and possible hurt feelings arising among friends in Example 9:

Example 9 (Setting: Persons W, A, C, and D had spent the evening together, playing cards and talking. Person D visits W and A on a regular basis, but it is rare for C to accompany him. At the beginning of the evening, C and D (spouses) had brought a large Raggedy-Ann doll that C had spent months making. During the evening, several jokes were made about C spending so much time working at her job and sewing that D hardly had a chance to spend time with her. C and D left at the end of the card playing. Several minutes later, there was a knock on the door. The following discussion ensued.)

Utterances	*Interpretations*
1 **D :** C left her doll.	
2 **W:** Oh, sure you don't want to leave it?	(That's a joke. C would *kill* him after the time she's spent making it.)
3 **D :** No:::oo thanks! She'd *kill me!*	
4 **W:** OK. (Hands D the doll.) Whenever C isn't around . . .	(Don't forget that now you have a "companion" for those lonely hours while your wife's at work. Ha, Ha . . .)
5 **D :** (frowning) Oh, OK. Goodnight.	(Hmmm. Why does W want me to visit when C's not around? Maybe he doesn't like C and would prefer that I stop

over by myself in the future.
That's strange . . .)

Throughout the evening, discussions about the doll and C's work habits had provided W and D with shared knowledge. In both of W's turns (2 and 4), this background understanding was used to make two attempts at humor. D (turn 3) clearly recognized A's first humorous comment. However, W's "Whenever C isn't around . . . " confused D. D interpreted W's utterance as serving the function of a "good-bye" (e.g., "Hope to see you soon," "Stop over again when you feel like it," and so on). However, D was confused as to whether the presuppositions underlying this utterance might have excluded C from joining him in a future visit: Do W and A dislike C? If so, what implications might this have for W and D's relationship? Whether D decides to directly confront W with his confusion (as he did at a later date), and how to go about confronting, are commonsensical decisions indicative of D's social construction of reality.

It is clear that within a group setting, interactants need not (and often do not) share the same background understandings. Example 10 evidences yet another possible outcome, namely, how S breaks a rule that is idiosyncratic to W and A's relationship:

Example 10 1 **S :** Well, you have a *bunch* of convention papers, Jesus.
2 **A :** (to W) He said *Je*sus!
3 **W:** (laughs, looking at S)
4 **S :** I think I've uncovered a previous discussion here.
5 **A :** (to S) See, the background is . . . (A continues to fill in S.)

Unknown to S, W and A had negotiated an understanding of not referring to "Jesus Christ" as an exclamation or tag term in everyday conversation. In essence, S unknowingly broke the rule and received a comment from A (turn 2), confronting S with a language puzzle in need of solution: What do W and A know that I don't, and how should I react? S apparently realized that the key to the puzzle was to discover the nature of this presupposed knowledge as rooted in the substance of a previous W-A discussion. A then proceeded to inform S of the negotiated rule adhered to by W and A on a normal basis.[5]

Of interest here is how conversation can be used as a reflexive, multifunctional vehicle for (1) figuring out why immediate utterances are connected as they are, (2) rendering previous discussions as legitimate topics for inspection, and (3) building coherence by filling in unspoken presuppositions, currently at work, by reference to explicit conversational negotiations *in the past.* Moreover, background understandings can function as meaningful resources for legitimizing current activities, as revealed through S's comment one week after the occurrence of Example 10:

> **Example 11   S:**   I can't believe all the snow, *Christ* (pause) oooops!
> (pause) Are you going to write that one down too?!

S was reflexively aware of his usage of "Christ," and his, "Are you going to write that one down too?!" makes sense *only* in light of the previous discussion one week earlier.

Examples 2 through 11 were employed to illustrate how interactants work reflexively with discourse presuppositions and methodically confront the problems initially raised with Example 1: Because sequential coherence is replete with "normatively residual ambiguities," interactants regularly use language *in* contexts to *build* contexts in which "what is 'said' is obscure; what is 'meant' is obvious and clear" (Goffman, 1976, p. 258). Of course, coherence is not always obtained; we have also attempted to show how such phenomena as ambiguity and reality disjunctures influence practical, everyday understandings.

BACKGROUND UNDERSTANDINGS AND TELLING-EXPANSIONS

The discourse segments examined thus far were reconstructed from natural settings. They are relatively short sequences within which the working of background understandings and shared knowledge were shown to be evident. As conversations become expanded, background understandings also function as resources allowing for the meaningful possibility of these expansions. The sequential organization of turn-taking can be understood, at least in part, from the perspective of how interactants reconstruct past experiences and/or render descriptions of shared or common knowledge. These reconstructions and descriptions function to make current discussions more informative, detailed, exciting, relevant, and understandable in general (or so it appears in a majority of cases). They have been widely characterized as "tellings" or "accounts,"[6] wherein interactants go about producing mini-ethnographics about people, places, events, and their constituent features.

Group Tellings

Background understandings give rise to tellings throughout diverse social occasions. It is exceedingly normal for interactants to integrate past experiences — individual and/or relational — into present interactional circumstances. This normality is evident in the following video-transcribed segments, drawn from small groups whose task it was to study conversational organization in small group decision making.[7] Natural language is reflexively used to make sense of past sense-making experiences descriptively, as seen in Example 12 where D attempts to *show the relevance* of his telling to other group members:[8]

Example 12	1	**A:**	Who's having the FAC?
	2	**B:**	It's Sig Eps//or not Sig Eps
	3	**A:**	Oops, they'll be there//she'll go
	4	**B:**	No (0.5) hey (0.5) it's Kappa//Sigs and Sigma Nus and their little sisters
	5	**C:**	(0.1) boyfriends?
➤	6	**D:**	This is//
	7	**A:**	Oh//
➤	8	**D:**	just like the tape!
	9	**C:**	What (1.0) *our* tape!
➤	10	**D:**	"Oh, you're goin to the bars?"
➤	11	**C:**	Ya, I thought about that, too
➤	12	**D:**	"No, they canceled that" [GP1, 121-125]. (C acknowledges D's reconstruction through nodding and eye contact, and the group continues with its discussion.)

As D was monitoring turns 1-5, he noticed that the present discussion was similar to an earlier taped discussion that had been analyzed in class. The classroom tape also included an "FAC sequence." In D's first two turns (6, 8) he identified the resource presupposed in his following reconstructions (turns 10, 12). Vague as D's moves might appear to the uninformed reader, C appeared to recognize that D was attempting to integrate the current discussion with a prior classroom experience. D's telling, then, required C to work with presuppositions rooted in their shared knowledge.

Reflexive monitoring can also promote ambiguity through tellings. In Example 13, *confusion* is treated through *clarification:*

Example 13	➤1	**A:**	I think he's been the *least* quiet in the group, don't you think?
	2	**B:**	Um hum
➤	3	**C:**	Ge::zz, *really?*
	4	**A:**	Who do you think has been (0.5) ya you have (2.0) who do you think has been the most talkative in our group?

   ⟶ 5   **C:**   I won't say anything but wait (1.0)*le:::ssst* quiet?
        6   **A:**   Ya, you're the//
        7   **B:**   No, most//quiet
        8   **A:**   You're the most quiet
   ⟶ 9   **C:**   I didn't think so [GP1, 395-400].

It turns out that in Example 13 there is no real substantive disagreement, because A (turn 1) made a later corrected mistake (turn 8) in saying "least quiet" rather than "most quiet." For C to have recognized A's mistake, of course, presupposes that his background knowledge of group interaction was different from A's initial characterization in turn 1. Through this clarification sequence, *current* definitions of C's *past* behavior are collaboratively brought into an agreeable form.

Substantive disagreements do occur, however, as with Example 14, where A offers a telling that B finds problematic. The following is yet another instance of an interactional reality disjuncture:

Example 14 1 **A:**   And we decided to take off and go to another party because it was so boring//
            2 **B:**   (to C) I was havin' a pretty good time aktuly and really didn't wanna drive all over town when it was snowing and icy
            3 **A:**   = You were *bored,* too!
            4 **B:**   Not really bored//
            5 **A:**   And you told me//
            6 **B:**   cuz I was watchun TV and lsnin to music
            7 **C:**   (to A) Don't look at me! I wasn't there
            8 **A:**   (to B) You *told* me you were ready to go, remember? [GP4, 227-230,].

Tellings can promote *compliments* rather than disjunctures, however, as in Example 15 where B and C tell A and D about their past writing of the group paper (being revised by the group in turns 1-11):

Example 15 1 **C:**   OK, should we revise that?
            2 **A:**   Maybe a little bit//um
            3 **C:**   In general or//
            4 **D:**   For the majority of
            5 **A:**   Most people (1.5) the majority of people
            6 **C:**   Or generally speaking
            7 **A:**   Right
            8 **C:**   Or *some*thing like that
            9 **A:**   Generally desire to take a turn and um (1.0) this taking turns *can* fulfill a person (2.0) I would

say *can* or not that's good "Aids in fulfilling a persons" (2.5) and uh this kinda gets kinda confusing//

10 **C:** Yep (0.5) very

11 **A:** But as soon as you get to this that's//pretty clear

12 **B:** (laughing) You shuduv been there when we were trying to do it=

13 **C:** ="How do I word this?" (1.0) "How do we word this?"

Telling 14 **B:** Ya

Sequence 15 **C:** "What's a good big word?!"

16 **A:** (mimicking C) What's a good big word

17 **C:** "We're gonna make this so confusing//you won't be able to understand it"

18 **A:** You guys (1.5) I think you did a really nice job on this

19 **D:** Yep (nodding)

Compliment 20 **C:** Sue did a nice job typing

Sequence 21 **B:** It wasn't too hard//really

22 **A:** Good job, Sue (patting her on the shoulder) [GP2, 645-654].

Note C's *reconstructions* (turns 13, 15, 17) of the kinds of comments C and B were making at an earlier meeting. It is presupposed that these utterances do not refer directly to the present context, except to add detail and to reexperience their work for their own as well as A and D's benefit. The telling sequence (turns 12-17) sets up the compliment sequence (turns 18-22); the latter is reflexively tied with the former. Note also how C and B *downgrade* the (18-19) compliment and agreement in turns (20-21) (see Pomerantz, 1978).

Example 16 also involves compliments and a telling, yet in this instance the compliments appear first and the telling is employed as an expansion indicative of *shared knowledge:*

(Group is talking about organizing their paper.)

Example 16 1 **A:** Right, cuz if you just//start out

2 **C:** Ya you'd havtuh tie it all together

3 **A:** If ya just start out with speech acts//

→ 4 **B:** Ahhh!=

5 **A:** =you kinda lose that initiation=

6 **C:** =You have some//thing to say?= (to B)

7 **D:** What?

→ 8 **B:** OK uhh (2.0) hhm:::mm (2.0) my ideas come
            and go so quickly
→ 9 **C:** You shaved your *bee::ard!*
10 **B:** Ya
11 **D:** Oh my *God* you//di::dd!!=
12A **and C** (laugh simultaneously)
→13 **A:** Didn't you notice that?=
14 **B:** Ya
15 **C:** Aa::::hh!
→16 **D:** God, ya I noticed//something was difrent (1.0)
            but//
17A **and C:** (laugh simultaneously)
18 **B:** Ya
19 **C:** OK
20 **B:** Wednesday I did it
→21 **D:** Looks very nice (0.5) looks very//nice
→22 **C:** Yes it does
23 **B:** Thank you guys
→24 **C:** Larry's startin//to grow his back, ya know
            Larry, *Kristi's* Larry? Larry and Kristi of Kristi
            and Larry fame?
→25 **B:** Oh ya [GP2, 807-816].

In turn 8, D "spaces out" what he was going to say next, but is miraculously saved from embarrassment because in turn 9 C notices that B had shaved his beard. In turn 13, A questions C and D's background knowledge, which D justified somewhat in turn 16. D them compliments B (turn 21) on his appearance, and C agrees. C then offers a brief telling to B in turn 24, apparently (but not assuredly) because C and B both know Larry and Kristi.

Examples 12 through 16 only begin to reveal how tellings are rationally ordered and oriented-to by interactants. As interactants reflexively monitor the conversational sequencing of which they are a part, background understandings function as an integral resource for describing past experiences and mutual acquaintances, and for integrating them into the ongoing stream of interaction. At times such tellings can be successfully enacted for purposes of providing detail and elaborating points, creating a sense of interactional cohesiveness, and for *altering* the future course of interaction:

Example 17   1 **D:** We should probly get to work though instead of
                    messin around

  → 2 **A:** He *said* we could do whatever we feel like doin, even telling jokes if we feel like it (1.5) Wanna hear//a joke?

     3 **B:** I think we got (0.5) oh (looking at A)

  → 4 **C:** (scoffing to A) OK, go ahead. But did you remember the punch line?

  → 5 **A:** *Yes* I did! (laughing and slapping C on the shoulder)

     6 **D:** Oh ya, tell us

     7 **C:** No//

     8 **D:** Tell us//

     9 **C:** Nope
              (1.5)

   10 **B:** Why?

   11 **C:** Cuz
              (2.0)

   12 **A:** It's really funny

   13 **B:** Do::oo (0.5) *do* tell

   14 **A:** OK

 → 15 **C:** Oboy! (as though he can't believe A was really going to tell the joke on tape)

   16 **A:** OK (1.0) ya think I should?

 → 17 **C:** Well it's up to you//but who knows who can see this? (hesitantly)

   18 **B:** Why not? Why na::uught?

   19 **A:** No, I can't

 → 20 **C:** (chuckling) I *knew* it//good

 → 21 **A:** It's really bad (C and A laugh together)

   22 **B:** (frustrated) Would you *tell* us the joke?

   23 **D:** Tell us a *nice* joke then

   24 **A:** I don't have any (C and A chuckle) (2.5) OK, well, Sue, do *you* want to tell us anything?
            [GP1, 200-203,].

This segment reveals how A's background knowledge, displayed in turn 2, altered the course of the conversation for at least 22 turns at talk. A justified "messin around" by reporting that the professor (who is presupposed in this sequence) wouldn't mind "even telling jokes if we feel like it" (turn 2) and then "baited" the group by uttering, "Wanna hear a joke?" C than displays further background knowledge in turn 4 by asking, "Did you remember the punch line?" Note how A and C collaborate on laughing and chuckling, apparently because A has told C the joke before. As is obvious, group interaction can be organized in and through multiple levels of background understandings working simultaneously to structure turn-taking. Tellings such as Example 17, then, are indicative of what Churchill (1978, ch. 7) terms "procedural problems" as the course of a conversation sequence is negotiated. Moreover, while the telling of a dirty joke is comprised of various structural properties (see Sacks, 1974), this sequence evidences how *not* telling a joke is itself an organized accomplishment. The joke's telling is withheld because of C's (turn 15, 17) concern about the appropriateness of such a telling as captured on videotape, A's being influenced by C's concern, and the nature of their shared knowledge about the unspoken joke.

B-K Conversation

In the Appendix we are informed that B and K were both members of a class and a small group who worked together on a project for a complete semester. They are not strangers and must share some knowledge about common experiences and each other, yet the extent of their relational history is not readily apparent. One must look at the discourse to glean an understanding of their social relationship, recognizing at the outset that any given conversational segment — regardless of duration — only glosses more complex histories presupposed (and frequently ignored) by interactants as they structure turn-taking. With these considerations in mind, certain features can be identified that reveal how B and K utilize background understandings to organize coherent exchange.

First, natural language users of a given culture possess a certain amount of pragmatic knowledge about that culture, such that interactants need not know one another to exchange this information coherently. It should come as no surprise, therefore, that B and K generate sequences in which cultural presuppositions assume a major role:

Example 18	012	**K:**	Oh. What kind of sandwich is that.
	013	**B:**	Turkey.
	014	**K:**	Very Thanksgiving of you/
	015	**B:**	Appropriate.
	016	**K:**	((barely audible)) Yes.

The connections between "Turkey," "Thanksgiving," and "Appropriate" are rationally accountable by reference to the season of the year and those foods indicative of Thanksgiving festivities, both of which are presupposed in this sequence. In another sequence (045-066), B initiates a telling about her father in such a way that is recognizable to K, as evidenced in the "correctness" of her question:

| **Example 19** | 058 | **B:** | It seems like long. It's gonna be two weeks. |
| | 059 | **K:** | Hmm::! |

060 **B:**   [
            My father and I haven't spent two weeks
            together in quite some time ((snicker))
061 **K:** A real challenge? ((pause)) Or will it be fun.

            [
062 **B:**   He's a
            challenging person . . .

Pragmatically, K relied upon the content *and* tone of B's first utterance (058) to paraphrase and reflect her understanding of B's relationship with her father. Her utterance (061) is also reflexively tied to B's,
"My father is the main problem.=" (turn 022), and the following
"father" sequence (turns 023-033), itself being a resource for background understandings created throughout mutual interaction.

Second, B and K use *reconstructions* to build coherence, similar
to those employed in Examples 12 and 15, to better integrate past
events with present topics:

Example 20 023 **K:** =*Yes.* I have that same problem. I finally
                        resorted to saying ((louder, mock
                        exasperation)) "Dad? What do you *want.*"
                        ((high pitch, comical)) "I don't need
                        anything."

              030 **B:** I mentioned that problem to my father on his
                        birthday. He said "I don't want anything, I
                        don't need anything save your money," so I did
                        and I just sent him a card and he was
                        tremendously hurt and upset. ((laugh))

              073 **K:** So I got him one the other day an'ma I- showed
                        my mom it, an' she said ((raised pitch,
                        animated)) well what *size* did you get'em. An'I
                        j's I picked it up and looked at it sa- Oh! A
                        medium. I got him one to fit me. She *wha::t?*
                        Well by summer he'll be wearing the same size
                        I am. He wears the same size shoes.

Third, this conversation appears lubricated by tellings, given their
frequency and the detail in which they are rendered across topics. As
a result of B's turns (e.g., 112, 233) and K's turns (e.g., 209, 213, 314,
337), previous experiences are granted privileged status to make
current interaction more interesting. Getting a handle on the past can
set the stage for more meaningful here-and-now relationships and also
can be therapeutic for speakers and hearers. Of course, these functions can be fulfilled through less extended and elaborate tellings
(e.g., B's 243/245, 257; K's 189, 226/228) as topics are initiated,

maintained, and terminated. Notice, however, that the vast majority of tellings noted above are rooted in either B's or K's *individual* rather than *shared* (B-K) experiences. The presuppositions in this conversation also appear more cultural than relational (i.e., restricted code-specific, since rules idiosyncratic to this relationship are in initial phases of development). Thus one might conclude that these tellings were used practically to inform each other about their personal backgrounds, and in so doing to advance the relationship beyond current levels of nonintimate involvement. Mutual interaction and shared knowledge should not necessarily be translated into relational intimacy; B and K possess the former, but not the latter (or so it appears and can thus be hypothesized).

CONCLUSION

The researching of conversational organization is constrained by many of the same variables influencing everyday interaction. As natural language users, social scientists must rely on their their private, shared, and common knowledge about particular relationships and the social world in general in order to make coherent sense of how language and meaning are inextricably woven together. The process of inquiry presupposes a necessary reliance upon extralinguistic and extrasituational information as sequences of conversation are deciphered and unraveled. Much as normal interactions, this investigative work is inherently ambiguous, especially when attempts are made to ascribe inferences and presupposed meanings to those scenic practices constituting exchange. As Cicourel (1980, p. 101) notes:

> Forms of reasoning are viewed as central to the researcher's understanding of the way speakers and hearers presumably understand one another. The forms of reasoning we attribute to the participants of discourse parallel the reasoning we employ as researchers in making sense of the speech acts we record and listen to in arriving at some form of analysis. But as researchers we can, of course, specify formal aspects of discourse, produce systematic descriptions, and note emergent properties of the interaction. Yet we cannot attribute such properties unequivocally to the knowledge base of the participants. . . . The general point is that the communication we attribute to discourse and any paralinguistic and nonverbal activities is part of a complex, multi-level, not always integrated setting. Multiple sources of information are always operative and so our analysis of discourse must necessarily simplify or reify many aspects of social interaction as well as what we are calling discourse.

While practical experience informs us that utterances are routinely connected by natural language users and that this common-sensical work is frequently accomplished with relative ease, a pragmatic view reminds us of the problematic tasks confronting researchers wishing to investigate *how* sequentially achieved understandings are regulated in context. The 20 examples and corresponding analyses in this study, presented as partial evidence of the existence and workings of conversational coherence, are best viewed as simplifications or reifications of the settings from which they were drawn. Moreover, the insights offered about these instances are not *incorrigible readings* (see Wootton, 1976) in so far as they were not intended as finalized knowledge claims. Rather, each discourse segment is open to alternative readings and formulations, just as any given sequence of utterances might be interpreted differently by a variety of hearers in everyday interaction.

The three data sources previously discussed — reconstructed instances observed and experienced by the author, video-transcribed segments of small groups working on a class project for the author, and the B-K transcript supplied to all authors by the editors of this volume — each possesses its strengths and shortcomings. First, the reconstructed instances allowed for the possibility of first-hand interpretations and observations of these events, as well as the accessibility of asking others how they rendered these instances as socially meaningful. Through the author's background understandings, various interactional presuppositions could be identified beyond the utterance themselves. Yet, this technique faces the danger of being little more than a personal recapitulation of the author's (possibly) idiosyncratic interpretive and conversational practices across a fairly limited sample size. Consequently, it is essential that such reconstructions include the collaborative efforts of those involved as efforts are made to transform talking into textual data.

Second, the video-transcribed segments permit detailed transcriptions of longer interactional sequences and also the freedom of observing how these segments both preceded and followed other sequences. The use of precise notation symbols begins to capture the subtle nuances and various turn-taking operations representative of natural language. The explicit use of background understandings, then, are describable as embedded structures within the ongoing flow of interaction. Tellings are seen as being accomplished in numerous ways, through various interactional mechanisms and strategies, and conclusions can be drawn about how tellings contribute to the structuring of sequential order. The mere identification of structure, however, need not lead to pragmatic explanations of rational actions. At times it is useful to have access to interactant's knowledge base, even though this access is only partial. The groups in this study consisted of students within the author's classes, so some degree of shared knowledge was available as evident in some of the insights employed (e.g., Example 12). Yet recordings of unknown but natural interactions will not lend themselves to interpretations through shared knowledge. In such cases researchers must rely upon their common knowledge and basic competence as natural language users. They must also be willing to recognize *and* tolerate trade-offs concerning the richness of findings generated solely structurally and/or pragmatically (i.e., where discourse structures also document underlying presuppositions).

Finally, the B-K conversation forces the researcher to rely fully on the discourse itself as an indicator of the relationship between these interactants as well as a structural display of degrees of conversational coherence. The influence of background understandings must, out of necessity, be inferred only from those interactional mechanisms used to structure exchange. The detailed organization of turn-taking is thus essential to the identification of various mechanisms (e.g., reconstructions, tellings). Moreover, the transcribing process provides an excellent opportunity to become aware of the sequential workings of turn-taking mechanisms, and when researchers rely upon other's transcripts — not generated, for example, with the same or similar transcription notation symbols — this awareness is short-circuited and the only options available involve the utilization of "what's there." The most important function of having numerous researchers examine the same transcript, therefore, is to point out that available data can be legitimately understood from multiple perspectives.

Little has been said in this study about the strategic employment of background understandings for such purposes as deceiving, avoiding, purposely creating ambiguity, and other practical accomplishments having to do with identity and appearance management in face-to-face occasions. Social knowledge is often used for purposes of *not* revealing interactional presuppositions, or revealing only those in line with interactant's goals. The correspondence of actions and meanings is frequently subject to manipulation. Conversational coherence is often attained but not recognized, or simply not attainable as interactant's background understandings differ radically in their presuppositional status. Much could be gained by systematically examining instances where coherence is *not* displayed, so as to gain a fuller appreciation of those situations made possible because of a mutually coherent sense of social structure.

NOTES

1. One might add to this list spiritual, moral, and ethical commitments. In this case Coulter's (1979) formulations of beliefs, as presuppositions informing degrees of certainty about truth claims, are particularly useful. Similarly, Clark and Marshall (1981) argue for the relevance of *co-presence heuristics* (i.e., physical and linguistic co-presence, community membership) as interactants use their knowledge to infer mutual beliefs. Clark and Carlson (1982) extend the notion of a mutual belief induction schema by analyzing the coordination of such collective directives and joint acts as requests and informatives. (See also Note 5.)

2. Garfinkel's indebtedness to Schutz's (1962, 1964) views on "schemes of interpretation," the "stock of knowledge at hand," and "intersubjectively shared experiences" is most clearly evident when examining how *interactional* understandings are made possible because of the assumed or presuppositional status of any given normative order.

3. Grice's (1969, 1975) seminal work on the cooperative principle and attending maxims for successful communication (i.e., quantity, quality, relevance, manner), as well as his views on conversational implicatures and indirectly conveyed meanings, have been widely cited by language researchers interested in conversational coherence and comprehension (e.g., Clark & Haviland, 1977; Clark, 1977). Searle's (1969) elaboration of "felicity conditions" giving rise to certain speech acts, and the interface of illocutionary and perlocutionary dimensions of utterances, draws attention to the utility of simultaneously examining the interpretive (e.g., intentional) and structural variables of discourse. For example, as Bach and Harnish (1979, p. 12) have noted, "People do rely on others to have identifiable intentions in their utterances, and they expect others to rely on them to have such intentions." Basic to their speech act schema is the communicative presumption that speakers typically produce utterances with the intention of performing an illocutionary act decipherable to hearers. This is the case even when speaker's utterances are ambiguous and do not seem literally stated nor directly spoken. Thus, speakers can perform subtle hints with the intention that the hearer can identify an act being performed but not necessarily the indirect purpose underlying the hint per se. In such cases the perlocutionary effect intended by the speaker may differ from the hearer's uptake (or identification of the act being performed). Nevertheless, successful communication has been achieved "if the hearer identifies the attitude expressed in the way the speaker intends him to identify it. This requires the hearer to make an inference, an inference based partly on the supposition that the speaker intends him to make it" (Bach & Harrish, 1979, pp. xv-xvi).

4. Kreckel (1981, ch. 10) refers to such skills as "metalinguistic abilities," or the competence required to make sense of how others are making sense in and through context-dependant speech. Schiffrin (1980) identifies how such sense making is situated in actual discourse by examining how it is not simply talk, but talking about talk — metatalk — that functions in both refential and expressive fashions.

5. Relying heavily upon Bernstein's (1972) research on restricted (context-dependant) and elaborated (context-independant) *speech codes,* Kreckel (1981, ch. 4) displays how social relationships possess unique role relationships. Relationship rules are essentially viewed as language codes, through which interactants structure and negotiate their roles, which define the presuppositional nature of relevancy and appropriateness for any given utterance or action. Example 10 is one instance of an outsider (S) unknowingly breaching a rule, becoming aware of this breach by observing how A and W *interactionally treat* this breach, and then recognizing that he is not privy to W and A's shared knowledge.

6. A more thorough discussion of *storytelling* research, and an elaboration of how interactants time-travel in order to make points, plan activities, and report ordinary experiences may be found in Beach and Japp (1983).

7. Small group tasks involved (1) the audio-recording of small groups in a natural setting (e.g., homes, dorms, bars, committees); (2) systematically listening to and reflecting upon the recording; (3) the transcription and analysis of a small segment of the recording (e.g., thirty seconds to two minutes); (4) the writing of a paper integrating the chosen segment(s) with how small groups construct their social reality in and through turn-taking and the use of speech acts, and how conversational organization is related to the ways in which groups accomplish decision making communicatively.

8. Transcribing conventions were generally borrowed from the notation system developed and refined by Gail Jefferson. This system appears in full in Sacks, Schegloff, and Jefferson (1974). Specific conventions are as follows: The double oblique (//) indicates the point at which a current speaker's talk is overlapped by the talk of another; the equals sign (=) indicates "latching" — that is, no interval between the end of a prior and start of a next piece of talk; numbers in parentheses indicate elapsed time in tenths of seconds; colons (:) indicate that the prior syllable is prolonged, while multiple colons (:::) indicate a more prolonged syllable; italics (*terribly*) indicate various forms of stressing, and may involve pitch and/or volume; finally, to represent reconstructed, projected, and/or personified utterances, we chose to employ quotation marks ("").

<<<<<<<<<<<< >>>>>>>>>>>>

11

Language, Coherence, and Textuality

<< DONALD G. ELLIS >>

< < < An adequate understanding of human com- > > > munication is impossible without a working knowledge of the organizational features of the linguistic system. Such a system, which is composed of arbitrary symbols and rules for their usage, operates on a number of levels (phonic, morphemic, syntactic, pragmatic), all of which combine to produce a meaningful message. Understanding how the various elements of a linguistic system combine and cohere is the key to understanding how meaningful messages are produced. The relationships among linguistic units are complex and operate on multiple levels such that one structural level (e.g., morphemics, semantics) contextualizes another and seeks its own context in other units. I argue below that language is organized around a series of structural levels and the nature of the organization is responsible for coherent language use. More specifically, language and discourse serve the *functional* requirements of communication and cannot be separated from an extralinguistic context (situation). The act of tying language to a situation is the essential communicative act and any quality of language use, even syntactical structures, is a function of larger discourse requirements.

The term "coherence" is very broad and the study of any number of issues can fall under its rubric. Coherence implies the presence of some organizational structure or relational principles, and any theorist is either explicitly or implicitly concerned with the sensible organization of phenomena. The goal of systematic inquiry is to render a phenomenon coherent. But the trick to understanding coherence lies in identifying the constructional elements of the subject of interest and in stating relationships among these elements. The purpose of this chapter is to explore the interrelationships among language, coherence, and textuality. The symbols that constitute language are organized in accordance with principles of coherence and it is my contention that the functional requirements of communication and the general strain for meaning provide the impetus for the coherent and communicative use of language. I will argue in this essay that coherence operates at various linguistic levels and that textuality results from the intermingling of these levels.

The term "textuality" is necessarily abstract because it refers to that quality of being a whole text. Textuality is the sense one has that some corpus of language use is unified and exists as a whole. A book, speech, verbal exchange, essay, journal article, group discussion, and so forth all represent situated language use that functions in some systematic manner and can be recognized as having boundaries, artificial as they may be. Textuality results when there is actual functional unity between language and the world created through processes of decision and selection. It is not the case that textuality depends on the sentence as its primary constructional unit. A text could be no more than a single word, or any system of elements that do not have sentence status (advertisement, sign), and still signify textuality (deBeaugrande, 1980; Pike, 1967; Jones, 1977).

Although coherent discourse is a semantic notion, coherence is realized in *cohesion;* that is, when some aspect of a discourse is dependent on another (Halliday & Hasan, 1976). Cohesion, according to Halliday and Hasan (1976), "is part of the system of language" (p. 5). And although they claim that cohesion is not a structural aspect of texts, Halliday and Hasan are essentially *text based:* They emphasize the system of reference that is natural to the language. Cohesion is a tie or a relation between two elements such that one assumes the other and is at least partially dependent on it for interpretation. Pronomialization is the most commonly cited example. For example, in the B-K conversation, B says, "I mentioned that problem to my father on his birthday. *He* said, 'I don't want anything . . . '" (turn 027). The word *"he"* depends upon a relationship with something else for its interpretation. It depends upon "father" in the preceding sentence, and the relationship between "father" and the pronoun "he" lends coherence to the two utterances and contributes to textuality. I will retain Levy's (1979, p. 184) distinction between "cohesion" and "coherent" by using coherent to mean "comprehensible." Where cohesion refers to the particular mechanisms of structural binding, coherent connotes the mental processes that allow a discourse to be sensible and understood by the participants. What follows is a discussion of how coherence contributes to all levels of language use. I will proceed by delineating functional levels of language use, discussing the nature of coherence at each level, and concluding with some proposals for future lines of work.

Much of the work in traditional linguistics is concerned with cohesion or relationships among elements of the language. It is possible, even if for demonstrative reasons only, to organize the foundational features of language hierarchically to show how linguistic phenomena are patterned. Beyond the syntax level the strength of this hierarchical organization weakens, but it is useful for showing the nature of cohesion with respect to phonology, morphology, and syntax. These three subfields comprise traditional linguistics and each is rendered coherent — that is, sensible — by identifying the discrete units that define the subfield and the combination rules that account for their operation. These combination rules can be complex and varied in form (e.g., descriptive, prescriptive, transformational, recursive, and so on), but they all state some regularity and a relationship among elements. Coherence is conceptually tied to these rules by virtue of a rule's ability to state a relationship between two or more elements of a phenomena, and for the relationship to be understood by language users. I will avoid a detailed discussion of the nature, scope, function, type, and value of rules (see Shimanoff, 1980) except to say that these rules are normative and assist language users with the process of interpretation and sense making. So, in turn 027, the pronoun "he" is recognized as a substitution for an earlier referent. The hearer is instructed to retrieve the fully lexicalized meaning of the term elsewhere. This pronomialization rule tells the hearer that the person performing the action in this utterance is a third person who is a singular male. The hearer must then return to the most sensible noun to understand who "he" refers to.

Phonemes are the building blocks of language and it is the relationship among phonemes, including articulatory principles and sequential structure, that constitute sound sequences that are a part of the coherence structure within the phonological system. In English, for example, any word beginning with three consonants will begin with an /s/. If /p/ is second then only /r/, /l/, or /y/ can follow. If the second consonant is /t/ then only /r/ can follow ("streak"). A sequence of sounds coheres and is thereby meaningful if the proper phonotactic rules are involved. Rule deviations that apply to other languages and exceptions are easily recognizable by users. For instance, the /ts/ arrangement of phonemes does not occur in the word-initial position in English, but it does in German. Moreover, spelling conventions that result from phonemic loans can find their way into a language, for example, the combination /ts/ in the initial position in tsetse, a word borrowed from Bantu. But language users know these rules and are struck with confusion when they are violated.[1]

Morphology is the next hierarchical level respectively. As soon as a sound or series of sounds acquires meaning it is a morphological element. Morphemes — meaning-bearing parts of a word — are the fundamental elements of morphology, and the way morphemes are tied to one another and form other words is labeled derivational morphology. Any morphological rule (e.g., adding the bound morpheme "est" to form the superlative, as in "quick" becoming "quickest") can serve as an example of how the morphological system in the language creates coherence.

Up to this point we have been principally dealing with the arrangement of elements into order (i.e., sequential connectivity). When we move to the next hierarchical level the importance of sequential connectivity begins to subside. While sequential connectivity is important in syntax, it cannot fully account for the structure of a sentence. In a sentence such as, "The man in the building wants to have lunch," it is impossible to explain how the sentence is well formed or coherent by referring to the sequential (syntagmatic) aspect of language alone. "Building" and "wants" are adjacent but not functionally related since a building cannot "want," and "want" refers to "man," which appears much earlier in the sentence.[2]

Relations among language elements become increasingly complex at the level of syntax, and the complexity is intensified when considering relations among sentences or sentence groups, that is, discourse. It is no surprise that the most well-developed areas of linguistics are those that have identifiable segments (e.g., phonemes) and a relatively restricted range of combination rules. The reason for this increasing complexity is the importance of meaning when considering syntax and discourse. For years language theorists avoided the thorny issues of meaning and semantics and treated meaning as if it were like the phoneme level; that is, decomposable into minimal segments (Katz & Fodor, 1963; Nida, 1975). So the analogue to a phoneme was a "sememe" or a semantic marker (Kempson, 1977). However, meaning cannot be decomposed into neat units and there are any number of issues that present inordinate difficulties (see Rieger, 1975; Wilks, 1977; Winograd, 1978).

An important response to segmentation approaches to meaning has been use theories of meaning as advanced by Wittgenstein in the 1930s. Use theories hold that the meaning of an expression is determined by its use in a language community. This is a very significant shift in perspective and one that I want to pursue and extend to general principles of coherence. A use theory of meaning is important because the question of how a discourse is organized and coherent becomes a matter of language functions rather than language structure. Where phonemics and morphemics can be decomposed into primitive elements with structural relations, this is not the case when considering discourse. Discourse is inextricably tied to communicative intent, purposes, and goals; it is based on pragmatics or the rules that apply illocutionary force (meaning) to utterances and utterance parts. Discourse coherence is both conceptual and empirical in that it is concerned with meaning and conventional knowledge on the one hand, and reliant on the observable properties of language and context on the other.

The argument that language and discourse are fundamentally communicative devices and can be manipulated by human beings is receiving serious attention (Givón, 1970a, Sanders, this volume), especially with respect to syntax. Nevertheless, it is an important argument to pursue because it reassigns communication to the central influence on language behavior and relegates internal linguistic constraints to a subordinate position. Moreover, I would like to take the argument a step further and show how functional variation is *intrinsic* to the nature of language; it is a fundamental property of language and can account for the distribution of grammatical units and, more important, for the particular texture of a discourse. A functional approach to discourse does not simply mean that some message serves a communicative purpose, but that communicative purposes and social requirements constrain the particular organization and expression of language. An utterance can be multifunctional. It must be possible for more than one principle to assign meaning to an utterance. Functional coherence, then, implies that even though meaning relations are bound together in a very dense framework, these relations cannot be segmented and governed by a few combination rules; rather, coherence operates at a number of levels and we must understand the contribution of each level before a proper interpretation is possible.

I have stated previously (Ellis, 1982) that coherence and language use must be examined on a variety of levels, and that coherence mechanisms reflect a functional relationship between the peculiar characteristics of an utterance and discourse requirements. A functional relationship means that the organizational qualities of an utterance are a consequence of something else, namely, communicative intent. Garcia (1979) and Givón (1979a) have shown how such a functional relationship can account for even the most definite structures of a sentence. The disparity between this position and more traditional Chomskian grammar cannot be stressed too much. Transformational grammar restricts syntax to the sentence and posits the autonomy of syntax; that is, grammaticality is separate and independent of communicative purposes. However, something cannot be both independent and the result of something else, so if it can be demonstrated that communicative requirements do explain certain qualities of structure then such a demonstration will have significant implications for the functional relationship between language use and interaction.[3] The functional nature of language organizes coherent linguistic relationships at all levels and creates a discourse text, and while I am most interested in the interactive aspects of coherence even the most stable syntactical structures are sensitive to more general communicative requirements.

COHERENCE LEVELS

The role of meaning becomes increasingly important at the syntax level, so this is the proper place to begin the analysis. It is possible to show how all aspects of a sentence or utterance cohere to render the unit sensible or interpretable by a competent language user. Garcia (1979) and Givón (1979a) offer some convincing demonstrations of how certain communicative qualities have become grammaticalized; that is, found their way into the syntactic structure of a language. These authors, among others (Li & Thompson, 1976; Schachter, 1976), explain how the properties of sentence subjects are topic properties and that the topic requirements of a discourse have become grammaticalized into sentence subjects. In other words, all sentences are about something and this topicality has its roots in the most rudimentary forms of communication. Speakers in early oral cultures uttered phrases that were about something (topic) and they then commented on the topic of their utterance. This topic-comment structure was a response to communicative needs because all communications say something about a general topic. This topic-comment organization found its way into the nature of formal sentences as a subject-predicate structure. Moreover, Garcia (1979) has shown the order of the nominative case verses a second case in old English is a function of communicative considerations of the author and not a simple fact of old English grammar. Again, this indicates how even some of the most technical aspects of syntax, which are typically thought to be unresponsive to context, vary as a function of the communicator's desires, preferences, and so on. Language use of any type is a response to human interaction and this functional perspective means that standard interaction routines play a more important role in explaining the nature of language and how it coheres. To claim that the intrinsic structure of syntax explains what a speaker does implies that speakers communicate in the *only* way they can. However, if the facts of language structure must be explained by appealing to communicative requirements, then coherence becomes a function of interaction among communicators and not an a priori property of the language. Such a perspective directs attention to the contributions of individuals, relationships, contexts, and topics to coherence; a contribution that has been largely ignored in the past.

Case markers (Givón, 1975) have influenced the theory of language and were proposed as an effort to introduce meaning into transformational grammar and syntactical structure. Cases are conceptual and help explain how meaning and communicative intent have worked their way into the structure of language. The case of a noun or pronoun indicates its function in a sentence as it relates to verbs; nouns or pronouns can be the subject of verbs, the possessor, or the object. They contribute to coherence in a sentence by syntacticizing typical relations that a communicator may want to express. For example, I might express the relationship between a noun and a verb and communicate my message by simple serial positioning. In this situation the relation between a noun and a verb is maintained because propositions precede or follow one another and there is some sensible relationship between the two. So someone might say, "TAKE BALL THROW." When the relation is syntacticized as in, "He threw the ball," there is one complex verb that communicates time (tense) and a relation between the verb and the noun (a transitive verb that takes an object). The morphological and syntactical structure of the language is sensitive to communicative requirements. Again we can see how the facts of language can be explained as a response to communicative needs. As communicators needed to express more with respect to time and relationships among objects and events, mechanisms for doing such became available and were incorporated into the language system. These mechanisms are a form of cohesion and one way to explain how syntax is responsive to the strain for meaning that is the essence of textuality.

I want to propose three levels of coherence analysis; that is, three levels of language functioning that must be governed by principles of various types. Before I do it is necessary to be more specific about the difference between coherent and cohesion and to explain how this difference finds its way into all three levels of language functioning. The distinction between "coherent" and "cohesion" generates two aspects of any analysis of coherence, and while it is impossible to ignore either, an analyst can emphasize one or the other. Coherence is fundamentally dependent on *text-based* and *mind-based* principles. Text-based analyses focus on the properties of language (e.g., reference, ellipses) and are associated with more traditional linguistics. Mind-based analyses emphasize mental representation and are the typical focus of cognitive psychologists and artificial intelligence researchers. It is important to stress that a full and complete understanding of discourse coherence results from the convergence of both text-based and mind-based perspectives. The mental processes of speakers are realized in language and language and mind have a reflexive relationship; it makes little sense to talk about one and not the other.

Depictive Level

A detailed analysis of a particular discourse would be a tedious process indeed. So I plan to use a portion of the B-K conversation and hope that it is representative of the issues I want to address. I will use the opening segment of the conversation beginning with utterance 001 and ending with utterance 016. The points I want to make can be illustrated in any segment of the conversation; I have chosen this initial segment because it is clear and relates well to the general categories of coherence. Consider the following utterance:

Example 1   012   **K:**   What kind of sandwich is that?[4]

This is a well-formed English question and a conversationist could imagine any variety of utterances that might legitimately precede the utterance or follow it. For now we will consider the sentence in isolation and move to its discourse relationships later.

The first function of coherent language use it to portray the world. I have termed this the *depictive* function. Before an utterance can express a communicative desire, or relate in any way to other verbal contributions, it must bear some symbolic resemblance to the real world. It does this by portraying objects, describing processes, characterizing events, expressing relations, and so on. I have termed this the *depictive* function because it more accurately captures the descriptive and "portraitive" nature of language. This is different than simple representation, which is usually presented as a basic function of language, because it avoids the connotation that language involves some one-to-one relationship between sound and object or concept. To represent implies that language *re-presents* or acts as an agent for the world; depiction, on the other hand, retains a sense of the ontological nature of language. So utterance 012 can be schematized as follows:

Example 2

What kind	of sandwich	is	that
nature, character	identify and name class of objects	state of identity between object	object understood from context

What is an interrogative adjective, and combined with *kind* it is understood as an attempt to inquire about the distinguishing qualities of a thing. *What* + *kind* is a conventional device used to inquire about the nature or type of an object. The expression makes no sense until a class or group of objects are identified. Typically, the class of objects that *kind* is referring to will follow. In this sentence *of* names the class of objects and the noun class comes next *(sandwiches)*. Now given the situation, the sandwich is present in the environment and *is* + *that* relates the general class *(sandwiches)* to a particular object in the environment. At the most basic level the utterance depicts the world. There are things called sandwiches and these things have qualities and attributes; moreover, there are kinds of sandwiches where some aspect of the object changes. There are linguistic conventions for referring to objects in the environment (e.g., exophoric, *that;* naming things, *of;* inquiring, *what;* and so on).

Utterance 012 easily depicts recognizable phenomena and processes in the world. However, we really have to elaborate on this because so much of our communication is imaginative and creative. It must be possible to account for metaphorical and novel uses of language. For example, K says, "Very Thanksgiving of you" (014). Again, the sequential character of the interaction is important to a full semantic interpretation, but it is still necessary to explain how the depictive level of coherence contributes to the full realization of a text. *Thanksgiving* is a noun that refers to the act of giving thanks or to a particular American holiday. Although *thanksgiving* can be used as a descriptive adjective (e.g., thanksgiving day, thanksgiving parade), it almost always refers to the holiday and very rarely describes the dispositional state of a person. The use of the term here is quite metaphorical because its meaning is transferred to a novel or atypical context. In the broad sense switching from a noun to an adjective is metaphorical, but this switch is built into the structure of the language. Another layer of meaning is added because of the special use of the word "thanksgiving" involving a class of objects and behaviors typically belonging to one occasion that are transferred to another.

Coherence in this case is still depictive because the sense of the utterance is determined by the fit between the lexical item and the occasions of its use. Adjectives usually describe things so it is possible to describe a person as having thanksgiving-like qualities even though it is somewhat odd. The term "thanksgiving" implies a reasonably autonomous situation and acts as a frame (Minsky, 1975). The depictive level of coherence is more than a direct semiotic relationship such that one thing is a sign for another. A single term, such as thanksgiving, establishes conventional knowledge and activities, causes and consequences, and part/whole relationships. The entire frame must be shared if the utterance is to be coherent. Moreover, the peculiar use of the term accounts for the whimsical quality of the utterance. Even without detailing the prosodic features of the conversation, a casual listener could attest to the light-hearted manner in which the utterance was offered. K is implicitly aware of the rather clever extension of the thanksgiving frame and takes some delight in its use. These paralinguistic qualities also contribute to the interpretation of the word because the hearer is cued to the unusual metaphor. The depictive level is essentially reliant on a relationship between expressions and objects, situations, and processes. However, discourse and language function at another level of abstraction; they express action based on purpose and intentionality.

Speech Act Level

Simply depicting the world is one function of language but beyond that sentences or utterances perform larger communicative functions. If we look again at utterance 012, it is immediately recognizable as a question. The utterance is not viewed as a depiction of our experience but as a basic move in the social interaction process; it is an act or something that is carried out with speech. The meaning is, "I request you to provide me with information about the nature of the object in that place." The meaning, then, is different than the depictive level because it is more abstract and corresponds to a speech function that is either appropriate or not in a particular context. Where an utterance may depict reality in a stable manner across a variety of contexts, a speech function may be appropriate in one context but inappropriate in another. I have termed this the *speech act* level because it is language as action rather than language as depiction.

The speech act function of language and coherence is analogous to the work on speech acts by Austin (1962) and Searle (1969) so I will not dwell on it here. However, the coherence issues emerge from theories of action. To say that we do something when we speak (e.g., promise, question, assert, and so on) is a long way from producing sounds that combine into words or sentences that depict the world. Yet, there is a correlation between sounds and action and this correlation is the central concern of the study of pragmatics. This decision on the part of a speaker to produce certain sounds comes from the speaker's intentions with respect to what he or she wants to communicate to a hearer, and these intentions derive from the speaker's decisions about what is going on in the communicative situation and what the hearer should know. In other words, control of the more fundamental properties of the language (phonetics, syntax) comes from the larger social acts. Again, the communicative and general discourse function of language is the primary organizing element. The task of doing coherence analyses is a matter of formulating the conditions that comprise a successful speech act that has illocutionary force. This involves analyses of reference, propositions, clauses, morphemes, phonemes, and the performance of the speech act. The speech act is coherent if the result of the act is an acceptable token of the intended act. The success of the act (its perlocutionary effect) is unimportant at this point. If the communicator executes language in accordance with the conventions of the intended speech act, then the act would be deemed coherent.

The elementary structure of the coherent relationships for speech act is as follows: I perform X (action) by doing Y (speaking, depicting, sounding). There is both a mind-based (coherent) and a text-based (cohesion) dimension to this relationship. Action is essentially dependent on mind-based structures such as the beliefs, wants, and conventional knowledge of the speakers and hearers. To ask a question, such as the one in utterance 012, depends on the speaker's knowledge of the context, knowledge of the hearer, assumptions that the hearer possesses the relevant information, politeness norms, knowledge about how to perform the speech act, and so on. The text-based dimension depends on the extensional and intentional definitions of the lexical items and how the speaker utilizes formal linguistic conventions to recover knowledge and meaning. For example, interrogative noun sequences might give rise to an expectation that one was asking a question about an object (e.g., a sandwich). In short, the coherent performance of a speech act depends on the interaction of participating mind systems and language systems, each of which is governed by the conventional nature of the act, and the conventional nature of the units and structure rules.

Discourse Level

To provide the final balance among language functions we must consider the discourse function of language. It is possible to argue that the discourse level cannot be meaningfully separated from speech acts because they rely on contexts; nevertheless, the distinction is useful because the discourse level addresses issues in structural binding beyond sentences or clause units. Discourse issues lend thematic organization to interaction and such organization is central to textuality. Speech acts and their constituents signal the elementary meaning units in interaction and the discourse structure lends more general semantic organization. This is true even with respect to cohesion because even the most precise structural tie functions to preserve semantic continuity. So the discourse level of coherence requires linguistic units beyond the sentence proposition and is based on the interpretation of one sentence, clause, or utterance relative to another. There is a fundamental notion of "connectiveness" vis-à-vis the *n*-wise relations among units. The issues in coherence at the discourse level pertain to one of three general categories.

The first is a general system of structural relations that characterize the semantic properties of discourse. A sentence, utterance, or whatever unit of interest must be understood in relation to an understanding of some other unit. It is theoretically possible, then, to propose a discourse model, and the model is satisfied when all possible relations have been identified and values attached to them. The analyst's task is to show how a discourse is coherent by specifying the various types of connectivity. DeBeaugrande (1980) describes the two general components of discourse structural relations as being concerned with either sequential connectivity and/or conceptual connectivity. Although deBeaugrande offers some precise operationalizations of these issues, he is essentially referring to the tasks of arranging language elements into working order, and stating how underlying concepts promote meaning and a sense of understanding. Sequential and conceptual connectivity are not analogous to text-based and mind-based approaches respectively because the latter set of terms are points at which one can enter the problems of connectivity. It is possible, in other words, to take a text-based approach to conceptual connectivity or a mind-based approach to sequential connectivity. I offer some examples below but the key point here is that coherence at the discourse level must begin with a statement of formal semantic relations that organize discourses. Such a statement relies on the intersection of two paths: one establishes conditions for possible relations and the other provides conventional content based on knowledge of the world.[5]

A second organizing principle of discourse coherence, and one that has generated a fair amount of commentary, is the notion of topic of conversation. Topicality, and its various attendant issues, has been used to define connectedness of sentences and coherence of discourse. The basic topic-comment structure is fundamental to all discourse and has even found its way into the essential definition of a sentence (Givón, 1979b). Topicality contributes to coherence and textuality because it has semantic status. It functions to determine what is being said and is associated with what is assumed or already known about an utterance. The subject-predicate nature of a sentence, which derives from the topic-comment nature of discourse, has explicit *syntactic* status and can conceivably be different from the topic of a sentence. K says (006): "No. Thanks. I've finally got my apple." The sentence is not about "I" (K) but about not wanting half of a sandwich. The semantic status of topicality is especially evident when we consider how easily the topic can change simply by reassigning vocal stress:

> **Example 3** **a:** Í've finally got my apple.
>   **b:** I've fínally got my apple.
>   **c:** I've finally got mý apple.
>   **d:** I've finally got my ápple.

The topic of the utterance could be who got the apple (I), when the apple was obtained (finally), whose apple was obtained (mine), or what object was obtained (apple).

Topicality is logically related to the connectivity issues of discourse as discussed above because it contributes to coherence via both sequential and conceptual connectivity. It is often difficult to decide just what the topic of an utterance is, but this is mostly true when sentences are considered in isolation. The sequential connectivity aspects of topicality can be ascertained by examining preceding utterances. Sequential connectivity concerns the linguistic, logical, propositional, referential relations, and so on, that adhere between temporarily related utterances. (e.g., utterance 005 topically contextualized utterance 006). We are now talking about the relationship between the topic of an utterance or the topic of a conversation or discourse, and this is a more complex notion than the topic of a sentence. Discourse topics are related to conceptual connectivity and function at a different level of abstraction from sentence topicality. While it is possible, although cumbersome, to explicate topical continuity between utterances (via reference, ellipses, semantic categories, etc.), relating a series of particular verbal contributions to a more macro-topic is especially difficult. It can only be done by demonstrating that a macro-proposition is logically and semantically related to particular sequences in a conversation; moreover, the relationship must be hierarchical because the individual elements of the conversation must be part of the more general topic. So in utterances 005 through 016 of the B-K conversation, for example, the macrotopic is food and it must be theoretically possible for this topic to generate interaction pertaining to types of food, times for consumption, effective reactions to food, holidays that imply certain foods, and so on.[6]

The third class of issues that bear on coherence at the discourse level pertain to the more precise linguistic mechanisms that do the work of coherence. Most research has been concerned with these matters (see, for example, Halliday & Hasan, 1976; deBeaugrande, 1980). The central concern is with the precise nature of a meaning relation. After all, to say that two or more sentences or conversational turns cohere because of some meaning relation is not very precise. Almost any collection of utterances might cohere from some perspective, bizarre as the perspective might be. However, it is critical that one be able to identify specific coherence relations and how they help develop textuality. Halliday and Hasan's (1976) work is quite well known and most representative of this type of work. They discuss referential ties, conjunctions, lexical cohesion, substitutions, and ellipses.

One problem with this line of work is the extent to which tie mechanisms can have ambiguous interpretations. A typical conjunction such as *and* can serve a variety of semantic functions; it can tie elements of a discourse in some very different ways and the exact nature of the tie is not apparent from the conjunction itself. Halliday and Hasan (1976) explain numerous conjunctive relationships but they do little to solve the problem of multiple uses and how the same grammatical morpheme (e.g., *and*) serves numerous functions. Consider, for example, the use of *and* in turns 030, 031, and 033 in the B-K conversation. The conjunction that begins 033 is continuative and allows the speaker to extend on the content of the utterance. However, both uses of *and* in turn 030 are consequential and instruct the hearer to understand the subsequent phrase as a result of what went before it. A third use of the conjunctive *and,* in turn 031, is additive. Birthdays are to be added to Christmas as holidays that K's father enjoys. The conjunction *and* can serve so many purposes because it is not semantic. Unlike topics or lexical relations, the term is purely structural and coordinative and relies on the semantic relations among the words or clause units that it coordinates. *And* simply expresses a conjunction of two propositions and coherence is achieved on the basis of the known conceptual relation between the propositions.

FURTHER ISSUES IN COHERENCE

One dimension of the entire discourse coherence question that has received very little research attention is the difference between within-speaker turn coherence versus between-speaker turn coherence. That is, what meaningful differences emerge when coherence functions to organize the on-line construction of a message by a speaker, as opposed to messages that are responsive to previous turns at talk? Moreover, are there unique or special coherence strategies designed for either? Again, it is useful to make the distinction between text-based approaches and mind-based approaches to either cohesion or coherence. Issues in cohesion probably do not vary significantly with respect to within-turn or between-turn coherence, especially when considering particular grammatical ties such as conjunction, lexical cohesion, and referential relations. These forms of structural binding work the same way whether they are organizing within-in turn or between-turn utterances. However, the frequency with which a particular form occurs will vary according to within- or between-turn utterances. It is rare, for example, to use a conjunction such as *and* to tie two turns at talk or even to indicate that one turn is connected to another. *And* functions to coordinate propositions according to relationships (e.g., additive, continuative, consequential) and it is rarely used as a sign that one speaker is establishing these same relationships with the propositions of another speaker. It is, of course, possible for one speaker to continue the flow of the previous speaker with a conjunction such as *and* but, as evidenced by the B-K discussion, this hardly ever occurs.

It is interesting to note that a conceptual issue that distinguishes between cohesion functions has implications for when such devices are used in a conversation. Consider the difference between two cohesion mechanisms, namely, reference and conjunction. In the case of reference, information is being signalled for retrieval. The thing being retrieved is referential *meaning* or the class of objects or things being referred to. Reference is a *semantic* relation and coherence lies in the continuity of reference. A conjunction, on the other hand, is a type of semantic relation but not one in which the instruction is to retrieve the information elsewhere. A conjunction does not stand for prior information; rather, it specifies how one thing is to be systematically related to another. It is instructive to examine the use of various references and conjunctives in the B-K discourse, and how these inform the differences between within-turn and between-turn coherence. Referential ties are fairly common at the beginning of turns because they maintain topical continuity. Although the demonstrative *that* occurs within turns and can perform exophoric functions, it relates two different speaker turns when it appears in the beginning of an utterance and refers anaphorically to something that preceded it. Utterances 145, 163, 180, 220, 284, 289, 302, 308, and 315 all begin with the demonstrative *that* and essentially begin the process of relating the current turn on the floor to the immediately preceding one. *That* also implies distance between the speaker and the proposition and is typically used to refer to something that someone else said, a strategy that is necessary for between-turn coherence. Although *this* can refer to something that has preceded it, there is a tendency for *this* to be used when the speaker is referring to something near or to something the speaker himself said. Utterances in the B-K dialogue begin with *this* on two occasions (utterances 153 and 338); in the one case (153) it reflexively refers to something the speaker said and in the other it exophorically refers to something current and near.

The conjunctive *and* almost never serves as a tie to the preceding utterance, unless the speaker is extending on the specific content of the previous speaker. There is one instance of this in the B-K conversation (turn 074) where B offers a future consequence of K's brother outgrowing his shirts. The conjunction *and* is in the initial position of an utterance in turns 033, 082, 087, 114, 206, 219, 245, 251, 257, 261, 276, and 283. A close examination of the transcript shows how these turns are really continuations by the same speaker. In each instance the *and* is a grammatical extension of the same speaker's previous subject matter. Utterance 033, for example, is a simple addition to the subject matter in utterance 031. This is true of all the other turns listed above. So *and* is more of a conceptual organizer than a conversational one; it connects semantic relations within a speaker's turn but is very unlikely to assist with the organization of sequential connectivity between turns.

There is yet another issue with respect to coherence that might prove to be an interesting avenue of research. It concerns an individual communicator's predispositions to construct messages that cohere in a particular way; that is, individual differences that might account for strategies of coherence. In some senses this is an odd question to ask because the coherence system is a defining aspect of the language system and is not something communicators are very reflective about. People are not consciously strategic about how they organize their within-turn or between-turn utterances. Nevertheless, various cohesion mechanisms and coherence relationships are not equally distributed throughout the population of language users. It is probably possible to assume a correlation between the coherent organization of discourse and various individual differences and predispositions. The explanation for this correlation requires a deeper understanding of the relationship between discourse and mind, or text-based and mind-based coherence. Individual tendencies to organize their discourse in a particular way are not analogous to personality or trait variables, rather they are a reflection of cognitive structure and processing.

Given the intimate relationship between language and mind, it should not be surprising that differing psychological realities have correlates in coherence issues. Labov and Fanshel (1977) utilize such a perspective in their analysis of therapeutic discourse. They reason from the verbal text of a patient to her cognitive representations of the world and her private characterizations of people, relationships, and problems. One way to do this is through the analysis of typical cohesion mechanisms. Consider the following example from Labov and Fanshel (1977, p. 99):

Example 4   **Th.:**   Does it have anything to do with . . . your . . . weight?
　　　　　　 R.:   No, I don't think so!

The *so* in R's response is a clausal substitute and refers anaphorically to the fact that *it has nothing to do with my weight!* The task of the discourse analyst is to expand the utterance to make the implicit explicit. While such a task is simple for the above example, the value of the activity becomes apparent when the analyst must devise a technique of tracking the coherence system of a particular individual. In the therapeutic setting this is often the exact goal of the therapist's diagnosis and analysis. As Labov and Fanshel (1977) indicate, there is typically no simple rule that allows one to make the connection between utterances. The problems of moving from filling out the cohesive nature of elliptical responses to a portrayal of a person's psychological reality are formidable indeed.

Bernstein (1971) and Kreckel (1981) also speak to the issue of individual qualities and their relation to cohesion in discourse. These authors present a theory of codes based on language rules and individual speech codes that regulate interaction and an individual's discourse. It is at this point that much of the work in discourse cohesion can work in concert with more individually based concerns. A subcode is a person-based way of organizing reality. It is, according to Kreckel (1981, p. 37), "an open-ended system whose elements, signs, receive their value by paradigmatic and syntagmatic relations that reflect the communicative context, i.e., the history of priorities of the social group and social function(s) to which speech is subjected within this group." The definition emphasizes cognitive categories or the predominance of principles of organization. A speaker, given his or her code, selects language features from alternatives on the basis of cognitive organizing principles, and thereby represents his or her individual reality in interaction. Language use in this case is not simply representative of what is out there. Rather, communication is a portrayal of the interplay of what is in there and what is in between (Kreckel, 1981; p. 38). The systematics of such analyses are a bit difficult to imagine. Nevertheless, it should be theoretically possible to use principles of cohesion and individual preferences for particular cohesive devices, as an index of how a language user is creating and maintaining meaning.

CONCLUSION

In this chapter I have tried to show how the properties of language derive from functional requirements and organize according to a set of organizational principles. These principles are essentially what account for coherence in discourse and it is the sense of coherence that makes for textuality in language use. Textuality is what makes a discourse recognizable as a clearly identifiable semantic unit; it is a general property of language use and is apparent when a discourse has a unified relationship with its environment. Principles of cohesion and coherence, along with individual language users, are what account for such a unified relationship. And although there are any number of methodological and research issues to work out, it is important to establish a reliable presuppositional base for the pending solutions to these puzzles.

NOTES

1. It is important to keep in mind that orthography (spelling) is responsive to a different set of rules than pronunciation. Alphabets do not represent sounds in a direct way.

2. Any book on syntax can provide a complete explanation of this (Akmajian & Heny, 1975).

3. In fairness to Chomsky, I should note that given his interests in understanding the human mind and not communication, the assumptions of an autonymous syntax are sensible.

4. The terminal punctuation used here (?) differs from that of turn 012 in the Appendix (.). Here the utterance is written in regular form, as a question. Punctuation in the Appendix is used to indicate intonation patterns; thus the period that terminates 012 indicates that the speaker used a full-stop falling intonation. — *Eds.*

5. See Goddard and Routley (1973) for more on this type of logic.

6. I should note that what counts as a topic can vary in abstraction. The food topic in utterances 005 through 016 is nested in larger topics (see the topic change in 017). The entire B-K conversation is about something even though quite a variety of specific topics are subsumed by more general ones.

<<<<<<<<<<<< >>>>>>>>>>>>

IV

CONVERSATION AS A GENRE OF DISCOURSE

<<<<<<<<<<<< >>>>>>>>>>>>

12

Tactical Coherence in Courtroom Conversation

<< ROBERT E. NOFSINGER >>

<<< Witnesses in civil and criminal trials in the >>> United States typically say what they are expected to say.[1] During direct and cross-examination, witnesses' answers to questions predominantly display the information that the lawyers intend them to give. Departures from this pattern usually involve cross-examination of a witness hostile to the questioning lawyer's case or, from the witness's perspective, cross-examination by a hostile lawyer. The witness in these situations often phrases answers unsatisfactorily for the lawyer or gives incomplete answers, but even here it is clear that the witness knows roughly what answer is expected. Of course, in any trial there is often some adjustment of answers to questions and vice versa. Conversation analysts call this *alignment*. Most of the time, witnesses' answers substantially match the intent of lawyers' questions. In addition, people observing these lawyer-witness conversations in the courtroom, whether they be spectators in the public gallery or members of the jury, usually have the feeling that they know what the questions and answers mean and even where they lead.

Assuming these descriptions of lawyer-witness conversations are accurate, two inferences are warranted. First, witnesses for the most part understand lawyers' questions in the usual sense of knowing the semantic meanings of words and the syntactic relationships within and between sentences. Often, witnesses also understand what the lawyers are getting at, where they intend to go with their questions, and what use they might make of the answers. Second, lawyers for the most part understand how their questions will be interpreted by witnesses and can anticipate to a large extent that the answers will either be on target or will be intendedly off target. While it might be argued that the lawyers and witnesses have heard and said it all before (in depositions, preliminary hearings, and rehearsal), this is not generally true of spectators in the public gallery, and certainly is not true of the jury. Jurors, in fact, are usually selected through a process that screens out anyone who has heard pretrial testimony. Since they, too, understand what is being said and what its import might be, it seems that processes of understanding in the courtroom rely on something other than repetition.

These assertions about lawyer-witness conversation in the courtroom are likely to be accepted by anyone who has examined a witness, given testimony, served on a jury, observed trials, or studied court transcripts. It is readily apparent that court participants experience lawyer-witness talk as orderly and meaningful most of the time, and that they utilize that sense of meaningfulness to perform their respective roles and to make judgments about the progress of the trial. This sense of the meaning and direction of questions and answers in the courtroom is termed *coherence.* Lawyer-witness talk that produces testimony (that is, direct- and cross-examination) has many important similarities to everyday conversation, and is accordingly termed *courtroom conversation.*

I shall assume the existence of coherence in courtroom conversation unless evidence to the contrary is present. My purpose here is not to prove that courtroom conversations cohere but to present the claim that recognizing an utterance as part of a tactical plan for reaching a known goal (which a lawyer or witness is pursuing) contributes to that coherence. The following sections of this chapter describe the strategic perspective from which the study is done, characterize courtroom conversation in more detail, examine the tactical (goal-oriented) aspect of conversational coherence in the courtroom, and compare it to the coherence of everyday small talk.

THE STRATEGIC POINT OF VIEW

Courtroom conversations will be characterized in the next section as directed toward primarily informational goals and as involving the orderly exchange of talk between a restricted set of participants. It will be shown that the talk is exchanged within identifiable spatial and temporal boundaries and is designed to achieve a restricted set of communicative functions. It therefore seems best to adopt a strategic model or point of view from which to investigate coherence in the courtroom. The same point of view will be applied to everyday small talk.

One model of the communication process that seems compatible with the character of courtroom conversation is Frentz and Farrell's (1976) language-action paradigm. It is a *strategic* point of view in that it assumes communicators — called *actors* — are oriented toward one or more communication *goals* (objectives, results). During conversation the actors have or develop a sense of each other's goals, including some they usually have in common. Actors also have a sense of the rules that constrain and define their behavior as well as a sense of what communicative actions they can take to pursue their goals. Frentz and Farrell's (1976) basic framework and many of their concepts are in current use by communication researchers (e.g., Krueger, 1982), and with some modifications to be mentioned later, the language-action paradigm provides much of the basis of the strategic point of view adopted here.

To use Frentz and Farrell's (1976) terms, the examination of a witness by a lawyer (a courtroom conversation) is a communication *episode:* "a rule-conforming sequence of symbolic acts generated by two or more actors who are collectively oriented toward emergent goals" (p. 336). The concept of an episode reflects findings reviewed by Gumperz (1972, p. 17) that members of a society are typically able to view certain stretches of conversation as distinct wholes having specific rules, communication patterns, and beginning and ending boundries. The *symbolic acts* that constitute the episode (Frentz & Farrell, 1976, pp.340-341) are conversational actions performed through talk (although some could be performed nonverbally) by actors with the intention of achieving their goals. As described in the next section, symbolic acts that predominate in lawyer-witness episodes in the courtroom include requests for information, requests for clarification, statements or assertions, and the like. Searle's (1969) work on speech acts is usually the basic reference on these conversational actions, and other communication theorists use his term (e.g., Cronen, Pearce, & Harris, 1982; Jacobs & Jackson, this volume, who also focus on Searle's, 1969, narrower concept of illocutionry acts).[2] For a view somewhat different than Searle, see Bach and Harnish (1979).

Symbolic acts are typically about something; that is, they have semantic and syntactic meaning, a certain sense and reference. Frentz and Farrell (1976) call this *propositional force.* When we understand *what* a lawyer has asked or *what* a witness has stated, we understand the propositional force of that actor's symbolic act. The conversational function of the act — taken in the context of the particular episode of which it is a part — is what Frentz and Farrell (1976) call its *episodic force*. When we understand that a lawyer has *asked* or that a witness has *stated* something, we have recognized the episodic force of that symbolic act. This depends on our recognition of the actor's intention to produce the force of requesting, clarifying, stating, or whatever (Bach & Harnish, 1979, p. 15; Searle, 1969, pp. 43, 47). For example, if a witness were to follow a lawyer's question with the utterance, "I didn't hear that," we would probably recognize the witness's intention to request the lawyer to repeat the question. We would thereby recognize the witness's act to have the episodic force of a request for repetition (rather than, say, an assertion of fact). While Searle (1969) and others (Bach & Harnish, 1979; Jacobs & Jackson, this volume) use the terms "illocutionary force" and "illocutionary act" for this, Frentz & Farrell's (1976) term reminds us that it is only the interpretation of an act within the context of an episode that has any relevance to the present analysis. For this reason, Frentz and Farrell's (1976, p. 340) concept of an astitituational (out-of-episode) force will not be used here.[3]

A final assumption of the strategic point of view is that at any point in an episode, some symbolic acts are well designed to achieve actors' goals, and other acts are not. The question of which symbolic acts would result in the most progress toward the goal at a given point in the episode is the question of *tactics*. Frentz and Farrell (1976) do not explicitly discuss tactics (although Rosenfield, Hayes, & Frentz, 1976, pp. 36-43, do), but the concept is implied by their discussion of the effects or consequential force of symbolic acts.[4] Actors who have a sense of each other's goals and who are competent conversational communicators can judge (with varying degrees of accuracy) the relative effectiveness of different symbolic acts for advancing toward those goals.

In the terms of the strategic point of view, then, courtroom conversation is an episode between a lawyer, a witness, and a number of listeners (jurors and, to a lesser extent, other courtroom participants). These actors, within the constraints of certain rules, are engaged in the pursuit of one or more communication goals to which they are collectively oriented. To this end they make tactical choices among symbolic acts and then produce and interpret those acts that seem best calculated to achieve their goals. The nature of these goals, the types of symbolic acts employed, and the general characteristics of courtroom episodes will be further described in the next section.

THE COURTROOM CONVERSATION

This study is part of a continuing project focusing qualitative research methods (Spradley, 1979, 1980) on interactive (face-to-face, conversational) communication in civil and criminal trials, primarily in the northwestern part of the United States.[5] Five types of data collection procedures are used, though not all five can be used for every trial. These include after-the-fact reflections about actual participation in the courtroom process, observation within and just outside the courtroom, interviews with courtroom participants, collection of public comments about a trial, and detailed analysis of trial transcripts.[6] From examination of these types of data, and from previously published accounts of communication patterns in trials (Bennett, 1978, 1979; Bennett & Feldman, 1981; Danet, 1980; Dicks, 1981; Pollner, 1979; Yarmey, 1979), the following general description of courtroom conversation seems warranted.

Courtroom conversation is generally assumed to be goal oriented. Judges and lawyers usually espouse the goal of a fair trial, and during the jury selection process, prospective jurors come to espouse it also. Within this constraint a trial is assumed to be a competitive communication event. Participants generally perceive the lawyers for the various sides as being oriented toward goals that befit their client's side of the case. The *overall* communication goal of each side is seen as incompatible with that of the other side(s). Participants also perceive that this competitiveness extends to the communication of some, if not all, witnesses. At least some witnesses appear to pursue the same general goals in their testimony as do the lawyers who called them to testify. Other witnesses appear oriented toward personal goals: to avoid self-embarrassment or self-incrimination, to avoid perjury, to appear cooperative and competent, to present a particular version of events related to the case, and so on. Despite their recognition of the incompatibility of actors' goals, however, courtroom participants strive to present themselves as reasonable and cooperative. They recognize an overriding norm that their goals must be pursued in a way that will not infringe upon the rights of others to pursue their own legitimate communication goals in the trial. Courtroom competition must be enacted cooperatively.

The general character of goals oriented to by lawyers, witnesses, and jurors is understood to be informational. Jurors are usually instructed that they are to judge the facts of the case. Lawyers' opening statements often project that certain facts will be developed through the testimony of witnesses and the introduction of physical evidence, and jurors are often told what some of those yet-to-be-presented facts will be. Thus, jurors share in the goal orientation of lawyers and witnesses by being made aware that each side intends to produce in them certain states of knowledge which will result in their voting for a certain verdict.

Communication goals in the courtroom, then, relate to the development or alteration of the knowledge states of the jurors. *Knowledge state* (used basically as a primitive term by Lehnert, 1978, and Schank & Abelson, 1977) refers to the structure of facts, assumptions, inferences, and value judgments related to the events coming to trial and held (believed) by any courtroom participant. Lawyers and witnesses seek primarily to affect the knowledge states of jurors (rather than each other's knowledge states), despite being in conversation with each other. The overall goal of testimony and other courtroom communication, as described by Bennett and Feldman (1981, pp. 4-10) is the production in each juror's knowledge state of a *story* that is favorable either to the plaintiff's or the defendant's case. Thus, the goal operative in any particular lawyer-witness episode is the construction, definition, or validation of a major component or connection in the overall story (Bennett & Feldman, 1981, p. 117; Bennett, 1978, 1979).

Lawyers and witnesses pursue their goals through the taking of conversational turns and the exchange of talk (see Sacks, Schegloff, & Jefferson, 1974, for a discussion of the organization of talk exchanges). Compared to everyday conversation, the range of conversational functions they employ is relatively restricted. For the most part the symbolic acts exchanged consist of requests for information, requests for clarification, requests for restatement and confirmation, statements of information, restatements, confirmations, corrections, and accounts for why actors are asking certain questions or answering in certain ways. The sequencing pattern of most of the lawyer-witness (L-W) episodes is what one would expect in a rather formal two-party conversation: a speaker alternation of L, W, L, W. There also are clear spatial and temporal boundaries to these courtroom conversations. Each one usually takes place in a restricted area of the courtroom, begins when the witness is called (or recalled) to the witness stand and sworn in, and ends when the witness is excused by the judge. These constraints are more narrow than those of everyday small talk, but probably not very much narrower than in everyday business meetings, interviews, and so on. There is one respect, however, in which lawyer-witness episodes are strikingly different from most types of everyday conversation, whether small talk (see Knutson, 1982) or otherwise: Some participants must be listeners but are prohibited from being speakers.

While the lawyer and witness carry on an apparently dyadic conversation, interrupted occasionally by the judge or another lawyer, the jurors participate as intended and recognized listeners. As indicated above, if the lawyers and witnesses of either side are to achieve their goals, their symbolic acts must be designed so jurors can understand. Yet jurors are not ordinarily allowed to talk as part of the courtroom conversation. Occasionally, a juror will tell the judge, the lawyer, or the witness that the jury cannot hear or cannot see an exhibit, but otherwise, jurors sense that *they* are not to ask for information or clarification, nor assume the speaker's role at all. Of course, jurors can and do give nonverbal cues that lawyers and witnesses interpret as evidence of understanding, misunderstanding, puzzlement, and so on, but this is not the same as being a full fledged conversational actor.

One final peculiarity of courtroom conversation should be noted: Sometimes the immediate goal to which lawyers (and perhaps some witnesses) orient does not relate as much to establishing a point in jurors' knowledge states as it does to getting the point into the record. Lawyers routinely attempt to get certain information expressed in so many words, a direct and literal statement, so that it will appear explicitly in the trial transcript. This tactic is designed to provide the basis for a future appeal or legal motion to the judge or to forestall such appeal or motion by the other side. Courtroom participants quickly become adjusted to these pedantic sequences of talk, and usually infer (if they do not already know) that the real goal is not the jury's understanding, at least not primarily. However, a witness or spectator who has never experienced trial testimony before sometimes fails to recognize the tactical objective of the moment. Such a failure can lead to confusion about a symbolic act or a larger segment of a courtroom episode and suggests the need for closer examination of the relationship between tactics and coherence.

TACTICS AND COHERENCE

It is quite possible for one actor in a conversation to understand what the other is saying, and to recognize what symbolic acts the other is using, but to still be puzzled about the speaker's talk. Such a conversation has less than satisfactory coherence for the listener if he or she cannot anticipate such things as: what response the speaker expects the listener to give, what use the speaker might make of that response, or which of several technically correct responses would be most appropriate for the speaker. In Example 1, which is *not* a courtroom conversation, speaker A begins a conversation with her husband about a major research project he is about to undertake.[7]

Example 1 01 **A:** B_____, is there any particular place that would be better for you to be for your sabbatical?

02 **B:** Well, my agreement with the provost doesn't specify any particular place, just anywhere there are trials.

03 **A:** Would a metropolitan area be better? There might be more trials going on.

04 **B:** It might be. . . .

05 **A:** (pause) Would you consider using your sabbatical as a trial separation for us?

In interpreting this conversation, B experienced confusion about A's first two utterances, 01 and 03, despite his clear recognition that she was requesting information about locations where B might conduct his research and the possible advantages of his going to a large city. B felt sure that A knew he had no specific locations planned. He also sensed that she was not *merely* gathering information (he perceived that she had no interest in his research); nor was she merely making small talk (she put down a book to initiate 01). B realized that he did not know what A was getting at with her questions. Her 05 revealed to B that A had been preparing to suggest a marital separation. She had been attempting to elicit information from B that could then be used to show that his research sabbatical provided a workable opportunity for such a separation. B's sense of the conversation was that it was not completely coherent even though he knew *what* A was asking — until A's 05 showed *why* she was asking.

Ongoing examination of courtroom transcripts suggests, as does B's sense of coherence trouble, that the coherence of a symbolic act involves more than an understanding of its propositional force. Certainly, a kind of coherence is produced by people's ability to process such semantic and syntactic relationships as reference, substitution of pronouns (e.g., "they," "one," "it") and pro-verbs (e.g., "do"), ellipsis, conjunction, and the like (see Halliday & Hasan, 1976). Comprehension of propositional force would also be impaired without our sense of the functional relationship among the major parts of a sentence, such as the goal-agent-action-attribute relations embodied in Schelsinger's (1977, pp. 9-15) I-marker analysis. Of course, our background knowledge of everyday events contributes greatly to our understanding of propositional force. Schank and Abelson (1977) developed structures of such background knowledge, called scripts, for their artificial intelligence and simulation computer programs.

Lehnert (1978) has designed a computer simulation of question answering that incorporates semantic, syntactic, and background-knowledge processing. The claim being advanced here is that our recognition of communicators' goals and of the tactical operations they employ to achieve those goals also contributes to coherence.

A key factor in courtroom participants' ability to hear testimony as coherent and to produce coherent testimony when so required is that they usually know what each side in the case is trying to do. As indicated in the preceding section, the basic nature of the case is routinely described during the jury selection process, and the plaintiff's (or prosecution's) side of the case is further outlined to the jury during the opening statement. The same is true of the defense's side of the case, although the defense occasionally reserves its opening statement until the plaintiff's witnesses have testified. In these opening statements the lawyers inform the jury (and others present in the courtroom) of what they intend the overall story to be from their side of the case: what they will try to prove. Thus, jurors have an advanced look at the knowledge structure each side intends to establish for them through witnesses' testimony. Everyone can see that the overall goal of each side is to produce a certain story, and everyone is made aware of the major points in each story. Bennett and Feldman (1981) argue that this communication process works because lawyers, judges, witnesses, jurors, and other participants have acquired the cultural knowledge necessary to understand stories: "Through the use of broadly shared techniques of telling and interpreting stories, the actors in a trial present, organize, and analyze the evidence that bears on the alleged illegal activity" (p. 4). Jurors and others are able to infer the goal of the actors involved in a particular lawyer-witness episode by relating the particular witness's expertise or involvement to the overall story structure. Since they can see the goal to which a particular courtroom conversation is directed, jurors and others are in a position to interpret the point of each symbolic act as a tactical objective designed to achieve that particular communication goal.

The coherence provided by this recognition of tactical purpose can be seen in Example 2, which is from a trial of rape and kidnapping charges.[8] The prosecuting attorney (L) began this conversation by eliciting general background information about the witness (W), and had just directed her (and the jury's) attention to the month and year in which the alleged assault took place. He then asked the witness where she was living at the time.

Example 2 01 **W:** I was living at 1428 M_____.
          02 **L :** Who were you living with?

> 03 **W:**   E_____ O_____.
> 04 **L :**   Has she changed her name since then?

The propositional force of the lawyer's last question, L's 04, seems unproblematic. We all know it refers to a possible change in the name of W's roommate from E_____ O_____ to something else. The episodic force of this particular symbolic act also seems clear: This is a request (of W) for information, or perhaps a request for confirmation. And yet, L's symbolic act would have even more coherence for us if we knew the point of developing this bit of information in this episode. We expect W's response to be some sort of affirmative answer, since L would not ask about a name change unless there had been one (or reason to suspect one), but what kind of affirmative? Has E_____ O_____ gone into hiding? Does she go through life using a set of aliases (as a criminal or police informant might do)? Has she joined a religious order that requires her to adopt a new name? Did she get married? And, above all, what relevance does the information, whatever it is, have to the overall story? What should W say in order to best further the goal toward which she and L are oriented? Even though L's 04 is coherent at two levels — propositional and episodic force — it remains a mystery at another level. Its tactical use in the episode is not clear unless we can see the rationale for employing this particular symbolic act at this time in this episode.

As this trial began, courtroom participants (and those of us reading the transcript) were informed that both W and W's roommate would testify. Knowing that E_____ O_____ will be called to testify as W's roommate, and knowing (from L's 04) that her name is probably not E_____ O_____ any longer, we can recognize L's tactic as a simple attempt to identify a later witness. L is using W's testimony to provide a connection (in each juror's knowledge state and also for the record) between the name the roommate will give when she is later sworn in and the name W used to refer to her. Knowing what L is attempting to accomplish, participants (including L and W) can project that an adequate answer to L's request for information would be something like, "she is married now and her name is E_____ R_____." This is, in fact, W's response. Recognizing an utterance as part of a tactical plan for the achievement of a known goal adds to its coherence.

In some situations, an actor's knowledge of the goal being oriented to in a particular episode allows recognition of an act as tactically coherent even in the absence of clear propositional force. This becomes especially obvious when the response is structured as a *completion* of the prior utterance. In Example 3, the witness has been called as an expert to testify about a component of a truck engine. The case is a complex civil suit arising out of a fatal truck-automobile crash.[9] The segment below begins with the sixth exchange between lawyer and witness, so it should be clear to all participants that the immediate tactical objective is the establishment of the qualifications of the witness.

Example 3 **01** L : What relation do you have with Jacobs Engine Company?
02 W: Jacobs Engine Brakes?
03 L : Yes.
04 W: I am a distributor.
05 L : You are the distributor for Jacobs Engine Brakes for . . .
06 W: Utah, Idaho, Wyoming, Colorado, New Mexico, and a portion of Texas and a portion of Nevada.
07 L : Would that include Boise, Idaho?

It is fairly clear that the episodic force of 05 is a request for information. The propositional force of 05 is clear only insofar as L is talking about W being the sales or installation outlet for this particular piece of equipment (the "Jake Brake"). Since L does not complete the sentence, part of the propositional force is obscured. What is being related, through the preposition "for," to the information "distributor," or "Jacobs Engine Brakes"? From the language L uses in 05, there is no reason to doubt that a response of "[brakes for] Cummins diesels" would have been appropriate. W and L both know (and other participants must begin to suspect), however, that the goal of this episode is to display W's expert opinion about the Jake Brake. They consequently know that the tactical objective at this early point in the episode is to show W's experience. L counts on W recognizing the tactical point of 05 despite its unclear propositional force. In turn, W produces a symbolic act, 06, that is propositionally coherent when taken together with 05 — and is also tactically coherent because it displays W's breadth of experience with the Jake Brake. W understands L's tactic. L's request for further elaboration in 07 shows that 06 was basically along the line L intended. Tactical coherence, then, is not wholly dependent on clear propositional force. We can recognize what a symbolic act *should* say or do in order to further the goal to which participants are oriented. We even complete truncated utterances and repair defective ones by calculating what the speaker must have intended to say in the pursuit of known goals.

Courtroom conversations can sometimes seem repetitious when judged by everyday out-of-court standards. Yet, when this happens, the reaction of jurors and other participants is not necessarily one of exasperation or puzzlement. People quickly adjust to communication rules peculiar to the courtroom, such as lawyers asking each witness to spell his or her name and to give a current address. As described in the preceding section, lawyers sometimes attempt to get information expressed with certain specific wording. Such a conversational exchange will produce a very direct, literal, and pedantic sequence of talk. In Example 4, the witness is an X-ray technician who has just testified that he took certain pictures of the body of R_____ M_____ (a three-year-old child) on the evening of September 19, 1981. The case is alleged first-degree murder; the child was the victim.[10] The prosecutor (L) is about to introduce the X-rays into evidence, and has elicited testimony about the process of W taking the X-rays. L now hands them to the technician.

Example 4	01	**L :**	Can you identify these?
	02	**W:**	They are the pictures I took.
	03	**L :**	And what are they of?
	04	**W:**	A three-year-old child.
	05	**L :**	And what was the child's name?
	06	**W:**	R_____ M_____.
	07	**L :**	And when were they taken?
	08	**W:**	The evening of September nineteenth, uh . . .
	09	**L :**	1981?
	10	**W:**	Yes.

Everyone in the courtroom probably understood from W's answer in 02 that the pictures he had been handed were those he had just testified about.[11] There was no lack of coherence in W's testimony through 02. L continues in 03, 05, 07, and 09 to elicit the same information again. The reason, of course, is L's goal of getting explicitly into the record a statement that these specific pictures, marked for identification and later to be offered in evidence, are the very same pictures that W has just testified about. This will forestall the defense from objecting to the admission of the X-rays on the grounds that they have not been adequately identified. Experienced witnesses usually provide such redundant information in concise form so that the explicit identification is quickly made. W, on the other hand, seems not to be aware of the goal operating here. During 03-04, W frowned and looked puzzled; during 05-07, he smiled but still looked puzzled.[12] At no point in this segment does W produce a clear statement for the record or give other evidence of recognizing L's tactical objective. It seems that this type of excessive repetition in everyday conversation might actually reduce coherence by raising doubts about what the communicators were trying to accomplish. Full coherence is achieved only with a sense of the conversational tactics being employed in the pursuit of actors' goals, at least in courtroom conversation (see Bennett & Feldman, 1981, pp. 8-9).

COHERENCE AND SMALL TALK

The strategic point of view also focuses our attention on the goals of participants in other types of conversational episodes such as everyday small talk. The goals oriented to by conversational actors in a context such as that of B and K (see Appendix) are likely to be different from those that operate in the courtroom (see Farrell, this volume, for a discussion of rhetorical aspects of conversation). For one thing, the overall goal of such actors is frequently the continuation of the episode. This is specifically true of the B-K episode: They have been instructed to keep talking. Thus, this type of episode is not as informationally dominant as the courtroom is. Everyday small talk tends to be *structurally* dominant (Frentz & Farrell, 1976, p. 338), in the sense that the *episode itself* is the overall goal. Of course, some information that the actors find useful gets exchanged, and their personal relationships get adjusted as well. But they are oriented primarily toward carrying on the episode. In Example 5, for instance, B apparently produces a request for information. Assume for the moment that B's goal is really to find out that piece of information.

Example 5   017   **B:**   K (pause) what are you giving ((laughing)) people
for Christmas this year? ((both laughing)) I've
started thinking about it'n - my - ability to be
inventive - without spending much ((laughing))
money is - very very small.
[ ]
018   **K:**   (oh)
019   **K:**   Like family? Friends?
020   **B:**   Family mostly.
021   **K:**   Family hhhoh:: (pause) What do you buy men in
your family for Christmas.
022   **B:**   My father is the main problem. =

B's request in 017 is accompanied by an account for why she wants to know, or so it seems. An insertion sequence follows in 019-020: K requests clarification and B provides it. Now, in an informationally dominant episode, with the clarification out of the way, the conversation would normally return to B's requested information. That does not happen in 021. Rather than supplying the information B asked for, K changes the focus slightly and turns the question back on B. In a courtroom conversation this kind of response would be tactically odd (although propositionally coherent enough) and might be interpreted as an attempt by K to avoid the issue. Even stranger would be 022 in which B goes along with this diversion and fails to reassert her initial request. In fact, the conversation does not return to the specific question of what K is giving her family for Christmas even through 033. Then, in 034, the topic changes to going home for Christmas vacation. Yet, this segment of talk does not seem at all strange in the context of this particular episode of small talk. When we recognize that symbolic acts in this episode are designed to keep the conversation going (by conveying information, to be sure, but not really *for* the information), 021 and 022 make perfect sense. They achieve the immediate tactical objective of raising or continuing talkable matters, thereby showing orientation and advancement toward the goal of keeping the episode going. Examining this small talk episode from the strategic point of view suggests that these utterances actually do what is called for here. In the courtroom, direct requests for information or confirmation, such as K's 105 ("Do you ski?") and B's 118 ("Do you ski?"), would be coherent in light of participants' recognition of a tactical objective: for example, to establish a witness's credibility. A tactically coherent response to such a request would be brief and to the point: "no," or "cross country only," or "yes, I'm on the U.S. Olympic Ski Team." The responses actually given in 106-108 and 119-121, rambling on as they do for approximately forty words, would not seem to fit courtroom episodic requirements (although their propositional force would be clear). However, because the tactical requirements of a small talk episode are different, these responses seem to us (and apparently seemed to K and B) not only propositionally coherent, but tactically coherent as well. They elaborate on talkable topics and thus further the goal of carrying on the conversation. Even in small talk, coherence involves a judgment about the purposes or utility of symbolic acts in relation to an assumed or recognized goal. What differentiates coherence in small talk from coherence in courtroom testimony is that the goals are different and thus require different conversational tactics. Small talk tactics seem to be designed less for constructing knowledge states in actors and more for perpetuating the episode than courtroom tactics tend to be.

CONCLUSION

Observation of courtroom proceedings and analysis of trial transcripts support the conclusion that coherence in courtroom conversation arises in part from participants' (jurors', lawyers', witnesses', and others') recognition that the speaker intends to produce, through the use of observed symbolic acts, a certain state of knowledge in the jury, or a certain direct and literal statement in the trial record. As Bennett and Feldman (1981) put it, "evidence gains coherence through categorical connections to story elements" (p. 8). This type of coherence presumes the ability of people to calculate the potential effectiveness of symbolic acts according to some conversational plan which they attribute to the actors in that episode.

Schank and Abelson (1977, pp. 69-78) posit that people know or can work out *plans* (general information about the sequence of steps by which goals are achieved) for a wide variety of activities involving a wide variety of goals. Some of these plans indicate general ways that people achieve communication goals. Such plans can then be used to find the tactical point of any given symbolic act. Indeed, it seems that effective tactics are actually possible because previous experience has established certain patterns of symbolic action which have become conventional and accepted as serving the pursuit of ordinary communication goals. Participants in the courtroom (and parties to everyday small talk) orient to the goals operative in their respective episodes and interpret each other as being so oriented. If an actor's talk cannot be recognized as accomplishing some tactical objective according to a conventional plan, it will not be fully coherent (see Jacobs & Jackson, this volume).

By the same token, actors wishing to be seen as competent communicators must produce sequences of symbolic acts that are recognizable as designed to further their immediate goals. That is, their conversational tactics must match some conventional plan for the achievement of communication goals. To the extent that this is not so, their talk will be less than fully coherent, and other participants may question actors' goals or doubt their conversational competence.

The implication of this for courtroom conversation is that actors should take care not only to display their goals for the jury (which they usually do), but also to display the tactical connection between their goals and the symbolic acts they employ, or at least to follow a communication plan that is conventional enough for the jury to infer the tactical connections for themselves. The risk of hiding one's plan (to achieve surprise or some other effect) is that talk may be rejected, misinterpreted, or forgotten and thus not produce the result that the plan envisions.

NOTES

1. Observations and transcripts providing the basis for this chapter are from state superior trial courts in the northwestern part of the contiguous United States.

2. Austin (1962) and Searle (1969) are largely responsible for the terms "speech acts" and "illocutionary acts." Frentz and Farrell's (1976) symbolic act is roughly the

same as a speech act, but reminds us that such acts can be written or nonverbal as well as oral. Episodic force corresponds to illocutionary force (or act), although Frentz and Farrell (1976) also discuss another type of force that seems similar to illocutionary force. See note 3.

3. Frentz and Farrell (1976) say that expressive force is an asituational force. They seem to intend what others refer to as illocutionary force, which is often discussed without a clear communication context. Since recognition (uptake) is the key to illocutionary success, and since this always takes place in a communication situation, we need be concerned only with episode force.

4. The idea of tactics is seen most clearly in game models of communication in which episodes are compared to ordinary games. L. W. Rosenfield presented a detailed paper on this at the Minnesota Symposium in Speech Communication, in 1968. See also Rosenfield et al. (1976); Farb (1975, pp. 4-8); and Jacobs & Jackson (this volume). Consequential force is what Searle (1969) and others refer to as perlocutionary force. Frentz and Farrell (1976) confuse episodic force with the consequences or perlocutionary force of an act. Their example (1976, p. 341) presents a *request* for a drink of water (from a child at bedtime) as being intended *to delay* going to sleep. The former is episodic force and the latter is an intended consequent or perlocutionary effect.

5. The examples used in this chapter happen to be from Idaho cases, although the basis of the study is broader than that. Even though trials are public, there would be no useful purpose served by further identifying the people, places, or actual cases used here. Accordingly, I have not cited the cases, and I have deleted all personal and some place names.

6. Transcripts used so far in this study are the official trial records generated in typed form when a case is appealed. Thus, all transcripts are from appealed cases. My actual participation in trial processes has been of two types. In 1981 I served on a jury in the state of Washington that heard a civil case arising from a fatal traffic accident. After the trial was completed I realized my growing interest in studying courtroom communication, and began to assess and describe my experiences as a juror. I have also been a casual spectator in the courtroom, which is an accepted role in our culture. My most extensive participation has been as a note-taking observer/participant in the public gallery.

7. Part of B's utterance is deleted from 04, as indicated by the ellipses.

8. The analysis summarized here is entirely from the trial transcript and official records. The witness is the victim. Her street address has been altered slightly.

9. This analysis is also based exclusively on official transcripts and documents. The ellipses in 05 indicate that the utterance ended there with an incomplete sentence.

10. This discussion is based on observing the trial, taking notes, and interviewing. The ellipses in 08 indicate that the utterance ended at that point.

11. Both 01 and 02 were fully coherent for me as an observer in the public gallery. Another spectator nearby indicated that she knew right away what W meant by 02.

12. As this segment unfolded, W seemed increasingly uncomfortable, and the jury seemed increasingly amused. From these brief observations I conclude that W did not understand what was required of him or why, but that the jury did understand.

<<<<<<<<<<<<< >>>>>>>>>>>>>

13

Aspects of Coherence in Conversation and Rhetoric

<< THOMAS B. FARRELL >>

Rhetoric is the counterpart of Dialectic.

Aristotle, *Rhetoric* (1354a)

< < < As we continue to sort out the principles and > > > criteria for conversational coherence, the increasing tendency among scholars in neighboring speculative disciplines (such as philosophy, social theory, hermeneutics) is to treat conversation as a privileged mode of interaction that somehow models or grounds the relational possibilities for ordinary discourse. To those of us absorbed with the routinized confusions of turn-taking, overlaps, and displaced references in actual communicative practice, this more speculative conversational turn is bound to seem odd, even ironic. Whether deliberately or not, such idealized readings of conversational form have often attributed its coherence to a kind of spirit or energy that is all but removed from the choices of real human beings. To take but one example,

> We say that we "conduct" a conversation, but the more fundamental a conversation is, the less its conduct lies within the will of either partner. Thus a fundamental conversation is never one that we want to conduct. Rather, it is generally more correct to say that we fall into conversation, or even that we become involved in it. The way in which one word follows another, with the conversation taking its

own turnings and reaching its own conclusion, may well be conducted in some way, but the people conversing are far less the
leaders of it than the led. No one knows what will "come out" in a
conversation. Understanding or its failure is like a process which
happens to us. Thus we can say that something was a good conversation or that it was a poor one. All this shows that a conversation
has a spirit of its own [Gadamer, 1975, p. 345].

While there is every reason to share Gadamer's respect for the mys-
teries of conversational coherence, my own interest in rhetorical
practice must prompt a cautionary note. It is usually the case when
we award honorific status to a single privileged discursive form (be it
dialogic, therapeutic, or poetic), that we are prepared to devalue,
even ignore, its less exotic family resemblances.

Thus it is that rhetoric, heir to a checkered history at best, has
been dismissed or openly disparaged by writers ranging from MacIntyre (1981), to Ricoeur (1978), to Apel (1976). Even Jürgen Habermas,
whose critical hermeneutics places such an important emphasis upon
language pragmatics, concludes that strategic speech is flawed or
distorted speech and therefore is not deserving of his felicity condition, "sincerity" (Habermas, 1979, p. 41). While the reasons for
rhetoric's devaluation vary, it may be important that each of the
authors I have mentioned holds to an ideal form of speech, wherein
truth and meaning tend to merge. Understandably, rhetoric suffers
somewhat by way of contrast. More to the point of our present
concern, important questions of coherence within conversation suffer
as well. When conversation is seen as the principle or only avenue for
attaining coherence, explaining coherence and its absence within
conversation is not easy. Either questions of coherence are begged
through the mythos of meaning (any intelligible content is, by communicative definition, coherent) or these questions are set aside (real
discourse is distorted by the world; only free, emancipated, unconstrained social worlds allow for coherent discourse).

The analysis of coherence offered by this chapter proceeds from a
view of rhetoric that has been influenced but not necessarily debili-
tated by the prevailing mood of speculative philosophy. Conversation
and rhetoric will be regarded as interdependent discursive arts with
analogous points of origin. As the opening words to Aristotle's
Rhetoric (and to this essay) suggest, these arts are counterparts to one
another. Despite their complementary relationship, however, the
traditions of conversation and rhetoric have given these arts characteristically different approaches to the problem of coherence, just as

these same arts have tended to acquire characteristic discursive forms. Central to our discussion throughout is the proposition that some potential coherence problems within conversation are resolved through the mediation of speech practices (i.e., figures, tropes, and stratagems) that have come to be regarded as rhetorical. The language-action paradigm of communication (Frentz & Farrell, 1976; Farrell & Frentz, 1979) is introduced in order to locate places ("topoi") within conversational discourse where the ambiguity of speech content derives not from a lack of coherence, but rather from an emerging rhetorical turn within utterance choices themselves. These are the moments when coherence becomes, as it were, a rhetorical proposition.

Following some preliminary definitions, our argument begins by observing some special problems of content *and* form within the development of conversational coherence. To the extent that semantic intelligibility and formal continuity provide insufficient conditions to explain conversational coherence, then we must allow for at least the theoretical possibility of a *rhetorical* mediation to some coherence difficulties within conversation. The body of the essay draws several important synchronic interrelationships among the characteristic discursive forms of conversation and rhetoric. Most important, junctures of intersection among these forms generate figures and stratagems (rhetorical tropes such as evasion, reduplication, bypass) that then may be applied to the coherence problems of several texts, including the B-K conversation (Appendix). Since the artistic proofs of rhetoric are made manifest within certain resources for language arrangement, then we might expect these same proofs, resources, and arrangement patterns to become the basis for coherence when conversations become rhetorical.

DEFINITIONAL PROBES

Coherence is obviously a difficult notion to define, suggesting aspects of form, propriety, intelligibility, and completeness that have all but disappeared as expectations of the modern age. It may be, as Foucault (1973) has suggested, that the very possibility of a scholarly discipline (an order of things, after all) is predicated upon a set of assumptions about coherence that are, for all practical purposes, obsolete. This much having been acknowledged, however, some opening probe remains necessary, if only to clarify the preferred agenda of this study. I consider coherence to be *an acquired feature of any complex phenomenon, such that there is some recognizable propriety of association among its otherwise variable elements.* For the sake of argument I should also like to preserve the sense of coherence conveyed by contemporary physics, wherein coherence is a coincident relation of wave sets that produces interference. The conversational corollary I wish to explore is that coherence may be a meaningful attribute of discourse only because certain forms of interference are also possible. By conversation I mean simply *the informal exchange of utterances by two or more parties in any setting.* As a working definition of rhetoric, let us attend to *that pragmatic capacity of discourse that allows agreements with interlocutors to be formed or anticipated in order to undertake collaborative action.* Generally speaking, rhetoric emerges in discourse as a reflective and anticipatory choice among options that are imposed upon us in a moment of uncertain contingency. The discursive impetus behind rhetoric is often intentional; it is always accountable, even as its successful enactment is always collaborative, that is, bound up within the confirmation and commitments of others.

What is most elusive and yet critical to this essay's argument is the markedly different manner in which the collaborative character of rhetoric takes its shape in discourse. In an ongoing research project building upon the language-action paradigm, Frentz and Farrell have argued that root differences in *duration* (the experience and articulation of time) are responsible for the fundamentally different approaches to meaning implied by conversation and rhetoric. For conversation, as Gadamer's reading intuited, the moment of thought and the moment of utterance are presumed to be simultaneous. This is why utterances that appear to be not only appropriate, but even elegant in their conjunction seemed (to Gadamer) to have a spirit of their own. In rather sharp contrast, rhetoric always seems to be at least one step removed from the immediate proceedings. Although fortuitous in its appearance, the art of rhetoric never appears to be a creature of fortune alone. It may be premeditative (i.e., thought through in advance of its expression), or anticipatory (looking forward to a sequence of utterances that has not yet come about). Frequently it is both of these at once. If coherence is, at least in part, a product of our own communicative expectations, then these expectations — our very rules for communicating — must undergo a discernable shift when we engage rhetorical discourse. Perhaps understandably, then, a proper understanding of rhetorical coherence must change the way we interpret and assess patterns of utterance exchange. Even though all conversational coherence is collaborative, the emergence of rhetoric within conversation presents us with an emphatic inventional moment in which we must collaborate as speaker and attending audience, so as to extend, complete, and even judge an implied message. As the several examples (from real conversations) are designed to illustrate, much is at stake in the practical collaborations provoked by rhetoric: the narrative continuity of episodes, the dignity of character, even the future of a human relationship. Rhetoric, for all its history of disparagement, is not an art to be taken lightly.

In order to appreciate properly the rhetorical dimension of conversational coherence, first we must demonstrate that rhetoric is not an accidental feature, or corruption of ordinary conversational exchange, but rather an inherent potential of any shared discourse. The aim of our first argument, then, is to uncover the limits to speaker content and discursive form as solitary determinants of conversational coherence.

CONTENT AND FORM IN CONVERSATION

Despite the best attempts of linguistic philosophy and science, it is apparent that conversational coherence can be reduced neither to signification (content) nor structure (form) alone. Moreover, I intend to demonstrate that, if intelligibility were held to be the sole governing criterion for conversational coherence, then two absurd consequences would follow: First, no truly coherent utterances would be conversational; and second, no truly conversational utterances could be coherent.

We begin with the commonplace that utterances perform multiple meaning functions within any conversation simultaneously (Farrell & Frentz, 1979). Add to this the finding of phenomenology and perceptual research that no one is able to attend to and comprehend multiple dimensions of meaning content (visual or otherwise) during the same temporal instant (Kosslyn, 1980; Steiner, 1982). In practice, participants and onlookers alike make snap appraisals based upon attributed background understandings as to the most intelligible placement for the utterance in question. However, this only confounds the problem of content. Consider the utterance, "Go to hell!" To the naive onlooker, the speech-act content of this expression might range from: a command, an answer to the question, "How do I get to the 'Third Circle'?", or what it most commonly is in Anglo-American culture, an informal insult, a curse. Yet once we expand our background understandings to include other interpretative horizons, namely episode, encounter, and form of life (Frentz & Farrell, 1976), the ambiguities expand accordingly. On an episodic level (where we consult prior and subsequent symbolic acts; i.e., the narrativity of discourse), the expression may have been delivered in jest in response to a purportedly amusing bit of repartee, for example, "Hey, terrific table manners! That's your salad fork, dummy!" On an encounter level (where we sort out continuous factors of time and place for conversationists as relational partners), this same utterance may cement the bonds of intimacy, "break the ice," or end the evening, perhaps the relationship. On the form-of-life horizon (where the historical praxis of a culture limits our more remote actional possibilities), there are issues of liturgy, mortality, guilt, and punishment that do not exactly bend with the wind of interpretative choice. The problem is complicated by the fact that the same utterance may abandon intelligibility on one horizon only to acquire what seems to be subsequent intelligibility or content on another level. This is especially the case with utterances that we typically take to be rhetorical (for example, promises or warnings). Not only do such utterances imply their own prioritized agenda of subsequent meaning and conduct; they may even suggest an interpretative horizon sufficiently forceful to transform the meaning of others' communicative conduct, for example, "Look, pal, you may only be kidding: but you go on talking like that and that's the end of our friendship, period." At the very least such utterances depend for their coherence upon something more than semantic content alone. If content alone is to be the criterion of conversational coherence, it may be the case that nothing and everything is coherent simultaneously.

Now it might seem that there is a relatively simple way out of our problem. Since it is obvious that some mutually understood (however mysterious) signification process occurs throughout conversation, this process is — in principle — open to the warranted consensus of the discussants themselves. Simply put, conversation always allows persons to ask each other what they mean. For instance, if I say to someone, "I want you to stonewall, cover up, do anything you have to do to save the plan," he or she can always reply, "Uh, I'm not sure I follow, sir. Could you run through that again?" Regretably, this movement from reciprocal meaning to truth (which both Gadamer and Habermas seem attracted to) will not do for several reasons. First, we should not overlook the fact that we have reverted to a formal feature of conversation (i.e., reciprocity) to disambiguate problems of content. Second, and I think more important, the exclusive formal preoccupation with meaning content would destroy conversational coherence. Recall that, with a very few onomatopoetic exceptions, the significations of language are established by wholly arbitrary conventions. Imagine what would happen if, in response to the utterance, "Go to hell," we were continually to inquire, "What do you mean?" Imagine what would happen if, after every equally ambiguous locution, we were to mount the same relentless inquiry. The result, I submit, would be a language that would repeatedly bump up against its own failed iconicity (the absurd), and a conversation that would be halted in mid-stride. In other words, the unbridled search for coherence through intelligible content alone would yield its exact opposite: nonsense, and incoherent discourse. By now, it should be apparent that a similar argument could be made about the proliferation of discourse, irrespective of intelligible content. Here the chattering would simply spin itself out endlessly in a kind of Derridean nightmare. This, too, would be nonsense (in conversational terms, at least); however, it would be nonsense punctuated by the silence of others and the eventual solitude of self.

As a first approximation of the problem of coherence in form and content, we have concluded that discourse that said only, exactly, and exhaustively what it meant would defy the bounds and possibilities of conversation, thus ending the prospect of conversational coherence. Discourse that talks only to fill the silence is nonsense of a different sort, but nonsense still. Perhaps we are entitled to a sense of relief that there is some slippage between utterances and their exhaustive signification. If we already knew everything we meant, there would not be much point in talking. Our brief excursus should also confirm the intricate conversational interdependence of content with *form*. Indeed, conversational coherence only seems to be a live possibility if our understanding of any discursive content is, at the given moment of its utterance, incomplete. Essential to conversation, then, is its sense of continual movement and transition; in short, a sense of *passage*. As I will soon clarify, we discover this whenever we ask our partner in a dialogue to repeat himself or herself. Hardly ever will exactly the same words return. More likely, the utterances (whether complaint, allegation, or proposal) will be more carefully hewn, qualified, cautious — as if they had been authored for the ages.

Once we turn our attention to the problems of intersecting content with form in ongoing conservation, we introduce that curious practical art, rhetoric. This is fitting, of course, since rhetorical quality has historically tended to be long on formal elaboration and most questionable on the level of intelligible content. I must ask my brethren scholars of conversational coherence to lay aside their suspicions about rhetoric, for the time being at least, so that we might explore some of the art's unexamined implications for problems in conversational form. In light of the preceding discussion, for instance, it is interesting to note that the content of rhetoric is usually a practical question of choice and avoidance, upon which other intelligible connections must depend. This question is usually made accessible through a type of background understanding that is analogous, but not reducible to the background understandings presupposed by conversation. Finally, instead of expanding interpretative possibilities, the form of rhetoric typically limits options, prescribes choice, forces concerned decision and action. The analysis that follows attempts to explain some of the traditional analogies and distinctions within the art forms of conversation and rhetoric.

ORIGINS AND INTERRELATIONSHIPS

Although it would not be easy to prove the matter, it seems likely that conversation and rhetoric share a similar point of conceptual origin. According to classical scholar Eric Havelock, the oldest form of discursive understanding was supplied by neither conversation nor rhetoric, but rather by the poetic narrative discourse of epic. He writes (1971, p. 191),

> The epic therefore is from the stance of our present quest to be considered in the first instance not as an act of creation but as an act of reminder and recall. Its patron muse is indeed *Mnemosune* in whom is symbolized not just the memory considered as a mental phenomenon but rather the total act of reminding, recalling, memorialising, and memorising, which is achieved in epic verse.

The traditional sense of poetic, in other words, was found in the reenactment of experience through the spell of continuous discourse, the monologue. And the only way to break the rhapsodic spell of words endlessly repeated was to separate the self (and the speaker) from the remembered word. How was this to be done? According to Havelock (1971), it "consisted in asking a speaker to repeat himself and explain what he had meant. In Greek, the words for explain, say, and mean could coincide" (p. 208). However we characterize this primitive interference, the interruptive question usually posits in root form the assumption "that there was something unsatisfactory about the statement and it had better be rephrased" (p. 209). Conversational dialogue, so conceived, began with the very first quizzical, "Come again?" Thus, the "poetic dream, so to speak, was disrupted, and some unpleasant effort of calculative reflection was substituted" (p. 209). Dialogue and thus dialectic could therefore be explained through the natural sense of breakage or disparity that emerges whenever a genuine other responds skeptically to a monologue.

With interference and the option of restatement also comes practical choice; and it is rhetoric, the practical art of *logos,* that makes the "unpleasant effort of calculative reflection" a worldly possibility. As Havelock (1971) concluded from his own investigation of poetic: "The story of invention belongs properly to the sphere of *logos,* not *mythos.* It was set in motion by the prosiac quest for a non-poetic language and a non-Homeric definition of truth" (p. 91). Today this quest is likely to seem more quixotic than prosaic to many. But despite the mythopoetic overtones to Havelock's own recounting of origins, an important original partnership between dialogue and rhetoric has been confirmed. Moreover, it seems that the same capacity that differentiated person from message has also made possible personal reflection with others and expanded the world of actional possibilities. I turn now to a more extended treatment of the formal interrelationships among conversation and rhetoric as discursive practices.

Figure 13.1 employs the interpretative horizons introduced by the language-action paradigm (Frentz & Farrell, 1976) in order to overview the synchronic interrelationships among the discursive practices of conversation and rhetoric. In speaking of the interrelationships among these modes of discourse as synchronic, I mean that although each form takes on its real-life existence as a succession of utterances over time, we are interested in logical junctures of intersection and determinants of coherence for ideal types of discourse, irrespective of their temporal priority. Note also that although there is considerable overlap in our diagram to acknowledge rhetorical and conversational intersection, both the presumed impetus and anticipated direction for each mode of discourse are emphatically different.

First, consider the impetus and destination of these two discursive practices. Conversation seems to emerge from the conventions and norms for exchange within the culture. We talk with people who share our ordinary life conventions. Moreover, conversation begins, in almost all cases, immersed in the conventions of language usage,

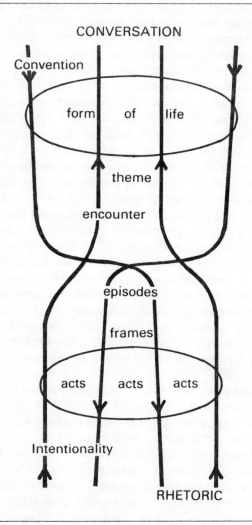

Figure 13.1 Language-Action Coherence

rituals of affinity and difference, and so forth. How richly nuanced or individuated meaning becomes must depend upon subsequent conversation. What is the destiny of conversation? For the most part, conversation is eminently perishable discourse, to be forgotten almost as its fragments are created. Occasionally, as may have happened when Wally dined with Andre in the film *My Dinner With*

Andre, a single conversation can have a decisive effect upon one's life. When this happens, conversation not only abandons its conventional origins, but moreover becomes an indelible part of that intentional consciousness known as memory. By rather striking contrast, the original impetus of rhetoric seems to come from the intentional consciousness (the practical intent to shape discourse toward extrinsic ends). This is also the sense of partisanship and wishful thinking we have come to associate with the purposeful rhetorical art. Yet we misunderstand rhetoric if we conclude that it begins and ends as directive or manipulative discourse. While this form begins by placing subtle emphasis upon its own intention, eventually intention must be set aside if preferable judgments are to be possible. The essence of rhetorical coherence, in short, is a special mode of collaborative address and engagement. Indeed, our most emphatic sense of rhetoric emerges in those moments of durational urgency where choice can be deferred no longer and the cooperative regard of others is necessary if meaningful action is to continue. When such moments arise, even the most forthcoming and reciprocal of conversational partners must act outside the zone of immediately intelligible meaning in favor of the more opaque prospect for contingent justification. So understood, the practical choices of rhetoric are redeemed through the extenuation of circumstance. What, then, is the destiny of rhetorical discourse? Alone among discursive practices, rhetoric rests its fate not only on the experience of hearers, but on the mysterious accord of events as well. In an oddly symmetrical counterpoint, then, truly lasting rhetoric (as rare as Wally and Andre's conversation) abandons the realm of intention entirely and becomes part of a culture's form of life: its ongoing conversation with history.

Second, there seems to be a marked difference in the way conversational and rhetorical discursive forms take on their respective directional shape. Even though our diagram suggests that each conversation includes a potential rhetorical impulse (involving, as it does, reasoning human agents), in practice, conversations may be virtually indeterminate in their acquired direction. They may involve, at various moments, polite chatter, philosophical dialectic (where form-of-life conditionals themselves are up for grabs), embarrassing but therapeutic disclosures, and the most painful relational confrontations. The reason for this fact apparently derives from the more or less spontaneous reciprocation and synthesis that takes place among at least two complex personalities in every conversation. By noticeable contrast, rhetorical discourse usually has some end in view or at least some zone of uncertain difference upon which discussion comes to rest. Accordingly, the sense of suspense in rhetoric has less to do with its actual manner of unfolding, and more with the uncertainty of its impending denouement. In other words, if conversation usually takes shape through an *emergent* sense of directionality, rhetorical discursive practice takes shape through a *proposed* sense of directionality.

Third among our preliminary contrasts between conversational and rhetorical discourse is the difficult matter of their respective "boundary conditions." In earlier research I have taken some pains to establish that everything is *not* rhetorical (Farrell, 1976, 1978, 1982). From Figure 13.1 and the discussion it should be apparent that there are large chunks of the world that are not conversational either. What appears most fascinating, albeit overly symmetrical, is the proportional relationship between each discursive art's boundary conditions and the other's point of origin. Conversation, despite Gadamer's anthropormorphic characterization, does not and cannot leave the bounds of intentionality imposed and expected by either partner. Whatever spirit emerges within conversational form would be impossible without the consciousness of the partners themselves. For its part, rhetoric always seems to be striving toward, but never beyond the form of life yielded by cultural history. This very worldliness of rhetoric has been subject to attack from the time of Socrates to that of Ricoeur. Still, it must be acknowledged that the practical limits which the world imposes upon rhetorical advocacy in general are no greater than those imposed upon most other human actions. Perhaps less obviously, these same limits also provide the last resource and grounding for coherence in meaningful communication.

The differences I have sketched among conversational and rhetorical discourse are sufficiently pronounced as to pose interesting questions about the coherence problems each discursive form tends to encounter. We know, for instance, that communicative coherence is largely a matter of acknowledging, following, violating, and sanctioning rules. Further, given the human origin and self-referential character of rules, it should not surprise that these stipulative constructs seem to defy the closure of our most elegant matrices. Some rules, for instance, the "third-person reference" rule (Farrell & Frentz, 1979), seem equally prohibitive for both face-to-face conversation and for public address. Still others, governing turn-taking, topic-shift, interruption, and so forth, are either applied or elaborated in radically different ways for the arts of conversation and rhetoric. The reasons for these differences are elusive, at best. To complicate matters, it seems there are times when the emergence of rhetoric within conversation poses severe, even irreparable, coherence problems for interactants. At other times virtually the same devices of rhetoric will emerge in the nick of time, as it were, to retrieve and crystalize muddled sequences of conversational discourse. In order even to begin an explanation of these curiosities, I turn directly to the difficult question of transformation, specifically, why conversations take on rhetorical characteristics.

If we remain consistent with the synchronic features of discourse discussed thus far, it is possible to locate junctures (or places) where the characteristics of rhetoric emerge; these junctures will be provoked by each of the following three types of development:

(1) Cases where the content or expected direction of conversation has been prepared in advance by at least one of the conversants.
(2) Cases where the emergent status of the conversation, as a potentially complete unit of discourse, comes to rest upon the reflective and collaborative practical choices of conversants themselves.
(3) Cases where conversational discourse becomes disputational.

It will become apparent shortly (if it is not already obvious) that there is considerable overlap among the sets of conditions envisioned by each type of case. For our present purposes, however, what is most important is that we must suspend or sharply modify ordinary coherence expectations in many of these cases.

To appreciate the rhetorical aspects of discourse that is prepared, we need only attend to the apparent distance between its point of origin and its moment of expression. The great surrealist poet André Breton (1972) once noted that the "speed of thought is not greater than the speed of speech"; this may be why we bring to conversations the expectation that thoughts will be triggered, formed, and expressed in closest proximity to the actual encounter. By recognizable contrast, discourse that has been prepared in advance of the encounter would at least appear to preempt the proximity of utterance formation and expression. Perhaps the corollary to Gadamer's mythos of falling into conversation, is that we must change our expectations whenever we sense we are being pushed. To illustrate this rhetorical development, I pause to consider a snippet of real conversation that was introduced in the initial language-action study (Frentz & Farrell, 1976). John Dean has just entered the Oval Office and is addressing Richard Nixon:

D: The reason that I thought we ought to talk this morning is because in our conversations, I have the impression that you don't know everything I know and it makes it very difficult for you to make

judgments that only you can make on some of these things and I
thought that —
P: In other words, I have to know why you feel that we shouldn't
unravel something.
D: Let me give you my overall first.
P: In other words, your judgment as to where it stands, and where it
will go.
D: I think that there is no doubt about the seriousness of the problem
we've got. We have a cancer within, close to the Presidency, that is
growing . . . [Presidential Transcripts, 1974, pp. 98-99].

Our first study of this passage was intrigued with the implications
of Dean's remarks for the unravelling of an institutional form of life
(i.e., that of the presidency). Note also the way that Dean imposes his
own anticipated reasons and interpretations upon the encounter; it is
apparent that he has something in mind. More than this, he goes so far
as to offer a reading of previous conversations as a thematic context
for this present encounter. Perhaps most interesting (in light of our
interference factor), the president tries and fails to *interrupt* Dean.
Rhetoric, as it is initiated here, seems to carry a temporary license not
to be interrupted. The rhetorical features of what I have called prepared discourse find clear parallels in our other two types of cases.

A second type of case arises when communicants are forced to
attend to the uncertain status of their own accumulated conversational discourse. Either there are unavoidable implications of the
conversation for the real world of prospective action, or the status of
the conversation imposes upon the uncertain relational or form of life
status of the participants. In each type of case, a still moment[1] of
contingent choice must arise, and we abandon our equation of spontaneous thought with expression in favor of a more deliberate interpretative horizon — of proposal and attendance, of advocacy and
audience. Here, for instance, is a particularly heated exchange:

H: Look, I just wish you would tell me what I've done wrong — I
mean, you're so damned angry!
S: Well, I'm not even sure I remember exactly what it was; it was
everything; you just really pissed me off, that's all — Anyway, I
don't want to keep going through it . . . I'm —
((interruption))
H: You're the one that keeps —
((interruption))
S: I'm saying things I don't even mean. Look, ask me tomorrow —
I'm sorry, I just lost it there for a while. . .
H: Ok.

While not particularly elegant stylistically, the utterances in this episode have undertaken a rhetorical burden that is not easily fulfilled: They are placing the conversation itself in a kind of interpretative perspective. There is no explicit referent for "it;" but unmistakably *it* conjures forth the entire apparently regrettable exchange. In questioning his own capacity to say what he means, S is proposing that a kind of productive ambiguity be restored to the proceedings. He goes further, even suggesting that the entire episode sequence be dropped, or filed for future reference. H is thus no longer a spontaneous dialogue partner, but rather a potentially complicitous audience. As such, H apparently assents to the proposal.

This dimension of practical choice in rhetoric is not always limited to conversational implications for future, real world conduct. Sometimes severe dislocations of level or continuity in episodic meaning force participants in a conversation to retrospect upon the entire ongoing discourse. Here, for instance, is a case where a relatively distant acquaintance has just disclosed his own extreme anxiety to an apparently sympathetic party. After awkward silences and uncomfortable cliches of reassurance, the episode nears an end:

T_1: Well, look, I know everything's going to go a lot better now — just talking this out, I'm a lot more confident now . . .

T_2: Err, ah, good, I'm sorry I couldn't be more help, but I . . .

No one can state with assurance what it is that has forced T_1 to get well prematurely. While most coherent conversations surely manifest a sense of reciprocity, that principle alone is not enough to explain an abrupt comic turn in this most bleakly revelatory conversation. Since the status of previous disclosure is clearly at issue in T_1's most optimistic prognosis, I can only submit that the practical choices of rhetoric are at work here, preserving conversational continuity and making room for future choice. Rhetoric is a comic art.

As the third type of rhetorical juncture within conversation, consider the disputational episodes that frequently erupt within otherwise civil discourse:

A Dinner Gathering

P_1: Well, I know we're all in a sorry state — everyone at work says so, too. But I just don't see how people can blame that nice man President Reagan — he's surely doing all he can do . . .

T_2: Yeah, well the key word there is "can" — I mean the guy has the brains of a Styrofoam cup!

V_1: Tommy, you promised you wouldn't . . . (Furious exchange follows).

It seems odd and perhaps somewhat disturbing that we go to such lengths to avoid disputation within "polite" conversation. Recently, even the ubiquitous Miss Manners etiquette columnists have been counseling fledgling interactants that they should always nod agreeably, and *never* say anything contentious. One is reminded of those pathological speech patterns where the patient continually repeats the last word in the therapist's previous utterance. André Breton (1972) maintained that conversation is always teetering over the abyss of such pathology, and that only the reminder of another's "difference" keeps us sane. For present purposes the most important characteristic of disputational junctures within conversation is that they usually do not erode the coherence of discourse. In fact, when conversationists begin to disagree, *and* disagreements become heated, consider what happens. We begin to move toward all the rhetorical features of our continuum: we relax turn-taking rules; whoever can hold the floor, through eloquence, persuasive acumen, or plain endurance, tends to keep the floor; and extended episodic fragments are considered acceptable conduct for individual social actors. Something else happens with conversational controversy: As each speaker says his or her piece, we begin to vary freely the contexts and actions that are at issue. We tell stories in which the other is or was at fault. We defend ourselves through narratives that help to excuse our lapses.

This tentative finding is consistent with an intuition I have already introduced about conversational coherence. Despite what Goffman (1974) and others have alleged about the egocentric content of conversation, the extension and sequencing of conversational form is a painstakingly collaborative affair. The proliferation of lapses, false starts, misfires, and dead ends should remind us that the very totality of discourse we observers require in order to make judgments about coherence is something unavailable to interactants themselves. For individuals who must communicate, coherence is something that must emerge from inductive and piecemeal choice, if it is to emerge at all. For this reason the very presupposition of coherence requires a benign conspiracy of communicants, or at least an act of faith. When we suspend more immediate expectations (of reciprocity, for instance, or agreement), other more remote anticipations must be introduced. As Dean sought to do with Nixon, perhaps, each of us tries to "give you my overall first." We do not cease to collaborate, or course. We grant the extension and compression of urgency and accounting. But we listen critically now, waiting for our chance to respond. We have slipped, unobtrusively, but undeniably, into the mode of rhetoric.

THE RHETORIC OF CONVERSATIONAL COHERENCE

The assumption throughout this essay has been that conversation and rhetoric are interdependent but distinguishable discursive arts. Despite the remarkable complementarity we have found within the origins, interrelations, and transformations of these modes of discourse, the contributions of each to coherence problems are not well understood. To that end several explanatory hypotheses relating the resources of rhetoric to the coherence problems of conversation will be introduced.

The fundamental paradox to be explained must still concern the purportedly suspect qualities of rhetoric when these are found pertinent to conversational discourse. From the examples we have considered thus far (ranging from preparation, to practical choice, to actual dispute), it should be apparent that rhetorical qualities of discourse are not inferior to but simply different from those of ordinary conversational interaction. When rhetoric happens to a conversation, we move from the relatively open stance of communicant to that of collaborative audience. Accompanying this difference in stance is an unmistakable difference in the way we are now expected to attend to messages. Since we are now *addressed,* we must affiliate with an unfolding message that we must complete and judge; we think about this message at a distance, in the sense that we must constantly construct our own discourse about what is being said. Critical to this new stance we are called upon to take is the fact that we are being addressed as a representative other, that is, as an exemplar of how others *ought to think.* Even when we are disputing or differing with others in conversation, this rhetorical contrast is evident. Either our own actions are appraised as typical of some larger class of conduct, or we are addressed so as to remove ourselves from immediate interest, and even to pass judgment on ourselves.

Given that the presence of rhetoric within conversation does seem to call for a different (but not necessarily inferior) mode of address and attendance, how are we to account for the apparent derogation of rhetoric in usual communication practice? To state the problem bluntly, an initial hypothesis could go so far as to claim that *the uncovering of rhetoric within conversation may pose serious, even lethal coherence problems to an ongoing discourse.* Here is a representative facsimile:

Phone Call
S: Hello, Mr. Farrell?
F: Yes, it is.

S: And how are you today, Mr. Farrell?

F: Oh, I'm fine . . . and who might you be?

S: Oh, I'm fine, too, Mr. Farrell (apparent misconstrual). Listen, I have just a couple of informational questions to ask you on energy, and I wonder if you'd be kind enough to help me out . . .

F: Well, I'm trying to watch the Dolphin game and this is the third call I've . . .

S: This won't take a minute Mr. Farrell. Then I'll let you get back to your game. . . . Do you know very much about energy consumption?

F: Actually, I know quite a bit — you'd be surprised. . . . What kind are you referring to?

S: In the home. . . . For instance, Mr. Farrell, what would you say is the cheapest and safest form of energy for home use right now?

F: Gas, which we already have. Listen, you said this . . .

S: (interruption) Wrong, Mr. Farrell. It's oil, oil-generated heating lamps to be specific. They're cheap, they're safe, they're con- . . . (interruption)

F: Alright, what firm is this? What do you want?

S: Kerosan home heating lamps, Mr. Farrell. We'd just like to send you some . . .

F: Look, I do business at the office . . . it's been nice chatting with you (click).

The episode sketched here may seem to have been ill-fated from the beginning. The parties are never properly acquainted and interruptions abound. Yet it continues after a fashion until the salesperson's avowedly rhetorical aim is detected. Each of us could cite instances, among more or less familiar conversants, where discourse itself is a pretext, and showing one's etchings is not the real aim of the conversational encounter. Yet the abrupt, unfinished, or hostile dislocation of discourse (all of which I am assuming must strain against formal expectations of coherence) is not the only fate of uncovered rhetoric. In *My Dinner With Andre* (Shawn & Gregory, 1981); Andre tells Wally that if things have gone dead in his relationship, then he should "become a hobo or something and go out on the road." Rather than being premeditated, and secretive, this utterance responds to an emerging contingent issue; that is, what should Wally do with his life? Rather than faltering, then, this dialogue seems to enrich its own developing meanings. Instead of disclosing an interloper, this singular exchange seems to reveal the anticipations of a prophet. Why the difference?

Without attempting to exhaust the rhetorical possibilities of conversation, several related premises may now be introduced to explain the shifting status of rhetoric. *First, it is the concealment of rhetoric that undermines its conversational legitimacy.* When we attempt to hide our rhetorical aims, or cover over real differences among interactants (as in diplomacy or highly ritualized exchanges), then the presence of rhetoric is rightly suspect, just as the coherence of conversation is always threatened. This is why the phone call episode collapses, while Andre and Wally's conversation enriches. What of the concealed rhetoric that works in conversation: the successful seduction, the slick con job? In each case what has transpired might be coherent, might even be rhetorically appropriate; but it is far from spontaneous in its appearance. For this reason it appears that *rhetoric cannot operate effectively within conversation unless there is an implied consensus from at least one of the parties to attend to the unfolding of discourse as an interested collaborative audience.* In other words, rhetoric cannot occur in such settings unless we let it. Now all intelligible conversation requires the assumption of certain background understandings that are available to interactants (Kreckel, 1981; Beach, this volume). I am suggesting, however, that a different order of more purposeful consensus must be taken for granted if the practical force of rhetoric is to play a constructive role within conversation. This is the postulate of *social knowledge*[2] that I have introduced and developed in ongoing research (Farrell, 1976, 1978, 1982). By consenting to the interpretative horizon offered by an advocate, the audience for rhetoric must suspend (for the time being) his or her individual biases and alignments in favor of a more critical attitude toward potentially generalizable interests. In conversational practice, of course, it is usually easier to recognize the retraction of social knowledge premises than to notice their emergence. Still, if it is true that semantic content and linguistic form are not always sufficient to assure coherence within conversation (and this is all I have argued), then it must follow that at least some conversational coherence problems (of intelligibility, or continuity, or reciprocation) are rife with potential for the warranted directionality that rhetoric might provide. Indeed, we are now prepared to be a bit more venturesome. If rhetoric is an art whose practices are manifest in certain figures, tropes, and topoi of utterance choice, then we might expect these very devices of rhetoric to become the basis of conversational coherence when premeditation, practical contingency, or disputation surfaces in such discourse; these are the places where conversation becomes rhetorical.

The most difficult question, as always, is that of procedure. Since rhetoric is typically a premeditative, practical, and disputational art, the figures and strategems of rhetoric traditionally have functioned so as not to call attention to themselves. How, then, are we as observers to attend to them? In the extended example that follows, I have tried to be particularly attentive to the narrative retrospections and anticipations of discourse because this seems to be where the episodic force of rhetoric is most readily detectable. Where recurrent narrative themes become apparent in communicative practice, we must assume either that premeditation or bad habits are at work. Where direct or indirect reference is made to the conversation as a collective unit, we should assume that some practical intersection with the worlds of the communicants is soon to follow. Where there are clear discrepancies between semantic and pragmatic functions of discourse, we must assume either that the conversation is incoherent (always a last resort) or that some broader rhetorical service is being performed by language choice. In particular, when the episodic force of utterances moves from that of expression to proposal, we should look for a conspicuous shift in the collaborative stance of interlocutors. An interpretative horizon of anticipated understanding will be offered by one of the speakers. However, it need not be accepted. The rhetorical speaker is also a reflective and accountable actor.

THE B-K CONVERSATION

Although there are apparent differences in background, communicative competence, conversational style, and individual personality between B and K, their conversation certainly seems to have been coherent. However, this sense of coherence was something of an achievement, in light of some potential threats to its intelligibility, continuity, and reciprocation. In the analysis that follows, I will contend that the rhetorical figures of evasion (opposite = *confrontation),* reduplication (opposite = *ellipsis),* and bypass (opposite = *ekphrasis,* the still moment of temporal choice) were all at work to some degree in lieu of more serious coherence defects. We begin, as formalistic critics might, with a narrative overview. However, we come to rest upon a critical stasis for the conversation itself, a moment where expression becomes proposal and rhetorical choice must be made.

In light of Figure 13.1 it is interesting that the conversation begins with ritualistic chitchat, rooted in the particularities of the lunch encounter and the generality of convention (pie, turkey, Thanksgiving). Yet even here B seems ill at ease. She laughs nervously at her own utterances (in fact, much clearer in the tape than the transcript is the fact that B punctuates the entire conversation with nervous laughter). Still, the first unmistakable sign of difficulty does not emerge until the apparently innocuous topic of Christmas shopping and travel plans:

034 **B :** Are you going home for Christmas?
035 **K :** Oh yeah. (pause) .hhh - Is there any other choice? =
038 **B :** Sure there's another choice/ Some folks don't go - home for
         Christmas/

Interestingly enough, B has responded with a curious admixture of confrontation and evasion. Now, instead of asking, "Where are you going?" as one might expect, K asks, "Oh, where's your Mom living?" This implies some prior knowledge by K of B's travel plans. When B observes, "He does. This will be the first time I have been to Florida" (052), K responds, "I meant to ask you the other day, are you flying down?" (053). Obviously, then, K knew that B was going to Florida over Christmas. What K apparently did not know was that only B's father was going to be there. Thus, the question (039 K), "Oh, where's your Mom living?" B's parents are divorced and K may need to tread lightly on this delicate subject. The first sign that she realizes this and chooses her words carefully comes with:

046 **B :** Um hmm/ Well he'll be in Florida by the time I get there.
047 **K :** What's he going t- does- Is this part of his business?

K has amended her question in midstream lest it appear to be too probing. What follows seems to confirm her rhetorical trope — ellipsis — as well chosen.

Following the question, "are you flying down?" (053), B offers: "Uh huh and I hate planes." K has heard this before and says so ("I know you said that." This is usually a mild rebuff). However, it turns out that B also has serious problems relating to her father (061-066); that she made a fool of herself while attempting to ski (106-116); that she is "terrified of heights" (122). For once K does not reciprocate: "I love the heights" (124). B also feels that the Midwest is "ugly" (204). If persons tend to thematize themselves in recurrent conversational narratives (Goffman, 1974), then the narrative portraiture of self offered by B does not present us with a very secure or satisfied person. Now in and of themselves such disclosures do not threaten the coherence of discourse. However, B finds herself punctuating even K's anticipated stories with unlikely morbidity. K's early California ballooning fantasy, "So that's what I want to do on my honeymoon. Go to California and- and balloon (laugh)" (145), leads B to observe, "If you missed you'd either hit the mountains or the ((laughing)) ocean ((laugh))" (150). B seems literally to be forcing the following unhappy dénouement:

217   **K:**   = So, I just walk out the back door and I can ski into the woods.
218   **B:**   Umm:.
              [[
219   **K:**   An:d spen:d two hours in the woods and never see anybody or hear anybody.
220   **B:**   That must be really fun, especially right around Christmas time.
                              [   ]
221   **K:**   Yeah it's nice.
222   **K:**   Um hmm/ =
223   **B:**   =When nobody's hunting ((laughing)) anything.
224   **K:**   Oh they can't hunt back there, it's not that - big.
                                                    [
225   **B:**   I thought they always sneaked in and did it anyway.

Although the construction of culturally significant narrative themes within natural discourse appears to be a rhetorical process, the very ubiquity of such themes within conversation must prompt some hesitancy in applying rhetorical terminology to each theme we encounter. In the case of B and K, however, it is the metaphorical consistency of themes that are repeated (highs and lows, terror of the unexpected, an incompetence at simple things, and so forth) that must arrest our attention. We need not attribute intentional choice to each specific instance in order to be struck by their implications as a collective story line. Debatable as observer attributions might be, there is no denying the moment when a conversational partner begins to predict, to anticipate, and eventually, to take account of such themes as implications for real life. The encounter of such a moment, its recognition, and its effective resolution relies upon the coherence resources of rhetoric.

In my reading of this complex text, one key rhetorical juncture occurs when B is recounting yet another tale of disappointment; this time a childhood experience at fox hunting:

247 **B:** . . . there were no foxes, they'd all been hunted to death years ago. . . .
249 **B:** So they had these special kennels where they'd raise ch-foxes and charge outrageous prices for them, and the foxes were often so tame they wouldn't ((laughing)) run (the rounds) ((laugh)) . . .
253 **B:** But the hunt club closed before I got good enough and old enough and ((voice fades)) all that to join- ((louder)) There's a whole etiquette that goes with that, which, I probably wouldn't have been very good at ((softly, laughing)) learning.
254 **K:** In other words if I had asked you if you would have enjoyed it you probably ((laughing slightly)) wouldn't've.

B, of course agrees. Now while the grammar of K's inquiry is flawed (and the tone of the question apparently humorous), K's utterance is the only subjunctive conditional question in the entire conversation. The very uniqueness of the conversational device suggests that K not only understands the themes of B's stories, but through a figurative temporal bypass K shows that she can also anticipate the ways these themes will repeat themselves. Perhaps more important, this rhetorical trope (of discursive bypass) has allowed K to circumvent a more uncomfortable confrontational question; that is, " Do you like *anything?*" Inadvertently or not, K's utterance has now placed her at one step removed from the discourse. This is particularly important as the interactants face the question of how to *end* the conversation.

If our instincts are correct here (and if we assume that K is not attracted by the prospect of indefinite repetition), then we might expect that this conversation will end on a note of polite but emphatic social distance. That seems to be what happens. In a concluding discussion of what to do in the winter in Madison, B offers, "I'm looking for somebody who — wouldn't be embarrassed to start skating. I'd like to skate with another beginner" (307). K concedes, "That's a (pause) a big thing, especially down on the campus area where there are places to skate" (308). She then adds, " . . . I don't really know! When I have free time I ski. I don't even think of anything else." Rather evasive. B immediately attempts another overture:

315 **B:** That sounds alright, we have this great big field near our house, - an:d you should come out and ski there sometime.

Umm: - there are two fields, connected by, a sort of path, next to a creek, through some woods.

317   **K:**   I was gonna say. There's gotta be - fields are pretty dull in themselves.

318   **B:**   Yeah -

[[

319   **K:**   The arboretum is fun. Things like that. Where there's trees and (hills) and - curves,

320   **B:**   These have - trees, and they're sort of hilly, and there's this creek, and there are also pheasants, and sometimes hawks, and lots of rabbits and things. . . .

The implied practical question (should we see more of each other?) has been met first with evasion and then — when there appears to be no other choice — by an implied metonymic judgment of B's dull fields. Overture, evasion, and circumspection continue for a time, and the conversation seems to close in Chekhovian fashion, as it were: in midstride, with our two interlocutors earnestly discussing the weather.

There is no way for us to know, of course, how many of the conversational actions I have described were intentional. While we can draw certain conclusions from within the text about what each of the parties must have known, the absence of anything more intimate than polite social distance inhibits us from naming complex interpersonal strategies. Yet, the synchronic relationship I have tried to sketch between conversation and rhetoric should not have to depend upon privileged insider information. The decision to put two and two together and therefore to use tact and circumspection is undeniably a rhetorical choice. The ellipsis of undesirable topics, the discovery of limits to the complementarity of world veiws, the anticipation of theme, and the evasion of commitments are all figures of discourse with critical rhetorical features. Did these devices help to preserve coherence? At the very least their periodic presence helps to alert the student of natural language to those moments within every conversation when coherence is a somewhat enigmatic achievement.

CONCLUSION

Along with the introductory hypotheses of this essay, my hope is to have begun a reappraisal of the unstable relationship between conversation and rhetoric. If we are prepared to grant rhetoric the parallel origin and status, as well as the conversational synchrony its tradition seems to deserve, then several more speculative possibilities might surface.

First, there seems to be something important, but unexamined, about the background understandings of conversation that allow rhetorical choices to emerge. While I have stressed the importance of social knowledge as a postulate contributing to the intelligibility of rhetoric, no attempt has been made to relate social knowledge to the more particularistic understandings that apparently contribute to the meaning of ordinary conversational discourse. In ongoing research I am exploring the hypothesis that rhetoric is always a background possibility for conversation, but that the reverse is much less frequently true: Conversation is only rarely a background possibility for public rhetorical discourse.

Second, an understanding of the characteristic differences between conversational exchange and the rhetorical mode of address ought to draw our attention to the ways in which researchers invite actual participants to make sense of their own utterances. If I am correct in assuming that rhetoric tends to emerge when we are called upon to reflect about contingent prospects for discursive conduct, then anyone who is asked to explain or account for his or her previous discourse is being placed in a kind of forensic rhetorical stance. Whether we participant-observers are doing much damage to the unfolding of real conversational discourse is a nagging and possibly unanswerable question. It is worth noting that Marga Kreckel's important recent study, *Communicative Acts and Shared Knowledge in Natural Discourse* (1981), found that every time one of her own respondents was asked to explain his or her conversational conduct (from videotape and manuscript), the respondent in question offered a narrative accounting. These persons became, for the moment, at least, rhetorical actors.

Finally, as a rhetorical theorist, I find that questions of discursive coherence and rhetorical propriety are never far removed from issues of character and responsibility. Rhetoric, in its very flamboyance, is always a risky proposition. For, in rhetoric, we speak to others in ways that must hold us acountable to them. The same presumption that prompts rhetoric to seek out a special form of attendance also must constitute a broad and unfinished commitment. This is another way of saying that rhetoric may offer figures, tropes, and strategems for resolving conversational coherence problems; but this is only at the risk of reminding audience and interlocutor alike of rhetoric's own ambivalent history. That history, checkered or not, speaks to remind us of a single, recurrent lesson. Conversation may and does disclose to us all the *state of the art* of human character. But rhetoric is the only art civilized persons have available to make up what human character may yet become.

NOTES

1. As will become apparent, the still moment refers to the rhetorical trope known as *ekphrasis*. With this trope, the usual sequential sense of continuity in language use, is slowed down, even decontextualized so that language choices — when they are made — seem to emerge within an enlarged interpretative horizon. While it cannot be proved in this essay, such still moments appear to arise when different zones of conversational meaning (form of life, encounter, episode) collide with each other.

2. "Social knowledge comprises conceptions of symbolic relationships among problems, persons, interests, and actions, which imply (when accepted) certain notions of preferable public behavior" (Farrell, 1976). In positing an essential relationship between social knowledge and the rhetorical utterance within conversation, the present essay alleges that social knowledge may be constitutive for what is distinctly meaningful about rhetorical practice.

14

Conversational Coherence

< <LEONARD C. HAWES > >

< < < What is entailed in the presumption that con- > > >
versation is coherent? As a way of approaching that question, *conversation* and *coherence* are developed in semiotic-diacritical terms; a discourse robust in the articulation of differences and contradictions. Conversation as discursive overdetermination replaces conversation as systemic interaction, and coherence as historical production replaces coherence as systemic rules.

CONVERSE/COHERE

Converse has its roots in the Latin terms, *con* and *vertere,* which mean to turn together in a continuing process of reversal. As such, conversing is a double-centered process; it simultaneously locates and positions the seams of difference articulating subject (speaker)/ object (listener, among other object types). For the moment, read "to turn together in a continuïng process of reversal" as a process of contradiction or the play of dialectical relations. As double-centered structuring, contradiction is a unity of two as opposed to a unity of one. To con-verse is to formulate in speech an object for subject; the formulating of object for subject is materially produced in the turning discursivity of double-centered speech (i.e., conversation). As such, conversing is a continuing process of contradiction.

The paradox of conversation is not that it is a double-centered structuring process but that neither center independently is capable of identifying its subject-ive location in discourse. Each center perpetually recenters itself in the turning of speaking conversationally. Independently, each center is both blind and invisible and thereby materially nonexistent; conversing is one method of recentering a decentered universe of significances. From the subjectivity of each center, meaning is a unity of one (right understanding).

Paradoxically, the production of single-centered meaning is possible only by means of double-centered practices; such practices, however, produce double-centered universes of significance necessarily read by each conversed center as differences evidencing decentering (i.e., trouble, problem, error, misunderstanding, confusion, conflict). The more the differences are thematized as single-centered structurings, the more differences there come to be articulated. It is from within such an infinitely elaborating process of contradiction that conversation produces its own motivated discursive movement. It is in this sense that conversation produces two from one; to converse, if even only one turn is spoken, is to con-textualize (i.e., inmix) subject/object as turning's pivotal position.

The object conversation presupposes is capable of understanding the difference being articulated. To converse is to attempt to produce unity from difference; the temporal unity produced is coherence and the difference produced is identity (i.e., the double structure of self/other). The unity of coherence also is a double-centered structuring; coherence is a temporary unity not in identity but in opposition. The dialectical structuring of coherence is the tension between truthfulness and appropriateness.

Jürgen Habermas (1979) claims that valid speech satisfies four conditions:

(1) an utterance (i.e., turn) must be spoken in a comprehensible language;
(2) an utterance must be a true representation of something in the world;
(3) an utterance must be a truthful expression of intention; and
(4) an utterance must be appropriate for socially recognized situations.

When some configuration of these conditions is satisfied, Habermas says that speech is more or less valid.

The question of the universal validity of speech is considerably more encompassing than the question of conversational coherence. Universal validity will not be considered here; nevertheless, the use of Habermas at this point is helpful in understanding conversing's production of coherence. Coherent conversation is conversation that is both truthful and appropriate; truthfulness functions to disclose subjectivity in *my* world of internal nature whereas appropriateness functions to establish legitimate interpersonal relations in *our* world of society.

Conversing problematizes the locus of meaning and re-solves the problem as centered subject facing the paradox of truthfulness/appropriateness. Any resolution of the double-centered structure of coherence is temporary; conversing produces possibility, not certainty. Any meaning is a temorary configuring of signifiers. Insofar as conversing is both the product and the practice of organizing and distributing discourse, the coherence of such discourse varies across its particular instances. In short, conversing is coproduced discourse the coherence of which is dialectical.

As an innocent-enough sounding example of the appropriateness/truthfulness dialectic and a method of its resolution, consider a story Liza Minelli told about her mother, Judy Garland, on Tom Snyder's *Tomorrow Show*. Miss Garland had been invited to an opening night performance by a well-known but unnamed actress friend. It is appropriate for a person in the position of having been invited to such a performance to go backstage and compliment the performer after the performance. Liza Minelli said her mother's difficulty was that the performance did not merit a compliment; not to go backstage, however, would have produced an insult. Judy Garland did not want to insult the friend nor did she want to compliment the actress. The pragmatic problem here is how to be truthful and at the same time appropriate. Miss Garland resolved these contradictory injunctions by going backstage, throwing her arms wide to the actress and exclaiming, "I don't know how you do it!"

Figuring centrally into the pragmatic success of that turn is the presumption that a compliment/acknowledgement is a two-turn practice; the compliment's recipient acknowledges the compliment by accepting it as gift and not pressing for elaboration or justification. The turn worked insofar as the context was overdetermined and formulary practices were sufficient to produce coherence as ambiguity. The ambiguity obscures the two centers one from the other. Miss Garland, as the story's centered subject, is decentered, producing the insight of a decidedly more double-centered reading. It worked insofar as it produced temporary unity of one in a double-centered context.

Wallace Shawn and Andre Gregory (1981), in their screenplay for Louis Malle's film, *My Dinner With Andre,* like Jürgen Habermas

(1979), are concerned about conversed relationships for which both centers are indexical and neither is reflexive. Andre is saying to Wally at one point during the dinner:

> What we *need* is to analyze our situation in the world with great clarity, so that we can act and respond appropriately, but instead when we get together, we fall into a kind of collective hysteria, in which nobody knows what's going on. And I mean, it may be, Wally, that one of the reasons we *don't* know what's going on is that when we're at one of those parties we're all too busy *performing*. We're concentrating on playing our own roles and giving a good performance, so we *can't* perceive what's going on around us. That was one of the reasons Grotowski gave up the theatre, you know. He just felt that people in their lives now were performing so well that performance in the theatre was sort of superfluous and in a way obscene [1981, p. 69].

To the extent that appropriateness of performance is of greater worth than truthfulness of utterance, both epistemological and ontological distortions are inscribed onto the surfaces of sociality. Andre is concerned that too few are willing, or able any more, to distinguish collective hysteria from coherent speech. At some point, if empirical/critical work is to have any connection with a material world, the materiality/ideality dialectic cannot be ignored. If truthfulness and appropriateness become conflated, trust is drained of its pragmatic vitality, and paranoia replaces it as social reality's founding presupposition. At best, the consequence would be speech disembodied from language.

The society Jerzy Kosinski (1970) characterizes in his novel, *Being There*, is founded on the materiality of disembodied conversation. Even if a bit overdrawn fictionally for our purposes, *Being There* can be read as critical theory. Benjamin Rand, the retired and dying corporate tycoon and friend of the president of the United States; EE, Rand's younger wife and Chance's would-be lover; the president of the United States, on the basis of a brief visit; and the Russian ambassador to the UN, who was convinced Chance spoke and read Russian; none of these subjects reflect critically on conversational coherence/validity. Kosinski describes Chance's conversational practices at one point when Chance and EE are talking:

> Thinking that he ought to show a keen interest in what EE was saying, Chance resorted to repeating to her parts of her own sentences, a practice he had observed on TV. In this fashion he

encouraged her to continue and elaborate. Each time Chance repeated EE's words, she brightened and looked more confident. In
fact, she became so at ease that she began to punctuate her speech
by touching, now his shoulder, now his arm. Her words seemed to
float inside his head; he observed her as if she were on television
[1970, p. 131].

TRUTHFULNESS/APPROPRIATENESS

Reading from the unreflexive center of either EE's or Chance's
subjectivity, coherence remains an untopicalized presupposition. The
possibility of performance never surfaces; coherency is presupposed
and thereby hidden from question. Insofar as both centers are unreflexive, the reciprocal deception produced is simply unavailable for
correcting precisely because the double-centeredness of reciprocal
deception is transparent to either single-centered subject.

Corrections in conversational speech are material evidences of
reflexivity's interrogation of its own validity claims. Correcting is a
double-centered practice of a subsequent utterance formulating some
prior utterance as either untruthful or inappropriate. On this view
untruthfulness or inappropriateness materialize as discursive articu-
lations of corrections. Practices producing appropriate, polite conversation probably evidence fewer corrections than practices producing truthful conversation. Conventional wisdom is vague on this
point; in some contexts it is not appropriate to correct; in others it is
not appropriate to overlook (i.e., not to topicalize) either inappropriateness or untruthfulness. The production of that dialectical seam
affords the analyst a diacritical vantage point from which to study the
practices of conversational coherence.

Conversation, as a process of opposing and contradicting, is a
chain of signifiers: furthermore, meaning does not lie beneath the
level of signifiers but is on the surface; on the configurings of signifiers
rather than in underlying signifieds. If meaning is on the surface of
sliding chains of signifiers, how is the sliding halted long enough to
produce the apparency of stable meanings of subject/object?
Grossberg (1979, p. 218) answers:

> To the extent that the available practices delimit our possibilities,
> our own self-existence as subjects is constituted by our necessary
> participation in those practices. These (material) practices of rela-
> tionship and differentiation, including language-use, construct our
> experience as transcendental subjects. The practices are not the

possession or creation of the human subject, but rather determine the possible positions in which the human psyche can exist in its relations with the other. For example, Foucault has argued that the notion of an author (or subject) is a device by which we stop the proliferation of meaning; that is, it is a particular modern practice of closing off the possibility of an endless series of readings.

Psychological subject as conversational center is a discursive resolution to the problem of how to halt, temporarily, the movement of the chain of signifiers and thereby punctuate its coherence. *Correcting* is one family of practices that halt the indexical sliding of conversation by turning back (to some prior turns), thereby locating reflexive subjectivity. Correcting might be a reflexive articulation, for it creates the very possibility of its own meaningfulness. Correcting, by its discursive nature, is a method of producing a reflexive turn, a turning back to that which correcting formulates as now standing in need of being corrected. Subject is located as responsible subject.

THE B-K CONVERSATION TEXT

My interest in this text (see Appendix) is in the pragmatic validity of its methods and practices of producing coherent conversation. Of course, Habermas's (1979) four validity conditions are not mutually exclusive; rather they form an ensemble of contradictory injunctions. I grant that the B-K conversation text, as an intersection of codes, satisfies comprehensibility. Of interest to me is the pragmatic region of speech animated by the contradictory injunctions of truth, appropriateness, and truthfulness productive of temporary coherence.

Three instances of correcting are examined at close range: turns 223-226; turns 267-277; and turns 277-287. But first, consider their discursive contexts. The 347 turns of transcribed speech evidence thirteen more or less clearly bounded movements. Figure 14.1 breaks out the text by movement, the corresponding inclusive lines of text, each movement's dominant speaker, if there is one, and the object(s) being formulated (i.e., the manifest topics talked about). Displayed in this fashion, several of its features stand out. First, subject as speaker corresponds quite directly to movement; B and K, as conversed subjects, become formulated in more or less alternating movements. Each movement is constituted by a configuring of one or more signifiers in the alternating of moving/halting. The moving of chaining signifiers is within-movement elaboration (i.e., indexical movement).

Movement	Turns	Subjective Object	Objective Subject(s)
I	001-004	B/K Greeting	B/K
II	005-016	B Offers/K Declines	Sandwich
III	017-034	B Characterizes	Christmas/Father
IV	034-039	K ''	Christmas/Choice
V	039-066	B ''	Mom/Dad
VI	066-079	K ''	Brother's growth
VII	079-085	B ''	Step-brother/Switzerland
VIII	085-096	K ''	Friend/Switzerland/Skiing
	096-105	B ''	Step-brother/Switzerland/Skiing/Olympic
IX	105-118	B ''	Her skiing ineptness
X	118-166	K ''	Cross-country skiing/Downhill skiing/Heights/Ballooning/Honeymoon/Graduation/Practicality/Internship
XI	166-228	K ''	Internship/Home/Flooding/Ugly city/State park/Transportation
XII	228-301	B ''	Skiing/Home/Rural Philadelphia/Horses/Riding ineptness/Ferriers/Lessons/Riding Accidents
XIII	301-347	K ''	Other winter activities/Skiing/Wisconsin weather/Pacific Coast weather

Figure 14.1 A Movement/Focus Display of B-K Conversation Text

The temporary halting of the chaining of signifiers is the between-movement bounding: the turning from one subject being positioned on the chain as speaker to another such subject as reflexive identity.

Second, as this conversation moves, each movement becomes more elaborated; compare Movement X with Movement III, for example. Later movements turn through more signifiers in their indexical development than do the earlier movements. As each movement articulates more turns, and perhaps more elaborate turns, subsequent turns, by their very production, disclose differences from previous turns. Such differences may be formulated as error, mistake, misunderstanding, lying, stupidity, naivete, or whatever.

My approach to each of the corrections is similar: First, I describe the pragmatic work of the lines immediately prior to the correcting; second, I describe the particular method by which each correction is produced; third, I display each method of correcting over against a field of possible methods with the aim of assessing the method of correcting actually produced; finally, I critique these instances of correction's work along the broader lines of pragmatic validity.

Correction 1.

215 **K:** Yeah   ((laugh . . .)) (pause)
         You're right though it isn't very pretty, - as - far as that goes, - it's a city. You know they're cities. But - like my parents live - right off - the state park.

216 **B:** Umm:::! =

217 **K:** = So, I just walk out the back door and I can ski into the woods.

218 **B:**   Umm:.
            [[

219 **K:**   An:d spen:d two hours in the woods and never see anybody or hear anybody.

220 **B:** That must be really fun, especially right around Christmas time.
                    [   ]

221 **K:**   Yeah it's nice.

222 **K:** Um hmm/=

223 **B:** =When nobody's hunting ((laughing)) anything.

224 **K:** Oh they can't hunt back there, it's not that - big.
                                          [

225 **B:**   I thought they
         always sneaked in and did it anyway.
         Uh'no:, it's - it's *nice* cuz like my: little brother and his friends all have - other friends around = the woods, on the other sides of the woods and they just roam through there, an' - and go out there to scream and holler to find kids an',-

Turn 215 is a turning from the prior elaboration of the signifier "city" to the signifier "state park" near where K's parents live. Turn 223 humorously qualifies 219. At this point there are a variety of possible turns the conversation may take: (1) 224 might elaborate 223's humorous characterizing of what goes on in state parks; (2) 224 might produce laughter, then silence; (3) 224 might denigrate 223's stupidity/naivete. Instead, 224 is a serious, as opposed to humorous, correction of 223's source of laughter (i.e., the suggestion that hunting takes place in state parks), thereby denying the attempt to formulate the topic humorously. A reason for the incorrectness is even produced: "it's not that - big."

Turn 225 is not a serious acknowledging of a prior mistake but rather elaborates the topic of hunting back in the primitive Midwest. Turn 226 corrects 225, and by implication 224, by first negating and then recharacterizing the characterizing of 215 through 222. The signifier "where my parents live" is not to be joked about but is to be about signifiers such as "nice," "brother," "friends," "woods," "little brooks," "bridges," and "all sorts of fun things." Turn 228 pivots the turn from Movement XI to Movement XII in which B becomes positioned in signifiers of "home/background."

Correction 2.

267 **B:** Yeah, yeah, in fact they were having a real problem because there was only one ferrier, otherwise known as blacksmith, =

268 **K:** = Yes.

269 **B:** uh::,

[

270 **K:**   Oh! - Ferriers are horse doctors.

271 **B:** Um::. Well, out there they're - they're mostly - concerned with the feet. The vet takes care of the horse from the ankles up.

272 **K:** Um::.

[

273 **B:**   But anything that is wrong with your horse's hooves, or, if it just needs to be shod, (   ) the blacksmith.

[

274 **K:**   ((cough . . .; cough))
I suppose they're a little more specialized, an - I just happened to pick up some books at the library every now and then on - ferriers =

[   ]

275 **B:**   ((laugh))

276 **K:** = an' - ((soft, "yawning" quality)) I was wondering what they were, so I finally - checked it out.

277 **B :**   They're the people who get paid outrageous amounts of
money to get kicked.

Turn 267 equates "ferrier" and "blacksmith"; 270 equates "ferrier" and "horse doctor"; 271-273 substitute "vet" for "horse doctor" in the process of differentiating "blacksmith" from "vet." The signifiers involved in the production of this correction of its error are, "ferrier," "blacksmith," "horse doctors," and "vet".

A rational reconstruction of this text discloses several alternative possibilities: (1) B might have accepted K's equation of the signifiers "ferrier" and "horse doctor" and in *not* correcting the proposed equation, *not* punctuate the chain reflexively; (2) B might have explicitly informed K that (a) the proper term for "horse doctor" is "veterinarian," (b) the proper form of "veterinarian" is "vet" and not "horse doctor," (c) K's proposed equation is a violation of truth inasmuch as a "blacksmith" is not a "vet"; (3) B might have laughed at K's naivete; or (4) B might have spoken some correcting practice less extreme than these three alternatives but more direct than the one actually in evidence. As it stands, however, an equation of difference is identified as incorrect by means of the correcting practices productive of the very incorrection they address.

A critical feature of this 11-turn segment is a possibility for correcting which passes uncorrected. Turn 274 acknowledges the "blacksmith/vet" difference. That same turn also reports an action:

I just happened to pick up some books at the library every now and then on ferriers. I was wondering what they were so I finally checked it out.

The truthfulness of that utterance is questionable. Assume that the prior correction is a truthful one; that is, that "ferriers" are different from "horse doctors." Further, assume that K did want to find out what "ferriers" were, and so checked out some relevant material. Clearly, then, K's checking produced an error that B corrects. More important, the reason(s) is/are not apparent for going to a library and checking out books from an apparent acontextual category: that is, "horses". What are the rational bases for the action? What motivates the interest in and curiosity about ferriers? The questions are relevant given that curiosity motivated action that produced error. K is formulated as signifying the signifier "ferrier," but with no other signifiers there is no movement, no sliding chain of signifiers; the significance reads as arbitrary and unmotivated. The questionable truthfulness/

appropriateness of turn 274's production is the apparent unfounded-ness (i.e., acontextuality) of the activity it formulates.

Notice, however, that turn 277 does not thematize the unfounded-ness of its prior utterance; instead, it elaborates humorously on the functionality of "blacksmith/ferrier." To thematize the truthfulness/appropriateness of turn 274 calls to question subjective validity; to do so, according to some conventional standards of appropriateness, risks a disruption of indexical interaction. "Why were you interested in ferriers if you don't ride horses or know much about them?" "What motivated your curiosity about ferriers?" Without answers, either implicit or explicit ones, turn 274 reads like bluff or pretense. In any case, its validity bases — its truthfulness and appropriateness — are not apparent and thereby are open to legitimate question and possible correction. Instead of correcting, however, turn 277 produces a cor-dial utterance complete with one-party laughter.

Recall Andre lamenting people's concern with their own perfor-mances, which blind them to what is, in fact, taking place. It may be that questionable validity claims go unchallenged because it is not worth the disruption of appropriateness to question the truthfulness of utterances such as turn 274's. What is the worth of commitment both to truthfulness and appropriateness? To what extent is unreflex-ive discourse easy to produce and, because of the ease of its produc-tion, thereby worth very little?

Correction 3.

277 **B:** They're the people who get paid outrageous amounts of money to get kicked.

278 **K:** Oo. ((laugh)) (pause) I suppose when you take lessons that's also when you - just sort of learn to - to y'just take it in stride, getting kicked and bit an' - I mean you don't like it, but - (you know it's)

279 **B:** When you ah - when you put a shoe on a horse, this is going to show up great on tape, - the horse's leg is here. The horse is facing that way, you face this way.

280 **K:** Um hmm/

281 **B:** You put your feet like this, and you pick his foot up between your legs.

282 **K:** Um hmm/

283 **B:** And then you put your legs together to hold it. Now if he kicks he's likely to kick up. And most ferriers being male, I don't ((laughing)) think it's the sort of thing you ever get used to or learn how to deal with.

        [   ]   [

284 **K:**   ((laugh))   That's-that's not what I was
talking about. But I mean just as a kid taking ho- lessons.
                                    [   ]
285 **B:**   ((cough))
286 **B:** Oh that kind of ((laughing)) lessons.
             [
287 **K:**   Y'know, learning - learning to groom horses an-
and things like that, w'you just get stepped on, and - an'get
kicked every now and then, by som- your horse or somebody
else's/

Turn 277 produces several validity concerns: (1) K's proposed
genus/species relation could be formulated as untrue in explicit terms
inasmuch as a "blacksmith" has no medical training and, in fact, is *not*
a "more specialized vet"; (2) K's proposed genus/species relation
could be allowed to pass with no further comment thereby implicitly
accepting it as true in its immediate discursive context; (3) the truthfulness of K's account of her knowledge of this bundle of signifiers
could be called ino question, giving the speech the sound and shape of
interrogation instead of polite conversation. Instead, turn 277 evidences a humorously formulated definition of the identity equation
"ferrier - blacksmith" — "They're the people who get paid outrageous amounts of money to get kicked."

Turn 278 is a critical transition is this conversing. Given that one
discursive consequence of humor, and more precisely of laughter, is to
punctuate topical completions, 278 is an opportunity for a topic
change. A relationship between "getting kicked and bit" and learning
to "just take it in stride," elaborates in a serious tenor the definition
produced in a humorous tenor in 277. Turn 278 changes the tenor of
the conversation; possibilities range from accepting the invitation to
join in the laughing and humorous characterizing to the other extreme
of commenting on the inappropriateness of the humorous tenor.
Neither extreme materializes; the moderate course is conversed.

Consider turns 279-283; they produce a graphic description of how
a blacksmith shoes a horse; it works as a reason for disagreeing with a
proposed relation concerning the normalcy of "getting kicked and
bit." As is now evidenced in turn 284, turns 279, 281, and 283 themselves evidence a misunderstanding and can thereby be corrected in
the pragmatically valid interests of truthfulness. Given the array of
practices available for the production of turn 279, the graphic description of horse shoeing is an adept choice. Because of its vividness it is a
clear lecture but its tenor does not patronize; instead, it humorously
implicates the reason(s) why turn 278's supposition cannot be true.

Turn 284 formulates turns 279 and 283 as predicated on the now evidently incorrect assumption that the "you" of 278 referred to the class of "blacksmith" defined in terms of "getting kicked and bit" in 277. Turn 284 corrects the incorrect assumption by reflexively reformulating 278 as having been a modulation from "blacksmith" to "you." It is unclear even now, however, whether the "you" of 278 is a first-person reference to B or a third-person reference to riders in general. Nevertheless, 284 is a rather direct correction and the basis for the correction is acknowledged in 286. However, 284 also constitutes the material evidence K formulates in not letting pass unthematized B's correction of K's prior supposition concerning the normalcy of "getting kicked and bit."

The intrigue of 267 through 287 is its two indexically reflexive structures: 267 through 277 is one such structure; 277 through 287 is the other. By *indexically reflexive structuring* I mean speech the reflexive objects of which are indexical particulars of prior utterances. Thus, 271 reflexively addresses the indexical assumptions of 270; 273 is a continuation of that reflexive address; 274 is structured similarly with respect to 271 and 273. There is an interleaving of reflexivity inasmuch as correcting appears to perpetuate correcting, for at least brief sequences of utterances. Turn 278 elaborates rather than corrects, but with 278 a sequence of corrections begins again. Such indexically reflexive structures reformulate prior speech rather than open it to the subsequent possibilities immanent in present speech.

To more fully appreciate B and K's positioning in mundane conversation, consider a method of correcting much more direct and at the same time much more opaque. David Mamet (1981), in his play, *Lakeboat*, has the Fireman, Joe, and Stan, shooting the breeze in the engine room:*

416	**Fireman:**	So, the way I hear it: she told him she was divorced. How about that.
418	**Joe:**	So what?
419	**Fireman:**	I'm divorced.
420	**Joe:**	Sorry
421	**Fireman:**	So they started to get really blind.
422	**Joe:**	My mother is blind.
423		*Pause*
424	**Fireman:**	And could he spare her some change, twenty for the kids, a saw for some groceries, you know.
425	**Joe:**	Yeah
426	**Fireman:**	And all of the time she's drinking this rum with coke and lime.

427	**Joe:**	Coke *and* lime?
428	**Fireman:**	That's what I heard.
429	**Joe:**	That's how they drink it in Italy.
430	**Fireman:**	You never been to Italy.
431	**Joe:**	Now how the FUCK do you know?
432	**Fireman:**	I . . .
433	**Joe:**	How the everlasting cocksucking FUCK do you know I never been to Italy?
434	**Fireman:**	Jesus
435	**Joe:**	Don't do shit all day and tells me where I never been
436		*Exit*

Here line 430 thematizes the correctness of line 429's proposition by means of assuming that its speaker, never having been to Italy, would not have access to the knowledge to validly ground such a proposition in truth. Consequently, line 430, in asserting that Joe has never been to Italy, is accusing Joe of not speaking the truth — of not knowing what he is talking about. In line 431, Joe rather forcefully corrects the Fireman's assumption; however, instead of (1) providing evidence of having been to Italy and thereby being in a position to know, or (2) of demonstrating that one could have such knowledge from sources other than pragmatic cultural experience, Joe continues to thematize the Fireman's entering assumption by deprecating its rational basis.

Conversation, as a sliding chain of signifiers and punctuated by subjectivity, produces what Jakobson (1962) might call langue-generated-parole — speech, the rationality of which is grounded in and motivated by language. On the other hand, speech more concerned with appropriateness is less likely to articulate material evidence of inappropriateness; instead, one might expect to find evidence of discursive practices for diverting speech away from those prior markers of potential mistakes. Jakobson might characterize such speech as parole-generated-parole, an argument David Lodge (1980) makes in characterizing the Marin County speech Cyra McFadden satirizes in her novel, *The Serial*. The relation of speech to language is superficially thematized, if at all, inasmuch as speech is perpetually drifting signifiers.

It is the region between identifying nonrationality but leaving it uncorrected and being incapable of recognizing nonrationality at all which is the domain of critical theory. In the B-K conversation text, coherence is formulated in part as humorously polite corrections. The seam dividing collective hysteria and collective rationality is a critical index of societal coherence and rationality.

APPENDIX: THE B-K CONVERSATION

BACKGROUND

The B-K conversation was recorded at the University of Wisconsin-Madison just after Thanksgiving 1979. Students in a course on small group communication were offered extra credit for participating in any of several research projects. B and K, two undergraduate women, volunteered together for a project on everyday conversation that would involve tape recording a half-hour conversation.

B, 27 years old, and K, 21, could be characterized as acquaintances. They had worked together all semester as members of a four-person project group in connection with the course. One can safely assume that they had previously talked about class work and had probably exchanged some personal information.

The conversation took place at noon in a small, quiet, unadorned room containing a desk and two chairs, with an audio tape recorder located on the desk. B and K were told that the researcher was interested in studying everyday conversation. They were asked to converse for a half-hour as they typically would, talking about anything they wished.

The B-K conversation may or may not be typical of conversations in general, but it is a discourse rich in many of the conversational phenomena discussed in this book. A transcript of the conversation was prepared and distributed to the chapter authors, who were asked to study it and comment from their varying perspectives. This procedure seems to offer several advantages: Each author is able to apply his or her approach to at least one complete, extended conversation that is available to the book's readers. Readers may then assess for themselves the validity of each analysis and the extent to which it sheds light on the discourse. Similarities and differences among analytical concepts and methods stand out in relief against the background of a common example. And the reader may sharpen his or her own skills of discourse analysis by applying them to the same example.

Before turning to the B-K transcript itself, we should mention certain issues related to transcription in general, and explain the notation system used in this particular transcript.

TRANSCRIPTION AS SELECTION AND ENCODING

Transcription is essentially a technique for representing discourse in order to facilitate its study by researchers and the communication of their findings to others. Discourse analysis involves the study of relationships among events that occur in conversations, often very subtle or minute events separated by intervals of time. Speech communication leaves no permanent record of itself except in fallible human memory. Audio and video recordings are useful means of capturing this evanescent phenomenon for analysis. Even so, analysts usually produce written transcripts of conversations that they wish to study intensively.

The written transcript is a useful supplement to direct observation and mechanial recording because it freezes events and displays the temporal process of communiction as a spatial arrangement on the page, where it can be examined at leisure. The very act of transcribing helps — indeed, forces — the analyst to attend closely to the details of discourse. Subtle events that may be difficult to perceive in real time, and relationships between events occurring at different times or in different conversations, become easier to study. The written transcript is also useful because it represents the discourse in an abstracted, symbolic form that is most compatible with the linguistic form of the analysis — for discourse analysis is itself a form of linguistic discourse, the products of which are often published as printed books and articles. But the written transcript is more than just a convenient way to publish conversational data. More profoundly, the transcript is a kind of half-way house between the phenomenon of communication and the theoretical concepts of discourse analysis.

A good transcript represents as closely as possible the conversation that actually took place. But an attempt to achieve *perfect* accuracy would ultimately lead to a paradoxical result. A perfect transcript, being a perfect representation of the discourse, would be just as unwieldy as the discourse itself — essentially useless for the purposes of a transcript. As the transcript became more complete, it would tend to lose the very qualities of accessibility and communicability that make transcription advantageous.

Transcription, then, if it is to serve its purposes, is best viewed as a technique involving *selection* and *encoding* of aspects of the communication process. The transcriber must select, from the rich phenomenon of communication, those aspects that will be recorded in the transcript. The barest transcript might include only some approximation of the words that were spoken. A more detailed transcript would be more precise and might include some indications of simultaneous or overlapping speech, some nonlinguistic vocalizations such as laughter, some details of disfluencies and nonstandard speech, some indications of timing, intonation, loudness, and voice quality, and, if the transcription is done from direct observation or a video recording, some gestural or other nonverbal behaviors or environmental events.

Just because the communication process is so rich in potentially meaningful phenomena that *might* be recorded, the selection of aspects for transcription must be done with great care. Any serious attempt to include *everything* would render the transcript unreadable and essentially useless for its purposes. On the other hand, because almost anything that occurs in a communicative situation is potentially meaningful, anything that one chooses to exclude from a transcript (or that one excludes inadvertently because of faulty memory, lapses of attention, lack of access, poor recording quality, or some other source of noise) might turn out to be important for interpretation of the discourse from some point of view. Analysts approaching the discourse with different theoretical or practical questions will find different aspects important. For this reason no transcript can be regarded as complete or final. Every transcript is a selective rendering of the discourse, with some finite degree of precision and accuracy, that serves some analytical purposes better than others. For many purposes the bare words that were spoken may be quite sufficient; for some other purposes one might even require a voice spectrograph to capture the precise sound of a word as spoken on a particular occasion (for example, see Labov & Fanshel, 1977).

Understandably, analysts often prefer to work from direct observations or mechanical recordings and do their own transcribing as needed. When, as in the case of the B-K conversation that is analyzed throughout this book, a general-purpose transcript must be used, analysts may find that aspects of the discourse in which they are particularly interested are not very accurately represented (Beach, Chapter 10, discusses this problem).

Transcription involves not only selection but *encoding* in that discourse must be represented by means of some system of graphic symbols, a code. This is an obvious point, but one that has important consequences. Because our ordinary system of writing is designed to represent correct language and lacks symbols for many phemonena (disfluencies, overlaps, loudness, intonation, vocal quality, etc.) that may prove important in discourse analysis, special symbols must be used. And because no fully standard system of transcription symbols for discourse analysis presently exists (and may not exist for a long time, because of the selectivity problem discussed earlier) analysts often find themselves inventing new symbols. The invention of transcription symbols is a *theoretical* problem; it requires that decisions be made about the elements of discourse that are worthy of attention, and the degree of precision with which those elements should be represented. It is also a *practical* problem because of the dilemma discussed earlier: Any invented symbol that makes the transcript more accurate is also very likely to make it less readable, thus restricting the potential audience for the analysis.

The transcription symbols used for the B-K conversation are explained in the next section. Chapters of the book use various slightly different transcript notations. Authors were asked to define any important symbols other than those used in the B-K transcript.

EXPLANATION OF SYMBOLS USED IN THE B-K TRANSCRIPT

The transcription system used here is largely based upon one described by Schenkein (1978, pp. xi-xvi). The system emphasizes certain aspects of turn-taking, vocal timing and emphasis, and intonation.

Even though the notion of a "turn at talk" is somewhat problematic theoretically, the numbered segments of the B-K transcript are referred to throughout the book as turns. Overlapping speech is indicated by square brackets placed between turns at the points where the overlap begins ([) and ends (]). Cases in which the two speakers began talking simultaneously are indicated by double left brackets ([[). The equal sign (=) placed at the end of one turn and the beginning of a subsequent turn indicates that the transcriber heard them as a continuous stream of speech with no overlap and no temporal break or pause between. This sometimes involves a change of speakers (e.g. 040-041, 089-090, 092-093); in other cases it means only that the transcriber broke a single utterance into more than one turn in order to make room on the transcript for overlapping utterances of the other speaker (e.g. 114-116, 155-157, 157-159).

The notation ((pause)) between turns indicates that the transcriber heard a noticeable (longer than normal) period of silence. Brief pauses *within* turns are noted with a hyphen; longer ones (more than about one second) are indicated by (pause), single parentheses. A hyphen attached to the end of a word (e.g. 024, 031) means that the brief pause began with an abrupt halt or clipping off of that word. Pauses were not timed precisely in this transcript, but no pause of more than a few seconds occurred.

The colon (:) is used to indicate prolongation of the preceding syllable, the number of colons corresponding roughly to the length of prolongation (e.g. Wha:t, 010; hhhoh::, 021; Hmm:::, 023). Italicized words were spoken with strong vocal emphasis (e.g. *bonus*, 011; *Yes*, 023). Noticeable exhalations are indicated by two or more contiguous aitches (hh), the number corresponding roughly to the length of exhalation; for an inhalation, the aitches are preceded by a period (e.g. hhh .hh, 145). The apostrophe — unless, of course, it denotes the possessive case — indicates a contraction, whether standard (e.g. don't, 005), or not (e.g. it'n, 017).

Intonation patterns are among the less well-understood aspects of English; yet they clearly are meaningful (Coulthard, 1977, pp. 117-137). Terminal punctuation marks — the period (.), question mark (?), slash (/), and exclamation point (!) — are used in this transcript to indicate *intonation* patterns rather than grammatical sentences. The period denotes a full stop falling intonation. The question mark indicates standard question intonation (relatively high pitch throughout the utterance, rising still higher at the end). The slash also indicates terminal rising (or sometimes falling-rising) intonation, but the utterance in general is of lower pitch than a standard question. Utterances following this (/) class of intonation patterns (e.g. 001, 008, 014, 038, etc.) often seem to convey a sense of presumed redundancy or already-shared understanding, as if to imply, "I hardly need say this, but . . ." The exclamation point denotes animated delivery, typically high pitch falling slightly at the end. The comma (,) represents a nonterminal continuation intonation, often a brief rising-falling-rising pattern followed by a slight pause.

Transcriber comments or brief descriptive notes are enclosed in double parentheses. The phenomenon most frequently noted in this fashion is laughter. The note ((laughing)) embedded in an utterance (e.g. 017, 041) indicates that the remainder of the utterance (until the next terminal punctuation mark or the end of the turn) was laughed or intermixed with laughter.

Utterances or parts of utterances are enclosed in single parentheses (e.g. 007, 018) to indicate uncertainty about the accuracy of the transcription. Empty parentheses (e.g. 029) indicate that the transcriber heard something that could not be interpreted.

Finally, a caveat: The transcript, despite many editings, undoubtedly contains a few outright errors and still more segments that different transcribers would hear differently. Every time one listens to a tape such as this, one tends to hear something new. Labov and Fanshel (1977) report that they continued to edit their transcript over a period of many years. In this sense too, no transcript is final.

TRANSCRIPT OF THE B-K CONVERSATION

((Tape begins with closing words of instructions, departure of the experimenter, and various sounds and sotto voce comments as the conversants ready themselves.))

001	**B:**	It's alright/
002	**K:**	So how are you doing?
		((pause, rustling sound))
003	**B:**	((laugh)) As well as can be expected this time of the semester. How about you.
004	**K:**	((animated)) Umm good.
005	**B:**	Are you sure that you don't want half? This is huge.
006	**K:**	No. Thanks. (I've finally) got my apple.
007	**B:**	(Umm, alright.)
		((pause))
008	**K:**	I didn't think I'd have time for lunch at all, so this is - a real treat/
009	**B:**	Umm (pause) a bonus. ((extended laugh))
		[ ]
010	**K:**	Wha:t?
011	**B:**	A *bonus*.
		((pause))
012	**K:**	Oh. What kind of sandwich is that.
013	**B:**	Turkey.
014	**K:**	Very Thanksgiving of you/
015	**B:**	Appropriate.
016	**K:**	((barely audible)) Yes.
		((pause))
017	**B:**	K_____ (pause) what are you giving ((laughing)) people for Christmas this year? ((both laughing)) I've started thinking about it'n - my - ability to be inventive - without spending much ((laughing)) money is - very very small.
		[ ]

018 **K:**   (oh)
019 **K:** Like family? Friends?
020 **B:** Family mostly.
021 **K:** Family hhhoh:: (pause) What do you buy men in your family
       for Christmas.
022 **B:** My father is the main problem.=
023 **K:** =*Yes*. I have that same problem. I finally resorted to saying
       ((louder, mock exasperation) " Dad? What do you *want*. "
       ((high pitch, comical)) "I don't need anything. "
024 **B:** That's exact - I think we've got the same father. ((laugh))
                                            [
025 **K:**   I think
       everybody's father must be like that at some point
026 **B:** Hmm:::
               [
027 **K:**   y'na - he doesn't so you end up buying him - something
       that - he really doesn't need - or want.
028 **K:** Um hmm?
029 **K:** But (pause) (   )
               [
030 **B:**   I mentioned that problem to my father on his
       birthday. He said "I don't want anything, I don't need
       anything save your money," so I did and I just sent him a card
       and he was tremendously hurt and upset. ((laugh))
                                                    [
031 **K:**   Um hmm?
       (pause) I don't think my dad would be hurt. Cuz he really
       doesn't he- enjoys - Christmas and birthdays - just - as a
       family activity.
032 **B:** Um Hmm
033 **K:** And he'd ra- much rather give. (pause) But (pause) it's just
       not the same.
       ((pause))
034 **B:** Are you going home for Christmas?
035 **K:** Oh yeah. (pause) .hhh - Is there any other choice?=
                           [   ]
036 **B:**   (You'll be up in Illinois?)
037 **K:** =((laugh)) - um hmm?
038 **B:** Sure there's another choice/ Some folks don't go - home for
       Christmas/
039 **K:** Oh where's your mom living.
       ((pause))
040 **B:** ((laugh))=
041 **K:** = You weren't supposed to take a bite right ((laughing)) then.
       ((pause))
042 **B:** My mother lives in Minneapolis.
043 **K:** Hmm::!

044 **B:** Which is easy and I visit her on vacations a lot.
045 **K:** Um hmm? And your dad lives in Philadelphia but he's now in Florida?
046 **B:** Um hmm/ Well he'll be in Florida by the time I get there.
047 **K:** What's he going t- does- Is this part of his business?
048 **B:** No, uhm, he works - he's a lawyer but he works part time - as an assistant district attorney. And for that job he gets - I think it's three weeks or a month or something of vacation every year.
049 **K:** Hmm::!
        [
050 **B:**   He hates winter.
051 **K:** Ah:::. So you leave!
052 **B:** He does. This is the first time I'll have been to Florida.
053 **K:** Hmm::! I meant to ask you the other day, are you flying down?
054 **B:** Um hmm, and I hate planes.
055 **K:** I:: know you said that.
        ((pause))
056 **B:** Yup/
057 **K:** Are you going to be gone long?
058 **B:** It seems like long. It's gonna be two weeks.
059 **K:** Hmm::!
        [
060 **B:**   My father and I haven't spent two weeks together in quite some time. ((snicker))
061 **K:** A real challenge? (pause) Or will it be fun.
                    [
062 **B:**   He's a challenging person.
        ((laugh)) He um - he's a lawyer so he only listens to as much as he needs to of what you're saying to make an argument against it. And if there is no argument going at the time he provokes one.
063 **K:** Ah:::!
064 **B:** Every once in a while you have to just sit down and tell him to back off. ((snicker)) .hhh That's done if you're willing t'either burst into tears or duck. ((laugh))
065 **K:** Oh::heheh
066 **B:** He uh - he doesn't like being told things like that. After - ten or fifteen minutes he cools down and listens but - the first few minutes are difficult. ((laugh)) (pause) How bout you you - you have brothers and sisters, don't you?
067 **K:** Brothers, two brothers, y'nger.
068 **B:** Ah. So they're still at home?
069 **K:** Well, no, one is in college. He's - he'll be home though too - and the other one's - little - yet.

070 **B:** ((slight laugh))
071 **K:** In my estimation I bought him a - tee shirt. Ahm, every year -
it seemed like my other brother goes to a small college - and,
we always bring him home a shirt from our school? Each of
us? So he's got - a collection of Wisconsin shirts that he's
outgrown cuz he's - thirteen so he's in the growing stage, and
he's got a collection of Northwestern shirts that he's
outgrown over the years.
072 **B:** (I know)
073 **K:** So I got him one the other day an'ma I- showed my mom it,
an' she said ((raised pitch, animated)) well what *size* did you
get'em. An' I j's I picked it up and looked at it sa- Oh! A
medium. I got him one to fit me. She *wha::t?* Well by summer
he'll be wearing the same size I am. He wears the same size
shoes.
074 **B:** And then when he outgrows it you'll have it.
075 **K:** Uh huh/
076 **B:** Um Hmm/
077 **K:** I'm getting to that stage where if I go home - and - needs a-a
sweater to wear:: or: - a grubby shirt to wear I w'jus' go
rummaging through his closet and see what's: a little big for
him an' - dig it out.
078 **B:** ((slight laugh))
079 **K:** ((cough)) You don't have any brothers d- and sisters do you?
080 **B:** No I have uh two step brothers and a step sister. But (pause)
my father divorced their mother, so we don't see each other
too much.=
081 **K:** = Umm:::.
082 **B:** And we didn't before cuz they went to school in Switzerland
so we only saw each other on vacations. Must be tough, huh?
083 **K:** Um hmm/ (pause) Spe-
        [
084 **B:**   *I* never got to go to school in
Switzerland. ((laugh))
        [
085 **K:**   Speaking of Switzerland a good friend of mine is going
there for Christmas. He's an AFS student,
086 **B:** Oh:::
        [
087 **K:**   and he's been home for a year and a half and he's going
back, and he's just on cloud nine.
088 **B:** Where in Switzerland.
089 **K:** Mountains. They're going skiing.=
090 **B:** =((laugh))
091 **K:** He's been packed for I don't know how long/
092 **B:** Hmm=

093 **K:** = He really - he worked hard though he worked like sixty
hours a week all summer - so he could afford - to go to school
and go to Switzerland - and he's still working while he's in
school.

094 **B:** N'yuk.

095 **K:** You have to really want to go ((laughing)) badly. =

096 **B:** = Um hmm/ (pause) Yeah my youngest step brother, B_____
- uh:: - did a lot of skiing when they were in Switzerland, and,
in fact, - they used to go to France for skiing, on vacations -

                                                                 [   ]

097 **K:**   Um hmm/

098 **B:** rather than staying in Switzerland but he::uh - he was -
actually, - asked to be on both the French and the American
Olympic teams

099 **K:** Wo::w! =

100 **B:** = in skiing and decided on the American teams - broke his
knee in training and couldn't do it.

                                       [

101 **K:**   ((snicker)) (pause) Um:::. =

102 **B:** = The only thing that saved poor little B_____ from growing
up to be a ski bum.

103 **K:** ((laugh)) Which I'm sure his family was ((laughing)) glad of/

104 **B:** Um hmm/ Um hmm/

105 **K:** Do you ski?

106 **B:** No. I skied once, I tried to ski, - I went part way down the
slope and sort of - tipped over. ((laugh))

                                     [

107 **K:**   ((laugh)) - That
was it. ((coughs))

        [

108 **B:**   Everybody, ev::erybody in the whole (skis-) class had to-
first learn to fall down and than stand up again?

109 **K:** Um hmm/

110 **B:** Everyone else including a nun wearing complete habit down
to the ground

111 **K:** Oh my go::d/

             [

112 **B:**   was standing up. I was rolling around
((laughing)) in the snow, with my feet tangled/ After twenty
minutes of this the instructor finally gave up, and picked me
up, but I never did learn to get up once I'd fallen down. I
never learned to stop so I'd ski down the hill, I can do that, -
and I'd get to the bottom it would be time to stop or I'd come
up to an obstacle that I couldn't get around, and the only
thing to do would be to fall over. =

113 **K:** = Um hmm/

114 **B:** And then I'd have to wait there for ((laughing)) somebody to
come and pick me out of the snow:: .hhh and I hated it, I got =

                                      [   ] [   ]

115 **K:**   .hhh   Oh no.

116 **B:** =very cold and unhappy ((laughing)) and quit.

117 **K:** .hhh Tha:t would be about my reaction too. Do you ever

                                                         [

118 **B:**   Do you ski?

119 **K:** Cross country.

120 **B:** Um::.

121 **K:** But I don't- I'on't think I could handle down hill. (pause) I've
- decided ((laughing)) I'm very uncoordinated and uh, (pause)
jus- doesn't seem like fun. I'm not a speed enthusiast. The
daring - adventure type things don't - get to me - at all.

122 **B:** I don't mind speed on- on the flat but I'm - terrified of heights.
Which makes me a ((laughing)) bad candidate for skiing.

                                    [   ]

123 **K:**   (I love)

124 **K:** I love the heights.

125 **B:** Umm.

              [

126 **K:**   (Tha's)

127 **B:** Umm.

((pause))

128 **K:** .hhh - .hhh I'm gonna learn how to balloon or something like
that so I can - see the world.

              [

129 **B:**   That's always seemed like fun to me. I keep
seeing ads in the paper for hot air ballooning now?=

130 **K:** =You know there's a class?

131 **B:** Nnn!

              [

132 **K:**   In - Madison? (pause) Uhm, there's a ground school
class? ((rustling of paper in the background through
beginning of 133)) And then (pause) they- also (pause) the air
part of it but it gets really expensive. I was reading up on it
one day.

133 **B:** I think it's in here there was a- an a:d. Maybe it's not in here.
There've been a number of ads in these: uh:: Cardinals and
Badger Heralds and things lately - about - learning - about hot
hair- hot air ballooning from some sort of a club. Y'know
having a meeting. And I've been - tempted

                                    [

134 **K:**   Do they meet like over
at the - IMC: or:

135 **B:** I don't know.

              [

136 **K:**   s:omething? Or in the extension office I think. I- I
might've even read it in there - too but then I read some other
stuff on it.
((pause, rustling resumes))

137 **K:** I w'd yes, that's tempting.
                    [
138 **B:**   I don't (really) know but it looks like great fun.

139 **K:** hhh

140 **B:** Anything.
                 [
141 **K:**   So colorful?

142 **B:** Um hmm/ (pause) Bright and pretty and this time of year
wouldn't you love to just sort of drift ((laughing)) away?

143 **K:** I don't know about this time of year I think it would be
awfully cold - up there - cuz you're not doing anything.

144 **B:** Hmm. I was thinking of - an excuse to get away from exams
and ((snickering)) papers and stuff.
                         [
145 **K:**   Oh well *tha:t* would be ni:ce/ hhh .hh
I al'ys thought- California's supposed to have- when I- first
started getting interested in it - they had - they were one of the
few places that had - pla- where you could go, and, someone
would either take you up or learn- teach you how to do it and
you could go. So that's what I want to do on my honeymoon.
Go to California and- and balloon. ((laugh))
                                  [
146 **B:**   ((laugh)) (pause)
Hmm::.

147 **K:** But it would have to be someplace pretty.
((pause))

148 **B:** California would be interesting.

149 **K:** (I don't know)/
                    [
150 **B:**   If you missed you'd either hit the mountains or
the ((laughing)) ocean ((laugh))
((pause))

151 **K:** Hmm::.

152 **B:** Have you picked out the long-suffering man who is going to
put up with that kind of a honeymoon yehhht?

153 **K:** Oh:. This is just a dream I mean
(someone can plan this type things)
              [
154 **B:**   You've just designed this honeymoon ((laughing)) without
having anyone in mind ((laughter . . . .))
              [ ]   [

155 **K:**   tt   .hhh I don't even want to get married, you know
              hhh (pause) .hhh I just thought that would alwa- that just
              always appealed to me. Oh, I'd - cuz I read it something- in
              something that was - in a McCalls or something one time that
              was - y'know=
                        [   ]
156 **B:**   Hm.
157 **K:**   =these are really neat things to do for honeymoons'n - or
              just=
                                                      [   ]
158 **B:**   hhfff
159 **K:**   =for weekends that you want to go and - have a good time.
160 **B:**   Maybe you could get your parents to give it to you for a
              graduation present.
161 **K:**   No:,
162 **B:**   One balloon lesson?
                        [   ]
163 **K:**   that's not - too practical.
164 **B:**   No::/
              ((pause))
165 **K:**   Nah, it's not worth it. I'm in to ((laughing)) practical - a lot of
              times/
166 **B:**   Umm. (pause) Have you heard anything about your
              internship. Speaking of practical.=
167 **K:**   =Um:::. No I forgot to call about that.
168 **B:**   Um hmm/ ((tone of mock reprimand)) And that was very bad
              you'll have to call about that today.
              ((pause))
169 **K:**   Yes mom ((laugh))
                    [
170 **B:**   Important to know about these things ((laugh))
                                                            [
171 **K:**   .hhh It
              would be nice to know before Christmas when I'm supposed
              to be there.=
172 **B:**   =Or before it *starts,* er ((laugh))=
173 **K:**   =Well, I might have to do it during part of exam week. Which
              would make it (pause) (well) the first part.
                              [   ]
174 **B:**   How could they do that.
175 **K:**   I don't have exams until Thursday. So I could easily go
              Monday Tuesday and Wednesday, put in an eight hour day/
              It's less than what I'm putting in now.
176 **B:**   They can do that, they can ask you to show up during exam
              week?
177 **K:**   No, I, schedule it when I want it - basically.
                              [   ]

178 **B:**   *Um::.*   Um:.

179 **K:** But I hafta kinda go along with what they want too. Like- I'd
really like to do it over the week of New ((laughing)) Years
but

180 **B:** That's always a boring week.

181 **K:** Well it'd be - in some ways it'd be good because I could be
shown around - the office and the ins and outs and there
wouldn't be a lot of interruptions. As far as, you know, think I
could - *learn* - things. Sit ( ) and talk to somebody for an hour
or two. But, its also there's nothing going on.

182 **B:** What office would this be?

183 **K:** Uh it would be in the extension office in Rock County.

184 **B:** Where's Rock County.

185 **K:** Southern Wisconsin, it's about - an hour south of here?
Janesville, Beloit, -
          [   ]

186 **B:**   Hmm.   Hmm.

187 **K:** area?

188 **B:** Um hmm/

189 **K:** Yeah, and that's where I grew up. So it'd be neat. Because I'd
be home, over New Years, where- when- the kids I went to
high school would still be home/

190 **B:** Hmm:. I thought you grew up i- in Illinois somewhere.

191 **K:** Un un, my family moved there after I started college.

192 **B:** Mm::.
((pause))

193 **K:** So, going to Illinois is no big thrill. (pause) In itself.

194 **B:** Well I had always thought that but I didn't think that - it
would be politic to tell you ((laughing)) if that was where you
were from.

195 **K:** Well, actually like where my parents live in Western Illinois,
it's - four large cities/ Bump bump bump/

196 **B:** What cities.

197 **K:** The quad c- uh, Moline, Davenport Iowa, - Bettendorf
y'kno-=
                    [   ]

198 **B:**   Hmm.

199 **K:** =they're really - it's really *f:un* to to there when you're=
          [   ]

200 **B:**   Yeah.

201 **K:** =from a town of thirty-five thousand to go to a- an
accumulation of - I don't know how many people.

202 **B:** N'yeah, East Moline is the one that stands out in my mind
that's really a thrill.
((pause))

203 **K:** Why.
          [

204   **B:**   One of the uglier places ((laughing)) on - on earth I th'nk.
            I- I went through there once after it had flooded.
205   **K:**   Umm.=
206   **B:**   = And, there was mud, and water up to here, and just oh:: a
            ((laughing)) filthier place I've never seen.=
207   **K:**   =When I was home, two years ago, they flooded really bad.
            A-at Christmas time. No at spring break. And, one of the
            roads we=
                        [   ]
208   **B:**   ((laugh . . . . . .))
209   **K:**   =had to go - through to get back up to Wisconsin, was: oh:
            maybe twenty feet above the riv- above the river in Iowa. It
            wasn't the main river, but a small river. And it was flooded
            over with at least a foot of water. And this was after it had
            gone down a lot. There's just so- but there's so much to *do* in
            those towns. Theaters, little theaters that are affordable for
            college students. Uh'there's - like four or five colleges in the
            area, so there's young people/ Uhm, like Augustana is a
            liberal arts college. More or less. And, they've got a lot of
            little theater productions and musicals, and concerts, - and
            things like that that are - you know, free or very nominal cost.
            ((pause))
210   **B:**   Can you get around easily there?
211   **K:**   I can, I have a car. But, no. Their -
                        [
212   **B:**   You take your car down then when
            you go.
                [
213   **K:**   mass transit system is not good for as big as the
            communities are. But it's very - I don't get lost down there, at
            all, because all the streets, it's- so neat! All the streets are
            numbered, - streets go this way, in, you know li- increasing
            number and avenues go this way in increasing number.
            There's no names of streets. Y'know like how do you find
            Washington Avenue, or West Main, y'know. There *aren't*
            any. They're all numbers. And they're all, in order, and it
            goes from - in Illinois it goes like Moline an' Rock Island are
            both - they're just - right next to each other, and you start over
            again when you get in to Moline, with one, after you go from
            forty-seven or sixty-two, and it starts over at one, but -
            they're still, like the ones that - run parallel, though the
            towns, are - seventeen and seventeen, twenty-three and
            twenty-three an'it's - just - you can't get lost. Until you go
            into Davenport. And ((laughing)) then you can get lost.
                [

214 **B:**   ((laugh . . .)) (pause) I wasn't - driving when we
went, so I - didn't think about getting lost, you know,
somebody else dealt with ((laughing)) those things.
              [   ]   [
215 **K:** Yeah.   ((laugh . .)) (pause)
You're right though it isn't very pretty, - as - far as that goes, -
it's a city. You know they're cities. But - like my parents live -
right off - the state park.
216 **B:** Umm:::!=
217 **K:** =So, I just walk out the back door and I can ski into the
woods.
218 **B:** Umm:.
        [[
219 **K:**   An:d spen:d two hours in the woods and never see anybody
or hear anybody.
220 **B:** That must be really fun, especially right around Christmas
time.
                        [   ]
221 **K:**   Yeah it's nice.
222 **K:** Um hmm/=
223 **B:** =When nobody's hunting ((laughing)) anything.
224 **K:** Oh they can't hunt back there, it's not that - big.
                                              [
225 **B:**   I thought they
always sneaked in and did it anyway.
226 **K:** Uh'no:, it's - it's *nice* cuz like my: little brother and his
friends all have- other friends around - the woods, on the
other sides of the woods and they just roam through there,
an'- and go out there to scream and holler to find kids an', -
227 **B:** Mm::.
228 **K:** there's little brooks, and bridges, and - all sorts of fun things.
Did you grow up in Philadelphia?
229 **B:** In the Philadelphia area. Not really *in* Philadelphia. (pause)
Uhm, (pause) this is embarrassing to admit, I was a Main
Line kid. (pause) In the uh - n'there's a stream - of - of cities or
towns - that go around Philadelphia.
230 **K:** Um hmm/
231 **B:** That are called the Main Line and (pause) they range from
suburban to rural.
232 **K:** Um::!
233 **B:** As rural as you get - in Philadelphia an'the, - Pennsylvania
farms don't look anything like Wisconsin farms. You don't
see a lot of - of fields with - wheat and corn. You see a few, -
but - there are a lot of horse farms, a lot of rolling hills and
very manicured looking lawns. They look much more like
golf courses than they do like farms.

234 **K:** ((high pitch)) Hmm!

235 **B:** Beautiful sculpted trees, y'know, - the trees are bigger and lusher there than they are here i' - it never gets quite so cold. And the vegetation is different and looks somewhat lusher. I=

       [   ]

236 **K:**   Um. Yeah.

237 **B:** =mean it's not - doesn't hold candle to Virginia for example, but- also it's a much - moister climate than here (pause) Well, you can't get much moister than Madison summers I guess, but-
    ((laugh))
      [

238 **K:**   Madison winters are worth a lot more (that)=

239 **B:** =((sniff)) Yeah,

240 **K:** could be done.

241 **B:** But yeah I'd- I'd never been - within touching distance of a cow, - but I grew up around horses. ((soft)) So:,
              [

242 **K:**   Is-is that where you learned to ride?

243 **B:** ((soft)) Yeah, an' - yeah when ((louder)) I was four or five or something I was given a junior membership in the - children's branch of the local hunt club.

244 **K:** ((snicker))
    [

245 **B:**   And I was expected to go out and ride a pony and pretend we were chasing foxes and learn how to jump and stuff so- eventually (   )
     [

246 **K:**   It's like kids getting library cards around ((laughing)) here.

247 **B:** Exactly! Yes and in fact, there were no foxes, they'd all been hunted to death years ago.

248 **K:** ((snicker))
    [

249 **B:**   So they had these special kennels where they'd raise ch- foxes and charge outrageous prices for them, and the foxes were often so tame they wouldn't ((laughing)) run (the rounds) ((laugh))
      [

250 **K:**   ((laugh, softly))
     [

251 **B:**   .hhh An'a bad time was had by all. It was very sad.
                [

252 **K:**   Oh:::/

253 **B :**   But the hunt club closed before I got good enough and old
             enough and ((voice fades)) all that to join- ((louder)) There's a
             whole etiquette that goes with that, which, I probably
             wouldn't have been very good at ((softly, laughing)) learning.

254 **K :**   In other words if I had asked you if you would have enjoyed it
             you probably ((laughing slightly)) wouldn't've.

255 **B :**   No, I think that I would have enjoyed the ride, but I would
             have enjoyed the ride more if it had been a- uh: - freer jumble
             of people out riding for the afternoon, and not so much -
             etiquette about who must follow whom, you know the senior
             members always go first however slow they are.

256 **K :**   Oh::.
             [[

257 **B :**   And eveybody else has to ride behind them in order of
             seniority, and - in order of their position within the club, and
             all that, uh::, - and you get sort of- mental brownie points
             detracted - for every little infraction on the rules, or if you go
             over a fence and fall or anything like that. 'N't's - seen -
             particularly - in a- a bad light if you go around a jump instead
             of going over it, it's a sign of either cowardice, or - weakness,
             or - sometimes it's seen as a sign, if they're being very
             charitable, of you just having a ((laughing)) rotten horse.
             ((laugh))

258 **K :**   Ah::. I was going to say, you- did you have your own
             (herse? - horse? or - herse.)
                         [

259 **B :**   No. Uh:m - one summer we leased a
             horse to see how it would work out but - I lived in one of the
             more suburban less rural areas.

260 **K :**   Um hmm/

261 **B :**   An::d, it was - about - forty-five minutes each way to get to
             and from the stable, an'eh, it was on the way - to the- the area
             where my father worked, so I could just go in with him in the
             morning and then come back in the afternoon but it stuck me
             at the stable all day and I couldn't have done it during the
             school year, - so: that we just settled for leasing horses.
             Which was=
                         [   ]

262 **K :**   Um:.

263 **B :**   =fine/ I enjoyed it/ It was fun. (pause) It saved you a lot of
             money in vet bills.

264 **K :**   ((laugh)) That's - undoubtedly very true. I don't know how -
             the prices are there, but -

265 **B :**   Quite high. ((laugh))
                 [

266 **K :**   as far as that's concerned, but I know they are here,
             so

267 **B:** Yeah, yeah, in fact they were having a real problem because
there was only one ferrier, otherwise known as blacksmith,=

268 **K:** = Yes.

269 **B:** uh::,

      [

270 **K:**   Oh! - Ferriers are horse doctors.

271 **B:** Um::. Well, out there they're- they're mostly - concerned
with the feet. The vet takes care of the horse from the ankles
up.

272 **K:** Um::.

      [

273 **B:**   But anything that is wrong with your horse's hooves, or,
if it just needs to be shod, (   ) the blacksmith.

          [

274 **K:**   ((cough . . . . cough)) I suppose
they're a little more specialized, an' - I just happened to pick
up some books at the library every now and then on -
ferriers=

          [   ]

275 **B:**   ((laugh))

276 **K:** =an' - ((soft, "yawning" quality)) I was wondering what they
were, so I finally - checked it out.

277 **B:** They're the people who get paid outrageous amounts of
money to get kicked.

278 **K:** Oo. ((laugh)) (pause) I suppose when you take lessons that's
also when you - just sort of learn to - to y'just take it in stride,
getting kicked and bit an' - I mean you don't like it, but - (you
know it's)

279 **B:** When you ah - when you put a shoe on a horse, this is going to
show up great on tape, - the horse's leg is here. The horse is
facing that way, you face this way.

280 **K:** Um hmm/

281 **B:** You put your feet like this, and you pick his foot up between
your legs.

282 **K:** Um hmm/

283 **B:** And then you put your legs together to hold it. Now if he
kicks he's likely to kick up. And most ferriers being male, I
don't ((laughing)) think it's the sort of thing you ever get used
to or learn how to deal with.

          [   ]   [

284 **K:**   ((laugh))   That's- that's not what I was
talking about. But I mean just as a kid taking ho- lessons.

          [   ]

285 **B:**   ((cough))

286 **B:** Oh that kind of ((coughing)) lessons.

      [

287 **K:**   Y'know, learning - learning to groom horses an-
                and things like that, w'you just get stepped on, and - an' get
                kicked every now and then, by som- your horse or somebody
                else's/

288 **B:**   I never did. I got - I've been stepped on twice and kicked
                once.

289 **K:**   That's- pretty good if you've been riding since you were four.

290 **B:**   Um, - uhm - the time I got stepped on, both times were my
                own fault. I just had my foot in the wrong place at the wrong
                time. Horses don't like to step on people.

291 **K:**   Oh, I'm sure not.
                        [

292 **B:**   It makes them (squeamish). ((cough)) The time I got
                kicked was fairly recently. It was early this fall.

293 **K:**   Hmm.
                        [

294 **B:**   It was a horse I'd never seen before.

295 **K:**   .hhh I remember when you said that! He attacked you.
                ((laugh))=
                                                    [   ]
296 **B:**   (Hm::)!

297 **B:**   =He did! He just came running up out of ((laughing))
                nowhere.

298 **K:**   ((coughs))

299 **B:**   But uh - I can guarantee he ((laughing)) won't do it again.

300 **K:**   You've lear:ned - fast.

301 **B:**   Yes, well - you just ((laughing)) don't go on the field without a
                baseball bat or a two by four. (pause) Do you do anything
                besides ski- besides cross-country skiing in the winter here?
                What do people in Wisconsin do for exercise in the winter.

302 **K:**   Uhm::, - that's a good question. Indoor (l'hh'ike)

303 **B:**   Hmm:.

304 **K:**   (in) pools. Um - my roommates all usually take up swimming
                in the winter, (pause) but=

305 **B:**   =I did that last winter but it was so hard to go into the water
                when I was already cold.
                ((pause))

306 **K:**   I get into taking showers that's about it. ((laugh))

307 **B:**   I take long baths. I'm looking for somebody who - wouldn't
                be embarrassed to start skating. I'd like to skate with another
                beginner.
                        [

308 **K:**   That's a (pause) a big thing, especially down on the campus
                area where - there are places to skate, there's usually places
                cleared off on the lake, there's Tenney Park, (pause) that's - I
                don't really know! When I have free time I ski. I don't even
                think of anything else.

309 **B:**   Hmm:.=

310 **K:** =Or take - long walks.

311 **B:** Where do you ski. Right- I mean you live right downtown.

312 **K:** On the lake, if I don't have a lot of time. Well last winter it was
         nice, cuz last winter, I worked a couple mornings a week, and
         I'd - just get up in the morning, -

313 **B:** Hmm.

314 **K:** I always wore jeans into work anyway, so it didn't matter, I
         just put my jeans and my ski sweater on, and I'd ski to work.
         And then I'd leave my skis, in the ro- in the office, and - when
         I got done, I had like one or two classes in the afternoon, and
         then I'd jus- ag-they were all down on Ag Campus, so I'd just
         go back to the library, pick up my skis, and ski home. And that
         was prob'ly the most skiing I got done sometimes last winter
         cuz it was so cold. When it - finally did freeze.
         ((pause))

315 **B:** That sounds alright, we have this great big field near our
         house, - an:d you should come out and ski there sometime.
         Uhm: - there are two fields, connected by, a sort of path, next
         to a creek, thru some woods.
                   [   ]

316 **K:**   ((cough))

317 **K:** I was gonna say. There's gotta be - fields are pretty dull in
         themselves.

318 **B:** Yeah-
         [[

319 **K:**   The arboretum is fun. Things like that. Where there's trees,
         and (hills), and - curves,

320 **B:** These have - trees, and they're sort of hilly, and there's this
         creek, and there are also pheasants, and sometimes hawks,
         and lots of rabbits and things. And of course other skiers that
         you=
                   [   ]

321 **K:**   Um hmm/

322 **B:** =can collide with if you're so inclined.
         ((both laugh slightly, pause))

323 **B:** This winter I've decided I'm gonna hafta get a - set- a pair of
         snow shoes so I can go tramping around with the dog without
         sinking in thigh deep/

324 **K:** ((laugh))
                   [

325 **B:**   I'm tired of that ((laughing)) struggling through the
         snow.
                                                      [

326 **K:**   You
         don't *like* that/

327 **B:** No. No. I don't like to get wet, when I'm ((laughing)) cold.
                   [   ]

328 **K:**   Have you ever

329 **K:**   Have you ever cross country skied?

330 **B:**   Un-un.

331 **K:**   You might like it. It's - more of an endera- endu*ra*nce type - thing than anything. There's not a lot of - talent to it at all. Believe *me*. .hhhhh

                  [

332 **B:**   Why, thank you.=

333 **K:**   =((laugh))=

334 **B:**   =((laugh))=

335 **K:**   =.hhh No. But I mean it's not something that'a- you could - pick it up in a morning. It's not something you have to spend - weeks and months learning how to do properly.

336 **B:**   Perfecting your technique.

337 **K:**   Yes. I mean, - I taught my little brother - up three years ago - how to ski. We rented some skis when he came up here, he used to come up with me in registration week, and spend the week with me. And, we rented skis for him, a couple days, and he just loved it. He wants skis so badly right now, except they don't really get a lot of snow. Like- they got more than we did so far but, ah, so,

338 **B:**   This is an exceptional year I hear.

339 **K:**   Well they usually get - about as much as - we do,

340 **B:**   Hmm:.

341 **K:**   because - well Madison is in one of these areas that's - too low for the northern storms an' - it's too far south for the northern storms and too far north for the southern storms, and we're just in this little bitty line that runs through there, that we don't get a lot of - snow. We get cold. Whereas- where my parents live they get - lots of snow. But it's gone in two days, because it doesn't stay cold.

342 **B:**   Hmm. (pause) I had forgotten that you knew all about all that weather stuff.

343 **K:**   ((laugh)) I really don't. I just pretend I do. ((pause))

344 **B:**   Tell me what you know about the weather - on: the Pacific coast. And the various parts of the Pacific coast. I'm- I have to go talk to A_____ D_____ about grad schools this afternoon, and would like not to get stuck somewhere that's got really horrible weather. An' I'd like to go somewhere on the - Pacific coast, probably the Oregon coast, - but, I've heard some parts of it just rain constantly and other parts just have

345 **K:**   Hmm.

346 **B:**   bizarre weather with earthquakes thrown in for - good measure and stuff like that.

347 **K:**   (I really haven't ever) studied anything that specific. There are some areas, (I think more like the Los Angeles area where because of the mount-) ((tape ends))

REFERENCES

Adato, A. Untitled manuscript, n.d.

Akmajian, A., & Heny, F. W. *An introduction to the principles of transformational syntax.* Cambridge: MIT Press, 1975.

Alberts, J., & Hopper, R. *Teasing: A conversational analysis.* Paper presented at the annual meeting of the International Communication Association, Dallas, 1983.

Aldrich, H., Sociability in Mensa: Characteristics of interaction among strangers. *Urban Life and Culture,* 1972, *1,* 167-186.

Apel, K-O. Sprechakttheorie und transzendentale sprachpragmatiik zur frage ethischer normen. In *Sprachpragmatik und Philosophie.* Frankfurt-Main: Suhrkamp, 1976.

Aragon, L. *Topics of conversation: A study of patterns in social discourse.* Unpublished manuscript, University of Pennsylvania, 1978.

Austin, J. L. *How to do things with words.* Cambridge: Harvard University Press, 1962.

Bach, K., & Harnish, R. M. *Linguistic communication and speech acts.* Cambridge: MIT Press, 1979.

Bales, R. F. *Personality and interpersonal behavior.* New York: Holt, Rinehart & Winston, 1970.

Barthes, R. *Elements of semiology.* London: Jonathan Cape, 1967.

Bates, E. *Language and context: The acquisition of pragmatics.* New York: Academic Press, 1976.

Bateson, G. A theory of play and fantasy. *Psychiatric Research Reports,* 1955, *2,* 39-51.

Bateson, G. *Steps to an ecology of mind.* San Francisco: Chandler, 1972.

Bateson, G. *Mind and nature: A necessary unity.* New York: Dutton, 1979.

Beach, W. A., & Dunning, D. G. Pre-indexing and conversational organization. *Quarterly Journal of Speech,* 1982, *68,* 170-185.

Beach, W. A., & Japp, P. M. Storyfying as time-traveling: The knowledgeable use of temporally structured discourse. In R. N. Bostrom (Ed.), *Communication yearbook 7.* Beverly Hills: Sage, 1983.

Beattie, G. W. Floor apportionment and gaze in conversational dyads. *British Journal of Social and Clinical Psychology,* 1978, *17,* 7-15.

Becker, A. L. A tagmemic approach to paragraph analysis. *College Composition and Communication,* 1965, *16,* 237-242.

Bellert, I. On a condition of the coherence of texts. *Semiotica*, 1970, 2, 335-363.

Bennett, R. G. The meaning of institutional life. In M. Leeds & H. Shore (Eds.), *Geriatric institutional management*. New York: G. P. Putnam, 1964.

Bennett, W. L. Storytelling in criminal trials: A model of social judgment. *Quarterly Journal of Speech*, 1978, 64, 1-22.

Bennett, W. L. Rhetorical transformation of evidence in criminal trials: Creating grounds for legal judgment. *Quarterly Journal of Speech*, 1979, 65, 311-323.

Bennett, W. L., & Feldman, M. S. *Reconstructing reality in the courtroom: Justice and judgment in American culture*. New Brunswick, NJ: Rutgers University Press, 1981.

Berlo, D. K. *The process of communication*. New York: Holt, Rinehart & Winston, 1960.

Bernstein, B. *Class, codes and control*. New York: Schocken, 1971.

Bernstein, B. Social class, language and socialization. In P. P. Gigliolo (Ed.), *Language and social context*. Harmondsworth: Penguin Books, 1972.

Betcher, R. W. Intimate play and marital adaptation. *Psychiatry*, 1981, 4, 13-33.

Birdwhistell, R. L. Contributions to discussion. In B. Schaffner (Ed.), *Group processes: Transactions of the second conference*. New York: Josiah Macy, Jr., Foundation, 1956.

Birdwhistell, R. L. *Kinesics and context*. Philadelphia: University of Pennsylvania Press, 1970.

Bochner, A. On taking ourselves seriously: An analysis of some persistent problems and promising directions in interpersonal research. *Human Communication Research*, 1978, 4, 179-191.

Bowers, J. W., Elliot, N. D., & Desmond, R. J. Exploiting pragmatic rules: Devious messages. *Human Communication Research*, 1977, 3, 235-242.

Breton, A. *Manefestoes of surrealism* (R. Seaver & H. R. Lane, trans.). Ann Arbor: University of Michigan Press, 1972.

Brockway, D. L. *Semantic constraints on relevance*. Unpublished Manuscript, Department of Linguistics, University College London, January 1979.

Brown, G., Currie, K. L., & Kenworthy, J. *Questions of intonation*. London: Croom Helm, 1980.

Brown P., & Levinson, S. C. Universals in language usage: Politeness phenomena. In E. N. Goody (Ed.), *Questions and politeness: Strategies in social interaction*. New York: Cambridge University Press, 1978.

Bruner, J. S. The ontogenesis of speech acts. *Journal of Child Language*, 1975, 2, 1-20.

Burke, K. D. (Nonsymbolic) motion/ (symbolic) action. *Critical Inquiry*, 1978, 4, 809-838.

Burton, D. Towards an analysis of casual conversation. *Nottingham Linguistic Circular*, 1978, 7, 131-164.

Cappella, J. N. Talk-silence sequences in informal conversations. *Human Communication Research*, 1979, 6, 3-17.

Chafe, W. L. Language and consciousness. *Language*, 1974, 50, 111-113.

Chomsky, N. *Reflections on language*. New York: Pantheon Books, 1975.

Christensen, F. *Notes towards a new rhetoric*. New York: Harper & Row, 1967.

Churchill, L. *Questioning strategies in sociolinguistics*. Rowley, MA: Newbury House, 1978.

Cicourel, A. V. Basic and normative rules in the negotiation of status and role. In D. Sudnow (Ed.), *Studies in social interaction*. New York: Free Press, 1972.

Cicourel, A. V. *Cognitive sociology.* London: Penguin Books, 1973.

Cicourel, A. V. Three models of discourse analysis: The role of social structure. *Discourse Processes,* 1980, *3,* 101-132.

Clancy, P. Analysis of a conversation. *Anthropological Linguistics,* 1972, *14*(3), 78-86.

Clark, H. H. Bridging. In P. N. Johnson-Laird & P. C. Wason (Eds.), *Thinking: Readings in cognitive science.* Cambridge: Cambridge University Press, 1977.

Clark, H. H., & Carlson, T. B. Speech acts and hearer's beliefs. In N. V. Smith (Ed.), *Mutual knowledge.* London: Academic Press, 1982.

Clark, H. H., & Clark, E. *Psychology and language.* New York: Harcourt Brace Jovanovich, 1977.

Clark, H. H., & Haviland, S. E. Comprehension and the given-new contract. In R. O. Freedle (Ed.), *Discourse production and comprehension.* Norwood, NJ: Ablex, 1977.

Clark, H. H., & Marshall, C. R. Definite reference and mutual knowledge. In A. K. Joshi, I. Sag, & B. Webber (Eds.), *Elements of discourse understanding.* Cambridge: Cambridge University Press, 1981.

Clark, R. A. The impact of self-interest and desire for liking on the selection of communication strategies. *Communication Monographs,* 1979, *46,* 257-273.

Cline, T. R. A Markov analysis of strangers', roommates', and married couples' conversational focus on their relationships. *Southern Speech Communication Journal,* 1979, *45,* 55-68.

Coulter, J. Beliefs and practical understanding. In G. Psathas (Ed.), *Everyday language: Studies in ethnomethodology.* New York: Irvington, 1979.

Coulter, J. *The social construction of mind: Studies in ethnomethodology and linguistic philosophy.* Totawa, NJ: Rowman & Littlefield, 1980.

Coulthard, M. *An introduction to discourse analysis.* London: Longman, 1977.

Coward, R., & Ellis, J. *Language and materialism: Developments in semiology and the theory of the subject.* London: Routledge & Kegan Paul, 1977.

Cronen, V. E., Pearce, W. B., & Harris, L. M. The coordinated management of meaning: A theory of communication. In F. E. X. Dance (Ed.), *Communication theory: Comparative essays.* New York: Harper & Row, 1982.

Cushman, D. P. *Rules theory: Ten years later.* Paper presented at the annual meeting of the Central States Speech Communication Association, Milwaukee, WI, April 1982.

Cushman, D. P., & Pearce, W. B. Generality and necessity in three types of theory about human communication with special attention to rules theory. *Human Communication Research,* 1977, *3,* 344-353.

Cushman, D. P., & Whiting, G. C. An approach to communication theory: Toward consensus on rules. *Journal of Communication,* 1972, *22,* 217-238.

Danes, F. (Ed.) *Papers on functional sentence perspective.* Prague: Publishing House of the Czech Academy of Sciences, 1974.

Danet, B. Language in the legal process. *Law and Society Review,* 1980, *14,* 445-564.

Dascal, M., & Katriel, T. Digressions: A study in conversation coherence. *PTL: A Journal for Descriptive Poetics and Theory of Literature,* 1979, *4,* 203-232.

de Beaugrande, R. *Text, discourse and process: Toward a multidisciplinary science of texts.* Norwood, NJ: Ablex, 1980.

Derrida, J. *Positions.* Paris: Editions de Minuit, 1972 [Also, Translated and annotated by A. Bass, Chicago: University of Chicago Press, 1981].

Detweiler, R. *Story, sign, and self: Phenomenology and structuralism as literary-critical methods.* Philadelphia: Fortress Press, 1978.

Dicks, V. I. Courtroom rhetorical strategies: Forensic and deliberative perspectives. *Quarterly Journal of Speech,* 1981, *67,* 178-192.

Dominick, B. A. Don't be afraid of silence. *Today's Speech,* 1958, *6*(1), 13-15.

Donaldson, S. K. One kind of speech act: How do we know when we're conversing? *Semiotica,* 1979, *28,* 259-299.

Donohue, W. A., Cushman, D. P., & Nofsinger, R. E. Creating and confronting social order: A comparison of rules perspectives. *Western Journal of Speech Communication,* 1980, *44,* 5-19.

Duncan, S., Jr. Some signals and rules for taking speaking turns in conversations. *Journal of Personality and Social Psychology,* 1972, *23,* 283-292.

Duncan, S., Jr. Toward a grammar for dyadic conversation. *Semiotica,* 1973, *9,* 29-46.

Duncan, S., Jr., Brunner, L. J., & Fiske, D. W. Strategy signals in face-to-face interaction. *Journal of Personality and Social Psychology,* 1979, *37,* 301-313.

Duncan, S., Jr., & Fiske, D. *Face-to-face interaction.* Hillsdale, NJ: Lawrence Erlbaum, 1977.

Eakins, B. W., & Eakins, R. G. *Sex differences in human communication.* Boston: Houghton-Mifflin, 1978.

Ellis, D. G. Language and speech communication. In M. Burgoon (Ed.), *Communication yearbook 6.* Beverly Hills: Sage, 1982.

Erickson, B., Lind, E. A., Johnson, B. C., & O'Barr, W. M. Speech style and impression formation in a court setting: The effects of "powerful" and "powerless" speech. *Journal of Experimental Social Psychology,* 1978, *14,* 266-279.

Farb, P. *Word play.* New York: Bantam Books, 1975.

Farrell, T. B. Knowledge, consensus and rhetorical theory. *Quarterly Journal of Speech,* 1976, *62,* 1-14.

Farrell, T. B. Social knowledge II. *Quarterly Journal of Speech,* 1978, *64,* 329-334.

Farrell, T. B. Knowledge in time: Toward an extension of rhetorical form. In J. R. Cox & C. A. Willard (Eds.), *Advances in argumentation theory and research.* Carbondale: Southern Illinois University Press, 1982.

Farrell, T. B., & Frentz, T. Communication and meaning: A language-action synthesis. *Philosophy and Rhetoric,* 1979, *12,* 215-255.

Fillmore, C. J. Pragmatics and the description of discourse. In P. Cole (Ed.), *Radical pragmatics.* New York: Academic Press, 1981.

Firth, J. R. On sociological linguistics. In D. Hymes (Ed.), *Language in culture and society.* New York: Harper & Row, 1964. [Orig. pub., 1935.]

Fisher, B. A., & Hawes, L. C. An interact system model: Generating a grounded theory of small groups. *Quarterly Journal of Speech,* 1971, *57,* 444-453.

Fitzpatrick, M. A., & Indvik, J. The instrumental and expressive domains of marital communication. *Human Communication Research,* 1982, *8,* 195-213.

Foucault, M. *The order of things: An archaeology of the human sciences.* New York: Vintage Books, 1973.

Foucault, M. What is an author? *Partisan Review,* 1975, *4,* 603-614.

Fowler, R. *Literature as social discourse: The practice of linguistic criticism.* Bloomington: Indiana University Press, 1981.

Frentz, T. S., & Farrell, T. B. Language-action: A paradigm for communication. *Quarterly Journal of Speech,* 1976, *62,* 333-349.

Gadamer, H-G. *Truth and method.* New York: Seabury Press, 1975.

Garcia, E. C. Discourse without syntax. In T. Givón (Ed.), *Syntax and semantics, Vol. 12: Discourse and syntax.* New York: Academic Press, 1979.

Garfinkel, H. *Studies in ethnomethodology.* Englewood Cliffs, NJ: Prentice-Hall, 1967.

Giles, H., & Powesland, P. F. *Speech style and social evaluation.* New York: Academic Press, 1975.

Givón, T. Serial verbs and syntactic change: Niger-Congo. In C. Li (Ed.), *Word order and word order change.* Austin: University of Texas Press, 1975.

Givón, T. From discourse to syntax: Grammar as a processing strategy. In T. Givón (Ed.), *Syntax and semantics, Vol. 12: Discourse and syntax.* New York: Academic Press. 1979.(a)

Givón, T. (Ed.) *Syntax and semantics, Vol. 12: Discourse and syntax.* New York: Academic Press. 1979.(b)

Glaser, B. G., & Strauss, A. L. *The discovery of grounded theory: Strategies for qualitative research.* Chicago: Aldine, 1967.

Goddard, L., & Routley, R. *The logic of significance and context* (Vol. 1). New York: Halsted Press, 1973.

Goffman, E. *The presentation of self in everyday life.* Garden City, NJ: Doubleday Anchor Books, 1959.

Goffman, E. *Encounters.* Indianapolis: Bobbs-Merrill, 1961.

Goffman, E. *Strategic interaction.* Philadelphia: University of Pennsylvania Press, 1969.

Goffman, E. *Relations in public.* New York: Harper & Row, 1971.

Goffman, E. *Frame analysis: An essay on the organization of experience.* New York: Harper & Row, 1974.

Goffman, E. Replies and responses. *Language in Society,* 1976, *5,* 257-313.

Goldberg, J. A. *Discourse particles: An analysis of the role of y'know, I mean, well, and actually in conversation.* Unpublished Ph.D. dissertation, Cambridge University (England), 1980.

Goldberg, J. A. *Track that topic with "y'know"!* Paper presented at the University of Nebraska Summer Conference on Conversational Analysis and Discourse Processes, Lincoln, 1981.

Goldberg, J. A. Hey, y'know, have I got a topic for you. *Psycholinguistic Newsletter,* 1982, *7,* 1-11.

Goodenough, D. R., & Weiner, S. L. The role of conversational passing moves in the management of topical transitions. *Discourse Processes,* 1978, *1,* 395-404.

Goody, E. N. (Ed.) *Questions and politeness: Strategies in social interaction.* New York: Cambridge University Press, 1978.

Gottman, J. M. *Marital interaction: Experimental investigations.* New York: Academic Press, 1979.

Grice, H. P. Meaning. *Philosophical Review,* 1957, *66,* 377-388.

Grice, H. P. The causal theory of perception. *Proceedings of the Aristotelian Society,* 1961, (Supplementary Volume) *35,* 121-170.

Grice, H. P. Logic and conversation. *William James Lectures.* Unpublished, Harvard, 1967.

Grice, H. P. Utterer's meaning, sentence-meaning, and word-meaning. *Foundations of Language,* 1968, *4,* 1-18. [Also in J. R. Searle (Ed.), *The philosophy of language.* Oxford: Oxford University Press, 1971.]

Grice, H. P. Utterer's meaning and intentions. *Philosophical Review,* 1969, *78,* 147-177.

Grice, H. P. Logic and conversation. In P. Cole & J. L. Morgan (Eds.), *Syntax and semantics, Vol. 3: Speech acts.* New York: Academic Press, 1975.

Grice, H. P. Further notes on logic and conversation. In P. Cole (Ed.), *Syntax and semantics, Vol. 9: Pragmatics.* New York: Academic Press, 1978.

Grimaldi, S. J., W. M. A. *Aristotle, Rhetoric I: A commentary.* New York: Fordham University Press, 1980.

Grimes, J. Topic levels. In D. Waltz (Ed.), *Theoretical issues in natural language processing 2.* Urbana, IL: Coordinated Science Lab, 1978.

Grimshaw, A. Mishearings, misunderstandings, and other nonsuccesses in talk: A plea for redress of speaker-oriented bias. *Sociological Inquiry,* 1980, *50,* 31-74.

Grossberg, L. Language and theorizing in the human sciences. In N. K. Denzin (Ed.), *Studies in symbolic interaction* (Vol. 2). Greenwich, CT: JAI Press, 1979.

Gumperz, J. J. Introduction. In J. J. Gumperz & D. Hymes (Eds.), *Directions in sociolinguisitics.* New York: Holt, Rinehart & Winston. 1972.

Gumperz, J. J. *Discourse strategies.* Cambridge: Cambridge University Press, 1982.

Haas, A. Male and female spoken language differences: Stereotypes and evidence. *Psychological Bulletin,* 1979, *86,* 616-626.

Habermas, J. *Communication and the evolution of society* (T. McCarthy, trans.). Boston: Beacon, 1979.

Haley, J. *Strategies of psychotherapy.* New York: Grune & Stratton, 1963.

Halliday, M. A. K., & Hasan, R. *Cohesion in English.* London: Longman, 1976.

Hancher, M. The classification of cooperative illocutionary acts. *Language in Society,* 1979, *8,* 1-14.

Haslett, B. *Making sense of sense-making: A reply to Hopper.* Paper presented at the annual meeting of the Speech Communication Association, Lousiville, Kentucky, November 1982.

Havelock, E. A. *Preface to Plato.* New York: Universal Library, 1967.

Haviland, S. E., & Clark, H. H. What's new? Acquiring new information as a process in comprehension. *Journal of Verbal Learning and Verbal Behavior,* 1974, *13,* 512-521.

Hawes, L. C. How writing is used in talk: A study of communicative logic-in-use. *Quarterly Journal of Speech,* 1976, *62,* 350-360.

Heap, J. Non-indexical action. *Philosophy of Social Science,* 1975, *5,* 393-409.

Heritage, J. C., & Watson, D. R. Formulations as conversational objects. In G. Psathas (Ed.), *Everyday language: Studies in ethnomethodology.* New York: Irvington, 1979.

Hewes, D. E. Finite stochastic modeling of communication processes: An introduction and some basic readings. *Human Communication Research,* 1975, *1,* 271-283.

Hewitt, J., & Stokes, R. Disclaimers. *American Sociological Review,* 1975, *40,* 1-11.

Hoban, R. *Riddley Walker.* New York: Summit Books, 1980.

Hofstadter, D. R. *Gödel, Escher, Bach: An Eternal golden braid.* New York: Basic Books, 1979.

Holmquest, A. *Cardinal Richelieu's rhetoric of conversation: A more natural public address.* Paper presented at the annual meeting of the Speech Communication Association, Anaheim, CA, November 1981.

Hopper, R. *Human message systems.* New York: Harper & Row, 1976.

Hopper, R. The taken-for-granted. *Human Communication Research,* 1981, *7,* 195-211.

Hopper, R., Knapp, M. L., & Scott, L. Couples' personal idioms: Exploring intimate talk. *Journal of Communication,* 1981, *31,* 23-33.

Hurtig, R. Toward a functional theory of discourse. In R. O. Freedle (Ed.), *Discourse production and comprehension*. Norwood, NJ: Ablex, 1977.

Hymes, D. Editorial introduction. *Language in Society*, 1972, *1*, 1-14.

Hymes, D. *Foundations in sociolinguistics: An ethnographic approach*. Philadelphia: University of Pennsylvania Press, 1974.

Jackson, S., & Jacobs, S. *Adjacency pairs and the sequential description of arguments*. Paper presented at the annual meeting of the Speech Communication Association, Minneapolis, November 1978.

Jackson, S., & Jacobs, S. Structure of conversational argument: Pragmatic bases for the enthymeme. *Quarterly Journal of Speech*, 1980, *66*, 251-265.

Jackson, S., & Jacobs, S. The collaborative production of proposals in conversational argument and persuasion: A study in disagreement regulation. *Journal of the American Forensic Association*, 1981, *18*, 77-90.

Jacobs, S. *The practical management of conversational meanings: Notes on the dynamics of social understandings and interactional emergence*. Paper presented at the annual meeting of the Speech Communication Association, Washington, DC, December 1977.

Jacobs, S., & Jackson, S. *Strategy and structure in conversation influence attempts*. Paper presented at the annual meeting of the Speech Communication Association, New York, November 1981.

Jakobson, R. *Selected writings*. The Hague: Mouton, 1962.

Jefferson, G. Side sequences. In D. Sudnow (Ed.), *Studies in social interaction*. New York: Free Press, 1972.

Jefferson, G. Sequential aspects of storytelling in conversation. In J. Schenkein (Ed.), *Studies in the organization of conversational interaction*. New York: Academic Press, 1978.

Jefferson, G. A technique for inviting laughter and its subsequent acceptance/declination. In G. Psathas (Ed.), *Everyday language: Studies in ethnomethodology*. New York: Irvington, 1979.

Jones, L. *Theme in English expository discourse*. Lake Bluff, IL: Jupiter, 1977.

Just, M. A., & Carpenter, P. A. (Eds.) *Cognitive processes in comprehension*. Hillsdale, NJ: Lawrence Erlbaum, 1977.

Katz, J., & Fodor, J. The structure of semantic theory. *Language*, 1963, *39*, 170-210.

Keenan, E. O., & Schieffelin, B. B. Topic as a discourse notion: A study of topic in the conversations of children and adults. In C. N. Li (Ed.), *Subject and topic*. New York: Academic Press, 1976.

Kempson, R. M. *Semantic theory*. Cambridge: Cambridge University Press, 1977.

Kendon, A. Looking in conversation and the regulation of turns at talk: A comment on the papers of G. Beattie and D. R. Rutter et al. *British Journal of Social and Clinical Psychology*, 1978, *17*, 23-24.

Knapp, M. L., Hart, R. P., Friedrich, G. W., & Shulman, G. M. The rhetoric of goodbye: Verbal and nonverbal correlates of human leave-taking. *Speech Monographs*, 1973, *40*, 182-198.

Knutson, M. *Small talk: An exploratory study*. Unpublished M.A. Thesis, Washington State University, 1982.

Konigsberg, E. The fallacy of the first name. *Today's Speech*, 1957, *5*(1), 1-2.

Kosinski, J. *Being there*. New York: Bantam, 1970.

Kosslyn, S. M. *Image and mind*. Cambridge: Harvard University Press, 1980.

Kramerae, C. *Women and men speaking*. Rowley, MA: Newbury House, 1981.

_10,4_

Kreckel, M. *Communicative acts and shared knowledge in natural discourse.* New York: Academic Press, 1981.

Kress, G, & Fowler, R. Interviews. In R. Fowler, B. Hodge, G. Kress, & T. Trew (Eds.), *Language and control.* London: Routledge & Kegan Paul, 1979.

Kristeva, J. The subject in signifying practice. In *Semiotext(e)* (Vol. 1). New York: Columbia University Press, 1975.

Krivonos, P. D., & Knapp, M. L. Initiating communication: What do you say when you say hello? *Central States Speech Journal,* 1975, *26,* 115-125.

Krueger, D. L. Marital decision-making: A language-action analysis. *Quarterly Journal of Speech,* 1982, *68,* 273-287.

Labov, W., & Fanshel, D. *Therapeutic discourse: Psychotherapy as conversation.* New York: Academic Press, 1977.

Lakoff, R. *Language and woman's place.* New York: Harper, 1975.

Lakoff, R. You say what you are: Acceptability and gender-related language. In S. Greenbaum (Ed.), *Acceptability in language.* New York: Mouton, 1977.

Lehnert, W. G. *The process of question answering.* Hillsdale, NJ: Lawrence Erlbaum, 1978.

Leiter, K. *A primer on ethnomethodology.* New York: Oxford University Press, 1980.

Leone, E., & Martin, J. N. *Conversational topic and speech functions in initial interaction: Complementary and symmetrical patterns.* Paper presented at the University of Nebraska Summer Conference on Discourse Processes and Conversational Interaction, Lincoln, August 1981.

Levinson, S. C. Activity types and language. *Linguistics,* 1979, *17,* 365-399.

Levinson, S. C. Speech act theory: The state of the art. *Language Teaching and Linguistics: Abstracts,* 1980, *13,* 5-24.

Levinson, S. C. Some pre-observations on the modelling of dialogue. *Discourse Processes,* 1981, *4,* 93-116.

Levinson, S. C. *An introduction to pragmatics.* Unpublished Manuscript, n.d.

Levy, D. M. Communicative goals and strategies: Between discourse and syntax. In T. Givón (Ed.), *Syntax and semantics, Vol. 12: Discourse and syntax.* New York: Academic Press, 1979.

Li, C., & Thompson, S. Subject and topic: A new typology for language. In C. Li (Ed.), *Subject and topic.* New York: Academic Press, 1976.

Lieberman, P. *Intonation, perception and language.* Cambridge: MIT Press, 1967.

Litton-Hawes, E. M. A foundation for the study of everyday talk. *Communication Quarterly,* 1977, *25*(3), 2-11.

Lodge, D. Where It's at: California language. In L. Michaels and C. Ricks (Eds.), *The state of the language.* Berkeley: University of California Press, 1980.

MacIntyre, A. *After virtue.* Notre Dame, IN: University of Notre Dame Press, 1981.

Malinowski, B. The problem of meaning in primitive languages. Supplement to C. K. Ogden and I. A. Richards, *The meaning of meaning.* New York: Harcourt Brace Jovanovich, 1923.

Mamet, D. *Lakeboat.* New York: Grove Press, 1981.

Mandler, J. M., & Johnson, N. Remembrance of things parsed: Story structure and recall. *Cognitive Psychology,* 1977, *9,* 111-151.

Manor, R. An analysis of a speech. *Theoretical Linguistics,* 1976, *3,* 125-143.

Matlon, R. J. *Index to journals in communication studies through 1979.* Annandale, VA: Speech Communication Association, 1980.

Matoesian, G. *Complaining about complaining: The anatomy of a conversational device.* Paper presented at the University of Nebraska Summer Conference on Discourse Processes and Conversational Interaction, Lincoln, August 1981.

McCall, G.J., & Simmons, J.L. *Identities and interactions* (Revised ed.). New York: Free Press, 1978.

McDermott, R. P., & Hall, W. S. The social organization of a successful and an unsuccessful school performance. *Quarterly Newsletter of the Institute for Comparative Human Development,* Rockefeller University, 1977, *1,* 10-11.

McHugh, P. *Defining the situation.* Indianapolis: Bobbs-Merrill, 1968.

Mead, G. H. *Mind, self, and society.* Chicago: University of Chicago Press, 1934.

Miller, G. R. The current status of theory and research in interpersonal communication. *Human Communication Research,* 1978, *4,* 164-178.

Mills, C. W. Situated actions and vocabularies of motive. *American Sociological Review,* 1940, *5,* 904-913.

Minsky, M. A framework for representing knowledge. In P. H. Winston (Ed.), *The psychology of computer vision.* New York: McGraw-Hill, 1975.

Mishler, E. G. Meaning in context: Is there any other kind? *Harvard Educational Review,* 1979, *49,* 1-19.

Mishler, E. G., & Waxler, N. E. *Interaction in families: An experimental study of family processes and schizophrenia.* New York: John Wiley, 1968.

Mohan, B. A. Do sequencing rules exist? *Semiotica,* 1974, *12,* 75-96.

Morgan, J. L., & Sellner, M. B. Discourse and linguistic theory. In R. J. Spiro, B. C. Bruce, & W. F. Brewer (Eds.), *Theoretical issues in reading comprehension: Perspectives from cognitive psychology, linguistics, artificial intelligence, and education.* Hillsdale, NJ: Lawrence Erlbaum, 1980.

Morris, G. H., & Hopper, R. *Symbolic action as alignment: Reframing a decade of rules research.* Paper presented to the International Communication Association, Boston, 1982.

Morton, J., & Jassem, W. Acoustic correlates of stress. *Language and Speech,* 1965, *8,* 148-158.

Mura, S. S. *An experimental investigation of the effect of gender and relative status on the use of deferential language style.* Unpublished M.A. Thesis, Ohio State University, 1980.

Naturalistic study of communication: A symposium. *Communication Quarterly,* 1977, *25*(3).

Nida, E. *Exploring semantic structures.* Munich: Fink, 1975.

Nofsinger, R. E. The demand ticket: A conversational device for getting the floor. *Speech Monographs,* 1975, *42,* 1-9.

Nofsinger, R. E. On answering questions indirectly: Some rules in the grammar of doing conversation. *Human Communication Research,* 1976, *2,* 172-181.

Nofsinger, R. E. A peek at conversational analysis. *Communication Quarterly,* 1977, *25*(3), 12-20.

Nofsinger, R. E., & Boyd, W. E. *Topic management procedures: Executing tactics and displaying adherence to rules.* Paper presented at the Western Speech Communication Association meeting, Los Angeles, 1979.

Nowakowska, M. Towards a formal theory of dialogues. *Semiotica,* 1976, *17,* 291-313.

Ochs, E. Introduction: What child language can contribute to pragmatics. In E. Ochs & B. Schieffelin (Eds.), *Developmental pragmatics.* New York: Academic Press, 1979.

Ochs, E., & Schieffelin, B. B. (Eds.) *Developmental pragmatics,* New York: Academic Press, 1979.

Onions, C. T. *Oxford dictionary of English etymology.* Oxford: Oxford University Press, 1966.

Parks, M. R. Ideology in interpersonal communication: Off the couch and into the world. In M. Burgoon (Ed.), *Communication yearbook 5*. Beverly Hills, CA: Sage, 1982.

Pearce, W. B. Consensual rules in interpersonal communication: A reply to Cushman and Whiting. *Journal of Communication* 1973, *23*, 160-168.

Pearce, W. B., & Cronen, V. *Communication, action, and meaning: The creation of social realities*. New York: Praeger, 1980.

Pike, K. *Language in relation to a unified theory of the structure of human behavior*. The Hague: Mouton, 1967.

Planalp, S. & Tracy, K. Not to change the topic but . . .: A cognitive approach to the management of conversation. In D. Nimmo (Ed.), *Communication yearbook 4*. New Brunswick, NJ: Transaction, 1980.

Pollner, M. The very coinage of your brain: The resolution of reality disjunctures. *Philosophy of the Social Sciences*, 1975, *5*, 411-430.

Pollner, M. Explicative transactions: Making and managing meaning in traffic court. In G. Psathas (Ed.), *Everyday language: Studies in ethnomethodology*. New York: Irvington, 1979.

Pomerantz, A. Compliment responses: Notes on the co-operation of multiple constraints. In J. Schenkein (Ed.), *Studies in the organization of conversational interaction*. New York: Academic Press, 1978.

Pomerantz, A. Telling my side: "Limited access" as a "fishing device." *Sociological Inquiry*, 1980, *50*, 186-198. (a)

Pomerantz, A. Speaker's claims as a feature of describing: A study of presenting the evidence for. Unpublished manuscript, 1980. (b)

The presidential transcripts (Edited by the staff of *The Washington Post*). New York: Dell, 1974.

Psathas, G. (Ed.) *Everyday language: Studies in ethnomethodology*. New York: Irvington, 1979.

Ragan, S. L. *Alignment talk in job interviews*. Unpublished Ph. D. dissertation, University of Texas at Austin, 1981.

Ragan, S. L., & Hopper, R. Alignment talk in the job interview. *Journal of Applied Communication Research*, 1981, *9*, 85-103.

Reichman, R. Conversational coherency. *Cognitive Science*, 1978, *2*, 283-327.

Ricoeur, P. *The rule of metaphor: Multi-disciplinary studies of the creation of meaning*. London: Routledge & Kegan Paul, 1978.

Rieger, C. Conceptual memory and inference. In R. Schank, N. Goldman, C. Rieger, & C. Riesbeck (Eds.), *Conceptual information processing*. Amsterdam: North-Holland, 1975.

Rogers, L. E., & Farace, R. V. Analysis of relational communication in dyads: New measurement procedures. *Human Communication Research*, 1975, *1*, 222-239.

Rogers-Millar, L. E., & Millar, F. E. Domineeringness and dominance: A transactional view. *Human Communication Research*, 1979, *5*, 238-246.

Rorty, R. *Philosophy and the mirror of nature*. Princeton, NJ: Princeton University Press, 1979.

Rosch, E. Classification of real-world objects: Origins and representations in cognition. In P. N. Johnson-Laird & P. C. Wason (Eds.), *Thinking: Readings in cognitive science*. Cambridge: Cambridge University Press, 1977.

Rosenfield, L. W., Hayes, L. S., & Frentz, T. S. *The communicative experience*. Boston: Allyn & Bacon, 1976.

Rumelhart, D. Notes on a schema for stories. In D. D. Bobrow & A. Collins (Eds.), *Representation and understanding: Studies in cognitive science*. New York: Academic Press, 1975.

Rutter, D. R., Stephenson, G. M., Ayling, K., & White, P. A. The timing of looks in dyadic conversation. *British Journal of Social and Clinical Psychology,* 1978, *17,* 17-21.

Ryave, A. L. On the achievement of a series of stories. In J. Schenkein (Ed.), *Studies in the organization of conversational interaction.* New York: Academic Press, 1978.

Sacks, H. *Lecture notes.* Unpublished transcripts. University of California, Irvine, 1968.

Sacks, H. On the analysability of stories by children. In J.J. Gumperz and D. Hymes (Eds.), *Directions in sociolinguistics.* New York: Holt, Rinehart & Winston, 1972.

Sacks, H. An analysis of the course of a joke's telling in conversation. In R. Bauman & J. Sherzer (Eds.), *Explorations in the ethnography of speaking.* Cambridge: Cambridge University Press, 1974.

Sacks, H., Schegloff, E. A., & Jefferson, G. A simplest systematics for the organization of turn-taking for conversation. *Language,* 1974, *50,* 696-735. [Also in J. Schenkein (Ed.), *Studies in the organization of conversational interaction.* New York: Academic Press, 1978.]

Sanders, R. E. Principles of relevance: A theory of the relationship between language and communication. *Communication and Cognition,* 1980, *13,* 77-95.

Sanders, R. E. The interpretation of discourse. *Communication Quarterly,* 1981, *29,* 209-217.

Sanders, R. E. *The role of meaning in producing an effect.* Paper presented at the Conference on Language and Discourse Processes, Michigan State University, 1982.

Sanders, R. E. The interpretation of nonverbals. *Semiotica,* forthcoming.

Schacter, P. Reference related and role-related properties of subjects. In P. Cole and J. L. Morgan (Eds.), *Syntax and semantics, Vol. 8.* New York: Academic Press, 1976.

Schank, R. C. Rules and topics in conversation. *Cognitive Science,* 1977, *1,* 421-441.

Schank, R. C. & Abelson, R. P. Scripts, plans, and knowledge. *Advance Papers of the Fourth International Joint Conference on Artificial Intelligence, Tbilisi, Georgia, USSR.* Cambridge, MA: Artificial Intelligence Lab, 1975, *1,* 151-157.

Schank, R. C., & Abelson, R. P. *Scripts, plans, goals and understanding: An inquiry into human knowledge structures.* Hillsdale, NJ: Lawrence Erlbaum, 1977.

Scheflen, A. E. Human communication: Behavioral programs and their integration in interaction. *Behavioral Science,* 1968, *13,* 44-55.

Scheflen, A. E. *Communicational structure: Analysis of a psychotherapy transaction.* Bloomington: Indiana University Press, 1973.

Scheflen, A. E. *How behavior means.* Garden City, NY: Doubleday, 1974.

Schegloff, E. A. Sequencing in conversational openings. In J. A. Fishman (Ed.), *Advances in the sociology of language* (Vol. 2). The Hague: Mouton, 1972.(a)

Schegloff, E. A. Notes on a conversational practice: Formulating place. In D. Sudnow (Ed.), *Studies in social interaction.* New York: Free Press, 1972.(b)

Schegloff, E. A. Preliminaries to preliminaries: "Can I ask you a question?" *Sociological Inquiry,* 1980, *50,* 104-152.

Schegloff, E. A. *Discourse as an interactional achievement: Some uses of "Uh huh" etc.* Paper presented at the Georgetown University Roundtable on Linguistics and Language Studies, March 1981.

Schegloff, E. A., & Sacks, H. Opening up closings. *Semiotica,* 1973, *8,* 289-327.

Schenkein, J. (Ed.) *Studies in the organization of conversational interaction.* New York: Academic Press, 1978.

Schiffrin, D. Meta-talk: Organizational and evaluative brackets in discourse. *Sociological Inquiry,* 1980, *50,* 199-236.

Schlesinger, I. M. *Production and comprehension of utterances.* Hillsdale, NJ: Lawrence Erlbaum, 1977.

Scholes, R. J. *Acoustic cues for constituent structure.* The Hague: Mouton, 1971.

Schramm, W. How communication works. In W. Schramm (Ed.), *The process and effects of mass communications.* Urbana: University of Illinois Press, 1954.

Schutz, A. *Collected papers I: The problem of social reality.* The Hague: Martinus Nijhoff, 1962.

Schutz, A. *Collected papers II: Studies in social theory.* The Hague: Martinus Nijhoff, 1964.

Scott, M., & Lyman, S. Accounts. *American Sociological Review,* 1968, *33,* 46-62.

Searle, J. R. *Speech acts.* London: Cambridge University Press, 1969.

Searle, J. R. A classification of illocutionary acts. In A. Roger, B. Wall, & J. P. Murphy (Eds.), *Proceedings of the Texas Conference on Performatives, Presuppositions and Implicatures.* Arlington, VA: Center for Applied Linguistics, 1975.(a)

Searle, J. R. Indirect speech acts. In P. Cole & J. L. Morgan (Eds.), *Syntax and semantics, Vol. 3: Speech acts.* New York: Academic Press, 1975.(b)

Searle, J. R. *Expression and meaning.* New York: Cambridge University Press, 1980.

Sennett, R. *The fall of public man.* New York: Vintage Books, 1978.

Shaw, M. Taken-for-granted assumptions of applicants in simulated selection interviews. *Western Journal of Speech Communication,* 1983, *47,* 138-156.

Shawn, W., & Gregory, A. *My dinner with Andre.* New York: Grove Press, 1981.

Sherman, S. J. On the self-erasing nature of errors of prediction. *Journal of Personality and Social Psychology,* 1980, *39,* 211-221.

Shimanoff, S. B. *Communication rules: Theory and research.* Beverly Hills, CA: Sage, 1980.

Sigman, S. J. *The social patterning of conversational topics: A nursing home example.* Unpublished M. A. Thesis, University of Pennsylvania, 1979.

Sigman, S. J. On communication rules from a social perspective. *Human Communication Research,* 1980, *7,* 37-51.

Sigman, S. J. *Some communicational aspects of patient placement and careers in two nursing homes.* Unpublished Ph. D. dissertation, University of Pennsylvania, 1982.

Silverman, D. Some neglected questions about social reality. In P. Filmer, M. Phillipson, D. Silverman, & D. Walsh (Eds.), *New directions in sociological theory.* London: MIT Press, 1974.

Sinclair, J. M., & Coulthard, R. M. *Towards an analysis of discourse: The English used by teachers and pupils.* London: Oxford University Press, 1975.

Sinclair, J. M., Forsyth, I. J., Coulthard, R. M., & Ashby, M. C. *The English used by teachers and pupils.* Final report to SSRC. Birmingham University (England), 1972. (mimeo)

Smith, D. H. Communication research and the idea of process. *Speech Monographs,* 1972, *39,* 174-182.

Snyder, L. *Beyond implications: Another look at Grice's maxims.* Paper presented at the Annual Meeting of the Speech Communication Association, Louisville, Kentucky, November 1982.

Speier, M. *How to observe face-to-face communication: A sociological introduction.* Pacific Palisades, CA: Goodyear, 1973.

Spradley, J. P. *The ethnographic interview.* New York: Holt, Rinehart & Winston, 1979.

Spradley, J. P. *Participant observation.* New York: Holt, Rinehart & Winston, 1980.

Stech, E. L. Sequential structure in human social communication. *Human Communication Research,* 1975, *1,* 168-179.

Stech, E. L. A grammar of conversation with a quantitative empirical test. *Human Communication Research,* 1979, *5,* 158-170.

Steiner, W. *The colors of rhetoric: Problems in the relation between modern literature and painting.* Chicago: University of Chicago Press, 1982.

Stokes, R., & Hewitt, J. P. Aligning actions. *American Sociological Review,* 1976, *41,* 838-849.

Strauss, A., Schatzman, L., Bucher, R., Erlich, D. & Sabshin, M. *Psychiatric ideologies and institutions.* New York: Free Press, 1964.

Street, R. L., Jr. Evaluation of noncontent speech accommodation. *Language and Communication,* 1982, *2,* 13-32.

Street, R. L., Jr., & Hopper, R. A model of speech style evaluation. In H. Giles & E. B. Ryan (Eds.), *Attitudes towards language variation.* London: Arnold, 1982.

Sudnow, D. (Ed.) *Studies in social interaction.* New York: Free Press, 1972.

Tracy, K. *The issue-event distinction as an aspect of conversational coherence: A rule and its scope conditions.* Unpublished Ph. D. dissertation, University of Wisconsin-Madison, 1981.

Tracy, K. On getting the point: Distinguishing "issues" from "events," an aspect of conversational coherence. In M. Burgoon (Ed.), *Communication yearbook 5.* New Brunswick, NJ: Transaction, 1982.

Tracy, K. The issue-event distinction: A rule of conversation and its scope condition. *Human Communication Research,* in press. (a)

Tracy, K. Staying on topic: An explication of conversational relevance. *Discourse Processes,* in press. (b)

Tracy, K., & Moran, J. P. *Competing goals and conversational extensions.* Paper presented at the annual meeting of the Speech Communication Association, Louisville, Kentucky, November 1982.

Tyler, S. *The said and the unsaid: Mind, meaning and culture.* New York: Academic Press, 1978.

van Dijk, T. A. *Text and context: Explorations in the semantics and pragmatics of discourse.* New York: Longman, 1977. (a)

van Dijk, T. A. Semantic macro-structures and knowledge frames in discourse comprehension. In M. A. Just & P. A. Carpenter (Eds.), *Cognitive processes in comprehension.* Hillsdale, NJ: Lawrence Erlbaum, 1977. (b)

Vuchinich, S. Elements of cohesion between turns in ordinary conversation. *Semiotica,* 1977, *20,* 229-257.

Warren, R. P. *All the king's men.* New York: Harcourt Brace Jovanovich, 1949.

Weiner, S., & Goodenough, D. R. A move toward a psychology of conversation. In R. O. Freedle (Ed.), *Discourse production and comprehension.* Norwood, NJ: Ablex, 1977.

Wieder, D. L. *Language and social reality* The Hague: Mouton, 1974.

Wiemann, J. M., & Knapp, M. L. Turn-taking in conversations. *Journal of Communication,* 1975, *25*(2), 75-92.

Wilks, Y. Good and bad arguments about semantic primitives. *Communication and Cognition,* 1977, *10,* 181-221.

Winkin, Y. *Patterns of intercultural communication: An exploratory ethnographic study of an American International House.* Unpublished M. A. thesis, University of Pennsylvania, 1979.

Winograd, T. On primitive prototypes and other semantic anomalies. *TINLAP-2*, 1978, 25-32.

Wittgenstein, L. *Philosophical investigations* (G. E. M. Anscombe, trans.). New York: MacMillan, 1953.

Wittgenstein, L. *The blue and brown books*. Oxford: Basil Blackwell, 1958.

Wootton, A. *Dilemmas of discourse: Controversies about the sociological interpretation of language*. New York: Holmes & Meier, 1976.

Yarmey, A. D. *The psychology of eyewitness testimony*. New York: Free Press, 1979.

Zabor, M. R. *Essaying metacommunication: A survey and contextualization of communication research*. Unpublished Ph. D. dissertation, Indiana University, 1978.

AUTHOR INDEX

SUBJECT INDEX

ABOUT THE
CONTRIBUTORS

WAYNE A. BEACH received his Ph. D. from the University of Utah and is Assistant Professor of Communication at the University of Nebraska — Lincoln. His articles have appeared in the *Quarterly Journal of Speech, Western Journal of Speech Communication,* and the *Communication Yearbook.* Among his current research interests are studies of conversational time traveling, reality reconstruction in the courtroom, and the role of ambiguity in appearance management.

ROBERT T. CRAIG, who received his Ph. D. in Communication from Michigan State University in 1976, is Assistant Professor of Speech at Temple University. His articles, reviews, and chapters have dealt with a variety of topics in communication theory. He is presently doing research on requests and working on a book about communication as a practical discipline.

BRYAN K. CROW is Assistant Professor of Speech Communication at Southern Illinois University, Carbondale. He received his Ph. D. in the Communication Research division of the Department of Communication and Theatre Arts at the University of Iowa in 1982. The study reported in this volume is part of his dissertation, "Conversational Pragmatics."

DONALD G. ELLIS (Ph. D., University of Utah, 1976) is Associate Professor and Chair in the Department of Communication at the University of Hartford. He has taught at Purdue University and Michigan State University. His published articles have included studies of language processes, discourse, and interpersonal communication.

THOMAS B. FARRELL is Associate Professor of Communication Studies at Northwestern University. He received his Ph. D. from the University of Wisconsin in 1974. Since that time, he has contributed numerous articles on rhetorical theory and criticism to journals such as the *Quarterly Journal of Speech, Philosophy and Rhetoric,* and *Communication Monographs.* His present research is concerned with the impact of social knowledge assumptions upon the durational demands posed by discourse (conversation, rhetoric, poetic).

JULIA A. GOLDBERG is a postdoctoral teaching associate in the Department of Speech Communication at the University of Illinois — Urbana. Dr. Goldberg received her Ph.D. in Linguistics from Cambridge University in England.

LEONARD C. HAWES (Ph.D., University of Minnesota, 1970) is Professor of Communication at the University of Utah. His current research is an investigation of conversation as ideology. Earlier work was concerned with group decision making and interviewing. In addition to research articles and reviews, he is the author of *Pragmatics of Analoguing: Theory and Model Construction in Communication* (1975).

ROBERT HOPPER is Professor of Speech Communication at the University of Texas, Austin. His long-range research interest is to make symbolic interactionist description empirical. His immediate research concerns "alignment talk" — the ways that people define situations and typify each other in conversation. One of his major concerns is with the use of talk as a social discriminator, say against women, minority-group members, and those victimized through communicative disorders.

SALLY JACKSON completed her Ph.D. at the University of Illinois at Urbana-Champaign. She is now Assistant Professor of Communication at Michigan State University.

SCOTT JACOBS completed a Ph.D. at the University of Illinois at Urbana-Champaign. He is now Assistant Professor of Communication at Michigan State University.

JOHN P. MORAN III received his Ph.D. from Temple University in 1979, and is currently an instructor at Temple. He has research interests in multiple goals and meanings in discourse, paradoxical discourse, and therapeutic discourse. He is involved in the ongoing study of therapeutic discourse with chronic hospitalized mental patients.

SUSAN SWAN MURA is a doctoral candidate in the Department of Communication at the Ohio State University. She is completing her doctorate in communication theory and rhetoric with a minor in psycholinguistics. Her research interests focus on the relationship between language and communication, particularly in regard to conversational coherence, symbolic interaction, and language and thought.

ROBERT E. NOFSINGER received the Ph. D. from the University of Iowa in 1973. He teaches language behavior and interpersonal, small group, and organizational communication in the Department of Communications, Washington State University. His primary research interests are conversation analysis, including courtroom interaction, and communication processes in the practice of law.

SANDRA L. RAGAN received her Ph. D. in interpersonal and organizational communication from the University of Texas. She is currently an assistant professor in the Department of Communication at the University of Oklahoma. Her primary research interests are conversation analysis and relationship communication.

ROBERT E. SANDERS is Associate Professor of Rhetoric and Communication at the State University of New York at Albany. His articles on language and communication have appeared in journals such as the *Quarterly Journal of Speech, Communication and Cognition,* and *Communication Quarterly.*

STUART J. SIGMAN holds a Ph. D. from the Annenberg School of Communications, University of Pennsylvania. He is currently an Assistant Professor in the Department of Speech Communication, the Pennsylvania State University.

KAREN TRACY received her Ph. D. in Communication Arts from the University of Wisconsin — Madison in 1981 and is presently on the faculty of the Department of Speech, Temple University. Her studies of conversation have been published in *Human Communication Research, Discourse Processes,* and the *Communication Yearbook.* Her general research interests are in discourse and cognition, and she is presently doing studies of request making, communicative competence, and comprehension of conversation.